Baseball Greatness

Baseball Greatness

*Top Players and Teams
According to Wins Above Average,
1901–2017*

David Kaiser

McFarland & Company, Inc., Publishers
Jefferson, North Carolina

The author may be reached at KaiserD2@gmail.com

LIBRARY OF CONGRESS CATALOGUING-IN-PUBLICATION DATA

Names: Kaiser, David E., 1947– author.
Title: Baseball greatness : top players and teams according to wins above average, 1901–2017 / David Kaiser.
Description: efferson, North Carolina : McFarland & Company, Inc., Publishers, 2018. | Includes bibliographical references and index.
Identifiers: LCCN 2017061210 | ISBN 9781476663838 (softcover : acid free paper) ∞
Subjects: LCSH: Baseball players—Rating of—United States. | Baseball players—United States—Statistics. | Baseball players— United States—History.
Classification: LCC GV865.A1 K33 2018 | DDC 796.3570922 [B]—dc23
LC record available at https://lccn.loc.gov/2017061210

BRITISH LIBRARY CATALOGUING DATA ARE AVAILABLE

ISBN (print) 978-1-4766-6383-8
ISBN (ebook) 978-1-4766-2862-2

© 2018 David Kaiser. All rights reserved

No part of this book may be reproduced or transmitted in any form or by any means, electronic or mechanical, including photocopying or recording, or by any information storage and retrieval system, without permission in writing from the publisher.

Front cover: Detroit Tigers centerfielder Ty Cobb, circa 1918 (Photograph by Paul Thompson)

Printed in the United States of America

*McFarland & Company, Inc., Publishers
Box 611, Jefferson, North Carolina 28640
www.mcfarlandpub.com*

To all those who struggle
with the burden of greatness

"I turn to the sports pages first because there I find a record of man's achievements, while on the front page I find only a record of his failures."

—Chief Justice Earl Warren

Table of Contents

Acknowledgments   viii

Introduction: Great Players, Great Teams   1

1. The Missionary and Lost Generation Era, 1901–1924   23
2. The Lost and GI Generation Era, 1925–1945   43
3. The GI and Silent Generation Era, 1946–1966   70
4. The Silent and Boom Generation Era, 1967–1983   116
5. The Boom and Gen X Era, 1984–2004   145
6. The Gen X and Millennial Era, 2005–2017   189

Epilogue: The Nature of Greatness   220

Appendix   227

Bibliography   230

Index   231

Acknowledgments

Three other men really made this book possible. I had been an intense baseball fan for 28 years when I picked Bill James's 1982 *Baseball Abstract* off the shelf at the Harvard Coop, but for me, as for so many others, that book and its successors opened up vast new perspectives that increased my understanding of the game many times over. James kicked off a scientific revolution in baseball statistics that continues to this day, and this book simply builds on the foundation which he laid down. He also provided, in a subsequent *Abstract*, the question that became the foundation of this book: "If this guy were the best player on your team, is it likely that you could win the pennant?"

The second key figure in the story was another pioneer in sabermetrics, Dick Cramer, whom I have come to know in long conversations at the annual convention of the Society for American Baseball Research. Dick combines very high intelligence and a very sympathetic and even temperament to an unusual degree, and I turned to him for advice at several key moments in putting this book together. But most importantly of all, it was he, about four years ago, who told me that Michael Humphreys had cracked the code regarding the evaluation of fielding in his relatively recent book, *Wizardry* (Oxford University Press, 2012). I immediately ordered the book and immediately agreed with him.

And thus, Michael is the third person who has made this book possible. Both he and Oxford University Press are to be commended not only for publishing *Wizardry*, which I cannot recommend too highly, but for making all the data behind it readily available for downloading in Excel spreadsheets on Oxford's web site. Having read the book, I immediately downloaded the data and began using it, together with other readily available material, to arrive at new evaluations of the careers of all-time baseball greats. One thing led to another, and the idea of this book was born. I finally got to meet Michael face to face at the SABR Convention in New York in 2017, and he has been an endless source of help and inspiration in many telephone calls. He is, in his own way, a giant in the field of baseball research.

Meanwhile, Sean Forman of baseball-reference.com and Dan Hirsch of seamheads.com also made the book possible by making so much raw data available on the web. Sean's own spreadsheets of player WAA were the basis for mine, although as I explain in the introduction and appendix, I modified his results in many ways. He very generously supplied individually crafted spreadsheets to make my work easier. His site was the source of invaluable data not only about individual player performance, but about the history of the minor leagues. Dan Hirsch has performed a huge service by using Michael Humphreys' Defense Regression

Analysis (DRA) method to calculate individual fielding data for every major leaguer for the years since *Wizardry* appeared. He too very kindly provided me with all that data in spreadsheet form. Pete Palmer provided excellent data on team runs scored, team runs allowed, and projected team runs scored.

Two other people provided critical programming help. One was my son Dan Kaiser, who wrote some Excel macros to make it easier to calculate the Wins Above Average of all the regular hitters and pitchers on individual teams. The second was Jordan Williams, a young IT professional whom I hired to write more complex programs through the site upwork.com. I could not have done it without them. The compilation, calculation, and transcription of the data in this book was an enormous task, one that would have been quite impossible without modern computers and software. I discovered many a slip that I had made along the way, and I am sure that some errors have found their way into the final text. I am confident, however, that they are minor and not of a character to affect the overall evaluation of any great players or teams. I will be glad to correct any that I can in the future.

My dear friend Jim Davidson, with whom I've been trading baseball statistics and insights for 50 years, provided some very useful help working with my data and some excellent criticism in the latter stages of the work. Over the past few years, the response of SABR members to talks I have given at the national convention and at chapter meetings in Massachusetts and Connecticut has been most encouraging. I will be delighted to reappear before them in 2018 with copies of the book in hand.

Last but not least, my thanks go to the men of exceptional talent who have devoted their lives to the game of baseball, providing an inspiring spectacle for their countrymen for well over 100 years, and providing the raw material for this study of greatness.

Introduction
Great Players, Great Teams

Was Barry Bonds a greater player than Babe Ruth? What is more important to the success of a team, pitching or hitting? Who managed the best Yankees teams: Miller Huggins, Joe McCarthy, Casey Stengel, Ralph Houk, Billy Martin, or Joe Torre? Was Mickey Mantle, at his peak, really better than Willie Mays?

Are the extraordinary statistics hitters compiled during the "steroid era" real evidence of greatness? What was the impact of successive expansions on major league baseball? Are there more, or fewer, truly great players today, and why? What are the key elements in putting together, and maintaining, a dynasty? What positions are most important to the success of a team? Have some overqualified players been left out of the Hall of Fame? Who among those still eligible deserves inclusion?

Even relatively casual baseball fans know that a flood of new statistical approaches to baseball has crested over the last few decades. Many fans understandably feel overwhelmed and bewildered, and find it easier to stick to traditional measurements such as batting average, home runs, RBIs, pitchers' won-lost records, and defensive reputations that often are not based on statistics at all. Yet it is not in the least necessary to familiarize one's self with all the advances in baseball statistics to answer all the questions listed in the first two paragraphs above, and a great many more besides. Thanks to breakthroughs in analysis, convenient web sites, and the magic of Excel spreadsheets, one statistic, Wins Above Average, suffices to answer them all. It is the basis of this book.

Thirty-five years ago, in 1982, after five years of self-publishing his *Baseball Abstract*, Bill James moved the public discussion of the game into a new phase. He signed with Ballantine, who would bring out James's annual for the next seven years, ensuring wider dissemination of his radical approach to baseball performance and evaluation. Although both major league baseball players and teams and most of the news media reacted very skeptically to his insights, he created an immediate sensation among the public and became a national figure. In the late 1990s, Billy Beane of the Oakland A's became the first general manager to build a team around some of the principles James had identified, and in 2002, the new owner of the Red Sox, John Henry, hired James himself, and won a world championship two years later. This is not the place to recapitulate the whole development of the science of sabermetrics, a word coined by James to refer to the sophisticated measurement of baseball performance. That was already done some years ago by the reporter Alan Schwarz in his fine book, *The Numbers Game*. Suffice it to say that most, if not all, major league teams now employ full-time statistical analysts, and a number of popular websites, including baseball-reference.com., seamheads.com, and retrosheet.org, have made sophisticated data widely available. Statistics like on-base percentage (OBP) and on-base plus slugging (OBS) now appear regularly in the columns of mainstream sportswriters and on the scoreboards of major league ball parks. Another breakthrough occurred in 2011, when Michael Humphreys, a tax lawyer, published *Wizardry*, the most accurate analysis yet developed of players' fielding skill, applied to all players from 1893 through 2009. Today it has become difficult to wade through the enormous mass of readily available data on contemporary and past baseball performance.

My own contributions to this new field of knowledge have included reviews of books by Bill James in the *New Republic* and the *Washington Post*, recent papers at the 2014–2016 SABR (Society for American Baseball Research) conventions, talks to local chapters, hundreds of contributions to the SABR mailing list, and comments on various web sites. They also included a book of my own, *Epic Season: The 1948 American League Pennant Race*, which appeared in 1998 and remains in print. Using my research skills as a diplomatic historian, I combined a detailed narrative of that season with what were then state-of-the-art statistics in an effort to explain not only how the Cleveland Indians beat out the Boston Red Sox and the New York Yankees in the most exciting pennant race in history, but why. In particular, I used relatively primitive methods to assess the positive or negative contribution of each regular on the three contending teams to their team's fortune. How much, I wondered, did Joe DiMaggio, Phil Rizzuto, Bob Feller, Lou Boudreau, Ted Williams, Junior Stephens, and many other players contribute to, or detract from, their team's performance in that thrilling season? That same question, asked across the entire history of major league baseball as we have known it, is the basis for this new book. It identifies the most valuable players from every generation since 1901 and analyzes their contribution to their teams. In so doing, it not only provides new answers to a host of perennial baseball questions about performance and contribution, but also sheds some light on more general questions of human performance and greatness, such as those addressed by Malcolm Gladwell in his book *Outliers*.

Like so much else in the field of sabermetrics, the genesis of this book began with something written by Bill James. The question of greatness in baseball is inevitably and intimately connected with the question of who ought to be enshrined in the Baseball Hall of Fame in Cooperstown, New York. In 1985, James wrote an essay in his annual *Abstract* in response to a letter he received arguing that Ken Keltner, the Cleveland Indians' third baseman in the 1940s, should be elected to the Hall. The essay answered a list of questions that James argued should be asked about any potential Hall of Famer. (He concluded that Keltner should not be elected—an argument with which I certainly agree—and he never was.) Among the 15 questions, which James reprinted in his book on the Hall of Fame,[1] one

---

1. Bill James, *The Politics of Glory: How Baseball's Hall of Fame Really Works* (New York: Macmillan, 1994), 274–275.

particularly caught my eye and has stayed with me ever since. "If this man were the best player on your team," he asked, "would it be likely that the team could win the pennant?" That, it seemed to me, was a critically important question, one that would identify the truly great players who decisively affected the fortune of their teams. And the more often a player turned in a performance good enough to lead his team to the pennant, it seemed to me, the greater a player he obviously was. I began working seriously on this book about three years ago because I thought that the statistical tools and the data necessary to identify those players over time had now become available. I have not been disappointed. The statistical answer to James's question—how good does a player have to be to make him a potential MVP on a pennant winner?—turns out to be 4 Wins Above Average, or 4 WAA. Such a performance will be referred to in this book as a superstar season. We shall now look at the derivation of that statistic.

Methods

This book will be very easily accessible to any serious baseball fan, including those who have never read a book by Bill James, have never gone to baseball-prospectus.com, and have never paid much attention to most of the new statistical measurements. The measurements I am going to use are both extremely simple and very powerful. The next few pages will lay them out, and an appendix will explain exactly how they are derived more thoroughly.

Baseball is, of course, a team game. While fans have always been fascinated, and rightly so, with individual performance, the job of individual players is to help their teams win games. A team wins any game in which it scores more runs than its opponent. Our analysis therefore begins with one of the foundations of sabermetrics, the formula that Bill James created to explain how the runs that a team scores on the one hand, and allows on the other, determine its won-loss record. That formula, which can be applied to all or any part of team's season, reads as follows:

Expected winning percentage = (team runs scored^2)/(team runs scored^2 + team runs allowed^2)

Using PCT to represent expected percentage, R for runs scored, and RA for runs allowed, we obtain the simpler equation:

$$PCT = R^2/(R^2 + RA^2)$$

For reasons obvious to anyone who remembers high school math, this formula is known as the Pythagorean formula. It has subsequently been modified, substituting 1.82 for 2 as the exponent, because that turned out to provide more accurate results. The formula, among other things, tells us how many runs a team has to score (or prevent its opponents from scoring) in the course of a season to create a reasonable expectation of winning one or more games. It turns out that depending upon the general frequency of runs—that is, whether the team is playing in a low-scoring era like the 1960s or a high-scoring era like the 1990s—it takes somewhere between eight and ten more runs to create each extra win.

Baseball is in part a game of luck, because a game—nine innings—is not long enough for superiority on the field to manifest itself consistently. That, it bears noting, is why millions of people attend, watch, and listen to games every day: there is no other way to find out who is going to win. The Pythagorean formula cannot therefore predict the winner of a single game, but over the course of a whole 162-game season the formula is astonishingly accurate. The 2017 Los Angeles Dodgers, to choose a non-random example, scored 770 runs and allowed 580. Plugging these numbers into the Pythagorean formula yields a winning percentage equivalent to 102 wins and 60 losses—just two games worse than their actual record of 104–58. This is in fact almost average: luck has either won or cost the average team four games, relative to its Pythagorean projection, over the history of baseball since 1901. Only 15 teams in that whole period have won ten or more games above their projection, and only one of those teams, the 1961 Cincinnati Reds, has won the pennant *because* of their luck. More often than not, the team with the league's or division's best record has the best Pythagorean percentage as well, although there have been important exceptions, such as the 1969 Mets and the 1975 Red Sox, which we shall take a look at in due course. In 2017, only the Boston Red Sox managed to win their division without posting the best Pythagorean percentage as well.

Playing with the Pythagorean formula yields another important piece of data. The average National League team's runs scored in 2013 was 718, and a team that scored and allowed 718 runs would obviously have a Pythagorean percentage of .500 and an expected record of 81–81. To raise that projected record to 91–71—ten wins better—it would have to score an additional 98 runs, about 9.8 per win. It may initially seem odd that it would require ten additional runs over the course of a season to increase a team's probable wins by just one game, but that is the impact of splitting more than 700 runs into 162 increments, distributed with a high degree of randomness. This is a critical number for our purposes, since it means that a hitter must create nearly ten additional runs, or a pitcher save ten additional runs, to be worth one additional win for his team.

It will not be necessary, however, to spend much time discussing the specific numbers of additional runs created by hitters like Ty Cobb, Babe Ruth, Ted Williams, Henry Aaron, Mike Schmidt, and Barry Bonds in various seasons, or the runs saved by Walter Johnson, Lefty Grove, Sandy Koufax, and Roger Clemens. Instead we can go directly to a simpler and more powerful statistic, Wins Above Average, or WAA—the statistic around which this book is built. Very simply, to credit a player with 4 Wins Above Average for a particular season (Josh Donaldson of the Toronto Blue Jays in 2016, for example), is to say that the Blue Jays probably won four additional games because they had him, rather than an average player, in the line-up. Let us just take a moment to show how WAA is computed for both hitter/fielders and pitchers.

The most valuable offensive player in the American League in 2017 was the Yankee rookie right fielder Aaron Judge, and his National League counterpart was first baseman Joey Votto of the Cincinnati Reds. Many formulas have been devised by Bill James, Pete Palmer, and other sabermetricians to measure the number of runs created by the walks, hits, and base running of an individual hitter. My basic data on offense comes from baseball-reference.com, which uses sophisticated formulas to estimate the runs created by a hitter at the plate (Rbat); the (usually very small) additional number of runs he created, or failed to create, because of his base running (Rbaser); and a third, also small, figure for runs gained or lost based upon the number of double plays he grounded into. Here are the 2016 figures for Judge and Votto.

Player	Rbat	Rbaser	Rdp
Aaron Judge	58	-1	-1
Joey Votto	59	-7	0

All these figures reflect the performance of these two men *relative to an average player*. In fact, both Judge and Votto created over 100 runs by virtue of their hits, walks, and total bases, but the figures of 58 and 59 represent their totals *above an average player with the same number of plate appearances*. This will enable us, in a moment, to assess their impact upon their team's performance in the standings.

We are not primarily concerned, in this book, about players' more traditional statistics. As it happens, Aaron Judge in 2017 batted .284, walked 127 times, hit 52 home runs, scored 128 runs, and batted in 114. Joey Votto batted .320 with 134 walks, 36 homers, 106 runs scored and 100 RBI. Any fan recognizes these as MVP-caliber figures, but we also know that such figures can be severely distorted by at least three factors. They can be distorted by the ballpark the player plays in. A player who hits 35 home runs for the Oakland Athletics is much more valuable than a Chicago Cub who does the same, because home runs are harder to hit in the Oakland Coliseum than in Wrigley Field. Such figures can also be distorted by the general level of offense in the league. Until the 1980s, anyone who hit 50 home runs in a season was, for that season, a superstar, but in the steroid era a number of players hit 50 or more homers without having that great an impact on their team's fortunes, incredible as that may seem, because homers had become so commonplace. RBIs in particular can also be distorted by the players' teammates. The Red Sox who batted behind Ted Williams had more RBIs than the Yankees who batted behind Joe DiMaggio, because Williams reached base so much more.

The advantage of the runs created totals generated at baseball-reference.com is that they correct for all these distortions and level the playing field within each league. When looking at the batting runs (Rbat) of Judge and Votto and comparing them with other players in their leagues, all runs are of equal value. We are almost ready to convert their totals into wins, but first we must deal with one of the most fascinating subjects of all: fielding.

Fielding skill has been notoriously difficult to measure since baseball began. By the 1980s, Bill James (him again!) and others had grasped that errors—balls that could have been turned into outs, but were not—were not a very important measurement. Instead, it was necessary to try to figure out how many batted balls a fielder turned into an out as a percentage of the balls the other team put into play. It was necessary, in short, to look at fielding the same way that we have always looked at hitting, with outs taking the place of hits, and batted balls taking the place of plate appearances. What made this so much more complicated was that, as was recognized early on, the number of balls which might fall within the reach of any particular fielder, be he shortstop, centerfielder, or what have you, was in part a function of independent variables. These included the tendency of his pitching staff to generate either ground balls or fly balls, the number of right- and left-handed hitters his team faced, and even his ball park. It was Michael Humphreys's success in solving these problems in his book *Wizardry*, published in 2011, which moved me to undertake this project. Humphreys explains all his methods very thoroughly and carefully in that book, and I will not try to do so here. I will merely focus on the results.

Essentially, Humphreys manages to calculate how many assists an average infielder would have, or how many putouts plus assists an average outfielder would have, given the number of balls put into play against his team, and adjusting for the independent variables I mentioned above. Humphreys does not pay any attention to putouts by infielders, because he believes, correctly in my view, that most of those come on popups and do not reflect greater skill on the part of the infielder. Popups are easy to catch, and the credit for generating more of them should go to pitchers, not fielders—and in this book, it does. What is important is that Humphreys's method gives him a figure for the number of hits saved by a better fielder or allowed by a worse one, relative to an average player at his position. He then converts that number of hits into a number of runs. I have combined Humphreys's fielding data with the baseball-reference hitting data to get my own measurements of total value for offensive players.[2]

Let us then add Humphreys's fielding data to our lines for Aaron Judge and Joey Votto.

Player	Rbat	Rbaser	Rdp	RField
Aaron Judge	58	-1	-1	5
Joey Votto	59	-7	0	16

Judge was a somewhat better than average right fielder, while Votto was an outstanding first baseman in 2017. We shall find that many fielders have saved their teams 20 or even 30 runs in a season, and a few have been great players for as much as four years mainly because of their fielding.

Adding up their various contributions, Aaron Judge improved total Yankee performance by 61 runs relative to an average player, while Joey Votto contributed 68 runs to the Reds that an average player would not have created. According to baseball-reference.com's calculation of runs per win, which I shall use throughout, Judge's 61 runs were worth exactly 6 extra wins to the Yankees, while Votto's 68 translated to 7.1 wins. In other words, Aaron Judge earned 6 Wins Above Average (WAA) in 2017, while Joey Votto earned 7.1 WAA.

Joey Votto, as it happens, has had 7 seasons of at least 4 WAA or more, our definition of a superstar season. Among active players that ties him with Miguel Cabrera for the second most such seasons (Albert Pujols leads active players with 11 superstar seasons.) That should, as we shall see, just about guarantee Votto a place in the Hall of Fame. Aaron Judge is of course a rookie, and unfortunately, he is already 25 years old. It will be interesting to see how long he can sustain a superstar level of performance.

---

2. For the years through 2009, Humphreys's fielding data is downloadable at the website of the Oxford University Press, his publisher. His data is available up to the present moment on the baseball gauge at seamheads.com.

Several people are now producing new sets of fielding statistics that actually count all the balls hit within a certain distance of each fielder and how many of them he turns into outs. These may be more accurate evaluations than Humphreys', but for obvious reasons, such data will never be compiled for players from earlier eras. Thus it makes more sense for me to use Humphreys' data throughout.

Now let's see how the system works with pitchers. Here baseball-reference.com has done even more of the statistical heavy lifting. Here is how I use their data to measure the Wins Above Average (WAA) of the best pitchers in the NL and AL last year: Max Scherzer of the Washington Nationals and Cory Kluber of the Cleveland Indians.

Max Scherzer in 2017 pitched nearly 201 innings and posted a 16–6 record with a 2.51 ERA. Baseball-reference.com first calculates that Scherzer surrendered 2.78 runs per nine innings, both earned and unearned, and names this stat RA9. It is the consensus of most sophisticated statistical analysts that the pitcher should be charged with all runs, not just earned runs. Then, baseball-reference calculates the number of runs per game that an average pitcher would have surrendered, pitching against the same teams, in the same parks, and, critically, with the same defense as Scherzer. In 2016 this came out to 5.08 runs per game. This stat is named RA9avg. That in turn leads to the conclusion that Scherzer saved the Nationals 50 runs, relative to an average pitcher, during 2016.

Exactly how I derive WAA from these numbers is too complicated to explain here in the introduction, and I am leaving it to the appendix. The calculation is complicated because while baseball-reference rightly tries to distinguish the runs saved or allowed by the Nationals' defense from the runs saved or allowed by their pitchers, it uses two different methods to calculate players' and teams' fielding skill, methods which often produce very different results from Michael Humphrey's DRA. As the appendix explains, correcting for this has been quite complicated, but I am satisfied that I have made my results for pitchers as accurate as I can make them. In this case they show Scherzer to have earned a league-leading (for pitchers) 4.4 WAA for the Nationals. This was the fourth season in which Scherzer has topped 4 WAA.

Meanwhile, in the American League, Corey Kluber had an even better season than Scherzer. Kluber, who pitched 203 innings with a 2.25 ERA, was estimated by baseball-reference.com to have saved the Cleveland Indians 55 runs, relative to an average pitcher. That, by my calculations, translated into a very remarkable 6.1 WAA. Scherzer was the only National League pitcher to earn more than 4 WAA in 2017, but Kluber was joined by Chris Sale of the Red Sox (4.9 WAA) and Marcus Stroman of the Toronto Blue Jays (4.2) in the AL.

Traditional hitting statistics usually, although not always, bear a fairly close relationship to an offensive player's wins above average. The same is not true of traditional pitching statistics, especially the won-loss record, which frequently give a completely misleading impression of a player's worth. Several variables determine whether a team wins a particular game. One is its hitting skill, which will help determine how many runs it scores. The second is the skill of the pitchers in the game, and the third is the skill of its fielders. The fourth—which is as important as any of the other three—is luck, which will largely determine how many runs are scored in nine particular innings. It is clear, when one thinks of it, that the skill of the starting pitcher accounts for well under 50 percent of the factors contributing to the outcome of the game. We shall find throughout this book that many pitchers—including not a few who have been rewarded with plaques in Cooperstown—have been systematically overrated because they had the good fortune to pitch for teams with dominating offenses. It is a great advantage of Wins Above Average that it corrects for this illusion.

So far this discussion has focused on outstanding players, and the rest of the book will largely do the same. But to understand how WAA relates to a team's record, we must keep in mind that every team includes a number of regulars whose performance is about average, and some—in some cases, more than half—whose performance is below average. As we shall see in a moment, there is no substitute for having a player who earns at least 4 WAA in a season, but his contributions can be, and often have been, more than counterbalanced by weaker players at other positions.

Wins Above Average and Different Eras of Baseball

One of the first breakthroughs in sabermetrics involved the need to evaluate both hitters and pitchers in context. It does not take much time glancing through a baseball encyclopedia or its modern equivalent, baseball-reference.com, to see that average performance levels change drastically over time. A .350 batting average in 1930, when the major leagues seem to have used the liveliest baseballs ever produced, was not worth nearly as much as a comparable average in 1957, when averages in general were much lower. Hitting generally ruled the majors in the 1930s, but the pitchers seemingly took over for most of the 1960s. In addition, a great pitcher's statistics can become even more extraordinary if he pitches in the right ball park (Sandy Koufax in Dodger Stadium, for example), and hitters for many years compiled much higher numbers in Fenway Park. To show how the single, simple, two-digit statistic of Wins Above Average allows us immediately to take account of all these differences, let's look at a couple of spectacular examples.

Let's start with two great seasons by Red Sox left fielders, Ted Williams in 1947 and Carl Yastrzemski in 1968. (Yastrzemski's greatest season was 1967, of course, and Williams's was 1942, but these two seasons provide the most revealing illustration of the point I am making now.) Williams in 1947 hit .343 (almost exactly his lifetime average), with 32 home runs and 162 walks. He scored 125 runs and drove in 114. Yaz in 1968—the "Year of the Pitcher"—led the league with a .301 batting average (the lowest league-leading average in major league history), hit 23 home runs, and walked 119 times. He scored 90 runs (no one in either league scored 100 in that extraordinary year) and drove in only 74. Surely this was an off-year for Carl Yastrzemski? Surely Williams in 1947 was much more valuable?

Well, as a matter of fact—no. Ted Williams in 1947 earned 9.5 Wins Above Average (WAA) for his team, and Carl Yastrzemski in 1968 contributed exactly 9.3. That is because hits, walks, and runs were so much more plentiful *across the whole American League* in 1947 than in 1968. Interestingly enough, the 1947 and 1968 Red Sox—both coming off of pennant-winning seasons—had almost identical records, 83–71 and 86–76. The average American league team scored 645 runs in 154 games in 1947, but only 553 in 162 games in 1968. And incredibly enough, Yaz's 1968 season was only slightly inferior to his more famous 1967 one, when he won the Triple Crown with a .326 average, 44 home runs, 121 RBI, 112 runs and 91 walks. That season was worth a full 10 WAA—the greatest season ever turned in, as it happens, by any hitter of Yastrzemski's generation, but less than a full win better than the apparently mediocre one he had in 1968, measured by its impact on his team's fortunes.

The 9.5 and 9.3 WAA which Williams and Yaz achieved in 1947 and 1968 puts those seasons within the top 60 seasons in the history of major league baseball. Only two other men have had seasons of exactly 9.3 WAA. One is Rickey Henderson in 1990 for the Oakland As, when he hit .325 with 28 homers, 61 runs batted in, 119 runs scored, 97 walks, and 65 stolen bases, and had an excellent year in left field. The second is Frankie Frisch for the St. Louis Cardinals in 1927, when he hit .337 with just ten home runs and 78 RBIs, walking 43 times, scoring 112 runs, stealing a league-leading 48 bases, and having a truly extraordinary year in the field, saving an estimated 60 runs at second base.

A more recent season makes the comparison more interesting. Barry Bonds in 2004 (again, not his greatest season, although quite close to it) hit .362 with 45 home runs and 101 RBI, walked an all-time record 232 times, and scored 129 runs. Yet these figures, in that high-offense era, added up to only slightly more WAA that Carl Yastrzemski's .301 season in 1968: 9.6 for Bonds, 9.3 for Yaz. Mark McGwire's 1998 season, in which he hit 70 home runs, earned the St. Louis Cardinals 6.9 WAA. That's a great season, but there have been 330 seasons at least that great in the history of baseball since 1901, almost exactly an average of three per season. McGwire broke Maris's record not because he was the greatest power hitter in baseball history, but because he was a fine power hitter (for whatever reason) in an era of extraordinarily inflated totals of home runs.

Several other important points emerge from this quick preview of what readers will find in this book. First of all, truly outstanding performances, measured by WAA, have occurred with roughly the same frequency throughout the history of baseball. The 27 seasons of 10 WAA or more have occurred in every era of major league baseball since 1901. Secondly, in every era, outstanding performances of 4 WAA or more have been more common among hitters than pitchers. Lastly, to say that Frankie Frisch in 1927 contributed as many wins to the St. Louis Cardinals as Ted Williams contributed to the Red Sox in 1946 does *not* mean that Frankie Frisch in that year was, in some absolute sense, as good as Ted Williams. That is an utterly unanswerable question, since they played in different leagues against completely different opposition. Unlike certain other analysts, I am generally going to stay away from the question of *absolute* merit in this book. Frisch and Williams each contributed 9.3 wins above average—that is, above .500—to their teams. That is all that mattered to either of their teams, and it's all that should matter, I think, to us, as well.

Wins Above Average, Wins Above Replacement, and Position Adjustments

As many readers will know, Wins Above Average as the measurement of a player's value is somewhat less fashionable than a related measurement, Wins Above Replacement (WAR). Both are readily available for any player and any season at baseball-reference.com (although as noted above, I calculate WAA differently in some respects than they do.) Wins Above Replacement is based upon an estimate of what a replacement-level player—presumably a player from the highest level of the minors—could be expected to contribute. There are two reasons why I vastly prefer WAA to WAR.

The first reason is that "replacement level" is an estimate, which cannot possibly accurately predict the quality of the player who would take the place of an injured star. Average performance level, on the other hand, is one of the things that can be calculated with nearly perfect accuracy.

The second and more important reason is that WAA instantly tells you what the impact of a player on his team's performance was, while WAR does not. We have seen that we can measure how many extra games the Reds and Indians could have been expected to win, thanks to Joey Votto and Cory Kluber. We know that a team of average players could expect to win 81 games and finish at .500.

To understand what makes a successful team, we must look a little more closely at the distribution of talent within entire leagues and at the role of average and below-average players. In 2016, of the 135 hitters in the AL with the most plate appearances—nine per team—44 were above average, earning between 1.0 WAA and 6.6 WAA. This book defines average as anything from +0.9 WAA to -0.9 WAA, in order to take reasonable account of randomness and chance. By that definition, 64 were average, and 26 were below average, earning -1 WAA or less. In addition, at the top end of the spectrum, 24 players earned 2 or more WAA, while at the bottom, only seven players earned -2 WAA or less. Only 19 percent of the regular players in the league, in other words, were significantly below average. Moreover, the next 30 players on the list ranked by plate appearance—those with 203–206 plate appearances—included about 27 more average players, suggesting that a more intelligent distribution of playing time could have reduced the number of below average players in lineups still further. Among the 96 starting pitchers with ten starts of more—about six per team—16 were above average (at least 1 WAA), 46 were average (0.9 to -0.9 WAA), and only 20 were -1 WAA or below. Thirteen of the above average pitchers earned at least 2 WAA; only five of the below average pitchers earned -2 WAA or less. Again, only 21 percent of the league's regular starters were at all significantly below average. These figures tend to confirm something that Bill James argued 30 years ago in an annual *Baseball Abstract*: that there is an ample supply of average to slightly below average players available to major league teams in the majors, to say nothing of the minors, if they are willing to look for them and give them a chance.[3] The National League had even fewer below-average regulars. Only 20 of its top 120 position players by plate appearance (eight per team) earned -1.0 WAA or less.[4] The distribution of National League starting pitchers was extremely similar as well, with only 23 of the top 96 scoring at -1 WAA or below. This is an extremely important point, since it means that in normal circumstances there is no excuse for keeping a player who is -3 WAA or worse in the lineup—yet we shall see that this happens all the time, and has wrecked the chances of more than a few teams with plenty of superstar talent.

The second difference between my calculations of WAA and those at baseball-reference.com relates to position adjustments. Baseball-reference.com adjusts the value of players depending on the difficulty of the defensive position they play. A shortstop with

---

3. Bill James, *The Bill James Baseball Abstract 1984* (New York: Ballantine, 1984), 113–116.
4. The reason for this is that average hitting in the NL is held down by pitchers, who do about 10 percent of the hitting in the league.

exactly the same offensive and defensive statistics as a left fielder will get a bonus that often amounts to a full WAA from baseball-reference.com. (This is listed as RPos in their tables.) I have eliminated those adjustments, because I think they distort the actual value of players, measured by the runs which they create and save.[5] We shall examine this point at length in the chapter on 1926–1945, when we first encounter Hall of Fame catchers.

As we shall see in a moment, superstars with at least 4 WAA are critical to a team's success, but other, slightly lesser players make critical contributions as well. Throughout this book, seasons of 2.0 to 3.9 WAA will be referred to as star seasons, and players who earn 1.0 to 1.9 WAA will be referred to as assets. The problem of putting together a winning team—and especially a superior pennant winner—consists of assembling enough superstars, stars, and assets, while keeping severely below-average players out of the lineup and off the mound.

Great Seasons—Great Players

A season of at least 4 WAA is a superstar season, representing the level which the best player on a pennant winner must normally exceed. It does not, however, represent anywhere near the limit of what great players are capable. In every era, at least one player has posted a season of more than 10 WAA. Still, a player who can earn 4 WAA in a season even once is a very rare bird. Since 1901, only 645 different men have done so, out of 19.000 who have played in the major leagues—in other words, about 3 percent of the total. Three hundred and two of them—nearly half—did so only once. One hundred forty-two did so twice, 56 three times, and 52 four times.

My standard for all-time greatness is at least five seasons of at least 4 WAA—a standard that has been met by 93 players in the history of baseball, or about half of 1 percent of everyone who has entered a major league game. Of this 93, 29 earned 4 WAA five times; 18 did it six times; eleven did it seven times; 11 did it eight times; three did it nine times, and 20, the best of the best, have had 4 WAA in from 10 to 17 seasons. The smoothness of that progression demonstrates that the ability to post seasons of 4 WAA or more is a very real skill that is most certainly not randomly distributed. Although, as we shall see the Hall of Fame includes many players with fewer than five seasons of 4 WAA or more, the standard of five seasons does bear some relation to selection of Cooperstown. Of the 51 players who had exactly four seasons of 4 WAA or more, only 18 have been elected to the Hall of Fame. Seventeen of the 39 players with 5 WAA have been elected, however, and if we eliminate ineligible players (including David Ortiz, Clayton Kershaw, and Mike Trout, who each earned his fifth season of 4 WAA or more in 2016) and players from the steroid era, we find that 17 out the remaining 28 are in the Hall. Of the 60 players with at least six seasons of

---

5. Let me be clear: the defensive runs saved of a shortstop is calculated, of course, in relation to other shortstops. The question at issue is whether 40 runs above average created at the plate by a shortstop are more valuable than the same number of runs created at the plate by a DH. In my opinion, they are not.

5 WAA or more, only 15 are not in the Hall, and more than half of them are ineligible (Joe Jackson), active (Albert Pujols and Miguel Cabrera), not yet eligible or tainted by steroids.

The vast majority of all-time greats by this measure—at least five seasons of 4 WAA or more—are hitters, not pitchers. Variance in pitching performance has always been considerably smaller than variance in hitting performance, and of the 1,773 superstar seasons in baseball history—4 WAA or more—1,214 of them were achieved by hitters and only 559 by pitchers. While in most cases the Hall of Fame standard for hitters is not too far from five seasons of 4 WAA or more, the Hall of Fame standard for pitchers is much, much lower. In the course of the book, we shall find exactly what it is that does and does not secure election to Cooperstown for pitchers.

Generations and Eras

Because we are dealing with the whole period of major league baseball since the formation of the American League in 1901, we need to divide up the period chronologically and divide players into specific groups. To do so, I shall use generations, following a model established in the 1990s by William Strauss and Neil Howe in their book, *Generations: The History of America's Future*. Men from seven different generations have played major league baseball since 1901.

The Missionary generation, which in a completely different context was largely the subject of my last book,[6] was born from about 1863 until 1883, and gave us most of the original players, and nearly all of the superstars, in major league baseball for the first decade of the twentieth century. Its most famous players include Christy Mathewson, Honus Wagner, Napoleon Lajoie, Rube Waddell, and Cy Young.

The Lost generation will be defined here as consisting of those born from 1884 through 1902. The first member of the lost generation to post more than 4 WAA in a season was Sherry Magee, a left fielder for the Philadelphia Phillies, who did so in 1907. Ty Cobb, one of their greatest players, won his first batting title that year. The Lost generation provided most of the first cohorts elected to the Hall of Fame, including Cobb, Walter Johnson, Grover Cleveland Alexander, Babe Ruth, Tris Speaker, and Rogers Hornsby.

It is now time to define our first era. One cannot define an era of baseball history based upon only one generation, because more often than not, the greatest players in any given year come from not one, but two different generations. Thus, for example, American League superstars of 1910 included Philadelphia pitcher Jack Coombs and Cleveland second baseman Nap Lajoie, from the Missionary generation—aged 27 and 35 at the time—and Ty Cobb and Eddie Collins, both 23, from the Lost Generation. In this book, every era will include superstars from only two generations. The era of the Missionary and Lost generations extended from 1901, the beginning of major league baseball as we know it, through 1925—only a little longer, clearly, than what is usually called the dead ball era.

---

6. David Kaiser, *No End Save Victory: How FDR Led the Nation Into War* (New York: Basic Books, 2014).

The boundary between the Lost and GI (or so-called Greatest) generations was rather fluid. Strauss and Howe originally put it at 1901, but I have concluded that they were mistaken and placed it a few years too early. The Lost generation was made up largely of cantankerous individuals who thought first and foremost of themselves; the GI generation were quiet, dedicated team players, the qualities that made them such outstanding soldiers in the Second World War. Lou Gehrig, born in 1903, embodied all the virtues of the GI generation, and thus for baseball purposes I have begun the GI generation in that year. Gehrig was the first member of his generation to post more than 4 WAA—a superstar season—which he did in 1926. We shall begin each new era with the first season in which a member of a new generation posts a superstar season, and thus the Lost and GI generation era begins then. The Lost generation was still dominating baseball at that time and its younger cohorts continued to do so well into the 1930s. Thus, our second era, the era of the Lost and GI generations, extends from 1926 through 1945, slightly shorter than the first era (20 years instead of 25.) The GI generation in baseball includes players born from 1903 through 1924, and the greatest GI players included Gehrig, Ted Williams, Joe DiMaggio, Bob Feller, Stan Musial, Mel Ott, Jimmy Foxx, Hank Greenberg, and Jackie Robinson.

The Silent generation was born between 1925 and 1942. Most of its oldest male members were drafted in the latter stages of the Second World War, although very few of them reached combat. The first member of the Silent Generation to post a superstar season was Philadelphia Phillies outfielder Del Ennis in 1946, marking the beginning of the GI and Silent generation era. The war had so disrupted the careers of the Silent Generation, however, that not until 1950, at the age of 25, did another of them, pitcher Ned Garver, post more than 4 WAA in a season. Their first superstar hitter, Richie Ashburn, did the same in 1951, when Mickey Mantle and Willie Mays, two of their greatest players, also made their debuts. Integration was the critical influence upon the Silent generation in baseball, and their greatest players included Willie Mays, Henry Aaron, Roberto Clemente, Bob Gibson, and Frank Robinson, as well as Mickey Mantle and Carl Yastrzemski. The era of the GI and Silent generations lasted from 1946 through 1966, 21 years.

The commonly accepted definition of the Boom generation—that it was born from 1946 through 1964—is a demographic one, because the United States' birth rate mushroomed in 1946 and plummeted in 1965. Strauss and Howe divided generations based on life experience rather than mere numbers, and concluded that the Boom generation included those born from 1943 through 1960—essentially, those Americans who could not remember Franklin Roosevelt but could remember John Kennedy. The first superstar seasons by Boomers were turned in in 1967 by Paul Blair, a potential Hall of Famer (as we shall see) whose career was tragically affected by a beaning in 1970, and two pitchers, Jim Merritt of the Minnesota Twins and 19-year-old Gary Nolan of the Cincinnati Reds. Merritt had been born in 1943, Blair in 1944 and Nolan in 1948. The greatest Boomer players included Rickey Henderson, Mike Schmidt, Reggie Jackson, Wade Boggs, Rod Carew, Joe Morgan, and Bert Blyleven. Because the Silent and Boom generations were the shortest, in terms of birth years, of those we are looking at, their era lasted only 18 years, from 1967 through 1983.

Generation X was born from 1961 through 1981 and grew up in a very different world from the Silent and Boom generations. Its first superstar season was turned in by Don Mattingly, born in 1961, in 1984. The greatest players of Generation X, based merely on the number of superstar seasons (at least 4 WAA) they put up on the board, were Barry Bonds, Albert Pujols, Roger Clemens, Jeff Bagwell, Randy Johnson, and Greg Maddux. The era of the Boom and X generations lasted from 1984 through 2004, and it coincides, of course, with the influx of performance enhancing drugs (PEDs) into professional sports. We shall find that their impact, while great, was not what it is generally thought to be.

In 1993, Strauss and Howe coined the term Millennial Generation, and it has now passed into common currency. We do now yet know when the youngest Millennials were born—only time will answer that question—but the youngest Millennials have not yet reached the major leagues. The first Millennial to post more than 4 WAA in major league baseball was a pitcher, Dontrelle Willis, in 2005. So far the greatest players of the Millennial generation, measured by their number of superstar seasons, are Miguel Cabrera of the Detroit Tigers, Joey Votto of the Cincinnati Reds, Clayton Kershaw of the Los Angeles Dodgers, and the extraordinarily precious Mike Trout. The era of the Xer and Millennial generations began in 2005 and is still going on as I write.

This book is designed both to identify the greatest player of each *generation* and to discuss how baseball has changed *from era to era*. Generations are defined *by birth years*, eras by groups of seasons. Both last in the neighborhood of 20 years.

Generations

Generation	*Birth years*	*First Superstar Season*	*Last Superstar Season*
Missionary	1863–1883	pre-1900	1920 (Babe Adams)
Lost	1884–1902	1906 (Sherry Magee)	1939 (Lefty Grove)
GI	1903–1924	1926 (Lou Gehrig)	1959 (Hoyt Wilhelm)
Silent	1925–1942	1946 (Del Ennis)	1980 (Jerry Koosman)
Boom	1943–1960	1967 (Blair, Merritt, Nolan)	1994 (Gwynn, Molitor)
Gen X	1961–1981	1984 (Don Mattingly)	2016 (David Ortiz)
Millennial	1982–(?)	2005 (Dontrelle Willis)	

Eras

Missionary and Lost generation era	1901–1925
Lost and GI generation Era	1926–1945
GI and Silent generation era	1946–1966
Silent and Boom generation era	1967–1983
Boom and Xer era	1984–2004
Gen X and Millennial era	2005–

Players and Teams

It is now time to introduce the real subject of this book: the impact of superstar seasons and superstars on their teams. There are two ways of doing this.

For most of the history of baseball, leagues have averaged about .7 superstar seasons per team per year. There is, however, a significant tendency, reflecting better financing or organization, for superstars to concentrate somewhat—and that is what creates great teams. Of the 1773 recorded superstar seasons since 1901, the teams for which the players with at least 4 WAA played averaged seven games above .500. That is more games than the average

WAA of those 1,754 seasons (5.4 WAA). These figures suggest, once again, that assembling seven regulars in the field (or six regulars and a DH) and a supporting cast of pitchers that is average, to complement one superstar, is not especially difficult.

A more detailed look at pennant winners yields even more striking results. The question that first inspired this project, once again, was, "If this man were the best player on your team, could you win the pennant?" As it turns out, over the history of baseball since 1901, it has been extremely difficult to reach the post-season without at least one player with at least 4 WAA.

The Chicago White Sox won the pennant in the American League's debut season of 1901 without a player with 4 WAA, even though there were a number of such players in the league. Four of the first six American League pennant winners also lacked a superstar (1901–1906), but after that, the next AL team to win the pennant without one was the 1944 St. Louis Browns, playing in a weak wartime league. And indeed, in the whole pre-divisional era of the American League (1901–1968), only 11 teams won the pennant without such a player. Most of those teams played in Yankee Stadium: the Yankees 1949–1951 and 1953, when American League superstars were only slightly more common than hen's teeth, and 1963. Pennant winners in the National League without superstars were even rarer from 1901 through 1968: there were only eight of them.

When the problem of reaching the post-season shifted in 1969 from winning a ten-team league to winning a six-team division, it became somewhat easier. Still, only 16 out of 96 division winners in the American and National Leagues in the period 1969–1993 lacked a player with 4 WAA, eight in each league, and only 17 percent of the total. (I have omitted the strike season of 1981 from these calculations.) Combining the two eras into the period 1901–1993, we find that 35 of these 234 teams had no superstar, or just 15 percent. To paraphrase Bill James, without a player with 4 WAA, it was extremely unlikely that your team could win a pennant or division championship from 1901 to 1993. It remained very uncommon for teams without such a player to reach post-season play until quite recently—for reasons that we shall examine in due course.

Baseball introduced the wild card team and three rounds of post-season play in 1994, but that season was not completed because of a strike, and although many, many players were on their way to superstar seasons at the time play ceased, we shall leave it aside because the teams did not play enough games to determine the winner. The shift from two to three divisions in each league, and the addition of first one and then two wild card teams, has obviously made it easier to reach the post-season, and more teams without superstars have managed to do so. The period 1995–2017—the era of one wild card in each team—divides in this respect into three parts. From 1995 through 2004, 16 out of 80 teams that reached the playoffs—20 percent—lacked a single superstar. In 2005–2011, after drug testing had begun and the number of superstars dropped suddenly for the first time in the history of baseball, 25 out of 56 teams—a full 45 percent—lacked even one superstar. In 2012–2017, with ten teams in post-season play every year, 33 percent of them have been without a superstar.

1,773 superstar seasons have been posted by individual players since 1901, an average of about 15 per year. During that time there have been 317 teams with two superstars, 68 with three, and only seven with four. They include the Cleveland Indians (then known as the Naps) of 1913 (Nap Lajoie, Joe Jackson, and pitchers Cy Falkenberg and Vean Gregg) and 1917 (Tris Speaker, shortstop Ray Chapman, and pitchers Stan Coveleski and Jim Bagby), both of whom failed to win the pennant; the Yankees teams of 1927 (Ruth, Gehrig, Earle Combs and Tony Lazzeri) and 1942 (Joe DiMaggio, Charlie Keller, Joe Gordon, and Phil Rizzuto); the 1963 San Francisco Giants (Willie Mays, Willie McCovey, Orlando Cepeda, and Juan Marichal); the Cincinnati Reds of 1972 (Johnny Bench, Pete Rose, Joe Morgan and Tony Perez); and the 2001 Seattle Mariners (Ichiro Suzuki, Bret Boone, Mike Cameron and Edgar Martinez).

To repeat, the Xer-Millennial era has witnessed a sudden decline in the number of superstar seasons. In the Missionary/Lost era of 1901–1925 there were 311 such seasons, an average of .78 superstar seasons per team per year. In the Lost/GI era of 1926–1949 there were 319 such seasons, an average of .76 per season per year—a decline of .02. In the GI/Silent era of 1950–1966, a further decline in superstar seasons, to .70 per team per year, took place. Thanks in part to the Baby Boom, that decline was reversed in the Silent/Boomer era of 1967–1983, when teams posted an average of .73 superstar seasons per year—nearly the same as in 1901–1925.

It is the assumption of most fans that steroids and other PEDs increased the number of outstanding performances in baseball. Yet in fact, although batting averages, home runs, RBIs and runs scored all soared, *above average performance did not.* In the 1984–2004 period, the Boomer/Xer era players posted only .72 superstar seasons per team per year, a decline of .01, essentially the same as in the previous era, even though the expansion of teams in the Boomer-Xer era (from 26 to 30) was smaller than the expansion in the Silent-Boomer era (from 20 to 26.) Then, something very dramatic and quite alarming began in 2005. From 2005 through 2013, the major leagues showed an all-time low of only .54 superstar seasons per team per league, a decline of a full 25 percent from the previous era. One would be tempted to attribute this decline to drug testing, were it not that the use of PEDs in the 1990s and early 2000s did *not*, as we have seen, significantly increase the number of superstar seasons. This will provide us with much food for thought and discussion at the end of the book.

Stephen Jay Gould Was Half Right

Many years ago, Stephen Jay Gould wrote a famous essay, "Why No One Hits .400 Anymore," arguing that .400 averages had disappeared because, as more and more young men played baseball, trained better, and benefited from better instruction, extreme performances became less extreme. While there was a grain of truth to this in one respect, it turns out that he was more wrong than right. This is one of the book's most important conclusions, and I think it best to share it up front.

A season of at least 4 WAA certainly qualifies as an extreme performance. We have seen that such seasons have occurred throughout most of baseball history at the rate of about .7 per team per season. Every team includes eight regular players (nine in the American

League since 1973) plus four or five starting pitchers, depending on the era, who pitch enough innings to achieve 4 WAA. That means that in an average year, seasons over 4 WAA represent about 6 percent of all regular or starting pitcher seasons. We are looking at the cream of the crop—and until 2005, the fluctuations in its size relative to the whole population of regulars were quite modest.

In two other respects, though, Gould had a point. In the Missionary/Lost era (1901–1925), which was essentially the era of the .400 hitter, the best players posted seasons further above average than in later years. Cobb, Ruth, Speaker, Alexander, and a few other players all posted seasons of more than 10 Wins Above Average, but there were only two such seasons (Ted Williams in 1942 and Stan Musial in war-torn 1943) from 1929 through 1966, and only three since then, by Yastrzemski (1967), Barry Bonds (2001) and Albert Pujols (2009). The most extreme performances, in short, became much rarer at almost exactly the same moment that .400 hitters disappeared, but the number of players who sustained superstar levels of performance for at least five seasons did not.

Meanwhile, although the numbers of truly great players have remained extraordinarily consistent from generation to generation, they have fallen significantly both as a percentage of the eligible population (which now includes millions of people born outside the U.S.) and as a percentage of the players in MLB. As I have mentioned, my definition of a great player is one who had at least five seasons of 4 WAA. In the Lost Generation (born 1884–1902), there are 11 hitters and four pitchers in that group. In the GI generation (born 1903–1924), there are 14 hitters and only two pitchers. In the Silent generation (b. 1925–1942) 14 hitters and two pitchers had at least five seasons of at least 4 WAA. In the Boom generation (b. 1943–1960), astonishingly, also had 14 hitters and two pitchers that made the cut. In Generation X, which is still playing but not putting up very many such seasons any more, 14 hitters and eight pitchers rank in that group. David Ortiz became the 14th and last of these hitters in 2016, posting 4.2 WAA at the age of 40, and although Albert Pujols remains a regular, it is quite possible that no one else from Gen X will again crack this charmed circle.

The pattern is even more striking if we focus on the real Olympians, the men with 10 or more seasons over 4 WAA. There were five of those among the Lost Generation (four hitters and one pitcher); four, all hitters, among the GIs (a total much affected by the Second World War); four more among the Silent generation (all hitters); just two hitters in the Boom generation, and three hitters and one pitcher in Generation X. As we shall see, with respect to their impact on their teams and leagues, the careers of Barry Bonds and Babe Ruth, Rickey Henderson and Roberto Clemente, and Willie Mays and Tris Speaker are extraordinarily similar. But proportionally, we don't seem to grow as many of these giants as we used to—perhaps because the number of young men seeking a career in baseball has dropped significantly over the last 75 years.

With the obvious exception of track and field, there are few if any human endeavors, inside or outside sport, in which performance can be measured as accurately as in baseball. And now, with more than a century's worth of evidence upon which to draw, using simple, powerful statistical methods, we find, generation after generation, an astonishingly small number of men who are much, much better than everyone else, and who indeed have shaped the broader story of winners and losers to a remarkable extent. The same pattern probably

The Quality of Teams

This book looks at every pennant and division winner from 1901 through 1993, and most of the teams that have reached the post-season since. Yet it is also a book about greatness, and thus distinguishes again and again among three different categories of pennant winners, defined by their winning percentage and the number of games that they won. In particular, it identifies three categories of winning teams: mediocre pennant winners, superior pennant winners, and great teams.

From 1901 through 1968, 136 teams won pennants. Of those teams, 71, barely over 50 percent, had winning percentages of at least .630 or more, equivalent to 97 wins out of 154 games (from 1901 to 1961 or 1962), or 102 games out of 162. The .630 cutoff comes closest to dividing the pennant winners into two equal groups. We shall refer to the 65 pennant winners with percentages *below* .630 as mediocre pennant winners, all the way down to the 1959 Dodgers, who had the lowest winning percentage (.564) of any pennant winner before divisional play. Using the terminology we shall employ throughout this book, such teams' overall performance represented between +9 and +19 WAA before 1961–1962, and between +11 and +21 thereafter.

Having divided the pennant winners of 1901–68 into two halves, we shall now divide the upper half somewhat more arbitrarily into two groups of their own. 41 of these pennant winners had percentages of between .636 and .661, which works out to between 98 and 102 wins in a 154-game season, and 103–107 games in a 162-game season. These teams rank as superior pennant winners. Their players had to earn between +20 and +25 WAA under the 154-game schedule, and +22 to +26 in 162 games. Lastly, 30 extraordinary teams have had winning percentages of .662 or more, equivalent to at least 103 wins out of 154, or 108 out of 162. They qualify as great teams. The same terms and definitions will be used to refer to teams in the playoff era.

As it turns out, particular eras in the history of the two leagues can easily be defined based upon the frequency of mediocre, superior, and great pennant winners. The 1900s in the AL, the 1910s through the 1940s in the NL, and both leagues in most of the 1960s, were dominated by mediocre pennant winners. The 1900s in the NL and the late 1920s through the early 1940s in the AL featured numerous superior and great teams. After the second round of expansion in 1969 and the division of the leagues into two divisions, mediocrity became much more common.

The Role of Luck

For teams as for players, skill is the most important determinant of success. Luck, however, is a closer second to skill than many of us would like to believe. For players, luck takes the form of balls that are hit just within or beyond the reach of fielders, balls and strikes that are wrongly called by an umpire, and much more. For teams, luck takes two main forms which will arise frequently during this book. They need to be explained, and certain terminology introduced, before we turn to individual seasons, players, and teams.

Two different kinds of luck can have a tremendous effect upon team performance over the course of a season. The first relates to the distribution of the team's runs, and its opponents runs, among the 154 or 162 games that make up a season. Close games, those decided by one or two runs, are especially critical here. The outcome of such games, it can easily be demonstrated, *bears a much looser relationship to the overall quality of the two teams involved than the outcome of games decided by many runs.* It is not at all uncommon for a team with a .600 winning percentage to have a .500 record, or worse, in close games, and a number of teams have lost (or won) a pennant because of a very good or very bad record in close games. Teams whose records in close games are exceptionally good or exceptionally bad will have unusual deviations in their actual winning percentage from their Pythagorean projection, as discussed above. For that reason, we refer to the luck that causes a team to finish six games, for instance, above its projection, as "Pythagorean luck."

No one, to my knowledge, has ever identified any factor other than luck that might allow a team consistently to win most of its close games and exceed its projection. There is no evidence, in short, that beating one's projection has anything to do with clutch hitting and pitching, superior character, better managerial strategy, or anything else. If it did, teams presumably would be able to beat their projection consistently over a period of years, and almost no team has ever been able to do that. Over the whole of the history of the major leagues since 1901, the average Pythagorean luck of every team is four wins, positive or negative—the equivalent of one superstar in or out of the lineup. It is not unheard of for it to miss or exceed it by ten wins.

The second kind of luck that affects the performance of teams will be called "run luck." Just as the number of games won is determined in part by the distribution of a team's runs among its games, the number of runs a team scores is determined by how well (or badly) it bunches its walks and hits during a game. Offensive run luck has been measured with a considerable degree of accuracy by researcher Pete Palmer, who has kindly made his data available to me. Palmer uses linear weights, which assign a run value to every hit, walk, stolen base, and out, to estimate how many runs a team should score in a season. He kindly provided me with his data, and over the course of major league baseball, 1901–2016, the sum of every team's deviations is so close to zero as to leave no doubt that his projections are accurate. As in the case of Pythagorean luck, however, teams often have 30–50 runs' worth of good or bad run luck and occasionally have as much as 100. Run luck, while it seems to emerge less frequently in winning or losing pennants than Pythagorean luck, can sometimes play a comparable role, as will be indicated when it arises.

Thanks to the data from baseball-prospectus.com, we can compute how many runs each hitter on a given team of hitters figured to create. If they had exceptionally good or bad run luck, there will be a discrepancy between the sum of those individual figures, and the actual number of runs the team scored. In several key instances, I have found that such discrepancies match the discrepancy Palmer found quite closely.

Every team also has defensive run luck—that is, the number of runs it *allows* depends on the ability of its opponents to bunch their hits and walks—or conversely, if you prefer, on the defensive team's pitchers' and fielders' ability to prevent them from bunching them. Unfortunately, I have no database comparable to Palmer's which measures defensive run luck for each major league team/season since 1901, by comparing how many runs their opponents' walks, hits, etc., *should* have generated to the number of runs the team actually gave up. Thus, my analysis attributes every extra run saved or allowed by every team either to its pitchers or its fielders. This has undoubtedly done some teams an injustice, but I cannot help it.

The reader will frequently encounter the phrases "good Pythagorean luck," "bad Pythagorean luck," "run luck," and "defensive run luck" while reading this book. He or she should also be prepared to put the book down with a much-enhanced appreciation of the enormous role that luck plays in the outcome of individual games, series, and seasons—as well as in life in general.

Team Statistics: Hitting, Fielding, Pitching

I will now return to the issue of team performance, around which much of the narrative of this book will be organized. Great players, together with stars of somewhat lesser value (2–3 WAA), make up great teams. Fortunately, our new metrics, led by Humphreys' DRA, allow us to identify and measure what part of a team's superiority came from hitting, pitching, and fielding. To understand exactly how we are going to do this, we need to return to the Pythagorean formula and its implications.

Let's begin with one of the truly great teams of history, the 1969 Baltimore Orioles. That team, featuring Frank and Brooks Robinson, Paul Blair, Mark Belanger, Boog Powell, and Jim Palmer, scored 779 runs and allowed 517 runs. Their Pythagorean percentage gave them 110 expected wins, and they actually won 109. Accepting luck as part of baseball and life, we shall consistently base our ratings of teams on their actual won-lost record, while always noting how many games it owed to, or lost to, Pythagorean luck—in this case, -1. With 109 wins, the Orioles were 28 wins over .500.

More interesting, however, is the disaggregation of the 1969 Orioles' 28-win edge. The Orioles' hitters, it turns out, created about 128 park-adjusted runs more than average in 1969. In the run environment of that year, those runs were worth +13 games. Using Michael Humphreys' fielding data for the entire team of fielders, we find that the Orioles' fielders saved 81 park-adjusted runs, equivalent to another +8 games. The Orioles' line-up in the field, in other words—Andy Etchebarren behind the plate, Powell at first, Dave Johnson at second, Belanger at short, Brooks Robinson at third, and Don Buford, Blair and Frank Robinson in the outfield—earned the Orioles +21 wins over .500. *With perfectly average pitching, as opposed to defense including both pitching and fielding*, the Orioles should have finished with 102 wins. But their actual projection should have earned them eight more. That was the contribution of the pitching staff. Throughout this book, the contribution of a team's lineup will always refer to the sum of the hitting and fielding contributions of its non-pitchers.

In my opinion, Michael Humphreys's measurement of fielding skill—which can be applied to an entire team as easily as to any individual player—is at least as accurate as any readily available measure of pure pitching ability. Thus I have decided to compute the contribution of pitching staffs simply by subtracting the number of runs the fielders saved from the positive or negative differential of total runs allowed for the team in question. This method is completely consistent with the conclusions of Voros McCracken, who found that individual pitchers have little or no influence on what happens to balls that they allow hitters to put into play. If McCracken is right—and I believe he is—the value of pitchers generally boils down to their ability to increase strikeouts, decrease walks, and decrease opposition home runs. In this analysis pitchers also receive credit, in effect, for their own assists and, more importantly, for popups in the infield, since Humphreys does not use infield putouts as part of his regression equations to measure infielder fielding skill.

Many readers will have been surprised to hear that the Orioles' fielders in 1969 won the team eight games, and their pitchers seven. The Orioles of that era were known for a great pitching staff, like the Milwaukee Braves in the late 1950s, the Oakland As of the early 1970s, and many Yankees teams. All those reputations, however, turn out to be highly misleading. No aspect of baseball mythology is more enduring than the supposed importance of pitching. Connie Mack reportedly said that pitching was 75 percent of the game. Both Pete Palmer and John Thorn, in *The Hidden Game of Baseball*, and Bill James, in developing his Win Shares system, assumed that team pitching skill was about twice as important as team fielding skill. All of them were wrong. The standard deviation for wins contributed by hitting over the history of baseball is eight wins. The standard deviation for pitching is six wins, and for fielding, four wins. That still makes pitching measurably more important than fielding, but again and again we shall find that dynasties owe most of their superiority to their hitting and fielding, not their pitching. And since the hitters and fielders are the same men, these standard deviations show that the eight (or now, in the AL, nine) non-pitchers in the line-up account for more than three times as much of the variance among teams as the pitchers do. In the history of baseball, there have been almost no dynasties that relied mainly upon their pitching staffs. The most striking exception to that rule, interestingly enough, is the Atlanta Braves from the late 1990s.

Of course, like a team's won-lost record, all these measurements are subject to luck as well. A player or a team can post extraordinary fielding numbers in a given season simply because a large number of batted balls happened to fall just within his, or their, reach. A hitter can, and often does, win the batting title thanks to seeing-eye ground balls, and a hitter could possibly win the home run championship because of a fluke string of windy days. But Humphreys found far too much consistency in his fielding data to doubt that he had identified true measurements of skill. This book will look at the greatest teams in baseball history and find what made them great. Fielding has been much more important than is generally supposed, and pitching much less so. And that leads us to the biggest anomaly in baseball statistics of all.

For 100 years pitchers have been evaluated mainly with two metrics: their won-lost record and their ERA. Both are extraordinarily dependent variables. The won-lost record is essentially their *team's* record in the games that they started, and the team's offensive performance is responsible for 50 percent of that. Their fielders are responsible for a good deal more, and their park, their era, and their fielders exert a huge influence on their ERA. As a result, our impression of who the greatest pitchers have been in any given season or era is highly misleading—as selections to the Hall of Fame show. While dominant pitchers exist in every era, the ones that wind up winning 200 games and getting to Cooperstown often do so out of a mixture of durability, on the one hand, and good fortune in having the right teammates on the other. Nearly every reputedly great pitching staff in history has in fact been a staff of average or slightly above average pitchers working in a pitchers' park with a strong offensive line-up. This applies to both the Orioles and the As or the early 1970s, the Yankees of the 1950s, and many more.

This book is about how great players make great teams. Historically, hitters have been more important than pitchers, all the more so because great pitchers very rarely remain great for very long. There is no substitute for developing a superstar and retaining him for the first 10–15 years of his career. This is a book not only for fans, but for managers and executives as well.

1

The Missionary and Lost Generation Era, 1901–1924

Major league baseball assumed its modern shape in 1901, when Ban Johnson transformed the Western League into the American League, joining the National League as a second major league, each with eight teams. It took several years for the leagues to recognize one another's contracts and start playing an annual World Series, and until 1904, both leagues played schedules of approximately 135 games in a season, not the 154 that became the standard from 1904 through 1960. Shorter schedules invariably generate more extreme performances by individual players. Expansion has the same effect, and the creation of the American League obviously involved a substantial dilution of major league talent. Two players, pitcher Cy Young of the Boston Americans and left fielder Jesse Burkett of the St. Louis Cardinals, led the two leagues in 1901 with 7.1 Wins Above Average apiece, a very high figure. Young went 33–10 with a 1.62 ERA on a team that played just 136 games.

The Missionary/Lost era of modern major league baseball coincides pretty closely with what is normally known as the dead ball era (1901–1919). It popularized the statistics that have dominated our understanding of the game, for better or worse, during most of the next 114 years, including batting average, home runs, and above all, pitchers' won-lost records. Individual pitchers had far more impact on their teams in this era than in any subsequent period. This was in large part because most teams, and especially most good teams, tended to rely almost exclusively on just five pitchers, and a great pitcher might pitch as many as 400 innings in a season—the equivalent of 44 games, more than ¼ of his team's total. Even in this era, hitters posted 179 superstar seasons of at least 4 WAA while pitchers had just 133, but this was the highest percentage by pitchers in any era. Yet because outstanding pitching seasons have such a pronounced tendency to occur at random, we shall find at the end of this chapter that pitching was only marginally more important in determining who would win the pennant than it was in subsequent eras. It accounted for only ⅓ of the variance among winning teams.

Offensive variance was already the most important part of the game, even though home runs were extremely rare and walk totals were much lower than in later eras. It is, unfortunately, impossible to evaluate the impact of stolen bases, which were numerous, before 1914, because no data on times caught stealing were kept. Interestingly enough, when the National League began keeping caught stealing data in 1913, they showed that only 56 percent of stealing attempts were successful, meaning that stolen bases overall cost each team a number of runs, although certain players probably gained their team a few runs by succeeding more than 66 percent of the time. Fielding variance was very great. Far more balls were put into play because of fewer strikeouts and home runs than later, defensive instruction was evidently primitive, and the variance of fielding skill at different positions was very high.

The National League was now the senior circuit, and it fielded the strongest teams in the first decade of the twentieth century. Three teams won all the National League pennants in the first 13 years of the new century: the Pittsburgh Pirates (1901–1903, 1909), the New York Giants (1904–1905, 1911–1913), and the Chicago Cubs (1906–1908, 1910). Never in those 13 years did a pennant winner fall below the level of a .630 percentage (97 out of 154 wins), the mark of a superior pennant winner. Those three teams also contested one of the first two great pennant races in modern baseball history in 1908, with the Cubs besting the Giants by a single game after winning a replay of the contest that had been declared a 1–1 tie, instead of a 2–1 Giants victory, thanks to first baseman Fred Merkle's famous base running boner. And like every dynasty, each of these teams was built around two or three superstars who repeatedly exceeded 4 WAA per season.

The Chicago Cubs started the new century slowly, but from 1904 through 1912 established themselves as an extraordinary dynasty, winning at least 91 games in every one of those seasons, topping 100 wins four times (1906–1907 and 1909–1910) and setting records that still stand with 116 wins and a .763 winning percentage in 1906. They won the pennant in 1906–1908 and in 1910 and set a record for a second-place team that still stands in 1909 with 104 wins. Although their pitching staffs had two of the greatest years in baseball history in 1905 and 1909, earning +19 and +14 wins above average, respectively, the Cubs failed to win the pennant in either of those years, and won their pennants primarily because of their hitting and fielding. Franklin P. Adams, it turns out, was showing genuine baseball acumen when he wrote his famous poem about the Cubs' infielders, Joe Tinker, Johnny Evers, and Frank Chance.

In 1906, the Cubs' record-setting, 116-win year, they were the first great fielding team in modern baseball history. (It turns out to be almost impossible for a team to achieve a run differential worth a winning percentage of .690 or more without vastly superior fielding.) Their fielders saved 95 runs, worth ten full games. Michael Humphreys discovered extraordinary variance among fielders in the early twentieth century, and with the sole exception of third baseman Harry Steinfeldt—the forgotten man of that famous infield—every regular on the team saved runs, relative to the league. Shortstop Joe Tinker saved +34 runs, second baseman Evers +22, and first baseman Chance +8. The forgotten outfield of Jimmy Sheckard, Jimmy Slagle and Frank Schulte saved +57 among them. The fielders were just as good in WAA in 1908 and in 1910, despite their advancing age. The Cubs' hitting was generally at least as superior as their fielding, earning them +17 WAA in 1906, just +6 WAA in 1907, +13 WAA in 1908, and +11 WAA in 1910.

The Cubs' lineup in these years turned in only a few individual superstar performances, but they were a team of stars in which most of their lineup often earned 2 WAA or more.

1. The Missionary and Lost Generation Era, 1901–1924

Combining hitting and fielding, Chance earned 5.5 WAA in 1906, Evers put up 5.7 WAA in 1907, and Tinker earned 6.3 WAA in 1908. The Cubs' pitching never earned the team more wins than their hitting in their pennant-winning seasons, but it remained an asset thanks to fantastic individual performances. Mordecai "Three Finger" Brown earned 3.8 WAA (and a 26–6 record) in 1906, 2.8 WAA in 1907 (20–6), 4.9 WAA in 1908 (when he went 29–9 in 312⅓ innings), 5.2 in 1909 (27–9), and 2.5 in 1910. Orvie Overall joined Brown with 2.9 WAA in 1907 and 4.3 in 1909, when the team was narrowly beaten by the Pirates. Leonard "King" Cole was the ace of the 1910 staff with 3.5 WAA (he went 20–4), but like so many others, apparently burned his arm out and never came close to that level in the rest of his brief career. The Cubs were the strongest dynasty of the era, although amazingly, their best team of all—the 116-game-winning team of 1906—lost the World Series to a mediocre crosstown White Sox club in six games.

Given that the record of the 1906 Cubs remains unsurpassed, they provide a fascinating test case for the kind of analysis that we shall apply to all the most successful teams of the past and present. The Cubs' positive run differential of 320 runs projected out to a record of 113–41, 36 wins over .500 (or 36 WAA). Pythagorean luck allowed them to win three more games, for a total of 116. Where exactly did those 36 WAA come from? The numbers tell the tale.

The Cubs' lineup—the players in the field—contributed +29 WAA, +17 of them at bat and +12 in the field. Although Frank Chance, with 5.5 WAA (most of them at bat), was their only superstar, every player in the lineup but one met the definition of a star, with at least 2 WAA. These included second baseman Evers (2.4 WAA, all from his fielding), shortstop Tinker (2.5, also in the field), third baseman Harry Steinfeldt (2.7, mostly at bat), and outfielders Sheckard (2.9), Schulte (2.4), and Slagle (2.2). Catcher Johnny Kling just missed the same distinction with 1.9 WAA of his own. These eight players' totals added up to only 22.6 WAA, and their reserves cost them some runs, but the Cubs scored enough runs to earn 29 thanks to run luck. Their hitting statistics projected to 630 runs scored, but they actually scored 704, indicating an extraordinary bunching of their hits and walks. The pitchers, meanwhile, added another +8 WAA thanks to Brown (3.8), Reulbach (2.3), and Jack Pfister (2.1). We shall find that both extraordinary fielding—which is probably in part due to luck, since it may reflect an unusual number of balls hit just within fielders' reach—and good fortune have contributed to all the greatest teams in history, the ones with a winning percentage of .700 or more.

The anchor of the Pittsburgh Pirates' dynasty, of course, was shortstop Honus Wagner, the greatest offensive player of the Missionary generation (born 1863–1882), the most dominant shortstop of all time, and the first player in the modern era to post the extraordinary figure of ten seasons of 4 WAA or more. Wagner's career had several amazing features. Showing a pattern that Roberto Clemente replicated 60 years later, he became even better after turning 30 in 1904. Wagner posted seasons of 4.9, 4.5, 5, and 4.9 WAA in 1901–1904, and 7.7, 7, 7.1, 7.7, and 6.7 WAA in 1905–1909, when he turned 35. His batting averages in those years ranged from .330 to .363, and he led the league in doubles or triples eight times in nine years. Most of his value came from his hitting, although he was a significantly above-average shortstop until 1907, and about average thereafter. A versatile player, he was a regular outfielder in 1902. Wagner was generally (although not always) the most valuable offensive player on the Pirates, and as in nearly every dynasty we shall encounter, the vast majority of the Pirates' superiority came from their hitting and fielding. Here are the contributions of the Pirates' hitters, fielders and pitchers to their four pennant-winning teams from 1901 to 1909.

Year	Hitting (games)	Fielding (games)	Pitching (games)	Won	Lost
1901	+13	+4	+7	90	49
1902	+22	+5	+7	103	36
1903	+11	+6	0	91	49
1909	+13	+8	+8	110	42

Two of these teams, in 1902 and 1909, were all-time great teams, with winning percentages of .741 and .724, respectively, putting them among the top 15 teams of all time. The 1902 team also featured third baseman Tommy Leach, who turned in his best season ever with 5 WAA, and pitcher Jack Chesbro, who earned 4.6 WAA with a record of 28–6. (The team, typical for that era, had only five pitchers with more than 30 innings pitched.) The 1903 team had pitcher Sam Leaver, who earned 5.3 WAA with a 25–7 record. Leaver was the first of many pitchers who managed to reach a superstar level only once. Meanwhile, outfielder-manager Fred Clarke and center fielder Ginger Beaumont contributed about two wins a year each. The 1909 team, like the 1906 Cubs, was extraordinarily balanced. Wagner was its only superstar, but three other regulars in the field (including Clarke) and three pitchers had 2–3 WAA each.

John McGraw's New York Giants won the remaining pennants of the first decade of the century in 1904–1905, and three more from 1911–1913. They won an impressive 105 and 106 games in 1904–1905 thanks to their lineups, which earned +26 and +20 WAA in those years. Their offensive superstars in 1904 were shortstop Bill Dahlen (4.5) and right fielder Sam Mertes (5.1), both of whom made most of their contribution in the field. Roger Bresnahan—in 1904 an outfielder, then a catcher—first baseman Dan McGann, third baseman Art Devlin and second baseman Billy Gilbert were stars as well. Mike Donlin, a new acquisition in the outfield, led the lineup with 5 WAA in 1905, and Mertes and Dahlen remained stars as well. And although the pitching staff was much less responsible for the team's success in the first decade of the century, their greatest player, of course, was one of the two greatest pitchers of the Missionary generation, Christy Mathewson, who between 1901 and 1913 nearly matched Wagner with nine seasons of 4 WAA or more, five of which topped 6 WAA. No single player was more responsible for his team's success. Mathewson was not the ace of the Giants' staff on their first pennant winner of 1904. Joe "Iron Man" McGinnity pitched 408 innings, earning 4.7 WAA and a 35–8 record, while the 23-year-old Mathewson had 1.7 WAA and a record of 33–12 in 367⅔ innings. But Mathewson surpassed McGinnity in 1905 with 6 WAA, while McGinnity, not surprisingly after two years over 400+ innings pitched, failed to reach average for the remainder of his career. Despite the brilliance of McGinnity and Mathewson in 1904–1905, the pitching staff in those years contributed only +4 and +8 WAA overall. Mathewson's 6 WAA represented most of the 1905 total, and he topped off 1905 with three shutouts in the World Series against the Philadelphia Athletics.

1. The Missionary and Lost Generation Era, 1901–1924

The Giants slumped a bit in 1906–1907, but in 1908 Mathewson had his greatest season, winning 37 games and earning 7.3 WAA, one-third of the 21 wins that the team finished over .500. Pitcher "Hooks" Wiltse added another 3.4 WAA, and the Giants' pitching staff totaled +9 WAA while the lineup added +14, led by Donlin's 4.2 WAA. Sadly for Mathewson, he was beaten, 4–2, by Mordecai Brown in the post-season replay that decided one of the most exciting pennant races in history. Mathewson posted 5.9 WAA as the Giants won 90 games and the pennant in 1911, and Rube Marquard added 4.7. They had star seasons of 3.8 and 2.3 WAA in 1912, when the Giants won 103 games, and Mathewson turned in 3.8 WAA pitching for his last pennant winner in 1913.

The 1911–1913 Giants, were a genuine pitching dynasty, the first of a very small number in the history of baseball. The better teams were consistently using only five pitchers with 100 or more innings pitched, and in 1911 Mathewson and Marquard were complemented by Red Ames, Doc Crandall, and Hooks Wiltse, all of whom contributed at least one extra win. The 1911 staff contributed +16 WAA to the team, compared to just +6 for the offensive players, who fielded badly. In 1912 Jeff Tesreau chipped in with 3 WAA, and in 1913 Tesreau and Al Demaree again joined Mathewson and Marquard as significantly superior pitchers. The 1912 pitchers contributed +13 WAA, the same as the hitters (their fielding was average), and the 1913 team had 10 WAA among the pitchers and the same number in the lineup. The 1911–1913 teams did not boast a single offensive superstar, but most of the regulars were at least average. Meanwhile, the balance of power between the leagues had changed. The NL's era of dominance ended in 1908, and the newer American League rapidly established a superiority that it did not relinquish until the 1960s.

The American League, founded by Byron Bancroft Johnson, got off to a wild and wooly start punctuated by lawsuits over players' contracts. For its first three years, both leagues played schedules of 135–140 games per season, finally settling on the standard 154 in 1904, a number they stuck to until 1961–1962. Although short seasons give players less time to accumulate WAA, they also result in more extreme hitting and pitching performances, since more games inevitably cause even the best players to regress towards the mean. The Chicago White Sox won the first American League pennant in 1901 without the benefit of a single superstar and repeated that feat in 1906—the last American League team to accomplish that feat until the 1944 Browns. After 1901, the next four pennants were divided between the Philadelphia Athletics (1902, 1905) and the Boston Red Sox (1903–1904). None of these clubs reached the level of a superior pennant winner, that is, a winning percentage of .630 or 98 wins out of 154 games. The strength of those Athletics teams was on the mound, featuring two left-handers of contrasting types. Rube Waddell had a similar fastball and career path to Sandy Koufax. For four seasons, 1902–1905, he was head and shoulders above every pitcher in the league, with WAA totals of 7.1, 7.0, 7.8 and 7.4—actually superior to Koufax's run in 1963–1966. Waddell pitched from 276 to 383 innings in those years, and he is now credited with 349 strikeouts in 1904, a figure first exceeded by Koufax in 1965.[7] The range of his win totals, from 21 to 27, almost exactly matched Koufax's in his peak years as

---

7. Bob Feller was credited with a new season strikeout record of 348 in 1948, when Waddell was thought to have struck out a few less batters.

well. The Athletics' other ace was "Gettysburg Eddie" Plank, who was more similar to Warren Spahn. While not nearly as dominant as Waddell, Plank was even more of a workhorse, and topped 4 WAA in three of these four years, peaking at 6.2 in 1904. The Athletics' pitchers accounted for nearly their entire positive run differential in 1905, earning+ 14 WAA while their hitters earned just +4 and their fielding cost them -3.

The Athletics would have been a true dynasty, surely, had they not lost the services of the American League's first all-time offensive great, second baseman Nap Lajoie, to the Cleveland Blues after the 1901 season. Lajoie was more dominant in the American League than Wagner was in the National from 1901 through 1908, nearly always leading offensive players in WAA with totals of between 6 and 9 WAA in six seasons. He was both a great hitter (lifetime BA of .336) and a fine second baseman whose fielding was twice worth more than 4 WAA in a single year. But he was the unluckiest superstar in the history of baseball. Cleveland lost the 1906 pennant by two games to a much inferior Chicago White Sox team, even though Lajoie, shortstop Terry Turner, and outfielder Elmer Flick combined for +21 WAA. They lost the 1908 pennant race to the Tigers by half a game, even though pitcher Addie Joss had 4.2 WAA and Lajoie 9. With ten seasons over 4 WAA, Lajoie is easily the most dominant player in baseball history never to have appeared in a World Series. Lajoie was unlucky again in 1913, when he was on the first team since the founding of the American League to have four different superstars—Lajoie (4 WAA), young Shoeless Joe Jackson (6.4), and pitchers Cy Falkenberg (4.0) and Willie Mitchell (4.0). Unfortunately the rest of the lineup was about -6 WAA, and Falkenburg and Mitchell represented the whole positive value of the pitching staff. The team won 86 games, finishing in third place.

The 1906 Chicago White Sox, who edged out Lajoie's Naps and the New York Highlanders for the pennant, were one of the luckiest pennant winners in the history of baseball. They had no superstars, and their run differential projected them to win only 89 games, while Cleveland figured to win 98. Amazingly, the White Sox finished four games ahead of their Pythagorean projection while the Naps missed theirs by nine games. And as if winning the pennant against the odds were not enough, they promptly defeated their crosstown rivals, the Chicago Cubs, who had just set a record that still stands with 116 wins and 36 losses, in a six-game World Series.

From 1907 through 1918, the American League was dominated by three dynasties. The Detroit Tigers won three consecutive pennants from 1907–1909, the Philadelphia Athletics won four in 1910–1911 and 1913–1914, and the Boston Red Sox won four pennants in 1912, 1915–1916, and 1918. Each of these dynasties was built around a single superstar: Ty Cobb of the Tigers, Eddie Collins of the Athletics, and Tris Speaker of the Red Sox. Cobb and Speaker were two of the three greatest players of the Lost Generation and two of the greatest 15 hitters of all time, posting 14 and 15 superstar seasons, respectively. They set a new standard for career greatness, one that only about three players per generation have been able to equal ever since. Collins ranks with Rogers Hornsby as the greatest second basemen of all time.

Born in Georgia late in 1886, Ty Cobb joined the Detroit Tigers briefly in 1905 at the age of 18 and played most of a season in 1906. He blossomed in 1907 at age 20, leading the league with a .350 batting average, 212 hits and 119 runs batted in. Cobb was credited with

12 out of 13 batting titles from 1907 through 1919, although modern research has concluded that he actually lost the 1910 batting title to Napoleon Lajoie. Although Cobb in that period never hit as many as ten home runs in a season, he also led the league in slugging percentage eight times and on-base percentage seven times. More to the point for our purposes, he had at least 6 WAA every year but two from 1905 through 1917, and topped 9 WAA—a truly astonishing figure—in 1909, 1910, 1911, and 1917 (when he set his personal record with 11.3). Cobb, who usually played center field, was a very fine outfielder from 1907 through 1911, saving 10–22 runs a year relative to average, and usually posted good figures in the field for the rest of his career. He was also the leading base stealer of his era, although because we lack caught stealing data for most of the early part of his career, we cannot tell how many runs his base-running added for his team. Data for 1912 and 1914–1916 show him caught in about ⅓ of his attempts, which, as we know now, means that the impact of his base-stealing was essentially neutral. One exception was 1916, when he stole 68 bases and was caught only 24 times. Given his extraordinary dominance, the biggest question suggested by his career is why the Tigers managed to win only three pennants during the 21 seasons he spent with the team—figures that almost exactly match those of another much later great, Willie Mays.[8]

Indeed, despite Cobb, only one of the three pennant-winners Cobb played on—the 1909 Tigers—was anywhere close to dominant. The Tigers won just 92 games in 1907 and, as we have seen, was very fortunate to finish above a superior Cleveland team in 1908 by just half a game, going 90–63. Led by Cobb, the offense provided most of their edge, with +14 WAA in 1907 and +11 in both 1908 and 1909. The second most valuable player was another outfielder, Sam Crawford, whose best years were behind him by 1907, but who nonetheless had more than 3 WAA in that year and in 1909. With three seasons over 4 WAA and five more of 3 WAA or more, Crawford, who still holds the career record for triples, was a reasonable if not overwhelming selection for the Hall of Fame as well. Pitchers Wild Bill Donovan in 1907–1908 and Ed Killian in 1907 and 1909 contributed 2–3 WAA each.

The 1909 team improved to 98 wins in, partly thanks to an important new acquisition, 21-year-old Donie Bush. Bush's remained Cobb's teammate for the next 13 years and set a pattern destined to be repeated many times in the future, one which might be dubbed Declining Shortstop Syndrome. While never one of history's greatest shortstops, Bush saved enough runs at shortstop to win the Tigers 1–2 games for the first four years of his career, and earned 3 and 3.8 WAA overall in his first two seasons. But then, with his reputation as a top shortstop firmly established, he slipped below average in 1913 and remained there—sometimes to the extent of -2 games—for the rest of his career. Reliable fielding statistics now confirm that this pattern has repeated itself in every era, from Bush through Travis Jackson of the Giants to Phil Rizzuto of the Yankees, Luis Aparicio of the Orioles and Red Sox, and Derek Jeter of the Yankees.

The Tigers' pitching collapsed completely in 1910, and the team slipped to 86 wins. Although Cobb had one of his greatest seasons with 10.1 WAA, the rest of his teammates in the field added only 3 more. In 1911 Cobb was nearly as good, hitting .420 (his highest

---

8. In 19 full seasons with the New York/San Francisco Giants, Mays was on three pennant winners and one division winner.

mark) with 9.9 WAA, but the rest of the lineup surrendered -6 WAA. Cobb hit .409 with 7.7 WAA in 1912, but only two other regulars were above average, and the team won only 69 games. They slumped further in 1913 when Cobb fell to just 5.8 WAA. In 1915, Cobb's 6.1 WAA led the strongest Tigers team he ever played on, but its 100 wins fell one game shy of the Boston Red Sox, who posted a slightly inferior run differential. That was the last time Cobb's Tigers came close to a pennant. From 1916 through 1922, Cobb's teammates in the lineup were at best average, and at worst (1920) a full 13 wins below average. The pitchers were also usually below average, and the Tigers' best showing was an 80–60 record in the shortened 1919 season. Cobb had begun having injury problems in 1918 and did not play as many as 130 games in any of the next four years. He had his last great season in 1922, with 6.4 WAA at the age of 35—another extraordinary parallel, as we shall find, to Willie Mays—and he was still a superstar in 1923, when he was joined by the even better Harry Heilmann, who posted 7.3 WAA to Cobb's 4.4. Heilmann remained a superstar during the next two seasons, but the Tigers could still not crack 90 wins. Heilmann was a late bloomer—he did not crack 4 WAA until his sixth year as a regular (1921), when he was 26—but he finished his career with five superstar seasons, amply qualified for election to the Hall of Fame.

After the 1926 season, Cobb was released as player-manager by the Tigers, following a scandal that erupted when retired pitcher Dutch Leonard revealed a letter implicating both Cobb and Tris Speaker in fixing a late-season game in 1919, the year of the Black Sox. After Commissioner Landis ruled, in effect, that the statute of limitations had passed, Cobb (and Speaker) spent two years with the Philadelphia Athletics. The Georgia Peach posted 3.6 WAA at age 40 in 1927 and 1.4 WAA in 1928—a performance that puts modern veterans like Pete Rose, Cal Ripken, Jr., and Derek Jeter to shame. He was still an asset when he got his last base hit.

Our survey of Cobb's career—altogether one of the half-dozen most impressive in baseball history—has taken us away from the broader history of the American League. His 1907–1909 Tigers gave way in 1910 to another dynasty, the first of two put together by Connie Mack's Athletics, which won four pennants in five years with an average winning percentage of .657, with three World Series wins to boot.

The 1910–1914 Athletics exceeded the .636 percentage of a superior pennant winner three times and just missed it in one other year. They were known for their "$100,000 Infield," composed of first baseman Stuffy McInnis, second baseman Eddie Collins, shortstop Jack Barry, and third baseman Frank "Home Run" Baker. Collins, only 23 in 1910, was the true superstar of the team and one of the five greatest players of the Lost Generation, and it was no accident that his two teams led the league in either wins or run differential in eight out of 11 seasons from 1909 through 1919. Helped by an extraordinary year in the field in 1910, he posted a remarkable 9.5 WAA, and followed it up with 4.7 in 1911, 6.8 in 1912, 7.8 in 1913 and 4.8 in 1914. Baker, only a year older than Collins, had three consecutive superstar seasons in 1912–1914, the only ones he ever had. That was enough, remarkably, to make Baker not only the greatest third baseman of the Lost Generation, but the best at that position until Eddie Mathews. Barry (also Collins' age) and McInnis (the youngest, just 19 in 1910, and not a regular until the next year) were above average players in those years as well. Their outfielders contributed more modestly. The Athletics' lineup, led by Collins and Baker, earned

+19 WAA in 1910, +17 in 1911, +26 in 1913, and +20 in 1914. It could have done even better, but Mack in 1910 made the astonishing blunder of shipping Shoeless Joe Jackson, then 22 years old, to the Cleveland Naps as a throw-in to complete an earlier deal.

Their pitching contributed much more modestly during these five years. In 1910, Collins's 9.5 WAA were supplemented by 5.7 from hurler Jack Coombs (31–9), who also beat the Cubs three times in the World Series. Although Eddie Plank and Chief Bender posted over 3 WAA in 1911, Coombs had the only superstar pitching performance of this dynasty. Overall the pitchers earned +5 and +8 WAA in 1910–1911, but they fell apart, slipping to -7 in 1912 and 1913. They rebounded once again to +3 in 1914 with the help of two youngsters, Bullet Joe Bush and Bob Shawkey. Hitting and fielding accounted for 66–80 percent of the Athletics' edge during these years.

Then came the deluge. The 1910s were the most contentious decade in player management relations until the 1970s, and entrepreneurs took advantage of the situation to form the Federal League in 1914. The reserve clause, of course, bound players in perpetuity to the team that had signed them, and Connie Mack knew the value of a dollar and was not about to write bigger checks when some of his stars threatened to depart after the 1914 season. Mack claimed in his autobiography that the team in late 1914 was split between loyalists and defectors, and implied that that contributed to their shocking, four-game loss to the Boston Braves in the World Series. Two of Mack's stars, Eddie Plank and Chief Bender, did sign with the Federal League for 1915, but Plank was 38 and could not have been regarded as a critical loss. What Connie Mack now did to his team, however, has occurred on only two other occasions in the history of modern baseball, and Mack himself was the author of one of them.

With the whole Athletics' infield still in its prime and two good young pitchers having just joined the staff, there was absolutely no reason why the Athletics could not have gone on winning pennants for at least five more years. In another inexplicable development, Mack's attendance had just fallen from 572,000 in 1913 (second in the league) to 347,000 in 1914 (fifth), despite their cruise to another pennant. Mack reacted rather drastically and disastrously—to say the least.

In the winter of 1914–1915, Mack sold Eddie Collins—one of the three greatest players in the American League—to the White Sox for $50,000. Collins did not want to leave Philadelphia and was still under a long-term contract, but Mack, working with league President Ban Johnson, appears to have brought the sale about. In the middle of the 1915 season, he sold Jack Barry to the Red Sox for $10,000, and Bob Shawkey, a pitcher with a fine career ahead of him, to the Yankees for just $5,000. Home Run Baker went to the Yankees for $37,500 in early 1916. Both the team and attendance had now collapsed—the Athletics lost a record 117 games and drew 184,000 fans in 1916—and Mack traded Joe Bush to Boston with catcher Wally Schang and outfielder Amos Strunk in early 1917 for a few warm bodies and $60,000. Stuffy McInnis, a Boston-area native, was traded to Boston 1918 for Larry Gardner, a quality player, and a couple of others. Charlie Finley of the Oakland A's tried to embark upon a comparable fire sale in 1976, after the era of free agency began, but Bowie Kuhn stopped him.

The results of Mack's fire sale were quite astonishing and, indeed, have never been duplicated. Fresh from 99 wins and a pennant in 1914, the 1915 Athletics set a record for negative run differential, giving up 360 more runs than they scored—a sum that has been topped only once, by the 1932 Boston Red Sox, in a year when runs were *far* easier to come by. And as if that were not enough, the 1916 Athletics, while improving their run differential to a still-amazing -346 (tied for sixth-worst in history), added five games worth of bad luck into the mix and finished with a record of 36 wins and 117 losses, almost the exact opposite of the Cubs' record-setting 1906 season and the worst percentage (.235) in modern baseball. They remained utterly dreadful through 1921 and improved only to respectably bad for the next two years, before reaching the .500 mark in 1924 and becoming a genuinely strong team in 1927. The effect of this was parallel to the effect of expansion in 1961–1962, 1969, and subsequently. Given that the average team stood to go 17–5 in its 22 games with Philadelphia, a series of close pennant races was very likely, and that indeed is what took place.

The Athletics' dynasty had already been interrupted by the Boston Red Sox, who returned to the top in 1912 with a record of 105–47, a record not surpassed in the American League until 1927. Their key player was center fielder Tris Speaker, who had broken in with a superstar season in 1909 with 6.2 WAA at age 21 and gone on from there. Speaker was a tremendous hitter who frequently finished second to Ty Cobb in the AL batting race and did beat him once with a .386 mark in 1916, when he also led the league in on-base percentage and slugging. He also established a reputation as the greatest center fielder in baseball, playing notoriously shallow—and that reputation was fully deserved. Speaker in 1909 saved the Red Sox 21 runs in the field and improved to 29 the next year, enabling him to post an eye-popping 8 WAA in his second full season. After an off-year in the field, he saved 27 runs in 1912, 30 in 1913, and a record-setting 47 in 1914, a record that was not broken for more than 80 years, when Andruw Jones topped it by a single run with eight additional games to work with. With the exception of another off-year in 1916, Speaker continued to save at least 20 runs a year through 1919, when he saved 32 at age 31. He then fell suddenly and dramatically to average and remained there for the rest of his long career. Speaker was in fact more valuable to his teams than Ty Cobb: he posted 15 superstar seasons of 4 WAA or more compared to Cobb's 14, and his top six seasons were also marginally superior to Cobb's.

Speaker in 1912 was half of one of the greatest one-two punches any team has ever had, since his 9.8 WAA were complemented by the 6.4 WAA of pitcher Smokey Joe Wood, who went 34–5. (Wood was, however, as we shall see, not even close to being the most valuable pitcher in that league.) The rest of the Red Sox lineup contributed about 4 more WAA at bat and in the field, while the rest of the pitching staff added about 6. Wood's arm went bad in 1914 when he was only 23, and the Red Sox slumped to just 79–71 despite Speaker's 9.2 WAA. In 1914 they were a two-man team again, as Speaker's 11.4 WAA (his best season) and pitcher Dutch Leonard's 5.3 WAA would have given them 94 wins with average teammates—instead of the 91 wins they actually posted. But in 1915 they rebounded to the pennant with a 101–50 record, helped by Speaker's 6.2 WAA and a resurgent Joe Wood's 3.5. Speaker was the only significantly above average hitter on the 1915 Red Sox, although his fellow outfielders, Duffy Lewis in left and Harry Hooper in right, were each worth more than 1 WAA. Overall the lineup earned +12 WAA and the pitchers, including Wood, Ernie Shore, Rube Foster, Dutch Leonard, and 20-year-old Babe Ruth, contributed +8. The team was also very lucky, since its run differential was slightly worse than the Tigers' and 34 runs worse than that of the White Sox, who were beginning five years at or near the top of the league. The team beat the Phillies in the World Series, whereupon in April 1916, in a shocking move, Tris Speaker was in effect sold to the Cleveland Indians for $55,000. Owner Joseph J. Lannin claimed that the club could not meet his $15,000 salary demand.

Without Speaker, the Red Sox lineup in 1916 turned out to be almost exactly average despite an outstanding season by right fielder Hooper, worth 4.1 WAA. Yet young Babe Ruth earned a remarkable 5.9 WAA on the mound—third best in the league behind Cobb and Speaker—with a 1.75 ERA in 324 innings pitched, and the pitchers overall earned 9 WAA. And for the second straight year, the Red Sox trailed the White Sox in run differential, this time by 34 runs, but beat their Pythagorean projection by five games while Chicago missed theirs by one. The 1915–1916 Red Sox were the only team in history to win two consecutive pennants while trailing rivals in run differential, and since both clubs won the World Series, they seem to have been as lucky as subsequent Red Sox teams were unlucky from 1946 through 2003. Not surprisingly, the team slumped to 88 wins in 1917 despite another superstar season from Ruth, who earned 4.5 WAA on the mound in 326⅓ innings pitched, and another .9 at the plate with 142 plate appearances. Then Ruth's role changed.

In 1918 Ruth came to the plate 382 times and pitched 166⅓ innings, earning 4.3 WAA at bat and in the outfield, and 1.4 on the mound for a total of 5.7. With Harry Hooper adding 5.4 in right field, the Sox took the pennant again in the shortened 1918 season with a 75–51 record (Ruth and Hooper accounting for all but two of the team's wins above average), and the best run differential in the league. That was the end of the Red Sox dynasty that won four World Series in seven years—the luckiest dynasty in history. Harry Hooper, the team's right fielder, has long been one of the most controversial selections in the Hall of Fame, but it turns out that he is a perfectly legitimate choice. Hooper's great reputation as a right fielder has been proven out by Michael Humphrey's DRA: Hooper saved more than 20 runs in the field in seven different seasons, an extraordinary record for a right fielder which turned him into a genuine superstar for four years. With four seasons of more than 4 WAA and two more of 3.9 (in a shortened 1919 season) and 3.8, Hooper has a much better record than many other Hall of Famers.

The pennants of 1917 and 1919 went to the strongest team of the second half of the decade, the Chicago White Sox, who as we have noted also posted the league's best run differential in 1915 and 1916. That team boasted two of the top offensive players of the Lost Generation, Eddie Collins and Shoeless Joe Jackson, bought from Philadelphia and Cleveland in 1915 and 1916. Collins began his White Sox career with 7.1 WAA in 1915, but slumped to 2.3 and .9 in the next two years, largely because his fielding deteriorated badly. He rebounded impressively in 1919, to 2.3 WAA, and even more so in 1920 at the age of 33, when he had 5.6 WAA for a team that was eliminated in the last week of the season after most of its lineup was suspended on suspicion of throwing the 1919 World Series. Jackson, who turns out to have been a mediocre outfielder, earned 4.9, 3.1, and 4.7 WAA in 1915–1916 and 1919 (he missed nearly the entire 1918 season) and 5.1 WAA in his last season of 1920.

The White Sox, however, got at least as much help from their pitching staff from 1915–1920. Although their offense (led by Collins) dominated in 1915, it slumped in 1916, but the pitchers, who spread the workload out among them, earned +11 WAA with the help of a good deal of luck in the clutch. In 1917 the ace of the staff, knuckleballer Eddie Cicotte, earned an amazing 7.9 WAA with a 28–12 record and 347 innings pitched, and the rest of the pitching staff, including Red Faber, Reb Russell, and Jim Scott, earned 8 more for a total of 16 WAA. Cicotte had a terrible season in 1918 when the team slumped, but he rebounded in 1919 with a 29–10 record and 6.5 WAA—one more than the pitching staff as a whole. The staff was better in 1920, when it featured four 20-game winners—Cicotte, Lefty Williams, Red Faber, and Dickie Kerr—but the hitting was worse, and the White Sox had the third-best run differential in that wild year by a wide margin. Like the next quartet of hurlers to win 20 games for the same team—the starters for the 1971 Orioles—these four owed their records mostly to good fortune and a good offense. Faber and Cicotte earned 3.4 and 3 WAA, while Williams and Kerr had 1.5 and 1.7. One myth about these White Sox involves Buck Weaver, who failed in a long (and, as it turns out, dubious) attempt to clear himself of any involvement in the 1919 World Series fix. In the three decades of his suspension, a myth grew that he was a great third baseman, but he turns out to have been average at best.[9]

The Athletics, Red Sox and White Sox had won all the American League pennants in the 1910s, but in the next five years, three of the four AL teams that had never won a pennant accomplished the feat, and the fourth and last was very unlucky not to do the same. The 1920 season marked the turn of the Cleveland Indians, led by superstar (and now manager) Tris Speaker. Three years earlier, in 1917, the Indians had had one of the most amazing seasons in baseball history, when they became the first in history to field four players with 4 WAA or more but did not come close to the pennant. On the mound, pitchers Stan Coveleski and Jim Bagby posted 4.7 and 4.4 WAA, respectively and a combined 42–27 record, but the rest of the staff was simply dreadful, costing the team a full -9 WAA. In the field, Speaker's 7.0 WAA were complemented by shortstop Ray Chapman's 5.1, but the team's starting lineup as a whole was worth just 4 WAA. Catcher Steve O'Neill and third baseman Joe Evans were the biggest liabilities. A team including Speaker, Chapman, Coveleski and Bagby and a supporting cast of average players would have been expected to win 103 games, but the Indians won 88 thanks only to six games' worth of Pythagorean luck.

The Indians won in 1920 because three of the same players turned in superstar seasons: Speaker (6.1 WAA), Bagby (5.2) and Coveleski (5.4). The rest of the pitching staff was a liability, costing the team about -3 WAA overall, while Coveleski and Bagby pitched 654⅔ innings and ran up a combined record of 55–26. The offense, however, was much stronger. This time, catcher O'Neill and outfielder Elmer Smith were each worth between 2 and 3 WAA, Chapman had already earned 2 when he was killed by a pitched ball in mid–August, and 34-year-old Larry Gardner added another. With an impressive run differential of 227 runs and 98 wins, the Tribe deservedly beat the Yankees and the White Sox, who were wrecked by suspensions in the last week of the season, and won the World Series. Speaker, as we have seen, was the second-greatest offensive player of the Lost Generation, with a total

---

9. See William F. Lamb, *Black Sox in the Courtroom: the Grand Jury, Criminal Trial and Civil Litigation* (Jefferson, NC: McFarland, 2013), on Weaver's actual role in the World Series conspiracy.

of 15 seasons of 4 or more WAA, and Stanley Coveleski was the Lost Generation's fourth greatest pitcher with five such seasons, behind Walter Johnson, Lefty Grove, and Grover Cleveland Alexander.

No one knew it at the time, but 1921 was the biggest milestone in the history of the American League. Through 1920, the New York American League team, known as the Highlanders and then the Yankees, had not won a pennant. They won 27 pennants in the next 44 years, including three in a row three times, four in a row twice, and five in a row two more times. Until 1965, the history of the American League was essentially a history of Yankees dynasties, each dominated by one or two all-time greats. The first (1921–1923) was led by Babe Ruth; the second (1926–1928 and 1932) by Ruth and Gehrig; the third and strongest (1936–1939 and 1941–1943) by Gehrig, Joe DiMaggio, and the strongest supporting cast; and the last three (1949–1953, 1955–1958, and 1960–1964) by Mickey Mantle. After a break of a decade, the Yankees created a new dynasty in 1976–1981, and began another long run at or near the top in 1995. No other major league team, of course, has ever posted a remotely comparable record.

Babe Ruth dwarfed his teammates from 1921 through 1924. Ruth had moved from the Red Sox to the Yankees in 1920 at the same moment as general manager Ed Barrow, at the near-prime age of 25. His sale by Red Sox owner Harry Frazee was, as we have seen, merely the last and largest ($100,000) such transaction in the previous decade, similar to the deals involving Eddie Collins, Grover Cleveland Alexander, Joe Jackson, and Tris Speaker. (Frazee had not owned the Red Sox when Speaker was sold.) Converted to a full-time outfielder, Ruth in 1920 batted .376, walked 150 times, hit a record-shattering 54 home runs, played slightly below average in the outfield, and finished with a league-leading 10.3 WAA as the Yankees finished third—all in just 142 games. The next year, he improved in nearly all those categories, hitting 59 home runs and earning 9.6 WAA, as the Yankees won 98 games to beat the defending Indians by four games. Ruth's teammates in the line-up contributed 10 WAA more. Although shortstop Roger Peckinpaugh cost the team about a game, second baseman Aaron Ward and right fielder Bob Meusel were stars, and the rest of the lineup was at least average, with team fielding accounting for 6 WAA. Setting the pattern that Yankees dynasties would show for most of the next 44 years, the pitching staff was quite mediocre, with just +2 WAA overall. Carl Mays and Waite Hoyt pitched 619 innings and combined for a record of 46–22 and 4.9 WAA between them, but Bob Shawkey (18–12) and Rip Collins (11–5) gave almost half of those back. Shawkey's 1921 season illustrates the arithmetic that has created so many 20-game winners, Cy Young Award winners, and even Hall of Famers. Shawkey's pitching was slightly worse than average, but he started 31 games—⅕ of the team total—for a team whose players in the field were worth 20 WAA over the season, or about 4 WAA in the 30 games he started. Under the circumstances, a record of 19–11 would not have been surprising—one game better than he actually posted. Yet to repeat, he was actually a below-average pitcher who could claim no credit for any of the team's wins over .500. Pitchers post misleading records of this nature every year.

The Yankees at the plate and in the field fell from 20 WAA in 1921 to just 9 WAA in 1922, with Ruth, who played only 110 games in an injury-plagued season, leading the decline, losing about 5 WAA all by himself. New shortstop Everett Scott, acquired from the Red

Sox, and second baseman Ward were average, although Pipp (2.4 WAA) and Meusel (2.2) remained stars. Baker, now 36, slumped to below average, and the bench was very weak. The pitching staff, on the other hand, improved from 1 WAA to 6, with Shawkey turning in 3.5 WAA, and the aging Joe Bush and younger Waite Hoyt contributing 2.4 WAA between them. Still, the offensive drought cost the Yankees about ten games' worth of run differential, and they were lucky to win 94 games. And they were luckier still that that sufficed to win the pennant, since the St. Louis Browns, fielding what was surely the strongest team in their long, sad history, posted a run differential of +233, 74 runs better than the Yankees, but won only 93 games, one less than the Yankees, because they missed their Pythagorean projection by six games.

The Browns' extraordinary season was in certain respects a fluke. They were a completely average team in 1920–1921, and again in 1923–1924. Their great star was first basemen George Sisler, a tremendous hitter who had posted 9.2 WAA in 1920, when he hit .407 with 257 hits, a record that stood until 2004, when Ichiro Suzuki broke it with the help of eight extra games. Sisler in 1922 tied Ty Cobb for the second highest batting average since 1900, .420, with another 246 hits, and posted 7.2 WAA, nearly three more than Ruth. Two other superstars rounded out the team. Left fielder Ken Williams hit .332 with 39 homers and 155 RBI, and edged out Sisler for the team and league MVP with 7.3 WAA of his own, one of only two superstar seasons in his career. Despite a disastrous -3 WAA season from 30-year-old shortstop Wally Gerber, the lineup finished with 14 WAA. The pitchers, led by Urban Shocker (3.8 WAA), contributed 8 more. Shocker posted superstar seasons for the Browns in 1921 and again in 1923. Had they won the pennant they performed well enough to win, then every American League team would have won a pennant between 1909 and 1924. As it was, the Browns waited for their only pennant until 1944.

The 1923 Yankees improved from 94 back to 98 victories. The improvement was more than supplied by Babe Ruth, who recovered from his off-year to post 11.6 WAA, the highest total ever posted by a non-pitcher, with the help of a .393 average, 170 walks, an OBP of .545, and 41 home runs. Ruth also had the first of two outstanding consecutive years in the outfield, saving the team +13 runs. The rest of the lineup was below average overall, with 30-year-old Everett Scott and third baseman Joe Dugan costing the team a dreadful -5.9 WAA between them. Second baseman Aaron Ward was the only other regular to make a significant positive contribution with 2.9 WAA. On the mound, Herb Pennock, a veteran recently acquired from the Red Sox, posted 3.4 WAA, the third-best pitching performance in the league. One of the more remarkable late bloomers in the history of baseball, Pennock, then 29, improved to 4.7 WAA the next year and added 3.5 or more twice more. While this was a strong record for a pitcher during the 1920s, it hardly constituted an overwhelming case of the Hall of Fame. Bush and Hoyt added 3.9 WAA between them, and the pitching staff overall contributed 6 WAA. The team won its first World Series over the Giants, whom they had lost to in the preceding two years.

In 1924, the Yankees won only 89 games and lost the pennant to the Washington Senators by three games. Seldom has a pennant contender owed its success almost completely to one man. Helped by another fine season in the outfield, where he saved 15 runs, Ruth, hitting .393 with a .545 on-base percentage, had another fantastic season with 11.3 WAA, enough to account for 88 wins with average teammates. The Yankees pitchers, led by Pennock, had another fine year, good for 6 WAA. But the rest of the lineup combined for -5 WAA, taking away nearly half of Ruth's value. Amazingly, center fielder Whitey Witt (-3.4 WAA), shortstop Scott (-3.1) and third baseman Dugan (-2.2) combined for -8.7 WAA. Under the circumstances, what happened in 1925, when Ruth had his famous physical collapse, played just 98 games, and earned just 2.6 WAA, was nearly inevitable. Despite the arrival of two promising rookies, Lou Gehrig and Earle Combs, the lineup plunged disastrously to eight wins below average, and the team finished with a record of 69–85. This paved the way, the following year, for one of the most remarkable turnarounds in the history of baseball—one that belongs in the next chapter.

The team that won the pennants of 1924–1925, the Washington Senators, featured the greatest pitcher of his era, Walter Johnson, whose nine seasons of 4 or more WAA tie him for fifth on the all-time list with his namesake Randy Johnson, behind Roger Clemens (12), and Mathewson, Grover Cleveland Alexander, and Lefty Grove (ten each.)[10] Johnson had reached the Senators in 1907, when he was only 19. Tall and very long-limbed, throwing with a side-arm motion and great rotation in his upper body, he immediately established himself as a star with a tremendous fast ball. He posted his first superstar season in 1910, when he led the league with 313 strikeouts, the first of 12 times that he would do so in the next 15 years, and put up 7 WAA. Until 1920, when offense suddenly took off, Johnson's annual ERA topped 2.00 only twice. His greatest seasons were 1912 and 1913, when had records of 33–12 and 36–7 with 369 and 346 innings pitched, respectively, and earned the Senators 8 and 9.9 WAA. He had more than 7 WAA in each of the next two years (1914–1915), and posted three more superstar seasons in 1916–1917 and 1919. In 1924, at the age of 36, he posted 5.5 WAA as the Senators finally won the pennant.

The Senators had not been as bad for much of Johnson's early career as has generally been believed. They went 91–61 and 90–64 in his two best years of 1912–1913, losing out to the great Red Sox and the Athletics for the pennant, and barely topped .500 during the next few years as well. The team's great weakness, ironically, was the rest of its pitching staff. Only twice, in 1915 and 1925, did the rest of the Senators' pitchers earn the team any wins above average, and on five occasions they were bad enough to more than make up for Johnson's enormous positive contribution. Part of the problem was Griffith Stadium, which had a huge outfield (400 feet down the left field line) and undoubtedly helped conceal just how bad most of the Washington pitchers were. The team in the field was bad in most of these years too, but not nearly so bad as the Washington pitching staff, less Johnson.

The 1924–1925 pennant winners were deserving but undistinguished, matching their Pythagorean percentage with 92 wins the first year, and exceeding it by six with 96 wins in the second. Remarkably, in both years the lineup contributed 11 WAA and the pitchers 5. The team's offensive superstar was Goose Goslin, 23 years old in 1924, who hit .344 with a .421 OBP that year, good for a 5.5 WAA. Both Goslin and center fielder Sam Rice had outstanding years in the field, and Rice earned about 2.5 WAA. Shortstop Roger Peckinpaugh, although

---

10. Johnson may be entitled to one more superstar season, which poor data from 1918 may have concealed. See Appendix A for a further discussion.

a poor hitter, had a fantastic year in the field in 1924, saving 38 runs and earning 2.7 WAA. Player-manager Bucky Harris outmaneuvered John McGraw to win the World Series, but hit poorly and cost the team a full -2.1 WAA during the season. Beyond Johnson, the rest of the pitching was average. Goslin and Rice almost exactly duplicated their performances the next year, and although Johnson could not, a new acquisition, Stanley Coveleski—formerly of the Indians—weighed in with 4 WAA. Harris improved, but remained a liability. Incredibly, Peckinpaugh's hitting remained mediocre and his fielding regressed to slightly below average in 1925, when he played only 126 games. Posting -.4 WAA, he was named the American League's Most Valuable Player, surely the worst selection in the history of the award.

Goslin was launched in a long, great, and very impactful career, featuring five consecutive superstar seasons with the Senators (1924–1928) and significant contributions to two Tigers pennant winners in 1934–1935. He was one of the most deserving Veterans Committee selections to the Hall of Fame during the era dominated by Frankie Frisch in the late 1960s and early 1970s. Rice had a fascinating career, and his selection to the Hall in the early 1960s is more questionable. He won election because he accumulated 2,987 hits in his 18-year career, but he had only one superstar season, in 1920 (5.6 WAA), thanks to a remarkable 37 runs saved in center field for the Senators. Beyond that he had five seasons of 3 WAA or more, two more of at least 2, and four more of 1-8 seasons of genuine stardom, but only one in the elite class. Rice had married a few months after his high school graduation, did not play in organized baseball until he was 22, and did not reach the majors until he was 25. That may account for his failure to sustain a higher peak.

The Senators played two of the most exciting World Series in history in 1924–1925, winning the first in the 12th inning of Game 7 against the Giants behind Johnson in relief, and losing the second in a rainy seventh game in Pittsburgh, 9–7, when Johnson failed in a bid for a third victory. Peckinpaugh, the mysterious MVP selection, committed eight errors during the series, and the Pirates became the first team to come back from a 3–1 deficit. Johnson's last good year, 1925, was also the rookie year of the only pitcher from the Lost Generation whose record compared with his. The Big Train, as he was known, retired after 1927 with 417 wins and 279 losses.

The National League, 1914–1924

The history of each major league can be divided into eras of greatness, dominated by one or more teams, and eras of relative mediocrity, in which most of the league has a real chance to win the pennant. The National League's first transition from one to the next began in 1914, when the "Miracle" Boston Braves brought the era of the Pirates, Cubs and Giants to an end. From 1901 through 1913, the pennant winner (always from Pittsburgh, Chicago or New York) won an average of 103 games; from 1914 through 1920, six different teams won pennants with an average of only 92 wins,[11] and the Giants, who won four pennants

---

11. That average was slightly reduced by shortened seasons from 1917–1919.

from 1921 through 1924, averaged only 93 wins. The 1919 Cincinnati Reds were the only team in 1914–1925 to reach the percentage of a superior pennant winner. Only the lowly St. Louis Cardinals were shut out during these dozen years. The shortage of great teams reflected a shortage of great players. While the American League included a number of all-time offensive greats from the Lost Generation during these years, including Ty Cobb, Eddie Collins, Tris Speaker, Joe Jackson, George Sisler, and Babe Ruth, the National League had only one, Rogers Hornsby, who toiled in obscurity for the Cardinals. Winning the pennant turned on getting extraordinary seasons from one or two players who usually were not destined for greatness. Often those players were pitchers.

The Boston Braves, who came from last place in mid-season to win the National League pennant in 1914, set this pattern. While most of the team was mediocre, the Braves got tremendous seasons from two pitchers, Bill James (26–7 with 4.6 WAA) and Dick Rudolph (26–10 with 3.2 WAA). Both James and Rudolph pitched about 330 innings, and neither ever approached this level again. A third superstar was shortstop Rabbit Maranville, just 22 years old, who saved 49 runs, worth five games, at shortstop and earned 4.5 WAA. The Braves scored 34 more runs than their statistics would have predicted, boosting their lineup to +10 WAA, but the rest of their pitching staff was substantially below average. They topped off their season with four straight wins over the dissension-plagued Philadelphia Athletics, several of whom were about to sign with the Federal League. Maranville literally parlayed this season into a place in the Hall of Fame. For most of the rest of the decade he was the third-best shortstop in the National League, behind Art Fletcher of the Giants and Dave Bancroft of the Phillies, and he regressed to average after that. He was never an asset as a hitter, but the combination of his 1914 season, his long career, and his colorful personality won him election in 1954, one of the worst selections ever by the BBWAA.

The 1915 Philadelphia Phillies featured three superstars, led by the great National League pitching find of this decade, Grover Cleveland Alexander. Alexander pitched 376 innings, posted a 31–10 record with a 1.22 ERA, and earned 5.3 WAA, the fourth of his nine seasons of at least 4 WAA. After coming to the Phillies in 1911 at the age of 24, Alexander pitched more than 365 innings in four of the next seven years, never dropping below 300. In 1918, he was essentially sold to the Chicago Cubs for two worthless players and $55,000 in cash—a transaction that has never been satisfactorily explained. The Phils won their first pennant in 1915 with the help of outstanding seasons from two other players, outfielder Gavvy Cravath (8.4 WAA) and first baseman Fred Luderus (5.3 WAA), neither of whom ever performed at that level before or afterwards. Since the Phillies won only 90 games, missing their Pythagorean projection by two games, the rest of the roster must have been a combined eight wins below average. The 1916 Dodgers won *their* first pennant with 94 victories, paced by outfielder Zack Wheat (5.3 WAA, a .312 batting average, 32 doubles, 13 triples, and 9 HR), and pitcher Jeff Pfeffer (a 25–11 record and 3.4 WAA). Wheat had only one other superstar season, and Pfeffer none. The Dodgers nosed out the Phillies even though Alexander's 7.6 WAA was nearly the equal of Pfeffer and Wheat combined. Pitching was the biggest asset of both the 1915 Phillies and the 1916 Dodgers.

The 1917 New York Giants were the strongest National League team since McGraw's 1913 club, a superior pennant winner that matched their Pythagorean projection with 98 wins. Their MVP, with 6.4 WAA, was one of the greatest utterly forgotten players in baseball history, their shortstop, Art Fletcher. Somewhat to his own amazement, Michael Humphreys in *Wizardry* found that Fletcher saved more runs annually than any shortstop in the history of baseball. 1917 was Fletcher's best season, and his 6.4 WAA narrowly trailed another shortstop, Rogers Hornsby of St. Louis, who led all National League hitters with 6.8. But while Hornsby hit .317 with 66 walks, Fletcher hit just .260. His value was almost entirely in the field, where he saved the Giants 37 runs relative to an average shortstop, or about four entire wins. Nor was this in the least unusual for Fletcher: his runs saved from 1915 through 1919 totaled 37, 32, 48, 37 and 47 runs, a string that no shortstop in baseball history has managed to match. The 1917 Giants boasted two other superstars in their lineup, outfielders George Burns (6 WAA) and third baseman Heinie Zimmerman (4.6). Their lineup accounted for 20 of their wins over .500, and their pitching just one.

Fletcher might have been even better than he was, since he was already 24 when he reached the majors in 1913 and took two more years to become a regular. But he finished his career with four seasons over 4 WAA, something which New York shortstops such as Pee Wee Reese, Phil Rizzuto, Travis Jackson and Derek Jeter did not come close to doing. Yet while all of them are (or soon will be) in the Hall of Fame, Fletcher never received more than three votes from the BBWAA. He was clearly more valuable than most of the shortstops in Cooperstown—almost entirely because of his fielding.

The Cubs, the Giants' great rivals ten years earlier, duplicated New York's return to the top in the shortened 1918 season, winning the pennant with a record of 84–45. Like the Phillies and Dodgers, they won thanks to their pitching, and more specifically thanks to Hippo Vaughn and Lefty Tyler, who respectively accounted for 6.7 and 5.8 WAA in the 129-game season. The rest of the pitching staff added about four more wins and the hitters seven. Vaughn had an amazing career: after several seasons as a slightly above average pitcher in the American and then the National League, he turned in four consecutive superstar seasons from 1917 through 1920. On May 2, 1917, Vaughn lost one of the most amazing games in baseball history, the double no-hitter, to Fred Toney of the Cincinnati Reds. Neither man allowed a hit for nine innings, but the Reds won the game in the tenth. Toney's performance was no fluke either: he had posted 5.2 WAA in 1915. The Cincinnati Reds became the sixth National League team to win a pennant during the teens in 1919, with a 96–44 record in another shortened season. Their only superstar was center fielder Edd Roush, with 4 WAA, but third baseman Heinie Groh was not far behind. The Reds' team in the field contributed about 13 WAA at bat and with their gloves, and the pitchers, led by Dutch Reuther, Slim Sallee, and Johnny Ring, 10 more. They became the first National League team to win the World Series since 1914 and only the second of the decade, at least partly, of course, because eight of the White Sox were throwing the Series.

The Dodgers won another pennant in 1920 with 93 wins and only one superstar, pitcher Burleigh Grimes (4.3 WAA). The standings were extraordinarily balanced, as the second-place Giants won just 86 games and the third-place Reds only 82. The Giants actually had a slightly better run differential than the Dodgers, but lost too many close games. In the field and at bat, the Dodgers were almost perfectly average, but Grimes and the rest of the pitching staff, including Leon Cadore and Sherry Smith, accounted for 13 WAA. Then, just as suddenly as it had begun in 1914, the era of the very balanced National League came to an end. From 1921 through 1924, John McGraw's New York Giants set a new record with four pennants in a row.

They did so without reaching the 97-win level of a superior pennant winner, winning 93 to 95 games every year. Once again, hitting dominated this dynasty, accounting for 14, 9, 12 and 18 WAA in those four years, while the pitchers never topped 3. The Giants' fielding was excellent in 1921–1922, earning +6 and +8 WAA, but fell to average after that. The Giants won these pennants with only three superstar seasons, two from second basemen Frankie Frisch in 1921 and 1924 (5 and 4.7 WAA), and one from shortstop Dave Bancroft, who had been acquired from the Phillies, and whose 4.3 WAA in 1922 came almost entirely from his work in the field. While not quite the equal of his predecessor Art Fletcher, Bancroft was a very fine shortstop, earning his team 2–3 WAA in six seasons between 1916 (when he was with the Phillies) and 1925 (when McGraw traded him to the Braves.) Frisch, who also had 3.9 WAA in 1923, was on his way to a truly great career with the Giants and (beginning in 1927) the Cardinals, with four superstar seasons and three more with more than 3 WAA. Bancroft and Frisch were consistently two of the three most valuable players on this Giants dynasty, and thus rank with Tinker and Evers as the only double play combinations to anchor a series of pennant winners.

Frisch, who also managed the Cardinals to a pennant in 1934, fully deserves to be in the Hall of Fame—but as Bill James showed at length in *The Politics of Glory*, many of the teammates whose election he managed to secure as a member of the Veterans Committee did not. One such was outfielder Ross Youngs of the Giants, who earned 4.8 WAA in 1920 and 4.1 WAA in 1924, but had only one other season over 2 WAA. Youngs was roughly as good as George "High Pockets" Kelly, the first baseman, who posted 3.9, 3.1, 2.9 and 2.8 WAA in his four best seasons, and whom Frisch also got into the Hall of Fame. The remainder of the 1921–1924 Giants' line-up was generally slightly above average, including third baseman Heinie Groh, outfielders Irish Meusel and Casey Stengel, and catchers Frank Snyder and Hank Gowdy. The Giants fielders, led by Frisch and Bancroft, contributed +6 and +8 WAA in 1921–1922, but the pitchers never secured more than 3 during the whole of these years.

The 1924 Giants won the pennant by a single game over their crosstown rivals, the Brooklyn Dodgers, one of the most remarkable teams ever to come that close. The Dodgers' three best players, all superstars, earned considerably more WAA than the entire Giants team: pitcher Dazzy Vance (7.3 WAA, with a 28–6 record and a 2.16 ERA), first baseman Jack Fournier (6.1 WAA, with a .334 average and 27 home runs), and outfielder Zack Wheat (5.3 WAA, with a .375 average and 14 home runs.) But their lineup also included one of the worst players ever to hold down a major league job, third baseman Milt Stock, who had OBP and SLG well under .300, fielded dreadfully, and cost the team -6.3 WAA. Outfielder Tommy Griffith subtracted another -.3.4 WAA. Beyond Vance, all but two of their other pitchers were below average, and as a result, a team with three superstars worth 18.7 WAA finished with a run differential worth only 81 victories. Only 11 games' worth of Pythagorean luck allowed the Dodgers to win 92 games. Dazzy Vance, a great pitcher and deserved Hall of Famer, had the most bizarre career path of any pitcher in the history of baseball. Starting his career at 1912 at the age of 21, he pitched briefly for two major league teams in 1915 and for the Yankees in 1918, but pitched about 1,641 minor league innings before cracking the Dodgers rotation in 1922 at the age of 31. After two years of stardom, he turned in his amazing 7.3 WAA in 1924 at the age of 33 and followed that up with three more superstar seasons in the next six years. He led the National League in strikeouts in seven straight seasons. Not until the 1990s was there ever a pitcher nearly so good who bloomed so late.

The National League was already known as the senior circuit, but its weakness relative to the American League, even during this first quarter-century of major league baseball as we know it, was quite remarkable. The greatest offensive players of the 1901–1924 era, measured in numbers of seasons of 4 or more WAA, were Speaker (15), Ruth (14), Cobb (14), Hornsby (11),[12] Collins (8), and Wagner (7 from 1901 onward.) Only Hornsby and Wagner were National Leaguers. Among pitchers the National League did only slightly better, with Mathewson and Alexander tied with ten superstar seasons apiece, compared to 11 for Walter Johnson.

The 50 pennant winners in both leagues, 1901–1925, averaged 10 WAA for their hitters, 6 for their pitchers, and 3 for their fielders. Even in the dead ball era, a truly superior team had to be based on a collection of very good hitters. That became even more strikingly the case during the next era of baseball, from 1926 through 1949.

---

12. Hornsby's career will be treated in the next chapter.

2

The Lost and GI Generation Era, 1925–1949

The GI generation, which began to be born in the early years of the 20th century, played a critical role in American history, battling the Great Depression in young adulthood with the help of the New Deal, providing the shock troops for organized labor in the 1930s, fighting the Second World War, and building new communities filled with large families beginning in 1946. For the most part, its members were polite, dedicated, and well-educated team players who understood the need for the individual to dedicate himself to the welfare of the group. Their long roster of baseball immortals had debuted in 1925, when Lou Gehrig, a 22-year-old who had attended Columbia University, became the Yankees first baseman and posted nearly 2 WAA in 126 games. In 1926 Gehrig transformed the Yankees, leading the first of two different Yankees dynasties to the pennant. He was the first of a flock of all-time greats, including Charlie Gehringer, Joe Cronin, Jimmy Foxx, and Mel Ott, who reached the majors in the late 1920s.

The American League from 1926 through 1932 featured the two most dominant major league teams ever to contend for pennants over a prolonged period of years. While the New York Yankees, who won in 1926–1928 and 1932, have a greater reputation, the rebuilt Philadelphia Athletics, who won in 1929–1931, were just about as good from 1928 through 1932. Indeed, each of these teams won a pennant in a year when its great rival had a better run differential: the Yankees in 1928, and the Athletics in 1931. And while no duo has ever matched what Ruth and Gehrig did during this period, the Athletics had not two, but three all-time greats: Lefty Grove, Jimmy Foxx, and Al Simmons.

Ed Barrow, the general manager of the Yankees, had presided over the weakening, and then the collapse, of the team that had won pennants from 1921 through 1923. In 1925 and 1926 he carried out an extraordinary housecleaning, filling the lineup with younger talent discovered by his chief scout, the legendary Paul Krichell, who had found Gehrig. Gehrig, as we have seen, became the regular first baseman in the late spring of 1925 and did not miss a game until 1939. In the same year, Earle Combs, a Kentuckian who had begun his baseball career at the age of 23 after graduating from Normal School (a teacher's college), took over in center field. In 1926, the Yankees fielded a completely new double play combination from the GI generation, 22-year-old second baseman Tony Lazzeri, who had played four years in the minors, and 21-year-old shortstop Mark Koenig, who had begun his minor league career at 16 in Moose Jaw, Saskatchewan. Pat Collins now toiled behind the plate. The only holdovers besides Ruth were third baseman Joe Dugan and left fielder Bob Meusel.

Not all the new acquisitions were very useful, and the 1926 Yankees were far from dominant. They edged out the Indians with just 91 wins. The team fielded poorly, -2 WAA overall, as Koenig was the only marginally superior fielder on the team, while Lazzeri and Dugan each cost the team about a game, and the outfield was entirely average. But Ruth, rebounding with a new conditioning program to 9.5 WAA, and Gehrig, with 4.5, contributed more than the line-up's entire +12 WAA. The pitching staff earned -1 WAA, as Urban Shocker, 35 years old, was the only significant asset, while Shawkey, Pennock and Hoyt were completely average. The Yankees' defeat at the hands of the Cardinals in the World Series was not much of an upset. The one-man team of 1924 had become a two-man team in 1926, but since the second man was Gehrig, that was enough to win the pennant in a weak league.

In the next year, however, the Yankees turned in the greatest season in the American League to date, one which remains one of the half-dozen greatest seasons in the history of baseball. Their run differential improved from +134 to +376, still the second highest in history, and their winning percentage of .721 (110–44) remains the sixth highest in baseball history. For many decades they were regarded as the greatest team in the history of baseball, and as we shall eventually find, they have nearly as good a claim to that title as any. How did they do it?

The Yankees line-up, not the pitchers, provided the bulk of the improvement. The hitters improved from +11 WAA to +19, and the fielders from -2 to +9. Ruth and Gehrig improved from 9.2 and 4.5 WAA, respectively, to 10.6 for Ruth and 9.0 for Gehrig, who enjoyed his greatest season and drove in 175 runs. No other pair of players have ever combined for 19.6 WAA for a single team, and it is rather astonishing that just two players contributed ⅔ of the positive value of one of the half-dozen greatest line-ups in history, but so it was. The rest came from two other players, center fielder Combs and second baseman Lazzeri, with 5.9 and 4.3 WAA, respectively. Combs's and Lazzeri's career years owed a great deal to spectacular marks in the field, where they saved 26 and 21 runs, respectively. Given that Combs had only one other positive season in the field in the whole of his career while Lazzeri had only two, it seems that both of them must have had a remarkable number of balls hit just within reach. Taken together, Koenig and Dugan on the left side of the infield, Meusel in the outfield (alternating with Ruth in left and right, depending on the park), and the three undistinguished catchers were average. The Yankees' pitching staff improved to +4 WAA thanks to Waite Hoyt and reliever Wilcy Moore, who earned 5 WAA between them, while Pennock and Shocker were average.

Under the circumstances, it was not surprising that the Yankees in 1928 lost 167 runs off of their run differential and needed two games' worth of Pythagorean luck to defeat the Philadelphia Athletics, whose run differential was slightly superior. Ruth and Gehrig did it again, with 10.1 and 7 WAA, accounting for the lineup's entire +17 WAA. Although Combs and Lazzeri each earned about 2 WAA, they were balanced out by Koenig, Dugan, two younger third basemen, and rookie shortstop Leo Durocher, who was terrible at the plate and mediocre in the field. On the mound, 35-year-old Herb Pennock's 3.3 WAA accounted for most of the plus value of the pitching staff. Yankees fielding once again became a liability overall, costing the team 4 wins. Still, they swept the World Series for the second year in a row, this time against the Cardinals.

The regression continued in 1929, and this time it did cost New York the pennant. Ruth, now 34, slipped to 6.1 WAA and Gehrig, still only 26, to 5.2 WAA. The rest of the lineup added just 1 WAA, and both the fielding and the pitching were completely average. Lazzeri and Combs remained stars, and rookie catcher Bill Dickey earned 1 WAA, but the left side of the infield remained bad. Winning just 88 games, the Yankees finished second by 16 games to a new great team, the Philadelphia Athletics.

The Athletics dynasty of 1929–1931 was built around four future Hall of Famers. In those three seasons, Lefty Grove, left fielder Al Simmons, and first baseman Jimmy Foxx turned in a total of eight superstar performances. Grove, born at the tail end of the Lost Generation in 1900, was with Walter Johnson one of the two greatest pitchers of his generation and was incomparably more dominant than *any* other pitcher of the era of 1926–1945. He did not reach the Athletics until 1925, after five very successful seasons with the Baltimore Orioles of the American Association, during which he pitched as many as 313 innings in a season. The handling of pitchers in the majors had changed by 1925. The American League had 12 pitchers with 260 or more innings pitched in 1915, but only four in 1927. Grove never pitched as many as 300 innings in a major league season, starting around 30 games a year, far less than Johnson, Mathewson, Alexander, or any of the greats of the 1960s and 1970s. Grove, who had turned in his first of a record-tying ten superstar seasons (for a pitcher) in 1926, had 4.6, 6.6, and 6.6 WAA in 1929–1931. In the last of those three years he went 31–4. Grove posted seasons of 6.2 and 3.8 WAA in 1931–1932, slumped badly in 1934 after being sold to the Boston Red Sox, but rebounded in 1935–1937 with three amazing seasons of 6.6, 8.5(his best), and 6.6 WAA at ages 35 through 37, following them with 3.4 and 4.8. *No other pitcher of his era had as many as five superstar seasons.* Grove led AL pitchers in WAA in every year from 1928 through 1933 and again from 1935 through 1938. He finished second in 1939 behind young Bob Feller, who was beginning a reign of comparable dominance—but one that lasted only four years. One may fairly define Grove, in his own context, as by far the most dominant pitcher in the history of baseball.

First baseman Jimmy Foxx, a Marylander like Grove, spent just two years in the minors and reached the Athletics at the age of 17 in 1925. After four part-time seasons, Foxx posted 5.2 WAA in 1929 and followed that up with 4.6 in 1930 (when he was still just 22) before slumping to 2.7 in 1931. Foxx's best years, typically, came in 1932–1935 at the ages of 24–27, when he put up Gehrig-like figures of 8.3, 8.2, 7.1 and 6.4 WAA, before he too was sold to Tom Yawkey's Red Sox by Mack. He had three more great seasons with them, finishing with nine superstar seasons, three fewer than Gehrig. The early 1930s was one of the two greatest offensive eras in baseball history, and many players posted batting averages and home run totals that gave a very exaggerated idea of their value—but Foxx was not one of those.

Al Simmons, the left fielder in the Athletics dynasty, had become a regular at 22 in 1924 after two years in the minors. He hit his peak five years later and batted .365, .381, .390 and .322 from 1929–1932, leading the league in 1930–1931, and hit about 35 home runs in three of those years. In 1988, in the first edition of his *Historical Baseball Abstract*, Bill James argued that Simmons was roughly comparable in value to Al Oliver and probably was not the equal of Jim Rice of George Brett. James was wrong, partly because Simmons turns out to have been a significant asset in the field. While Oliver never had a superstar season, Simmons had seasons of 6.1, 5.3 and 6.6 WAA in 1929–1931, and six such seasons overall—one *more* than either Jim Rice or George Brett.

The fourth Hall of Famer was catcher Mickey Cochrane, a .320 lifetime hitter with a .419 OBP who consistently caught about 120 games a season. Cochrane was the first of a series of catchers long thought key to dynasties and winning teams, including Bill Dickey, Yogi Berra, Roy Campanella, Johnny Bench, Carlton Fisk, Thurman Munson, Mike Piazza, Joe Mauer and Buster Posey. Cochrane was in fact a very fine player who contributed significant value to the A's—but he was not nearly the equal of Grove, Foxx, or Simmons, just as Dickey was far short of Joe DiMaggio, Campanella did not compare to Jackie Robinson or Duke Snider, and Munson was not nearly as important to the Yankees as Roy White or Reggie Jackson. The standard for true greatness in this book is five seasons of 4 WAA or more—*and not a single catcher in the history of baseball has ever met that standard.* There are two reasons for this.

The first reason, of course, is that the enormous physical demands of catching make it very difficult for a catcher to become, and especially to remain, a great hitter. Some have indeed managed to do so briefly, including Johnny Bench and Mike Piazza, but they are very exceptional, and no one has ever managed to do it for as long as the greats at other positions. Cochrane, like Joe Torre and Ted Simmons in their time, was a fine hitter, but he was a great hitter for only two years. That makes him very comparable to Bench and Piazza, as we shall see, who also reached that level for only two or three years.

The second reason, which is, when one thinks about it, fairly obvious, is that there is usually no way for a superior catcher to create a significantly higher number of outs than average on defense. The exception occurs in high stolen base eras, when he can throw out enough baserunners to win a couple of extra games for his team. Cochrane, Dickey, Campanella and Berra did not play in such an era. Catchers can also prevent runners from advancing from one base to the next by allowing fewer passed balls, and Michael Humphreys's DRA incorporates past balls in his evaluation of their fielding. A catcher's other defensive duties *once the ball is in play* are limited to catching pop-ups and fielding an occasional bunt or slow roller. While some people are undoubtedly handle these situations better than others, they simply do not occur often enough for superior skill to save a significant number of runs over the course of a season. Cochrane is a great example: according to Michael Humphreys's calculations, he never saved more than five runs in a season relative to an average catcher.

There is, of course, a long-standing mythology to the effect that certain catchers, such as Berra, Campanella, Jim Hegan, Bench, and many more, have a certain knack for calling pitches, "handling" pitchers, framing the strike zone, etc., that is of inestimable value to their teams. As it happens, most of those catchers played for teams that had good records because they had superior offenses, and many of their pitching staffs, as we have already seen for the Giants and Yankees in the 1920s, were only slightly above average. It is up to others to try to prove that these effects are real and meaningful. (It is interesting that no one, to my knowledge, has ever tried to give Javier Lopez particular credit for the success of the greatest pitching staff in history, the Atlanta Braves from about 1991 to 2004.)

Cochrane was extremely valuable, and there is every reason to think that he could have met the standard of at least five seasons of 4 WAA had he played a different position. But as it was, he had only two superstar seasons, in 1931 and 1933—which turns out to be one more than Yogi Berra and two more than Roy Campanella. From 1929 through 1931, Cochrane posted 2.1, 3, and 4 WAA. He peaked at 4.7 in 1933 and topped 2 on one other occasion. This is an outstanding record for a catcher, but it clearly does not make him as valuable as Grove, Foxx, or Simmons.

Some would argue that Cochrane's batting statistics are more valuable than they look precisely because he was a catcher, and might be far more superior to those of the average catcher than Foxx's were superior to the average first baseman, or Simmons' to the average outfielder. It is time to test that argument.

The argument turns out to have some validity, at least with respect to the period we are discussing, because the average American League catcher was so bad offensively. This was the era of the highest batting averages in history, but some first-string catchers still hit below .250. Cochrane in 1929 created 21 runs above average (about two games' worth) and totaled 2.1 WAA. The only other above-average player behind the plate, measured against the league's non-pitchers, was Bill Dickey, who earned a little more than 1 WAA. The average catcher was about -1.2 WAA, and Cochrane was therefore more than 3 WAA better than an average catcher. Turning to first basemen, we find that only one team, the Red Sox, had a below-average player there, and that the average for AL first sackers was 30 runs above average, or about three wins. That makes Foxx, with 57 runs above average, about 2.7 WAA better than an average first baseman—not quite as good as Cochrane, with the position adjustment.

What this means is that Cochrane was a rarer species, harder to come by, than Foxx, and that losing Cochrane might have cost the Athletics slightly more in their run differential than losing Foxx, depending on exactly who their replacements were. But that does not make him equally valuable in absolute terms. The Athletics' won-lost record depended on the total number of runs they managed to create and allow, and Foxx created 43 runs more than Cochrane did. This book began with Bill James's Keltner test: if this guy were the best player on your team, could you win the pennant? With or without the position adjustment, the answer for Cochrane would clearly be no in more than 90 percent of all baseball seasons. In the history of baseball, no team has won the pennant whose best player was a catcher with less than 4 WAA. For Foxx it would obviously be yes. All this does not mean that catchers are any less admirable than other players—it means simply that the nature of their position, whose physical demands make it much harder to sustain great offensive performance and whose duties give little room for the expression of superior fielding skill, means that their best performances almost always contribute less to their success than there the best players at other positions. Organizations with a catcher who shows promise as a great hitter should seriously consider moving him to another position.

Together, Simmons (the actual team MVP), Foxx, star right fielder Bing Miller and Cochrane contributed nearly 16 WAA to the 1929 Athletics, making the rest of the lineup slightly below average as a whole. Two disastrous part-timers, Sammy Hale and Joe Boley, subtracted -4.5 WAA between them. Center fielder Mule Haas and second baseman Max Bishop were average and third baseman Jimmy Dykes was a bit better. The pitching staff, however, was one of the greatest of the era, worth +14 WAA. Grove, of course, led with 4.5 WAA, but the other regular starters, Rube Walberg and George Earnshaw, combined for 6.8 WAA more. With the help of four wins of Pythagorean luck, the Athletics posted a great record of 104–46 and beat the Yankees by 16 games.

The same four Hall of Famers remained responsible for most of the Athletics' success during the next two years. In 1930, Foxx, Simmons, Bishop (who starred at second) and Cochrane had 15.7 WAA among them, while the line-up overall had only 10, with Dykes and Miller slipping below average. Grove had 6.6 WAA, but the rest of the staff added just one more. This time the team had even more Pythagorean luck—nine games' worth—so their record fell only to 102–52, still a superior pennant winner. The Yankees, as we shall see, were coming on strong once again, and in 1931 Mack's men were fortunate to beat them. This time Simmons, Foxx, Bishop and Cochrane earned 16.4 WAA (with Foxx slumping to 2.8), while the rest of the lineup was average. Grove's astonishing 31–4 season (with the weakest team of the last three years behind him) earned 6.6 WAA and represented nearly the whole positive value of the pitching staff. And this team was ten games better than its Pythagorean projection, allowing them to beat a superior Yankees club with a tremendous 107–45 record, their best yet. Should any researcher want to try to prove that beating the Pythagorean projection represents something more than luck, the 1929–1931 Athletics are the team to study. No other pennant-winning team has beaten its Pythagorean percentage for anything close to eight wins a year for three years in a row.

The rivalry between the Athletics and Yankees from 1928 through 1932 was the greatest long-term two-team rivalry in the history of baseball, measured by the quality of the teams involved. The Yankees in 1929–1930 presented a truly astonishing spectacle. In 1929, Ruth (.345 with 46 homers at age 34) and Gehrig (.300 with 35 homers and 122 walks) posted 11.3 WAA between them (the exact total of their counterparts Simmons and Foxx), and Lazzeri had his second and last superstar season with 4.1 WAA, but the rest of the team was below average overall. Combs cost the team a full game in the field, Durocher and Koenig were average at short, and the team had no regular third baseman. On the mound, the aging Hoyt, Pipgras and Pennock were all well below average on the year, and the pitchers cost the team -4 WAA, as the team won just 88 games. 1930 was the same, only more so. This was the biggest offensive season in history, and the Yankees set an all-time record of 1,068 runs, nearly seven runs per game. Ruth and Gehrig did even better, posting 8.4 and 6.0 WAA for a total of 14.4, but the team had a dreadful year in the field, where Lazzeri and new third baseman Ben Chapman led the way in giving up -6 WAA. The 25-year-old Red Ruffing, with 1.1 WAA, was the only above-average pitcher on the staff, and the pitchers overall gave away -4 WAA more. Manager Bob Shawkey, who had taken over for the late Miller Huggins, was deservedly replaced.

In the entire history of baseball, only 12 teams have had batting orders whose hitting was worth 20 WAA to their team. Thanks largely to Ruth and Gehrig, these include the Yankees of 1927–1928 and 1930–1932, and the hitters set the all-time record in 1931, under new manager Joe McCarthy, with +27 WAA. Although Ruth and Gehrig slipped slightly to 7 and 5.4 WAA—largely because both of them had very bad seasons in the field, where they cost the Yankees -4 WAA between them—Chapman, now switched to the outfield, and shortstop Lyn Lary starred with nearly 3 WAA each, and Combs added 2 more. But the big turnaround was on the mound. New pitcher Lefty Gomez, only 22 years old, earned 3.6 WAA, going 21–9 with a 2.67 ERA, and the rest of the staff was about average. As we have already seen, the 1931 Yankees also hold the record, in one sense, for bad Pythagorean luck: they had a better run differential than the Athletics, yet managed to lose the pennant by 13 games because they missed their projection by six while the Athletics exceeded theirs by ten. Interestingly enough, while the Yankees outscored the Athletics, 124–97, in the 22 games between them, the Athletics won half the games.

The Athletics still had essentially the same team in 1932, but this time the Yankees broke through. Even Pythagorean luck favored them this time, and they turned a projected four-game edge into a 13-game margin of victory, winning 107 games to the Athletics' 94. Although Ruth and Gehrig again had bad years in the field, they still posted 5.9 and 5.5 WAA, and the rest of the lineup, led by Lazzeri, Combs, and Chapman, contributed about 6 more, even though the still-aged team lost four wins' worth of runs in the field. Among the pitchers, Gomez slipped back to 1.4 WAA, but another relatively new hurler, Red Ruffing, suddenly blossomed at the age of 27 after eight totally mediocre years and had a superstar season with 4.2 WAA, and his contemporary Johnny Allen added another 1.9 WAA with a 17–4 record. All told, Yankees moundsmen contributed about 7 WAA, the most of any Yankees team in the entire Lost/GI era of 1925–1949. For the Athletics, although Foxx and Grove easily outdistanced Ruth and Gehrig with 6.2 and 7.3 WAA respectively, and Cochrane added 2.6 more, the rest of the team slumped across the board. Their attendance fell from 627,000 to 406,000, and for the second time in his long career, Connie Mack contemplated turning his biggest assets into cash.

On September 28, 1932, Mack sold Al Simmons, third baseman Jimmy Dykes, and center fielder Mule Haas to the White Sox for $100,000. Although Simmons alone had been critical to the team's success, this was the end of the Athletics' second and last dynasty in Philadelphia. Although Foxx (8.4 WAA), and Cochrane (4.7 WAA, his peak) remained great, the rest of the team, especially the pitchers, went to pieces, winning only 79 games in 1933. Grove and two other players now went to Tom Yawkey's Red Sox for $150,000, and Foxx followed him in another trade that netted $150,000 two years later, when he was still only 28. Mack had now sold five future Hall of Famers, four of them indisputable all-time greats, at or near their peak: Collins, Home Run Baker, Simmons, Grove and Foxx. As for the Yankees, Ruth was still a superstar, barely, in 1933–1934 at the age of 38 and 39, but he was sold to the Boston Braves in 1935 after losing a power struggle with manager Joe McCarthy, whom he had hoped to succeed. Gehrig promptly had one of his greatest seasons in 1935, the only year of his career in which he was indisputably the Yankees' greatest player, with 8.4 WAA. The loss of Ruth also dramatically improved the team's fielding, but the pitching staff was simply dreadful, and the team could win only 89 games. Help was on the way, but meanwhile, two other teams filled the gap in the American League from 1933 through 1936. Before turning to them, we must close the books on the Yankees dynasty of the Ruth years.

Ruth, as we have seen, was the key to the Yankees teams of 1921–1924, and no two players have ever had the long-term impact that he and Gehrig had from 1926 through 1934, when neither of them ever fell below a superstar level of 4 WAA, averaging more than 6 WAA a season each over those nine years. Ruth finished his career with an all-time record of 18 superstar seasons—three of them as a pitcher—while Gehrig had 12, tying him with Ted Williams and Stan Musial as tops for the GI generation. (He would almost surely have had more but for his fatal illness, which brought him below that level in 1938. He was only 36 in 1939.) Inevitably, thanks to the four pennants and three World Series they won together, their glow lit up some of their teammates. Four of them from the 1926–1928 teams—Combs, Lazzeri, Hoyt and Pennock—eventually found their way into Cooperstown. Pennock, a dominant pitcher in the mid–1920s, had a reasonably strong case, but Lazzeri had just two superstar seasons, Pennock had one (and three more over 3 WAA), Combs one, and Hoyt none. (We shall look at the credentials of Ruffing and Gomez later.) Hoyt finished his very long career with a 237–182 won-lost record and won 20 games only twice—with the 1927 and 1928 Yankees. His subsequent career as a broadcaster probably helped get him into the Hall, but Ruth and Gehrig did more than anyone to make his election possible.

From 1927 through 1932, the Yankees and Athletics won the American League championship, easily exceeding the level of a superior pennant winner (98 wins or more) every time. In 1933, a well-balanced Washington Senators team won the league with 99 victories, including five games' worth of Pythagorean luck. Their only superstar was their 26-year-old player-manager, shortstop Joe Cronin, who turned in his third superstar season in four years with 4.9 WAA. Cronin's career was strikingly similar to Cal Ripken, Jr.'s. Cronin had signed with the Pittsburgh Pirates in 1925, when he was 18, and played briefly for them in 1925–1926. They sold him to the minors in 1928, whereby Clark Griffith of the Senators immediately purchased him and made him a regular. He peaked very early with 7.3 WAA in 1930, helped by an amazing 45 runs saved in the field. He remained an outstanding fielder until he was 28 but was mediocre at best after that, continuing at shortstop as the Red Sox player-manager through 1941. In his last six seasons as a regular, his WAA ranged from -1.6 to 3.8. With a total of only three superstar seasons (the same as Ripken's), he is a reasonable but far from overwhelming Hall of Fame selection as a player. The Senators also got an amazing performance from center fielder Fred Schulte, who saved 35 runs in the field and earned 3.9 WAA, and solid contributions from second baseman Buddy Myer and outfielders Heinie Manush and Goose Goslin—the latter still a star. Their pitching was quite mediocre, and they lost the World Series to the Giants in five games.

Their successors as pennant winters, the 1934–1935 Detroit Tigers, were more similar to some of the Yankees and Athletics teams that had preceded them. In a remarkable display of consistency, the Tigers' line-up contributed +17 and +16 WAA in each of those years, while the pitchers added +5 in 1934 and +7 in 1935 as the team won 101 and 93 games. Their two superstars in each of those years were second baseman Charlie Gehringer (6.2 and 4.7 WAA) and first baseman Hank Greenberg (4.8 and 6.5.) Gehringer was the late bloomer of his era. Becoming a Tigers regular at 23 in 1926, he was a consistent .300 hitter but a mediocre to bad second baseman for seven seasons. Despite high batting averages, reflecting the high offensive level of the late 1920s and early 1930s, he was not yet of great value. Suddenly, in 1933, when he was 30, he blossomed both at bat and in the field, and earned 4.2, 6.2., 4.7, 5.4 and 6.1 WAA over the next five years, thereby earning a very deserved place in Cooperstown. Greenberg—of the players in the GI generation, one of the most affected by the Second World War—was even better, a tremendous power hitter along the lines of Foxx and Gehrig, and a better fielder than either one. He posted 4.5 and 6.5 WAA in 1934–1935, but a broken wrist in the 1935 World Series cost him nearly the entire 1936 season. He returned for four consecutive superstar seasons—three of them over 6 WAA—from 1937–1940, but drew one of the lowest draft numbers in the land in the fall of that year and did not play another full season until 1946, when he had 7.1 WAA. Without the war he would surely have eclipsed Foxx's nine superstar seasons, although he would not have equaled Gehrig's 12. The Tigers' other major asset was their catcher and manager, Mickey Cochrane, who posted 2 and 3.2 WAA in these two years despite missing 25–35 games in each. Goose Goslin, who had come over from Washington, was now only average, but shortstop Billy Rogell also had good seasons in 1934–1935. On the mound, Schoolboy Rowe and Tommy Bridges earned 3 and 2.7 WAA in 1934. No other Tigers pitcher approached that during these two seasons, but Tommy Bridges was a consistent asset. American league pitching had flattened out spectacularly during the Lost and GI era. AL pitchers posted only 33 superstar seasons from 1926 through 1942—fewer than two per season. One man, Lefty Grove, accounted for ten of them.

In 1936 the Yankees unveiled what became a new dynasty, one that very convincingly won seven pennants in eight years from 1936 through 1943. Although the Second World War prevented this team from matching the record of the Casey Stengel dynasty, which won ten pennants in 12 years, this one, built by Ed Barrow and managed by Joe McCarthy, was much more dominant. The 1921–1924 Yankees team had been built mostly through trades and player purchases. The 1926–1932 one had an all-time great, Gehrig, and two stars, Lazzeri and Combs, who had been signed by the team. By the 1930s, the Yankees had a large and growing farm system and an outstanding trio of scouts, Paul Krichell, Bill Essick, and Joe Devine. They were particularly active on the West Coast. For several years, new and younger players had been filling up the Yankees line-up. An outstanding catcher, Bill Dickey had become a regular in 1929 at 22 with only the briefest minor league experience, and had consistently earned 1–2 WAA during the early 1930s. Frankie Crosetti, a Californian, had taken over the shortstop position in 1932 at the age of 21 after four years with the San Francisco Seals. He remained an average player at bat and in the field, although nothing more, until 1939. Red Rolfe began his minor league career at 22 after graduating from Dartmouth in 1931, and became the regular third baseman in 1935, at 26. Rolfe was also only a slightly above-average fielder, but he hit .289 lifetime and was a genuine 2–3 WAA star in 1936 and 1938. Two of the three outfielders, George Selkirk and Ben Chapman, were also contributing at the 1–2 WAA level. Meanwhile, Gehrig had reacted to Ruth's departure by entering a second prime, turning in his best three-year run of seasons in 1934–1936 with 8.4, 7.7 and 8.1 WAA—largely, interestingly enough, because he had substantially improved his fielding, turning him from a liability at first into an asset. Lazzeri was still the second baseman, but his hitting had declined and poor fielding had pulled him down to an average level at best.

The Yankees line-up in 1935 was +10 WAA overall—indicating that Gehrig accounted for three quarters of its positive value. The second superstar whom the Yankees needed to regain dominance, Joe DiMaggio, arrived from the West Coast after three full years with the San Francisco Seals at age 21. DiMaggio was by any standard a very great player, but he was not quite as great as his reputation. His selection by MLB in 1969 as the greatest center fielder of all time and the greatest player then living was, as we shall find, indefensible: Willie Mays surely deserved the first honor, and a number of men had a far greater claim to the second. DiMaggio's 1936 rookie season was shortened to 138 games by injury, and he finished with an impressive 3.6 WAA. Then he blossomed in 1937 at bat (with 46 homers) and in the field (saving 13 runs), and turned in seasons of 6.7, 4.5, 7.6, 5.9, 8.6 and 4.4 WAA from 1937 through 1942. Yet the "Yankee Clipper" was to finish his career with only one more season of 4 WAA or more, leaving him with seven, the same number as Hank Greenberg, who missed most of five seasons during the war, while DiMaggio missed only three. The odd-even pattern of his early career suggests that he always had an injury-prone body, and that was going to prevent him, from 1946 onward, from ever approaching his peak levels of performance for a full season. He was a fine center fielder before the war, but average at best after it. Even within his own GI generation, both Ted Williams and Stan Musial had a much better claim in 1969 to the title of greatest living player than he did, to say nothing of Willie Mays and Henry Aaron. War or no war, it is most unlikely that DiMaggio would have broken the barrier of ten superstar seasons, as those two did, along with many more from the Lost, Silent and Boom generations. And other great players, who continued in 1937–1941 to arrive with extraordinary regularity, had just as much to do with making the Yankees the most dominant dynasty in history as he did.

With Hank Greenberg lost to the Tigers for most of 1936, the Yankees faced no serious competition for the pennant, which they won with 102 victories. While Gehrig dominated them with a .354 average, 49 homers, and 8.1 WAA, DiMaggio, Red Rolfe, George Selkirk and Bill Dickey all had more than 3 WAA. Because of good, though not outstanding, performances by four pitchers—Ruffing, Monte Pearson, Pat Malone, and reliever Johnny Murphy—their staff overall earned +5 more WAA. Their pitchers' won-lost records illustrate the advantages of playing for a team whose lineup earns +23 WAA. Ruffing, with 1.1 WAA of his own, finished with a 20–12 record; while Gomez, who was a dead average pitcher over 189 innings, went 13–7. Joe McCarthy's handling of his pitchers typified his era. He used a five-man rotation and rarely had any one with more than 250 innings pitched. Evidently he realized that the job of his pitchers was to hold the other team to a slightly below average number of runs, while his lineup of tremendous hitters put one game after another out of reach.[13]

The Yankees won 102 games again in 1937 with a different mix. DiMaggio had one of his greatest seasons, ending the year with 46 homers and 6.7 WAA, while Gehrig, now 34, did almost as well with 5.7. (For the Tigers, Greenberg, coming back from injury, was exactly as valuable as DiMaggio, and Gehringer was only slightly behind Gehrig.) The rest of the Yankees infield had substantial problems, with Lazzeri (now 33), Crosetti, and Rolfe combining

---

13. It is interesting that the strategy of a five-man rotation in which starters generally pitch 200–250 innings returned in the 1990s, but in that era, far more pitchers had dominant seasons than in the 1930s.

2. The Lost and GI Generation Era, 1925–1945   53

for -3 WAA. Dickey, reaching his peak relatively late and now 30, had the second and best of four consecutive seasons with more than 3 WAA, earning 3.7 in a career-high 140 games. (Bill James's assertion that Yogi Berra's career was far superior to Dickey's in his first *Historical Abstract* was false. Although Berra's best season was a little better, both men had just four seasons over 3 WAA.) The lineup as a whole earned +20 WAA and the pitchers added +7. Red Ruffing and Lefty Gomez had two of the greatest seasons of their careers, with 3.7 and 5.7 WAA, respectively. Luck must have been against Gomez: despite playing for a lineup worth 18 WAA, his 5.9 WAA translated into only a 21–11 record. The team almost exactly matched its Pythagorean projection with a 102–52 record.

The Yankees slipped very slightly in 1938, but still won 99 games. DiMaggio, who had a long and controversial holdout that ended when he settled for much less than he wanted, slipped to 4.3 WAA; Gehrig, stricken with his fatal illness in the second half the season, essentially closed out his career with 2.5 WAA, and Dickey had another excellent year with 3.5. Crosetti and Rolfe were both about average. The big news was the arrival of 23-year-old rookie second baseman Joe Gordon, yet another Californian who had spent just two years in the minors, and who began his great career with 3 WAA in 127 games thanks to +30 runs saved in the field. A new right fielder, 25-year-old Tommy Henrich, earned 1.6 WAA. On the mound, Ruffing and Gomez had fine seasons of 2.4 and 1.8 WAA, but the rest of the staff was average. The Yankees swept the Cubs, a strong National League team, in the World Series. The best was yet to come.

Nineteen thirty nine began with Gehrig's horrifying diagnosis and retirement. His replacement, Babe Dahlgren, was disastrous with -2.6 WAA, and Crosetti cost the team about three wins at bat and finished with -1.2 WAA. Nonetheless, the season ended with the Yankees posting their best Pythagorean percentage *ever*, good enough to earn them 111 wins and just 43 losses—better than the more famous 1927 team. (They missed their projection by six games.)[14] Fielding accounted for +11 WAA, hitting for +14, and pitching for +7. Not only did their recently acquired players continue to improve, but they made yet another Hall of Fame-caliber acquisition. Joe DiMaggio had a great year in the field, saving 23 runs, and turned in his best season with a .381 average and an astonishing 7.5 WAA in just 120 games. Gordon saved 35 runs at second base, hit well, and vaulted into the superstar category with 4.8 WAA. Crosetti, remarkably, had *his* best-ever year in the field too, saving 22 runs, and the fielders as a whole saved 111. Rolfe (3.6 WAA), outfielder George Selkirk (3.1), and Dickey (3.1) all had outstanding seasons as well. But the great revelation was Charlie Keller, another outfielder and left-handed hitter whom the Yankees had signed out of the University of Maryland two years earlier at the age of just 20. Keller earned 3.3 WAA in just 111 games in his rookie season, and he was about to get much better very quickly. With the exceptions of Dahlgren and Crosetti, *every regular in the Yankees line-up earned at least 3 WAA.* That, more than anything else, makes this Yankees team probably the most

---

14. It is difficult to break down the Pythagorean projection of a super team like the 1939 Yankees because of a peculiarity of the Pythagorean formula that is highly revealing about the nature of baseball. Essentially, the formula shows that when a team has won 100 or more games out of 154, each additional win takes more and more runs over the season to be likely. I have adjusted the figures for team hitting, fielding and pitching WAA in this case accordingly.

dominant aggregation ever to take the field. The pitching staff featured seven different hurlers who earned between 1 and 1.9 WAA, with Ruffing topping the list.

Neither Ruffing nor Gomez ever pitched 200 innings in a season after 1939. Thanks to their career won-lost records of 231–124 and 189–102 and their frequent World Series appearances, both are in the Hall of Fame. Yet Ruffing had only one superstar season and one more over 3 WAA. Gomez also had only three seasons over 3 WAA, although his two best earned 5.6 and 5.7. Both of them clearly reached the Hall only because they had the good fortune to spend their careers with the greatest dynasty in baseball history. Meanwhile, a contemporary, Wes Ferrell, pitched far more innings than either Ruffing or Gomez in an average year, posted five superstar seasons with weak teams in Cleveland and Boston in 1929–1930, 1932, and 1935–1936, but finished with a record of only 193–128. I have no doubt that Ferrell was a significantly better pitcher than Ruffing or Gomez, and is in fact one of only two pitchers from the GI generation with five superstar seasons. He never received as many as 4 percent of the votes in a BWAA Hall of Fame vote, and the Veterans Committee, while ignoring him, elected his brother Rick, a totally average catcher.

Closing the Books on the Lost Generation, 1906–38

The extraordinary Lefty Grove, born in 1900, posted his last superstar season in 1939 with 4.8 WAA, the last member of the Lost Generation to do so, 32 years after Sherry Magee did the same in 1907. The Lost Generation—unlike the older Missionary generation—was the first to spend its entire baseball career within the framework of the majors as we have come to know them. It is time to list the all-time greats of that generation as this book defines them: the hitters and pitchers who had at least five seasons with 4 or more WAA. Here they are, together with their best single seasons.

Player	No. of Seasons of 4+WAA	Best-ever season, WAA
Babe Ruth	17*	11.6 (1923)
Tris Speaker	15	11.4 (1914)
Ty Cobb	14	11.3 (1917)
Rogers Hornsby	11	10.4 (1924)
Eddie Collins	8	9.5 (1910)
Bill Terry	7	8.3 (1930)
Al Simmons	6	6.6 (1931)
Joe Jackson	6	10.0 (1912)
Goose Goslin	5	7.6 (1928)
Harry Heilmann	5	7.3 (1923)

Includes 2 superstar seasons as a pitcher

Nearly every great player's career has a similar trajectory, reaching a peak after several superstar seasons and then gradually declining. That is why there is a clear correlation between a player's best-ever season and the number of times that he managed to exceed 4 WAA. Of these ten players, seven were outfielders, two were second basemen, and one was a first baseman. No Lost Generation third baseman or catcher came close to a place on this list. All of these players but Joe Jackson, who was rightly barred from baseball for his role in the Black Sox scandal, were elected to the Hall of Fame, and only Goslin had to wait for the Veterans Committee to get him there. Of the entire list, only Heilmann never played in a World Series.

When we reach further generations we shall encounter quite a few players who had four, but not five, seasons with at least 4 WAA, but among Lost Generation hitters there are only four such: Frankie Frisch, forgotten first baseman Jack Fournier, who never reached post-season play, Giants shortstop Art Fletcher, and outfielder Kiki Cuyler. Only Frisch and Cuyler of those four have ever been elected to the Hall of Fame. So was Home Run Baker, who had only three superstar seasons, but who as we have seen ranks as the greatest third baseman not only of his era but of the whole first half of the twentieth century.

The list of pitchers is shorter.

Player	No. of Seasons of +4WAA	Best-ever season, WAA
Lefty Grove	10	7.6 (1931)
Walter Johnson	9	9.9 (1913)
Pete Alexander	8	10.1 (1920)
Stanley Coveleski	5	5.6 (1918)

Among these five all-time greats, Alexander, Johnson and Coveleski pitched in two World Series each, and Grove three. All of them are in the Hall of Fame. Three other Lost Generation hurlers, Nap Rucker, Dazzy Vance, and Hippo Vaughn, had four seasons with at least 4 WAA. Of those three, only Vance is in the Hall of Fame, although Herb Pennock and Waite Hoyt, whose records were much weaker than Rucker's and Vaughn's, are so honored.

The Lost Generation, the first whose entire careers took place within the context of the National and American Leagues, set the standard for greatness. In a famous article, the late Stephen Jay Gould wrote that .400 hitters had disappeared from baseball because of a general regression towards the mean. Using the far more accurate measurement of WAA shows that he was right: the most extreme performances by hitters and pitchers from the Lost Generation have never been duplicated. Ruth, Speaker and Cobb all had seasons of more than 11 WAA, and the only hitter to have reached that figure since was Stan Musial, who did it during wartime, in 1943. Only two subsequent pitchers have tied Alexander's record 10.1 WAA for pitchers in 1920. We shall find that subsequent generations have produced a few more great hitters, but the subsequent GI Generation, which already dominated baseball when Lefty Grove had his last great season in 1939, produced no pitchers with an impact comparable to Grove, Johnson, or Alexander.

What happened to the Yankees in 1940 was even more astonishing than their performance in 1939. Without unloading a single starter, the Yankees saw their run differential slip from +411 to +146. The team got off to a dreadful start, roared down the stretch, but eventually finished in third place, behind the pennant-winning Tigers and the Cleveland Indians, with an 88–66 record. The value of the lineup declined all the way from +33 WAA to +14, while the pitching staff improved by +3. This was all the more remarkable since DiMaggio earned 6 WAA, Keller, having his first of five superstar seasons, added 5.3, and Gordon had

4.1. The rest of the lineup was a full -4 WAA. The chief culprits were Dahlgren, Red Rolfe, and Crosetti, all well below average. Crosetti, still only 29 years old, batted .194 and finished the season about -3.3 WAA—a figure it would take a Yankees shortstop more than seven decades to worsen. Dickey slumped all the way to average. The pitching staff, only one of whom topped 200 IP, managed to improve, but it had never been critical to the team's success.

The Tigers team that beat the Yankees was equally uneven. The Tigers finished with a record of only 90–64, despite just missing having three superstars in their lineup. Greenberg, shifted to left field at age 31, came through with 6.0 WAA, and Rudy York, who took his place at first base, added 4.7. York had only one other superstar season in his career, a wartime one. Gehringer, now 37, gave up -21 runs in the field and was barely above average overall. Outfielder Barney McCosky (1.9 WAA) was the only other valuable player in the lineup, which overall earned only 4 WAA. Their pitching staff, however, was a remarkable nine wins above average, better than any Yankees pitching staff during the 1930s. Bobo Newsom earned 5.0 WAA in 264 innings, Schoolboy Rowe had 3.6, and Tommy Bridges added 3.4, as the staff earned the team a total of +10 WAA.

Two other teams with great young players played important roles in the 1940 race. The Cleveland Indians featured the second and last truly dominant pitcher of the 1925–1949 era, Robert William Andrew Feller. Losing the pennant to the Tigers on the final weekend of the season by a single game, the Indians were the closest thing to a one-man team ever to come so near to a pennant. Bob Feller, now in the middle of an extraordinarily dominant run of three seasons, pitched 320⅓ innings and emerged with 6.9 WAA, good enough to give the Indians 84 wins, one less than their Pythagorean projection entitled them to. Feller was only 21 years old in 1940, but during the years 1939–1941, and again in 1946, he was by far the most dominant pitcher that the GI Generation ever produced.

We have seen that in the big-hitting era of the late 1920s and early 1930s, Miller Huggins, Connie Mack and Joe McCarthy, who won most of the pennants for the Yankees and the Athletics, tended to use at least five starting pitchers and very rarely allowed any of them to pitch more than about 230 innings in a season. Meanwhile, however, some of the weaker teams in the league had pitchers like Bobo Newsom, who toiled for many years with the Senators but had superstar seasons with the Tigers in 1939–1940; Wes Ferrell, who had five great years with the lowly Indians and Red Sox between 1930 and 1936; Mel Harder of the Indians, who had one superstar season in the mid–1930s; and General Crowder of the Senators, who once threw more than 300 innings in a year. Feller—raised on an Iowa farm and trained as a pitcher by his father from a very early age—must have been one of the most remarkable physical specimens ever to play baseball. After two years of limited use in 1936–1937, he threw 277⅔, 296⅔, 320⅓ and 343 innings in the next four years, aged 19 to 22, before entering the Navy right after Pearl Harbor. Nor was this all. It is highly doubtful that any pitcher ever had as low a percentage of the batters he faced put the ball in play as Feller. From 1938–1941, he led the American League in strikeouts with totals ranging from 240 to 261, and in walks in three of those years, with 208, 142, and 194. (For some reason his walk total fell to 118 in 1940.) The number of pitches he threw, by modern standards, must have been mind-boggling, and Feller was one of few pitchers in his era with what we would call a big motion. In 1946, when he pitched a no-hitter against the Yankees, a reporter noted that he had thrown 135 pitches—which Feller personally described in his ghost-written autobiography as a pretty easy day's work for him.

Overall, Feller in 1939–1940 was quite simply the most valuable player in the American League, with 6.9 and 6.8 WAA, respectively, translating to won-lost records of 24–9 and 27–11. He accomplished those records, as well as 6.6 WAA more and 25–13 in 1941, with a very mediocre team behind him. The Indians played most of their home games in League Park, a hitters' park that looked rather like a reversed Fenway. They had had a number of high-average hitters during the 1930s, but their overall offensive performance had been mediocre at best, and in 1940 it was a dreadful -7 WAA. The 1940 team became known in mid-season as the "Cry Baby" Indians, after they tried to convince their owner, Alva Bradley, to fire manager Oscar Vitt for being too mean to them. Their real problem was that they were nowhere near good enough to win the pennant, despite Feller, and only four games' worth of Pythagorean luck allowed them to come within one game of it with a run differential of just +54. They fielded well (led by rookie shortstop Lou Boudreau) but hit dreadfully, and despite Feller's sensational pitching performance, the staff as a whole was below average. Feller turned in another big season in 1941 with 6 WAA, but the team regressed to just below .500. Feller enlisted in the Navy two days after Pearl Harbor.

The fourth team in the 1940 race was an interesting aggregation of Red Sox that featured five future Hall of Famers—two at the beginning of their careers, and three at the end. Their owner, Tom Yawkey, who came from a baseball family, had bought the team in 1933 after coming into a huge fortune on his 30th birthday. Within a few years he had essentially bought Lefty Grove and Jimmy Foxx from Connie Mack, and Joe Cronin from Clark Griffith in Washington. In 1939, outfielder Ted Williams, signed by general manager Eddie Collins, joined the team at the age of 20 after just two years in the minors. Incredibly, in 1939, Williams, Grove and Foxx turned in seasons of 6.1, 4.8, and 5.6 WAA, respectively, making them more valuable than the three best players on the magnificent 1939 Yankees team. The team also added 21-year-old Bobby Doerr, who had begun his minor league career at the age of 16, but who was so far only a marginal asset. But they were pulled down by outfielder Doc Cramer, who was nearly -2 in WAA, and the rest of their pitching staff, which negated all but one of Grove's 5 WAA, and won only 89 games. In 1940 Williams became the team's only superstar with 4.8 WAA as Foxx and Grove finally declined, but they also added 23-year-old outfielder Dom DiMaggio, Joe's brother, who had spent three years in the minors.

In 1941–1942 and again after the war interregnum in 1946–1950, the Yankees and the Red Sox both finished either first, second or third in the American League every season, winning every pennant but one. Competing in parallel, Ted Williams and Joe DiMaggio each won two MVP Awards during those years. The Red Sox, as it turns out, had the better player, but the Yankees usually had the better team.

Having seen their run differential fall from 411 to 146 between 1939 and 1940, the Yankees built it back up to 199 in 1941, added four games of Pythagorean luck, and won the pennant again with 101 victories, regaining the level of a superior champion. Turning once again to their farm system, they replaced Frankie Crosetti, a dreadful -3.5 WAA in

1940, with Phil Rizzuto, a 23-year-old New Yorker fresh from four years in the minors, who fielded brilliantly for the next two years and earned 2.4 WAA in 1941—a gain of almost six wins for the team relative to Crosetti. DiMaggio, who hit safely in 56 consecutive games in mid-summer, and Keller did an excellent imitation of Ruth and Gehrig with 8.6 and 6.4 WAA, respectively, and Henrich, blossoming with 3 WAA, made this probably the greatest outfield of all time, with a combined 18 WAA. Gordon added 2.8 WAA at second base, but Dickey and Rolfe were now average at best, and Johnny Sturm at first base was even worse than Dahlgren, with -3.6 WAA. The team's fielding was slightly below average for the second consecutive year, but the line-up contributed +15 WAA and the pitchers added +7. Relative newcomers Tiny Bonham and Marius Russo earned 4.4 WAA between them, and Spud Chandler and Atley Donald added 2.1, while Ruffing and Gomez dropped to average. The best player in baseball, however, played for the Red Sox. Williams hit .406 with 147 walks and 37 homers, and finished with 9 WAA. Although both Foxx and Cronin had star-quality seasons, the younger players performed less well and the pitching cost the team -2 wins. The Red Sox overall hit and pitched much less well than the Yankees, fielded slightly better, and won just 84 games.

By the time the 1942 major league season began, the United States was fighting in the Second World War and military draft calls were skyrocketing, but their initial impact on major league rosters was slight. It was larger in the American League, where Bob Feller joined Hank Greenberg (who had played just 19 games early in 1941) in a new uniform, taking away the league's greatest pitcher as well as one of its greatest hitters. Other 1941 regulars who were drafted included catcher Frankie Pytlak of the Red Sox, Soup Campbell of Cleveland, first baseman Johnny Sturm of the Yankees (one of the league's worst players), and Philadelphia Athletics Benny McCoy and Sam Chapman, both of whom were legitimate stars. The National League was much less affected, with no important pitchers and only two regular players going into the military in 1942, but it put on a remarkable pennant race in which the Cardinals defeated the Dodgers with 106 wins to the Dodgers' 104. Both leagues would observe the same kind of effect in 1946, when the stars had returned but the league had been struck by a dearth of young stars, and 1961–1962, when they expanded their size by 25 percent.

In the American League, two teams with a total of seven superstars contested the pennant race. Both teams were young and athletic, and both fielded brilliantly, the Yankees earning +9 WAA in the field and the Red Sox +7. The Yankees had Joe DiMaggio (4.4 WAA), Keller (5.9), MVP Joe Gordon (5.8), and Rizzuto (4.7 in his only superstar season). Although Henrich slipped to 1.6 WAA and the infield corners were average, the Yankees line-up as a whole earned a remarkable +27 WAA, 18 of them at bat. The pitchers added four more thanks to Tiny Bonham (2.4 WAA in 226 innings) and Spud Chandler (1.4 WAA), and the Yankees had 103 wins. In a shocking upset, they lost the World Series to the Cardinals in just five games. The Red Sox's top three were even better, including Williams, who won the Triple Crown with an astonishing 10.6 WAA, his best ever; Dom DiMaggio, who saved 41 runs in the field (compared to his brother's 5) and posted 6.4 WAA; and rookie shortstop Johnny Pesky, just 23, who saved 31 runs in the field, got more than 200 hits, and had 5.0 WAA. Oddly, neither Dom DiMaggio nor Rizzuto nor Pesky ever performed at that level again. Boston's pitching staff, alas, was a liability after Tex Hughson (3.1 WAA), costing the team -1 WAA, and although Doerr starred with 3 WAA at second base, third baseman Jim Tabor, outfielder Pete Fox and first baseman Tony Lupien (who took over for an injured Jimmy Foxx) were awful, costing the team -5.3 WAA. Despite the strongest three players ever fielded by a Red Sox team in the Williams era, they finished ten games behind the Yankees, winning 93. In 1943 the American League, and baseball generally, definitely entered into a new era, as most of its regular players began going into the military. Before discussing those years, however, it is time to see what had been happening since 1925 in the senior circuit.

Our previous chapter concluded with the end of the 1921–1924 Giants dynasty in the National League. The league remained far more balanced than the American for the rest of the 1920s and 1930s because it had fewer superstars, and they were not so concentrated as in the AL, where they clustered on the rosters of the Yankees, Athletics, and Red Sox. From 1926 through 1942, the American League had 124 superstar seasons, about seven per year. The National League had only 102, or six per year. That in turn suggests that average performance in the National League was lower than in the American. Together these facts explain why, from 1926 through 1942, the American League won 11 of 17 World Series, with five sweeps to the National League's none. Even within the National League, dominant teams were rare in this era, with only four clubs reaching the level of a superior pennant winner from 1926 through 1942.

We deferred discussion of the 1925 Pirates in the last chapter—the team that deprived the Washington Senators of a second straight world championship—because they also won the pennant in 1927. The two teams won 90 and 94 games. The superstar of the 1925 team was Kiki Cuyler, who hit .357 with 18 home runs and had a fine year in the field, giving him a total of 6.1 WAA. Cuyler was then 26, and because batting averages kept rising in the National League for the next half-decade, he finished his career with a .321 lifetime average and 2,299 hits, and was elected to the Hall of Fame at the height of the Frankie Frisch era in 1968. With four superstar seasons, he was at least marginally qualified. Other stars on the team included outfielder Max Carey (2.2 WAA) and third baseman Pie Traynor (2.2), and everyone in the lineup was at least average. From the 1930s through the 1960s Traynor was regarded, bizarrely, as the greatest third baseman of all time, and the BBWAA elected him to the Hall of Fame in 1948. That selection was questionable. Traynor also had only one superstar season and three star seasons of 2–3 WAA in his career, and he was a good, but not great, third baseman, leading the NL in runs saved only three times. The team overall fielded very well and the pitchers contributed +3 more WAA. The 1927 team's overall statistics were quite similar to 1925, but the cast of characters had changed somewhat. This time the team MVP was another outfielder, 24-year-old Paul Waner, who had joined the team at 23 in 1926 after three years with the San Francisco Seals. Waner led the league with a .380 average in 1927 and posted 6.4 WAA. He was a truly great player destined to post six superstar seasons between 1926 and 1936, making him an overwhelming candidate for the Hall of Fame. The same cannot be said, however, of his younger brother Lloyd, a rookie in 1926, who finished his career in 1945 with a .316 lifetime average, a .353 OBP, and a .393 slugging percentage. Lloyd never had a season of even 2 WAA and was a below-average player over his whole career. We have had occasion to remark that many players reached the Hall of Fame because they had the right teammates. Lloyd Waner appears to have been elected by the Veterans Committee in 1967 because he had the right brother. He was the worst player ever elected to the Hall. Pitcher Ray Kremer also contributed 3.8 critical WAA to the 1927 Pirates, but they were not surprisingly swept by the Yankees in the World Series.

Two axes converged for the 1926 St. Louis Cardinals, who won the pennant and the World Series. Their second baseman and manager, Rogers Hornsby, the greatest National League hitter from the whole Lost Generation, reached post-season play for the first of only two times. Meanwhile, the team's general manager, Branch Rickey, began one of the most successful and influential executive careers in the history of major league baseball. The 1926 team was actually quite mediocre, with a dreadful -5 WAA pitching staff, and won only 89 games. But the Cardinals, increasingly fueled by the game's first farm system, were going to win eight out of the next 21 National League pennants, filling the gap between the Giants and the Dodgers as the National League's dominant team.

Texan Rogers Hornsby had reached the Cardinals line-up in 1915 at the age of 19 after two years in the minors. Although frequently reputed to be a poor fielder, Hornsby actually performed adequately at shortstop for about four seasons, and posted his first superstar season with 6.8 WAA in 1917, when he hit .327. Switched to second base in 1920, he blossomed, leading the league in hitting five times in a row, three of them with figures of .401 (1922), .403 (1925), and the modern record of .424 (1924). That season was worth 10.1 WAA, the best for a National League hitter until 1943, and Hornsby topped 8 WAA on three other occasions. But he was the Walter Johnson of hitters for the first 11 years of his career; the rest of his team remained stubbornly below average, never coming within striking distance of their first pennant. Oddly, Hornsby himself slumped from 7.2 WAA in 1925 to just 2.4 in 1926, but the team won the pennant without a single superstar. Third baseman Les Bell, outfielders Ray Blades and Billy Southworth, catcher Bob O'Farrell and first baseman Jim Bottomley were modest assets at the plate, and the team fielded brilliantly (or luckily), led by center fielder Taylor Douthit and shortstop Tommy Thevenow, who saved 33 and 50 runs respectively. It was a good thing that they did, because Grover Cleveland Alexander, acquired in mid-season, was the team's ace with less than 2 WAA, and the pitching staff as a whole was one of the worst ever to win a pennant. The Cardinals edged out the Yankees—Ruth, Gehrig, and the seven dwarfs—in seven games in the World Series.

Success seems to have spoiled Rogers Hornsby. No sooner had he led his team to the pennant as player-manager than he got into a violent argument over money with his owner, Sam Breadon, who traded him during the off-season. The rest of Hornsby's career was somewhat similar to that of a modern player, Dick Allen. Both men were great talents (although Hornsby, in his time, was the greater) who had trouble getting along with management and had serious addiction problems—alcohol in Allen's case, gambling in Hornsby's. Like Allen after his departure from Philadelphia in 1969, Hornsby after leaving his first team went on a kind of progress around the league. Breadon got pretty good value for him in 1927, receiving Frankie Frisch, another future Hall of Famer, from the Giants, but Hornsby lasted only one year with John McGraw, who essentially gave him to the lowly Boston Braves for two extremely average players. Undaunted, Hornsby led the league in hitting once again in

2. The Lost and GI Generation Era, 1925–1945

Boston, whereupon he went to the Cubs for five unmemorable players and $200,000. Hornsby helped the Cubs win the pennant with his last great season in 1929, but missed most of the next three years with injuries. He received his release in 1932, returned to the Cardinals and finished with the St. Louis Browns. Over his career he piled up 11 superstar seasons, trailing only Ruth, Speaker, Cobb and Grove among his own Lost Generation. Like Johnson, however, he reached the World Series just twice.

Without Hornsby, the Cardinals in 1928–1931 won three pennants in four years, taking the flag with 95, 92 and 101 wins. They were a dynasty almost without parallel in baseball history, since their players turned in exactly two superstar seasons—4.2 WAA by right fielder Taylor Douthit (all of them in the field) in 1928, and 4.2 WAA by player-manager Frankie Frisch in 1930—during those four seasons. Essentially, they had a large number of good but not great players both in the lineup and on the mound. In 1928, the leading pitchers were Bill Sherdel (3.1 WAA), Jesse Haines (2.4) and Clarence Mitchell (2.0), while the line-up included Douthit (4.2 WAA), outfielder Chick Hafey (3.4), Frisch (3.2), and first baseman Jim Bottomley (2.9). Unfortunately, the four other regulars cost the team a combined -6.7 WAA, and the pitching staff deserved more of the credit for the pennant, earning +8 WAA. Only Frisch (4.3 WAA) and outfielder George Watkins (2.3) were significant assets in the lineup in 1930, when Bottomley and Hafey had disastrous seasons in the field that dropped them to average. Aging spitballer Burleigh Grimes anchored the pitching staff with 3.0 WAA in 152⅓ innings, and the hurlers matched the lineup with +9 WAA. Poor fielding held Bottomley and Hafey to 2.1 WAA each in 1931, and Frisch led the team with only 2.4. Now 33 years old, Frisch still saved the team +19 runs compared to an average second baseman. The legendary Pepper Martin, the hero of the World Series victory over the Athletics, was only +1 WAA. Branch Rickey, who had become general manager in 1925 (officially business manager), was just getting his farm system going, and he had not yet developed his aversion to players over 30—there were five such men in his lineup. Again the pitchers did better, with Wild Bill Hallahan, Grimes, young Paul Derringer and Syl Johnson combining for 6 WAA. The Cardinals did, however, manage to keep any drastically inferior players out of their lineup.

Forty years later, Frankie Frisch, by then the most powerful man on the Hall of Fame's Veterans Committee, arranged a series of most undistinguished inductions for his Cardinals teammates, complementing his teammates from the 1921–1924 Giants. They included pitcher Jesse Haines, who had two seasons over 2 WAA and none over 4; first baseman Bottomley, who had one superstar season in 1925; and outfielder Hafey, who topped 3 WAA two times, but 4 never. Frisch managed this, evidently, by stressing their batting averages: Bottomley finished his career a lifetime .310 hitter, while Hafey batted .317 over his career. But those figures were not enough to make a man a superstar in the 1920s and early 1930s.

It is somewhat astonishing that the Cardinals managed to win these pennants against a New York Giants team that consistently fielded two superstars of their own. In 1927 the Giants finished two games behind the Pirates despite the presence of first baseman Bill Terry (4.9 WAA), Hornsby (6.2), outfielder George Harper (3.7) and young shortstop Travis Jackson (3.2). Unfortunately, aging outfielder Edd Roush, third basemen Andy Reese and catcher Jack Taylor cost the team about -5 WAA, and dreadful pitching cost them -3 more. In 1928 the two superstars were pitcher Larry Benton (4.0 WAA) and third baseman Fred Lindstrom (4.4), but the Cardinals beat them by two games, as Hornsby made way for a very average Andy Cohen at second base. In 1929 the Cubs, as we shall see, fielded an unusually strong National League team, and the Giants finished well back. The Giants got extraordinary seasons from 20-year-old Mel Ott, on his way to establishing a new National League record for home runs (7.3 WAA), and Terry (4.3), but Travis Jackson (1.9 WAA) was the only other above-average player in the lineup. In 1930 Terry (8.3 WAA with a .401 BA, the last such mark in the National League) and Ott (4.8 with a .458 OBP) did it again, but the Giants lagged five games behind the Cardinals because their other players were two games below average. The chief culprit was one of the worst major leaguers in history, second baseman Hughie Critz, an inept hitter and fielder who cost the team -4.8 WAA. In 1931 Terry and Ott did their Ruth-Gehrig act yet again, with 6.3 and 3.9 WAA—but the team won just 87 games, meaning their teammates were average again. Only six Giants hitters played more than 90 games, and seven part-time players combined for -6.5 WAA in about 950 plate appearances.

The Giants had their most amazing season yet in 1932, when Terry (7.9) and Ott (6.6) were joined by left-handed screwballer Carl Hubbell with 5.3 WAA of his own. With an average supporting cast, they would have projected to win 97 games, but in fact they won just 72 games. Beyond Terry and Ott, the line-up did not boast a single player who was even average, led by Hughie Critz (-4.3 WAA) and Freddie Lindstrom (-2 WAA after being moved to center field). Nearly every pitcher but Hubbell was below average as well.

Bill Terry, who had become a great first baseman and thus must have had an excellent perspective on the performance of the rest of the infield, took over from John McGraw after 40 games of the 1932 season. In 1933 he let Lindstrom go and replaced him with George "Kiddo" Davis in center field, gaining +3.7 WAA at that position alone. In an astonishing turnaround, Critz, a very erratic second baseman, went from -22 runs to +45 runs on defense and +2.6 WAA overall. Although both Terry and Ott slumped in 1933 and fell out of the superstar range, these changes made up for part of their decline. Meanwhile Hubbell went 23-12 and 5.3 WAA, 21-year-old Hal Schumacher added 2.7 more, and the pitching became an asset. The Giants finished first in an extraordinarily mediocre league with only 91 wins. Chuck Klein of the Phillies was the only offensive superstar in the National League in 1933.

Now owned by Horace Stoneham, the Giants had established a tradition that would continue through Stoneham's tenure into the 1970s. For most of those 40 years, they had between one and three all-time greats on the roster, yet very rarely, under the circumstances, did they manage to win a pennant. Terry beginning in 1927 had seven superstar seasons, while Ott beginning in 1930 had 11, and Hubbell had 4, tying him for third among pitchers from the GI Generation. First baseman Johnny Mize came to the Giants from the Cardinals in 1942 and turned in four superstar seasons for them of his own. Starting in 1954 the Giants had Willie Mays, literally a perennial superstar, to whom they eventually added Willie McCovey and Juan Marichal. Yet with such enormous assets, the Giants won only three pennants in the 1930s, none in the 1940s, two in the 1950s and one in the 1960s, largely, it seems, because their stars somehow encouraged management to tolerate dreadful weaknesses at certain positions year after year.

In 1934, the Giants and the Cardinals faced off in a close pennant race. "In any voting on the Greatest Teams of All Time I have seen," Leo Durocher wrote 40 years later, "the 1927 Yankees have been ranked first and the 1934 Cardinals second. Which shows what the passage of time can do. In sheer talent, we weren't in the same class with a dozen teams I could name."[15] Durocher had no idea how right he was. Those Cardinals, for which he played a very poor shortstop (-13 runs), won 95 games and beat the Giants by two games only with the help of four games' worth of Pythagorean luck. Most of their positive value came from just two players. The first, of course, was 24-year-old Dizzy Dean, a very hard-throwing right-hander who posted a 30–7 record (four wins coming in relief) and 5.5 WAA, his first of two superstar seasons. Dean had 3.4 WAA in 1935 and 4.1 in 1936, throwing more than 300 innings every year. He was on the pace to post another such season in 1937 when his toe was broken by a line drive in the All-Star Game, but he faded very rapidly after that. Most of the pitchers of that era, clearly, did not try to throw very hard. In a surviving video about the 1934–1935 seasons, a sequence of shots of leading pitchers shows Dean to be the only one who does not look, by modern standards, simply to be warming up.

Dean's 5.5 WAA in 1934 equaled the pitching staff as a whole, including his brother Paul, who won 19 games. The biggest star of the team's line-up, surprisingly, was first baseman Ripper Collins, who accounted for nearly half its positive value with 4.7 WAA. Joe Medwick was headed for three consecutive superstar seasons in 1935–1937—his only ones—but he earned only about 2 WAA in 1934. Frisch, now 36, was below average, as was shortstop Durocher. Their legendary third baseman, Pepper Martin, had been significantly above average only once in his career, in 1933, when he had 2.8 WAA. Hubbell, Terry and Ott turned in three superstar performances once again for the stronger Giants club, but they lost the pennant despite a better projected record because of a poor record in close games.

The Chicago Cubs, meanwhile, had established themselves once again as the other power in the National League, taking the pennant in 1929, 1932, 1935 and 1938. The 1929 team featured Hornsby, who posted 8.4 WAA in his last superstar season, including +18 runs at second base; Kiki Cuyler, now 30, who had 4.5 WAA; outfielder Riggs Stephenson (3.7); and Hack Wilson, one of the more extraordinary combinations of strengths and weaknesses ever to set foot on a ball field. Wilson offensively created about half as many runs above average as Hornsby, putting him into the superstar category, but he was one of the worst center fielders in history. Having cost the team -26 runs in 1928, he cost them another -16 in 1929, giving him 3.3 WAA overall. The Cubs line-up as a whole was +20 WAA, meaning that the other regulars were average. It was poetic justice that Wilson cost the Cubs the fourth game of the World Series—and a chance to tie the series at 2–2—when he lost a fly ball in the sun, turning it into a three-run homer, in the midst of the Athletics' ten-run rally. What Wilson did the next year, in 1930, was even more incredible. The Cubs finished two games behind the Cardinals in the heaviest-hitting league in modern baseball, with a league batting average of .303. Wilson hit .356 with 56 home runs—a National League record that stood until 1998—and 191 RBI, an all-time record that has never been threatened. But he

---

15. Leo Durocher with Ed Linn, *Nice Guys Finish Last* (New York: Simon & Schuster, 1975), 81.

gave up almost half of the 76 runs above average he earned at the plate in center field, yielding -36 runs there, and finishing one of the most amazing batting seasons in baseball history with just 3.6 WAA. Wilson never had a genuine superstar season in his career, topping 3 WAA four times. But despite this and his short career, the Veterans Committee elected him to the Hall of Fame in 1979.

The 1932 Cubs were, quite simply, one of the most mediocre pennant-winning teams of all time, with no superstars and 90 victories thanks to four games' worth of Pythagorean luck. Their fielding contributed more to their success than either their hitting or pitching. The 1935 team, however, was the strongest National League team of the whole decade, missing their projection of 102 wins by only two games. They had two superstars in the lineup, left fielder Augie Galan (5.6 WAA) and second baseman Billy Herman (4.4 WAA.) Galan, although only 23, did not manage to match that performance until the Second World War, while Herman had one more superstar season in 1937. Other stars were catcher Gabby Hartnett, with an outstanding 3.9 WAA, and third baseman Stan Hack, with about 2.5. Hartnett had one other season over 3 WAA in his long career. Led by Galan, shortstop Billy Jurges, and Herman, the fielders earned +9 WAA to the hitters' +19 and the pitchers' +4. The 1938 team was entirely different, with a lineup that earned just 3 WAA, the lowest figure for a pennant winner in history. The pitchers, led by Bill Lee's remarkable 5.3 WAA, earned 8 WAA overall and allowed the team to lead a mediocre league with only 89 wins. With two superstar seasons and only one other over 2 WAA, Billy Herman was a somewhat questionable Hall of Fame selection, far inferior to the best second basemen of his generation. He was an average player by the time he reached the Dodgers in the middle of the 1941 pennant race and below average the next year.

The Cubs had been good enough to win four straight pennants from 1935–1938, but they were beaten out by the New York Giants both in 1936 (when their run differential was +151 to the Giants' +114) and in 1937 (when the teams' records were indistinguishable). Typically, some severe weaknesses limited the 1936 Giants to 92 wins (two from luck), even though they had three superstars: Hubbell (6.7 WAA in his last great year), Ott (5), and shortstop Dick Bartell (5.3), who saved 48 runs in 1936, 28 in 1937 and 14 in 1938. Bartell's record—reminiscent of Art Fletcher 20 years earlier—was all the more remarkable since he had spent about a decade at shortstop for the Pirates without posting above-average stats there. Center fielder Jo-Jo Moore also fielded brilliantly and earned 3.3 WAA, but Travis Jackson, switched to third base, hit .230 with no power and cost the team -4.2 WAA. The pitchers, beyond Hubbell, were average overall. Bartell and Ott slipped to 4.6 and 3.6 WAA in 1937, but they were the only assets in the lineup, and the latest Polo Grounds disaster was third baseman Lou Chiozza, who cost the team -3.9 WAA in only 117 games. Only five games' worth of luck enabled the Giants to edge out a virtually equal Cubs team with 95 wins. Hubbell slipped to 2.3 WAA, but the rest of the staff added +3 WAA.

The pennants of 1939–1940 were won by one of the most remarkable teams of all time, the Cincinnati Reds, managed by Bill McKechnie. Winning 97 and 100 games, the Reds owed most of their success to their fielders, who earned 8 of their lineup's 18 WAA in 1939, and an incredible, record-setting 15 out of 20 WAA in 1940, when luck must clearly have played a role. The men most responsible were All-Star second baseman Lonnie Frey

(+16 and +36 runs saved in those two years), shortstop Billy Myers (+14 and +9), third baseman Billy Werber (+16 and +25), right fielder Ival Goodman (+25 in 1939), and outfielders Harry Craft, Mike McCormick and Morrie Arnovich, who saved +41 runs among them in 1940. Pitcher Bucky Walters earned 4.6 and 2.5 WAA in those two years, and McCormick and Lonnie Frey, helped by their fielding, each had superstar seasons in 1940. The Reds were annihilated in four straight games by the fantastic 1939 Yankees team in the World Series, but it is not surprising that they prevailed in seven over the relatively mediocre Detroit Tigers the next year. The level of play in the National League, however, was about to improve markedly thanks to two owners: Branch Rickey of the Cardinals and Larry MacPhail of the Dodgers.

Although Rickey had created the modern farm system in the 1920s and expanded it in the 1930s, he had not been nearly as successful as Ed Barrow of the Yankees in developing great players, perhaps because his scouts seem seldom to have ventured very far from St. Louis. We have seen that his teams had won five pennants between 1926 and 1934, although only the 1931 team was truly outstanding. During the 1930s the farm system had produced Dizzy Dean, Joe Medwick, who turned in three superstar seasons, and the great first baseman Johnny Mize, who replaced Ott as the league's leading power hitter and posted eight consecutive superstar seasons for the Cardinals (1938–1941) and Giants (1942, 1946–1948) without ever reaching a World Series.[16] National League sportswriters in this era had a prejudice against home runs, and that must account for Mize's stature as the least recognized all-time great player in the history of baseball. It is simply incredible that Mize never received even a 50 percent vote from the BBWAA, and that he had to wait until 1981 to be selected by the Veterans Committee, one of the few occasions on which that body has rectified a genuine injustice.

Rickey, who shared a relatively small St. Louis market with the American League Browns, also had to keep a close eye on his bank balance, and he had concluded by the late 1930s that most players declined sharply around the age of 30. In early 1938, Rickey dealt Dean, who had hurt his arm, to the Chicago Cubs in exchange for Curt Davis, an above-average pitcher, two other players, and $185,000 Depression-era dollars. In June of 1940, Rickey essentially sold Medwick and Curt Davis to the Dodgers for another $125,000. Neither Dean nor Medwick, as it turned out, had that much to contribute to their new teams, but Rickey surely made a dreadful mistake at the end of the 1941 season, when the Cardinals had finished a close second, sending Mize, still only 28, to the New York Giants for three players who never amounted to anything and just $50,000.

New talent, however, had already arrived. In 1938, Enos Slaughter had come on the scene at the age of 22, after three years in the minors, and established himself as a slightly above-average outfielder during the next three years. After a shaky start in 1935, center fielder Terry Moore had reached about the same level by 1940. Most important of all, 20-year-old Stan Musial had a cup of coffee with the Cardinals in 1941 and became a regular the next year. He became the second-greatest hitter of the GI Generation, behind Ted Williams.

---

16. Mize did reach the World Series five times with the Yankees from 1949–1953.

The Dodgers, meanwhile, had ended a long period in the doldrums after Larry MacPhail had taken over running the club in 1938. MacPhail, a hero of the First World War with inherited wealth, had gotten into baseball in the early 1930s, running the Columbus Red Birds, a farm team of Rickey's Cardinals. He had become the general manager of the Cincinnati Reds in the mid–1930s but left for Brooklyn after some altercations with the local police, fights that owed much to his chronic drinking problem. MacPhail, who had introduced night baseball to the big leagues in Cincinnati, quickly put lights in Ebbets Field. Following a strategy opposite to Rickey's—and foreshadowing another New York owner from out of town, George Steinbrenner—he began acquiring high-priced stars from elsewhere. First baseman Dolph Camilli came from the Phillies in 1938, and MacPhail bought Medwick from Rickey, his old boss, in 1940, receiving Curt Davis as well. Leo Durocher became the manager, and Red Barber drew fans to Ebbets Field serving as the Dodgers' broadcaster. Meanwhile, the Dodgers owned potentially one of the greatest players of the GI Generation, Pete Reiser, who had reached them in a most unusual way.

In building his farm system—which eventually included two entire leagues that he controlled—Branch Rickey came up against the views of Commissioner Kenesaw Mountain Landis, who believed in independent minor league teams that would share in baseball's profits and give their local fans an honest effort to win. He periodically expressed his displeasure by freeing a few dozen players under contract to Rickey's teams—and Reiser, who had signed with the Cardinals in 1937 at the age of 18, was one of them in 1938. Reiser was, however, both an extraordinary prospect—a switch-hitter with great speed who could play almost any position—and a St. Louis native, and Rickey and MacPhail apparently struck a deal, promising to return him to the Cardinals in a few years. Durocher in 1940, after one of many violent arguments with his boss, managed to convince MacPhail to keep Reiser.

Reiser finally became the Dodgers center fielder in 1941, a year when everything went right in Brooklyn and the team won 100 games. They fielded three superstars. Reiser, now 22, won the batting title with a .343 mark, saved +30 runs in center field, and topped the league with 7.5 WAA. Twenty-nine-year-old Dixie Walker, a mediocre player for most of the 1930s, had the year of his life, hitting .310, fielding brilliantly in right field, and putting up another 6.3 WAA. First baseman Dolph Camilli, 34, had the last and best of three superstar seasons in his career with 6 WAA. Meanwhile, pitcher Whitlow Wyatt, 33, threw 288⅓ innings, finished 22–10, and put up 3.1 WAA of his own. Twenty-two-year-old shortstop Pee Wee Reese saved +30 runs in the field but gave nearly all of them back at the plate. Medwick earned just 1.4 WAA but Billy Herman, acquired from the Cubs, was average and catcher Mickey Owen cost the team -1.7 WAA. Overall, the line-up earned 21 WAA at bat and in the field. Fielding was the Dodgers' secret: somehow they had learned the secret of positioning themselves in their small ball park, and the fielders won them eight games over .500 while their pitchers, despite Wyatt, were only average. Kirby Higbe had a 22–9 record, his pitching was exactly average, and reliever Hugh Casey, the goat of the World Series against the Yankees, had cost the team -1.4 WAA in 162 innings. The three superstars and Wyatt accounted almost exactly for the team's 100 victories—the rest of the team, overall, was average.

Branch Rickey's Cardinals were lucky to finish only two games back in 1941. Their only superstar was Johnny Mize (4.2 WAA), although outfielder Johnny Hopp added 3.9. With Slaughter earning just 1.5 WAA, the lineup earned only +10 WAA to the Dodgers' +22, and their pitching earned +5 WAA. Rickey and his staff were known for looking for the best athletes available, and the young lineup earned a full +6 WAA in the field, but only +4 at bat. Rickey, oddly, reacted by unloading Mize to the Giants after the season was over. Like the Dodgers in 1941, however, the Cardinals in 1942 added a great rookie, Stan Musial, and the two teams fought out the most amazing two-team race in baseball history.

Like its American League counterpart, the 1942 National League season appears puzzling to the analyst. On the one hand, the impact of the military draft was even less in the National League than in the American. Only three 1941 regular hitters—third baseman Cookie Lavagetto of the Dodgers, Braves second baseman Bama Rowell, and Phillies outfielder Joe Marty—went into the military, and the draft did not take a single pitcher who had thrown as many as 150 innings. Total superstar seasons did not increase, yet the pennant race, in which the Cardinals won 106 games and the Dodgers tied the all-time record for a second-place team with 104, has all the hallmarks of an expansion year. The Cardinals won the pennant with three superstars. Pitcher Mort Cooper vaulted from nowhere to a 22–7 record in 278⅔ innings and earned 5 WAA. Two other pitchers, Max Lanier and Johnny Beazley, earned 2.2 WAA each, and the pitching staff overall contributed +12 WAA. In the outfield, rookie Stan Musial announced himself with a .315 average and 5.9 WAA, and Enos Slaughter blossomed with his first of two superstar seasons in his career with 4.8 WAA. The rest of the batting order was quite undistinguished, but the Cardinals lineup earned +15 WAA at the plate and +18 overall thanks to 46 runs worth of run luck, effectively bunching their hits and walks. The Dodgers, meanwhile, suffered an astonishing collapse in the field, thanks in large part to injuries to Pete Reiser, whose contribution in center field fell from +30 runs to -18. That explained the team's overall decline perfectly: the defense went from 8 WAA down to 2 WAA. Camilli (3.9 WAA), Reese (3.4) and Walker (2.4) were the only significant assets in the lineup. The pitching, on the other hand, went from average to 7 WAA. Wyatt fell to 1.1 WAA, but Larry French (2.7 WAA), Curt Davis (1.9) and relievers Max Macon (1.8) and Hugh Casey (1.4) more than picked up the slack. The Dodgers had even better run luck than the Cardinals, scoring 65 more runs than their hitting stats would have predicted. The rest of the league seems to have made a habit of giving these teams hits when they needed them most.

The Cardinals shocked the Yankees in the 1942 World Series, nearly overcoming a 7–0 deficit to tie Game One in the ninth inning, and winning the next four in a row. This was perhaps the climax of the second half of the Lost/GI Generation era, representing the peak of the GI Generation of ballplayers, who were now between 18 and 39 years old. During the last ten years, that generation had produced an extraordinary number of all-time greats, including Hank Greenberg, Dizzy Dean, Johnny Mize, Carl Hubbell, Joe DiMaggio, Joe Gordon, Charlie Keller, Lou Boudreau, Bob Feller, Ted Williams, and Stan Musial. Pete Reiser, if he could have stayed healthy, would probably have fit into that group too, and Pirates shortstop Arky Vaughan, who only once (1938) even came close to reaching the postseason, had posted four superstar seasons, equaling the best record for a GI Generation shortstop. There was a reason for this talent explosion. While about 10 percent of GIs were still excluded from organized baseball because of their race, there was never a time at which more young men began a professional baseball career at age 18 or so than in the 1930s. The minor leagues employed more young men than at any time in history, no other sport had remotely comparable appeal, and there was more chance, in short, of developing that rare group of supremely talented young men into real major league superstars than at any other moment in American history.

Because the Yankees clearly had by far the most extensive farm system and scouting operation in baseball, they drew upon this reservoir of talent to create the most dominant dynasty in the history of baseball. Thanks to DiMaggio, Gehrig, Keller, Gordon, Henrich and Rizzuto, the six Yankees pennant winners in the years 1936–42 averaged a winning percentage of .667. No other dynasty, including the Yankees teams of 1949–64, has ever achieved a remotely comparable level of dominance.

The war years, which we shall now look at, did much more than send most established players into the military. Equally importantly, they stopped the flow of 18-year-olds into organized baseball, and for various reasons, that flow never resumed at a comparable rate after the war. On the eve of the war in 1940, the minor leagues included 306 teams, or 19 for every single major league team. That number would be cut more than half during the 1950s, and the ratio of minor league to major league players has never come close to matching what it was in the 1930s in the decades since. Even now, nearly 70 years after segregation and decades after the opening of several Latin American talent pools, it is most unlikely that as many young men are devoting their lives to baseball as in the 1930s. Meanwhile, the size of the major leagues has nearly doubled.

The War Years

The war definitely hit baseball in 1943 and had transformed it by 1944 and 1945. Players who did not serve in the military became the exception, generally for one of two reasons. To begin with, several star players were ruled out for medical reasons, such as Cleveland shortstop Lou Boudreau (bad ankles) and Detroit pitcher Hal Newhouser (a heart defect). Some others, such as Stan Musial and Boston second baseman Bobby Doerr, were not called up until after the 1944 season. Lastly, the draft boards around baseball-mad St. Louis seem to have had a keen appreciation for the importance of the national pastime, and remarkably few of the players from the Cardinals and the Browns were drafted. This allowed the Cardinals to continue ruling the National League from 1942 through 1944, while the Browns rose from the depths of the American League to win their only pennant in 1944. Four of the regulars and two of the starting pitchers on the 1944 Cardinals had been part of the 1942 team as well. That was how the Cardinals managed to follow up their 106 victories in 1942 with 105 in each of the next two years. Meanwhile, in New York, the 1944 Yankees' line-up did not include a single player from their 1942 pennant winner, and they retained only two of the starting pitchers.

The Cardinals lost the last wartime pennant to the Cubs in 1945, while the Tigers won out in a close race in the American League. Both leagues, by then, had achieved a remarkable level of mediocrity. The Wins Above Average metric allows us to see exactly how much the two leagues declined during the war. Many players who had been mere stars before the war became superstars, while certain aging players turned in the best season, relative to the league, that they had ever had in their lives.

Outfielder Augie Galan had turned in one superstar season for the 1935 Cubs, but had declined, as would be expected, later in the decade. Suddenly, in 1943, at the age of 31, he earned 5.5 WAA for the Brooklyn Dodgers, and followed that up with 4.1 in 1945. In 1944, the great Mel Ott, now 35 years old, earned 4.3 WAA for the Giants. Stan Hack, long-time third baseman for the Cubs, turned in the first superstar season of his career in 1945 at the age of 35, helping his team to the pennant, with 4.2 WAA. For future Hall of Famers, the sky was the limit. Musial in 1943 and 1944 earned 11.1 and 9 WAA, the highest figures of his career, and Hal Newhouser had 6.2 WAA in 1944 and 8 in 1945, winning the MVP Award both times. While it is unlikely that Newhouser would ever have posted a record of 29–9, as he did in 1944, without the war, there is every reason to believe that he still would have finished his career as one of the two pitchers from the GI Generation with five seasons over 4 WAA. He added the other three superstar performances in 1946–1948.

Cleveland shortstop Lou Boudreau, who would also distinguish himself after the war was over, had 6 WAA in 1943 and 4 in 1944. One performer proved particularly deceptive, with fateful consequences. Joe Gordon was drafted in 1943, and Snuffy Stirnweiss took over as the Yankees second baseman. He batted over .300 and led the league in runs, hits, triples and stolen bases during both 1944 and 1945, earning 7.8 and 8.2 WAA. When Gordon returned in 1946, Stirnweiss was moved to third base, but Gordon got into a fight with the new Yankees owner, Larry MacPhail, and was traded to Cleveland for Allie Reynolds after the 1946 season. Stirnweiss quickly proved himself to be a completely average player under normal conditions, while Gordon remained a superstar in Cleveland. The trade of Gordon—undoubtedly prompted in part by an overestimate of Stirnweiss's value—almost surely cost the Yankees the 1948 pennant. Another player who enhanced his reputation during the war was pitcher Preacher Roe of the Pittsburgh Pirates, whose 1945 record (4.9 WAA) caught the attention of Branch Rickey, now an owner of the Dodgers. All in all, it would appear that the average level of play in both leagues must have dropped by the equivalent of at least 2 or 3 WAA by 1945, when first baseman Phil Cavarretta of the Cubs (4.5) and outfielder Tommy Holmes of the Braves (6.6) ranked among baseball's stars for the only time in their careers.

The biggest impact of the war, however, was the roadblock it put in the way of almost every talented young player born from about 1920 to 1926. With rare exceptions, such players found themselves in the U.S. Army rather than in the minor leagues after they turned 18, and after 1945 many of them surely abandoned any dreams of a baseball career at all. That was the beginning of a long drought in the production of outstanding players, one that continued well into the 1960s and had profound effects upon the game. The nation recovered rapidly from the war, but baseball—after a remarkable Indian summer in 1946–1950—did not.

3

The GI and Silent Generation Era, 1946–66

The turbulent baseball era of 1946–1966 witnessed integration, the decline of the minor leagues, the movement of teams to the West Coast, and the first round of expansion. But it was above all an era of dynasties, with just three franchises establishing a remarkable record of dominance in both leagues. They were of course the Yankees, who won 15 pennants in 18 years from 1947 through 1964; the Dodgers, who dominated the league, as we shall see, from 1949 through 1956 and won three of four pennants from 1963 through 1966; and the Braves, who had the best NL run differential from 1956 through 1959, even though they managed to lose the pennant on the last day of the season in the first and last of those years. For the most part, the story of these years is the story of those teams, along with the tale of a couple of other potential dynasties that rarely or never managed to break through, such as the Giants from 1959 through 1966 and the Phillies in the mid-1960s.

The Dodgers and Yankees dynasties dominated in large part because of the general mediocrity of the leagues. This in turn resulted from a shortage of both top-flight and even average talent, evidently a result of the Second World War and its impact on baseball and American life. We begin this new era in 1946 because in that year, the Silent Generation, born from 1925 through 1942, produced its first superstar, outfielder Del Ennis of the Philadelphia Phillies, who was only 21 years old. By comparing the subsequent years with those that followed the debuts of the GI generation at the top level of baseball performance, we can see exactly how devastating the war and its aftermath had been for the development of talent.

The first GI superstars, Lou Gehrig and Paul Waner, had reached 4 WAA or more in 1926, when they were both 23. During the next four years, nine other GIs had reached that level: Tony Lazzeri, Heinie Manush, Fred Lindstrom, Jimmy Foxx, Willis Hudlin, Mel Ott, Joe Cronin, Wes Ferrell, and Chuck Klein. The GI Generation, in other words, had produced 2.2 superstars per year for five years. Four of those—Gehrig, Waner, Foxx and Ott—were all-time greats with at least five superstar seasons in their career. But Ennis's 1946 season was equaled only twice by any other member of his generation in the next four years, by Richie Ashburn in 1948 and pitcher Ned Garver in 1950. In its first five years, the GI Generation produced 11 superstars and four all-time greats, while the Silent Generation produced just six superstars and two all-time greats. The shortage of younger players in the postwar years drove average ages upward. In 1941, the median age of hitters in both leagues with at least 300 plate appearances was 27.5 years; in 1948, it was 29.

Nor was this all. The Second World War, the Korean War, and the decline of the minor leagues clearly had a devastating effect on the development of baseball talent among all those born from about 1920 to 1940. Among the GI Generation, the youngest all-time great—that is, a player with at least five superstar seasons in his career—was Stan Musial, born in 1921. Among the Silent generation, the oldest all-time great was Richie Ashburn, born in 1927. The next three all-time greats from the Silent Generation, Willie Mays, Mickey Mantle, and Eddie Mathews, were born in 1931 and 1932 and reached the majors at the age of 20. By that time, the Korean War draft was already interrupting or delaying the careers of future superstars such as Mays, Ken Boyer, and Whitey Ford. Thus, nine birth years, from 1922 through 1930, produced only one all-time great. The years from 1931 through 1939 produced eight more, six of them black or Latin. The drought created a severe shortage of superstars during the 1950s and early 1960s, especially in the American League, which took very little advantage of integration.

Other developments in postwar baseball made the problem even worse. One was the bonus rule. During the Landis era, the commissioner's office had not allowed major league teams to sign amateur players out of high school, although the rule was widely evaded with the help of cooperative minor league teams. With Landis gone in 1944, the major league owners gave themselves the right to sign players directly, creating a bidding war for hot young prospects. Within a few years, a new rule required any major league team who signed a bonus baby to keep him on the major league roster for two full seasons—costing the team a player, in most cases, and delaying the prospect's development for two years. The total bonus that would trigger the rule was purposely set low to prevent the richer teams from signing too many prospects at the same time, on the correct theory that no team could afford to keep more than two untried youngsters on the bench for an entire season. From 1953 through 1965, about 60 players reached the majors via this route, many drawing handsome bonuses. Only about 12 of them ever became regulars, of whom three—Al Kaline, Sandy Koufax, and Harmon Killebrew—eventually reached the Hall of Fame. Kaline was the only one to have an immediate impact at a very young age. Meanwhile, while most of the money paid to these players went out of baseball to their families, the minor leagues were cut by about half in size.

This book has made clear that truly superior skill at baseball—*as in any complicated, demanding human endeavor*—is very rare. More than 20,000 men have played major league baseball, about 100 of whom rank as all-time greats with at least five superstar seasons— one out of every 200, or 0.5 percent. To locate the men with the necessary talent and dedication and give them a chance to develop, a very large sample has to enter organized baseball at a very early age. The minor leagues had been the iceberg from which the major league tip emerged for the whole of the twentieth century. In 1940, 306 different minor league teams at six different levels had provided the manpower pool for 16 major league teams. By 1943, only 66 minor league teams were operating, recovering slightly to 70 in 1944 and 92 in 1945.

Practically no one born from 1925 through 1927—the first three years of the Silent Generation—could begin a baseball career after high school, as most of the GI greats had done. Helped by an unprecedented postwar attendance boom, the major league clubs more than rebuilt their farm systems after the war, and by 1950 they were larger than ever—but that was too late to help the early Silent Generation cohorts. It was no accident that the first two offensive mega-stars of the Silent Generation, Willie Mays and Mickey Mantle, were not born until 1931 and reached the majors in 1951. And then came the Korean War and the return of the draft, and a drop in minor league attendance that reduced the size of the minors by 50 percent by 1955. Meanwhile, colleges had opened their doors to a vastly greater population, and other professional sports were starting to grow in popularity by the late 1950s.

Integration, of course, was a countervailing trend. Suddenly a new population was allowed into the majors, but it did not make up for the overall shrinkage of the talent pool. The Negro Leagues provided about half a dozen ready-made or budding superstars—Jackie Robinson, Roy Campanella, Monte Irvin, Willie Mays, Henry Aaron, and Ernie Banks—but they rapidly disappeared during the 1950s, and major league teams do not seem to have signed many black players born in the second half of the 1930s. This was especially the case in the American League, where superstars became nearly as scarce as hen's teeth in the late 1950s and early to mid 1960s. We shall find that the Dodgers, Yankees and Braves dynasties had their share of superstars, but they—especially the Yankees—dominated their leagues in large part because of a general shortage of top-grade talent.

Although 20-year-old Del Ennis of the Philadelphia Phillies introduced the Silent Generation to superstardom in 1946, that year was essentially a continuation of the prewar era. Especially in the American League, prewar stars—Williams, DiMaggio, Feller, Keller, Greenberg, and many more—still dominated the game. Meanwhile, the returning veterans among the public and their families, hungry for entertainment, flocked to ball parks in unprecedented numbers. The attendance boom of the late 1940s peaked in 1948, but rapidly collapsed in the early 1950s thanks to the baby boom, television, and the population's movement to the suburbs. By the early 1950s, a new generation of stars was finally emerging, and most, though not all, of the GI greats were retiring.

The Yankees bounced back slowly in the American League. The tempestuous Larry MacPhail had left the Dodgers and gone into the Army during the war, but returned in 1945 to purchase the Yankees as part of a three-way team including Dan Topping and Del Webb, who remained the owners for the next 20 years. In the spring of 1946, MacPhail immediately got into conflicts with manager Joe McCarthy, who quit, and four different men managed the Yankees that season. Joe DiMaggio, unlike his prewar rivals Williams and Hank Greenberg, did not fully bounce back, earning just 3.2 WAA, and Gordon, who was injured, earned only 1.2. Charlie Keller earned 5.7 WAA and wartime pitching sensation Spud Chandler earned another 3.1 at the age of 38, but Snuffy Stirnweiss, switched to third base, and Rizzuto were only average. So was the pitching staff as a whole, and the Yankees won 87 games and finished in third place, behind the Red Sox and the Tigers. Keller was, in more than one way, probably the unluckiest player of his generation. His superlative 1946 season (5.7 WAA) had given him five superstar seasons since 1940, peaking (with the help of the war) at 6.8

in 1943. But 1946 was not only his sixth full season, but his last. A serious back problem restricted him to part-time duty for the rest of his career. He and Wes Ferrell are the only members of the GI Generation with five superstar seasons who are not in the Hall of Fame, and in my opinion, his tremendous contributions to the Yankees dynasty would make him a deserving member. He had been their MVP in 1942 and 1943, when they won the pennant, and in 1946 when they did not. He was the Sandy Koufax of hitters.[17]

The 1946 Red Sox combined wartime stars and returning veterans, led by Williams, to post a great 104–50 record and romp to the pennant for the first time since 1918. They were not quite as good as their record suggested: Pythagorean luck gave them seven of their wins. Although a late-season slump cost Williams a chance at his second Triple Crown, he nonetheless finished with an amazing 10.3 WAA, his second-best figure ever. Shortstop Johnny Pesky had his second and last superstar season with 4.2 WAA, Bobby Doerr just missed with 3.9, and Dom DiMaggio added 2.9. The line-up was not superior to the Yankees' overall, however, because first baseman Rudy York was only slightly above average and four part-timers cost the team a combined -5.6 WAA. Pitcher Tex Hughson earned 3.7 WAA, and the rest of the pitching staff was roughly average. It was the pitching (+5 WAA) and their luck that gave the Red Sox their superiority over the Yankees. Second place went to the Detroit Tigers, who also had three superstars. Greenberg, now 35, returned with a vengeance after almost five full years in the Army, led the league in home runs and RBI, and earned 7.1 WAA. Newhouser showed his last two years were no fluke with 6.5 WAA more, and another pitcher, Dizzy Trout, posted his second superstar season in three years with 4.9 WAA. Neither Trout nor Newhouser, however, was the most dominant pitcher in the league.

Bob Feller returned to the Indians after four years in the Navy, and their new owner, Bill Veeck—the first owner from the GI Generation—decided to milk his main gate attraction for all he was worth. He signed Feller to a contract including an attendance bonus, and they agreed that Feller would pitch as often as possible in an attempt to break Rube Waddell's all-time single-season strikeout record, then listed at 343. Feller pitched 371⅓ innings and finished with a 2.18 ERA (third in the AL behind Chandler and Newhouser), a 26–9 record, a new record 348 strikeouts, and 6.6 WAA. That was Feller's fourth and, as it turned out, his last superstar season, even though his career had ten more years to run. These spectacular performances confirm that 1946, even more than 1942, resembled an expansion year more than a normal one, and that the players who returned to prewar form or who had played through the war were the exceptions.

A solid Yankees team returned to the top of the American League in 1947 as a superior pennant winner, missing 100 victories only because of three losses' worth of bad Pythagorean luck. They did it with only one superstar, Tommy Henrich, who had his best-ever season with 4.3 WAA. Joe DiMaggio had something of a fluke year, evidently because he was playing on a very bad heel. He earned nearly 4 WAA at the plate, but his overall value showed up below average because his fielding statistics showed him costing the team an amazing -42 runs in the field, relative to an average center fielder. As Michael Humphreys pointed out in

---

17. Keller's best superstar seasons were not as good as Koufax's, but he had five to Koufax's four.

Wizardry, however, his fellow outfielders—principally Henrich and Johnny Lindell—made up entirely for the slack, suggesting that they were catching every ball that they possibly could to save DiMaggio's heel. These extra contributions in the field allowed Henrich to reach 4.3 WAA, and Lindell, a dead average hitter, to earn 3.2.[18] First baseman George McQuinn had 3.3 WAA and Rizzuto rebounded with 2.1, giving the lineup +16 WAA overall. Meanwhile, the 1947 pitching staff was one of the better ones in franchise history, earning +6 WAA. This was truly a team effort. Only one pitcher, Allie Reynolds (acquired from Cleveland for the far more valuable Joe Gordon), pitched more than 180 innings, and he earned just 1.2 WAA. Reliever Joe Page (2.2), Chandler (1.6), rookie Frank Shea 1.7), and 39-year-old castoff Bobo Newsom (1.4), a late-season pick-up, all made it possible.

Meanwhile, in Boston, Ted Williams played every game, won the Triple Crown for the second time in three seasons, and posted his sixth consecutive superstar season with 8.6 WAA. His four-year run of 8.8 in 1941, 10.6 in 1942, 10.3 in 1946 and 9.5 in 1947 (after a three-year wartime interruption) was and remains the best in history. Yet having won the MVP Award in 1946, he lost it this year by one vote to Joe DiMaggio—whom as we have seen was far from the most valuable Yankee—because a Boston writer left him entirely off of his ballot. Williams' teammates did much worse. Pesky slumped badly, Dom DiMaggio missed time with injuries, and the team was very weak at first base and right field. The lineup as a whole was only +4 WAA. The pitching staff, led by Hughson, collapsed, costing the team -4 WAA. The Cleveland Indians actually had nearly as strong a lineup as the Yankees, led by their shortstop and manager Lou Boudreau, who earned 5.1 WAA, and new acquisition Joe Gordon, who had 4.1 of his own. Led by Boudreau and Gordon, the team fielded brilliantly, but most of the pitching staff was weak.

Although no one noticed it at the time, Bob Feller's career as a dominant pitcher apparently came to an end on the evening of June 13, 1947, when he was pitching against the Philadelphia Athletics. Threatening his own record of 18 strikeouts in a game, Feller struck out eight batters in the first three innings and made it nine when he fanned Barney McCosky to open the fourth. But according to Feller, he slipped on the mound and hurt his shoulder on the play. He pitched through the seventh inning, striking out 12 and running his record to 8–5. Through that game, Feller had pitched 109 innings and struck out 87 batters, a pace which, if maintained through the year, could have easily given him 6–7 WAA. But he tailed off significantly from then on, finished the season with fewer than 200 strikeouts and 3.6 WAA, and never again returned to anything like the dominant form he displayed from the beginning of 1939 through June 13, 1947.[19] For those five years he was without question the greatest pitcher of the GI Generation—and he had missed nearly four full seasons in the Navy.

---

18. Before any readers conclude that the figures for DiMaggio, Henrich and Lindell invalidate the methodology of this book, let me point out that neither Humphreys nor I has discovered a remotely similar anomaly in the whole history of major league baseball.
19. Feller told the story of his injury many times, including, in 1989, to this author. He exaggerated the immediate trauma of his injury, claiming that he had to leave the game on the spot and that he missed about a month of the season. His estimate of its impact on his career, however, appears to be entirely correct.

3. The GI and Silent Generation Era, 1946–1966

Nineteen forty eight was the year of the greatest three-team pennant race in history, in which the Cleveland Indians beat the Red Sox in a one-game playoff while the Yankees, eliminated on the last day of the season, finished two games back. Twenty years ago, I published an entire book devoted to that season, but without yet fully understanding the strengths and weaknesses of the various teams.[20]

The 1948 Indians' run differential of +272 in a pitchers' park was theoretically worth 104 wins, making them a truly great team, but they fell eight wins short of that projection thanks to bad Pythagorean luck and a miserable record in close games.[21] But like so many great teams in pitchers' parks, their pitching was actually the least of their strengths, earning them just +1 WAA. Their line-up, on the other hand, was one of the greatest in history, earning +15 WAA at the plate and a near-record +11 WAA in the field. They had one of the greatest infields of all time, anchored by shortstop and manager Lou Boudreau, who hit .355, walked 98 times, saved 20 runs at shortstop, and won the MVP Award with 7.6 WAA. This was Boudreau's fourth superstar season, including two during the war, tying him with Arky Vaughan of the Pirates and Luke Appling of the White Sox among GI Generation shortstops, and earning his place in the Hall of Fame. Second baseman Joe Gordon, acquired from the Yankees two years earlier, had slipped from his peak at 33, but still hit .280 with 21 homers, nine runs saved in the field, and 3.4 WAA. With five superstar seasons in his career, Gordon tied Charlie Gehringer and Jackie Robinson as the greatest second basemen of the GI Generation, and it was a terrible injustice that it took more than five decades to get him into Cooperstown. Bobby Doerr, Gordon's rival from the Red Sox, had four seasons of 3 WAA but never reached 4, and was a somewhat more dubious selection, as was Tony Lazzeri, who had two superstar seasons.

Third baseman Ken Keltner had been a star rather than a superstar so far in his career, but in 1948 he had the year of his life at age 31, with a .297 average, 31 homers, +24 runs saved in the field (more than Gordon or Boudreau), and 5.5 WAA. The team's third superstar was the first black player in the American League, Larry Doby, who alternated between center and right field and earned 4 WAA in just 122 games, including a brilliant 16 runs saved as a fielder. Doby, then 24, had played two seasons of Negro Leagues ball at second base at ages 18–19 before going into the military in 1944. Bill Veeck had brought him directly to the majors without a place to play him in 1947, but he blossomed the next year as an outfielder. He had just two more superstar seasons in his long career, with 4.6 WAA in 1950 and 6.3 in his greatest year, 1952, when he was the best everyday player in the American League. Together, Boudreau, Keltner, Doby and Gordon earned 20.5 of the lineup's total 23 WAA, and left fielder Dale Mitchell, a .336 hitter who saved a remarkable +20 runs in the field, earned 3 more. The rest of the lineup included no major liabilities. Given the team's age, a rapid decline was more or less inevitable, but the Indians remain one of the greatest clubs in history, and new players returned them to contention two years later.

---

20. David Kaiser, *Epic Season: The 1948 American League Pennant Race* (Amherst: University of Massachusetts Press, 1998).
21. That is, 104 wins out of 154 games. The Indians actually played 155 because of the one-game playoff with the Red Sox.

Among the pitchers, Bob Feller was no longer the Feller of old, turning in a dreadful first half, rallying down the stretch, but finishing with a perfectly average record. The real ace of the staff was knuckleballer Gene Bearden, who finished with a 20–7 record—including four wins in the last ten days of the season—and a league-leading 2.43 ERA. He owed much of that ERA to his defense, however, and earned only 1.9 WAA on his own, suggesting that his subsequent decline was no fluke. Twenty-seven-year-old Bob Lemon. a converted outfielder whose career had been delayed by the war, earned 1.6 WAA in 294 innings. The rest of the staff was evidently below average, but the great line-up carried the team. Forty-one-year-old Negro Leagues immortal Satchel Paige, signed in mid-season, earned more than 1 WAA in just 72⅔ innings.

We shall defer any discussion of the Red Sox, who finished the regular season in a tie with the Indians despite a significantly inferior run differential, for a few more pages, so as to look at their performance over the whole period of 1948–1950, when they lost three pennants by one, one, and four games. The 1948 Yankees team, which had a substantially better run differential than the Red Sox—though not better than the Indians—was most unusual. Its lineup earned 14 WAA. Its greatest strengths were Joe DiMaggio, who turned in his last superstar season with 39 homers, 155 RBI, and 5.1 WAA, and right fielder and first baseman Tommy Henrich, who had the second superstar season of his career with 4.2 WAA. Wartime superstar second baseman Snuffy Stirnweiss had now been exposed as an average major leaguer, and Phil Rizzuto had a dreadful year in the field and finished slightly below average. But the pitching was even better than in 1947, earning +8 WAA. No pitcher hurled more than 230 innings or had as many as 2 WAA, but Tommy Byrne, Allie Reynolds, Vic Raschi, Frank Shea and new acquisition Ed Lopat all earned a little over 1. The Yankees' run differential was better than the Red Sox and good enough to have won 98 games, but like the Indians, they were unlucky to the tune of five wins, and were eliminated by the Red Sox on the next to last day of the season, finishing two games back.

In 1949 the Yankees returned to the top of the league, defeating the Red Sox by a single game in the last game of the season and winning the World Series—their first of five consecutive pennants and World Series championships under Casey Stengel. They were, of all the winning teams in the history of modern baseball, the most difficult to analyze. Certainly the 1949–1953 Yankees were more than respectable pennant winners, finishing at or over the 97-win level of a superior pennant winner four out of five times, but they accomplished all this with only two superstar performances, both in 1952. Clearly this team warrants close investigation: how did they do it?

The lack of superstars was somewhat deceptive in the first of these seasons, 1949. Coming off great years in 1948, Joe DiMaggio and Tommy Henrich continued to perform at the same level in 1949, but Joe D. missed nearly the first half of the season after a botched heel operation, and Henrich played only 115 games himself. Together they earned about 5 WAA out of the total of 11 earned by the Yankees line-up. An equally critical though largely invisible contribution came from outfielder Cliff Mapes, who filled in for DiMaggio in center field for nearly half the season and saved +29 runs, or about three games' worth, contributing 3.5 WAA in just 111 games overall. Platooning in the outfield, Hank Bauer and Gene Woodling contributed about 1 WAA between them. Phil Rizzuto finished second behind

Ted Williams in the MVP voting because he was a media darling and the only Yankee to play the full season, but he was entirely average both at bat and in the field—a slight improvement from 1948. Yogi Berra finally won the catcher's job (which he had lost in the last months of the 1948 season), but played only 116 games and emerged with average value. The pitchers also fell off badly from 1948, slipping from 8 WAA to just 3. Reliever Joe Page earned 2.1 WAA in 135⅓ innings, Vic Raschi, Ed Lopat and Tommy Byrne contributed exactly 1 WAA each.

Another × factor, however, was contributing critically to the Yankees' success. This book has consistently distinguished Pythagorean luck—the random distribution of runs scored and allowed across 154 games that enables teams to win 5–10 games more or less than their raw totals would have predicted—from run luck. Only in 1949 did the Yankees narrowly win the pennant thanks to Pythagorean luck: the Red Sox's raw run totals were good enough to have beaten the Yankees by two games, but they lost by one. Offensive run luck, on the other hand, plays a role when the total number of a team's hits (of all kinds), walks, stolen bases, and other events contributing to offense produces significantly more or significantly fewer runs than a well-tested projection (like Pete Palmer's linear weights, which I have relied upon here) would have predicted. And from 1947 through 1953, the Yankees' runs scored exceeded their projections by 53 runs (1947), 42 runs (1948), 58 runs (1949), 51 runs (1950), 42 runs (1951), 6 runs (1952), 22 runs (1953), 69 runs (1954, when the Yankees had their best record yet under Stengel even though they lost the pennant, with 103 wins), 16 runs (1955), and 67 runs (1956.) Dick Cramer, one of the founders of sabermetrics, calculated that the odds that the Yankees achieved these results by chance are less than 1 in 100,000.

That was the end of this anomalous period, but from 1947 through 1951, and again in 1954, run luck provided the Yankees with four to seven extra wins, the equivalent of an extra superstar in place of average player, in every year. That is why, in contrast to other teams we have studied, the contributions of the various members of the lineup at the plate frequently do not seem large enough to create the number of runs that the Yankees actually scored. Somehow, Stengel's Yankees in these years (although not in the late 1950s) consistently managed to bunch their walks and hits so as to score more runs than their players' performances would normally have generated. Exactly how that happened is a matter for further research, far beyond the scope of this book.

Yankees pitching held steady in 1950, earning 3 WAA again thanks to Raschi, Reynolds, Lopat, and rookie Whitey Ford, while Yankees hitters earned another +15 WAA (about five of them from run luck) and the fielding held steady. Joe DiMaggio played in 139 games, hit 32 home runs, and finished as the team MVP with 3.7 WAA. Two other players narrowly trailed him. Phil Rizzuto had his second-best season, saving about one game's worth of runs at shortstop and finishing with 3.5 WAA. That was his last good year—he was never again significantly above average—and he finished his career with just one superstar season, in 1942, one season over 3 WAA in 1950, and one more over 2 in his rookie season in 1941. This clearly puts him well behind the truly great GI Generation shortstops—Vaughn, Boudreau, and Appling—and, as we shall see, leaves him about even with Pee Wee Reese from the National League, but he was elected into the Hall of Fame in 1994 after a long career as a broadcaster and Yankees icon. Last but not least, Yogi Berra had his first great season, batting .322 with 28 home runs in 151 games and earning a full 3.5 WAA, an outstanding figure for a catcher. The Yanks won a four-team race against the Tigers (who had six games' worth of Pythagorean luck, finishing second), the Red Sox, of whom more later, and the Indians.

In 1951, the Yankees won 98 games—a superior pennant winter—while the Indians could win only 93 and the Red Sox 87. The whole league had only three superstars: Ted Williams and shortstop Eddie Joost and first baseman Ferris Fain of the Athletics. The team's fielding was average and the hitters earned 14 WAA, led, astonishingly, by rookie Gil McDougald, who earned 2.7 WAA in 131 games at third and second base; Berra (2.5 WAA); platooned first baseman Joe Collins (2.2 in just 299 plate appearances); and outfielders Gene Woodling (2.1 in 120 games), Hank Bauer (1.9) and Joe DiMaggio (1.2 in his last year) also contributed, but rookie Mickey Mantle surrendered -25 runs in the outfield and finished with -1.8 WAA. Lopat, Reynolds and Raschi together earned 5.9 WAA, but Ford had gone into the Army and the rest of the staff gave back -2 WAA. The team's 42 runs of run luck were a more important contribution than any of their players.

The 1952 team nosed out the Indians (whom we shall look at in detail when we reach 1954), 95 wins to 93. Excellent balance again distinguished its line-up. DiMaggio had now retired, and thanks to Gene Woodling, Hank Bauer, and three young regulars—McDougald at third base, Billy Martin at second base, and Mickey Mantle in center—the team's fielding improved from average to 4 WAA. The line-up truly earned their 17 WAA this year without any run luck, and they did it the old-fashioned way, with two superstar performances. Saving 13 runs in the outfield, Mantle had the best fielding year of his life, sinking below average in the next year and rarely reaching it again. This fielding mark and a fine year at the plate enabled him to reach the superstar level for the first time with 6.2 WAA, just behind Larry Doby, the real league MVP among non-pitchers. (The award went deservedly to pitcher Bobby Shantz of Philadelphia, who had an amazing season with 6.5 WAA.) Gene Woodling managed 4 WAA of his own in 122 games, Hank Bauer added 2.2, Berra had 2.7, and Collins had 2.5. The three other infielders—Rizzuto, McDougald, and second baseman Billy Martin—were average. The pitching staff was a bizarre mixture of good and evil, adding +1 WAA overall. Allie Reynolds, long considered one of the team's aces, had his only really distinguished season with a 20–8 record and 3.1 WAA, the best Yankees mound performance in some time. Ed Lopat and Vic Raschi earned 3 WAA between them, but the rest of the staff combined for -7 WAA.

DiMaggio's retirement, Mantle's arrival, and Berra's emergence as one of the best catchers in baseball history had marked the end of the GI Yankees dynasty and the beginning of the Silent Generation one. That team really blossomed in 1953, winning 99 games despite two games' worth of bad Pythagorean luck. The hitters contributed more than 16 of the lineup's 19 WAA despite the lack of a single superstar. Though Billy Martin, the regular second baseman, cost the team -1.2 WAA, the lineup had five stars: Bauer and Woodling (3.6 WAA each), Mantle (3.2), Berra (3), and McDougald (2). Stengel's managerial technique of using the whole roster was now well established, and Rizzuto, Joe Collins and Irv Noren made small contributions as well. The pitching staff earned +7 wins thanks to Eddie Lopat

(2.0 WAA), former National League great Johnny Sain (1.6), and Whitey Ford (1.0 in his first full season).

We shall now look at the two teams that provided the Yankees with most of their competition in these years: the heartbreaker Red Sox of 1948–1950 and the Indians of 1951–1954, who finally stopped the Yankees' streak in 1954 and set an American League record with 111 victories, one that lasted for nearly half a century and still represents the highest American League winning percentage ever.

Ted Williams once wrote that the irony of the Red Sox of the late 1940s was that while they were not quite good enough to win pennants, they were good enough to convince people that they should have won them. He was right. The team appeared to have an overwhelming lineup, led by Williams himself, repeatedly leading the league in runs scored and posting a *team* batting average of .303 in 1950. The problem, however, as usual with the Red Sox in the second half of the twentieth century, was that those totals and averages owed a good deal to Fenway Park, and the team was never as offensively potent as it seemed to be. In 1948, 1949 and 1950, they led the league in runs scored with 907, 896, and 1,027 runs, but when park adjustments were added in, the Indians had the most potent offense in 1948 and the Yankees in 1949 and 1950. Despite their gaudy averages and some fine players, the Red Sox were consistently about one superstar short.

Williams, as we have seen, had led the American League in WAA, making him the real MVP, in 1941–1942 and 1946–1947 with astonishing figures of 8.8, 10.6, 10.3 and 9.5 WAA—the best four-year run of anyone, ever. Despite two injuries in the second half of the season in 1948, he still edged out Lou Boudreau, 7.9 to 7.6, and he earned 7.9 again in 1949, barely missing a third Triple Crown and receiving his second MVP Award in four years. He seemed on his way to another comparable season in 1950 when he broke his elbow making a catch against the left field wall in Comiskey Park during the All-Star Game. The injury kept him out of the lineup for most of the second half of the season, and he finished with 3 WAA in 89 games, the first time in his nine-year career that he had missed the superstar level—an unparalleled achievement. Although Williams, still recovering from his injury, had a mediocre year by his standards in 1951, he still finished that season with 5.8 WAA, tops in the league yet again. Then, early in 1952, he was recalled to service as a Marine Corps pilot and spent most of 1952–1953 in the Korean War.

The 1948 team that lost the one-game playoff to Cleveland featured center fielder Dom DiMaggio hitting .285; third baseman Johnny Pesky (switched from shortstop) at .281; shortstop Vern Stephens, acquired from St. Louis, who hit .269 with 37 homers and 137 runs batted in; second baseman Bobby Doerr, a .287 hitter with 27 homers and 111 RBI; and rookie first baseman Billy Goodman, who hit .310. All these players sustained roughly the same level of performance for the next two years, but in general, they were stars, not superstars. Dom DiMaggio was the greatest center fielder of his era, far superior in the outfield to his older brother Joe, and his play in the outfield was worth 1.5–2 wins a year until 1950, when age apparently caught up to him. Having posted superstar seasons of 4.6 WAA in 1941 and 4 in 1946, he put up 3.2, 3 and 3.2 WAA in 1948–1950. Shortstop Vern Stephens was another excellent fielder, far superior at this stage of their careers to Phil Rizzuto, and a power hitter who did break the superstar barrier once in 1949 with 4.3 WAA, after 2.6 in 1948. (Overall

Rizzuto had a slightly better top three seasons than Stephens, although neither one of them was in the class of Boudreau, Luke Appling, or Arky Vaughan.) Bobby Doerr had lost most of his edge in the field by 1948, but he still contributed 3.2 WAA that year and 3.2 the next before falling nearly to average in 1950. Pesky earned about 2 WAA a season as well. Goodman's value was largely illusory because he lacked power, and even in 1950, when he won the batting title with a .354 average in 110 games, he earned the Red Sox only 1.9 WAA. Although right field and catcher remained relatively weak positions, the Red Sox lineups earned 15, 14 and 14 WAA during these three years. But despite their gaudy averages and league-leading totals of runs scored, those figures lagged behind the Indians in 1948 by 12 games, and the Yankees in 1949 and 1950 by two and four games. Such was the distorting effect of Fenway Park, particularly in relation to pitchers' parks like Yankee Stadium and Municipal Stadium.

These Red Sox are also one of history's best illustrations of how misleading a traditional statistic—runs batted in—can be. Dom DiMaggio and Johnny Pesky, the first two hitters in the lineup, averaged on-base percentages over .400 during these three years, and Williams was not far from .500. That was why cleanup hitter Vern Stephens had 137 RBI in 1948, when he earned just 2.6 WAA; 159 in 1949, when he had his only superstar season with 4.3; and 144 in 1950, when he was a barely above average player overall. It is also the reason that rookie first baseman Walt Dropo tied Stephens with 144 RBI in 1950—while earning 1.1 WAA. Many observers, including myself, have wondered how Dropo's career could have been so mediocre after such a spectacular beginning. The answer is that he was never all that good in the first place. High RBI totals seem equally to be a function of a batter's slugging percentage on the one hand, and the on-base percentages of those batting in front of him on the other.

Just as the Red Sox's hitters were rarely quite as good as they seemed, their pitchers were always better. They earned the team about 2 wins in 1948, which ironically made them superior to the Indians, whose edge in adjusted runs allowed came from their fielders. And in 1949, left-hander Mel Parnell won the league ERA title and was nearly as valuable as Williams, earning 5.7 WAA, the best mark by any American League pitcher between Newhouser in 1946 and Bobby Shantz in 1952, in 295⅓ innings. Ellis Kinder, a journeyman, had by far his best season with 3.3 WAA, and the two men had a combined won-lost record of 48–13. Although the rest of the staff was mediocre, the Red Sox pitchers earned +8 WAA, compared to the Yankees' +3. The two teams' adjusted run differentials were in fact nearly identical in 1949, and it was appropriate that they decided the pennant on the last day of the season. Parnell barely missed another superstar season in 1950, and the Red Sox pitchers outperformed the Yankees' again with +5 WAA compared to +3—but better Yankees fielding more than made up for it, because the Red Sox were getting old.

Since 1950 was the last year that the Red Sox contended seriously for the pennant until 1967, it behooves us to look briefly at the remainder of the career of Ted Williams. While he only once became the same player he had been before he broke his elbow in 1950 and missed most of another two seasons in Korea in 1952–1953, he still remained at the very top of the American League for most of the rest of the decade. Returning from injury in 1951, he hit a mere .318 (for him) with 30 home runs, yet remained the genuine most valuable player in the American League with 5.8 WAA. In 1954, his next full season, he broke his collarbone in spring training and played only 117 games, but was still the second most valuable player in the league with an extraordinary 6.3 WAA. Injuries held him to 98 games in 1955, when Mickey Mantle finally surpassed him as the best player in the American League, but he still put up 5.7 WAA in that year. Under current rules Williams would have won the AL batting title in both 1954 and 1955, but he failed to get 400 at-bats in either season. After falling to a mere 4.6 WAA in 1956, he hit .388 with 38 home runs in 132 games in 1957—with 8.6 WAA. That was his last of 13 superstar seasons, but he topped 3 WAA again in 1958, when he won yet another batting title, and again in his last year, 1960, at the age of 42. Ty Cobb had also finished at 42, but he had earned only a little over 1 WAA in that season. The American League undoubtedly got stronger in Cobb's last years and weaker in Williams's, but Williams's achievement is still unequaled.

In 1950 the Cleveland Indians took over the role of bridesmaid from the Red Sox and finished second for four consecutive years. They broke through spectacularly in 1954 and returned to second in 1955–1956. They have been consistently known as a team with a great pitching staff. As so often happens, this was a half-truth due in large part to the characteristics of their park, which consistently reduced runs scored by about 8 percent until 1954. More often than not from 1950–1953, the Indians' line-up was nearly as good as the Yankees', thanks largely to their having signed a number of black and Latin players whom the Yankees spurned. Their pitching *cost* them the pennant in 1952 and 1953, before turning in three of the greatest seasons in history in 1954–1956.

Larry Doby, the first black player in the American League, was the Indians' most consistent offensive asset, earning 4.6 WAA in 1950—his second superstar season—slumping below that level in 1951 due to injury, turning in his greatest season in 1952 with 6.7 WAA (32 home runs and 14 runs saved in the field), and earning 2.7 WAA in 1953. He finished his career with three superstar seasons. The team's second major asset was third baseman Al Rosen. Like Ralph Kiner of the National League, Rosen was a great GI player who reached the majors late because of the war (and the presence in Cleveland of Ken Keltner) and who enjoyed a very brief, but spectacular peak. Rosen debuted in 1950 at the age of 26, saved 30 runs in the field (a figure he never remotely approached again), and earned 6.0 WAA. He slipped to 1.5 WAA the next year, but rebounded to 3.6 in 1952. He had a truly astonishing season in 1953, barely missing the Triple Crown with 7.9 WAA—the highest figure in the American League for any hitter not named Williams or Mantle from 1942 through 1960. Had the war not prevented Rosen from starting his career in his early twenties, he would probably have ranked by 1953 as the greatest third baseman in the history of baseball. As it was, Rosen faded quickly in the mid-1950s, and finished his career with just two superstar seasons.

In 1952 the Indians added new second baseman Bobby Avila, a Mexican, and black first baseman Luke Easter, who earned 1.7 and 3 WAA. Avila duplicated that performance the next year. All told, the Indians' lineups in 1950–1953 earned 12, 5, 18, and 16 WAA, compared to the Yankees' 18, 14, 17, and 19. They could have had a definitely superior lineup to the Yankees had they not unwisely given away Minnie Minoso, one of the three greatest American League players of the 1950s, to the White Sox in 1951. But while their lineup improved, their pitching deteriorated.

The pitching staff of the 1950 Indians was a mixed bag. Bob Feller and 30-year-old Early Wynn accounted for the entire positive value of the staff with 3.1 WAA, and Bob Lemon was average. In 1951, when the hitters slumped badly, the pitching staff earned 6 WAA. Wynn improved to 2.9 WAA, and Mike Garcia and Feller added 2.8 more, while Lemon remained average. Luck favored Feller, who now struck out just 111 men in 249⅔ innings, but emerged with a 22–8 won-lost record despite earning just a little over 1 WAA.

Although Lemon, Wynn and Garcia all won 20 games in 1952, Cleveland's pitching cost the team the pennant. Feller had an absolutely disastrous campaign, with -4.4 WAA in 192 innings, and despite 2.3 WAA from Garcia and 1.9 WAA from Bob Lemon, the pitching staff as a whole cost the team -2 WAA. The pitching was nearly as bad in 1953. Garcia led the staff with 2.3 WAA, and Lemon was second with just 1.2. Wynn pitched 286 innings and cost the team -1 WAA. Still, thanks to their lineup, Wynn and Lemon—the Gomez and Ruffing of the Indians of the early 1950s—finished with records of 17–12 and 21–15.

All this makes the 1954 Indians even more extraordinary—yet the first thing to understand about that team, winners of 111 games, is that they were not nearly as good as their record would indicate. The team's adjusted run differential of +240 was 34 runs lower than the Yankees' the year before, and *not as good* as the Yankees' in 1954 (+254). Their Pythagorean projection translated into 103 wins—the number the Yankees actually won—but a good record in close games earned the Indians 111. Neither their differential nor their projection was as good as those of the 1948 Indians—because while that team had three superstars, the 1954 team had only one. Meanwhile, the Indians' management had moved their fences in right-center and left-center closer to the plate, and Municipal Stadium suddenly became a neutral park instead of a pitchers' park.

The team's one superstar was Bobby Avila, who won the batting title, saved +26 runs in the field (more than the Cleveland fielders as a whole), and finished just ahead of Ted Williams with a very impressive 6.6 WAA. Doby (2.9 WAA), Rosen (3.3), and outfielder Al Smith (2.4) were stars, and first baseman Vic Wertz added 1.4 WAA in 94 games, but all the other at-bats in the lineup were taken up by below-average players, and the entire lineup earned just +12 WAA. The pitching staff, however, was sensational, earning +14 WAA without a single superstar. Wynn led with 3.1 WAA and a 23–11 record, Mike Garcia added 3.7 WAA more, Lemon went 23–7 with 2.2 WAA, and two relievers, Don Mossi and Ray Narleski, had 4.1 WAA between them in 182 innings pitched. In a tribute to good fortune, three veterans, Feller, former Tigers great Hal Newhouser, and Art Houtteman had a combined 35–12 record with 1.4 WAA between them. Of all the truly great teams in history, this one owed the most to its pitching.

The Yankees lineup was a full nine games better than the Indians'—+ 21 WAA—but their pitching staff was ten games worse, only +2. Although this race was not as close as the 1942 National League one and the Yankees missed the record for a second-place team by one win, the Indians and Yankees together won a combined 224 games compared to 210 for the Cardinals and Dodgers. No team vindicated Casey Stengel's managing style more strikingly than this one, which also had his best-ever won-lost record. Its only superstar was Irv Noren, who saved +15 runs at all three outfield positions, hit well, and emerged with 4.1 WAA in just 129 games. Berra was second with 3.4 WAA and Mantle, who had a dreadful year in the field, had 3.3. The first base platoon of Joe Collins and Bill Skowron had 3.4 WAA between them as well, Bauer had 1.9 and McDougald 1.7. Rizzuto was now a major liability, costing the team a full two wins in 127 games. Among the pitchers, Whitey Ford suddenly emerged as the ace of the staff but earned only 1.9 WAA. Rookie Bob Grim posted a 20–6 record—eight of the wins coming in relief—with just .7 WAA. Of such seasons are undeserved reputations made.

Avila was easily the real MVP in 1954, but he finished third in the voting with 203 votes, behind Doby, who had 210, and the winner, Yogi Berra—not even the most valuable Yankee—with 230. Lemon also drew 179 votes. In this case, one could not argue that Berra deserved the honor because he was a catcher, since the average catcher's performance was equal to the average second baseman's.

The Chicago White Sox finished third in this remarkable season with a record of 94–60. They included two of the players who have been most unfairly treated by the Hall of Fame. Bill Veeck had signed Cuban outfielder Minnie Minoso for the Indians in 1949, and the White Sox had acquired him two years later. He had barely played for the Indians before they inexplicably gave him away. Playing in a pitchers' park, Minoso had posted 4.6 WAA in 1953—second to Al Rosen in the American League—and followed up with 5.7 WAA in 1954, third behind Avila and Williams. He exceeded 4 WAA again in 1956 and again in 1958, when he had been traded to the Indians for Al Smith and Early Wynn. Minoso in 1954 had hit .320 with a .424 on-base percentage and led the league with 304 total bases. With four superstar seasons, he has a very strong, if not overwhelming, case for the Hall of Fame.

The White Sox's second-best player in this era was left-handed pitcher Billy Pierce, who was to the Silent Generation what Wes Ferrell was to the GIs. Although Pierce was injured and had a dreadful year in 1954, he had already posted seasons of 4.6 WAA in 1952 (with a most unlucky 15–12 record) and 3.8 in 1953 (18–12). In 1955 he had an ERA of 1.97, the only starting pitcher of the 1950s to reach that level, and reached his peak with 4.9 WAA, but went just 15–10. He finally won 20 games in each of the next two seasons, with 4 WAA in 1956, and added another 2 in 1958. His best four seasons were significantly better than Whitey Ford's four best, but Pierce, despite over 200 victories, is not in the Hall of Fame. Nellie Fox, the second baseman on this team, was eventually inducted, even though he had only one superstar season, with 5 WAA in 1958.

In the Bronx, 1955 marked the beginning of the era of Mickey Mantle, superstar. The young center fielder, still only 23, had reached that level only once in four seasons so far, but in 1955 he hit 37 homers, walked 113 times, and earned 7.2 WAA. This was the first of three seasons in which he *averaged* more than 8 WAA, a feat equaled by Williams in 1941–1942 and 1946, and he was the most valuable player in the American League in each of those years, even though he did not win the award in 1955. He was now an average center fielder. But Mantle was flanked by two excellent outfielders, Irv Noren and Hank Bauer, and Gil McDougald, switched to second base, saved +28 runs as well. Bauer and McDougald both cracked the superstar barrier for the only time in their careers, each with 4.2 WAA. Berra had an off-year with just 1.8 WAA. Overall the team's fielders earned +8 WAA and the hitters +12. Whitey Ford led a perfectly average pitching staff with 1.6 WAA.

The Yankees had slipped from 103 to 96 victories, but that was enough to beat the Indians by three games and the White Sox by five. No pennant race ever pitted one potent lineup against two such dominant pitching staffs. Led by Billy Pierce's 4.9 WAA, the White Sox pitchers earned +9 games, while the Indians, astonishingly, improved on their 1954 performance and earned +15. Early Wynn broke the superstar barrier for the first time with 4.2 WAA, and rookie Herb Score, one of the more tragic figures in baseball history, led the league in strikeouts and had 3.8 WAA. Garcia and Lemon contributed 1 more each and Mossi and Narleski, the relievers, had 3.2 between them. Only Doby and Smith among the lineup remained significant assets, however, as Avila regressed all the way to average and an aging Rosen fell below it. Thanks to dreadful fielding, the lineup as a whole cost the team -4 WAA.

The 1955 MVP voting in the AL was one of the most bizarre in history. The AL's most valuable players in 1955 were Mantle (7 WAA), second-year Detroit Tigers right fielder Al Kaline (6.8), Pierce (6.5), Ted Williams (5.3), and Early Wynn (4.7). Mantle was, however, rather unpopular with the writers at this stage of his career, failed to receive a single first place vote (out of 24 cast), and finished fifth in the voting. Kaline finished a deserving second and Williams a deserving fourth. Third place, however, went to the Indians' Al Smith, who earned about 2.8 WAA, and first place, almost unbelievably, went to Yogi Berra, who had hit just .272 with 27 homers and earned just 1.8 WAA, one of the poorer seasons of his career. The early 1950s was the era of the mystique of the catcher in the press boxes of both leagues. This was the third MVP Award in five years for Berra, who had yet to post a single superstar season (a barrier he broke for the only time in 1956). He had won in 1951 with 2.5 WAA, when rookie Gil McDougald had almost 3, and Williams and Ferris Fain of the Athletics were the league's best players. He had won in 1954 with 3.4 WAA, when Avila and Doby split the votes for the Indians, and Irv Noren was the best player on the Yankees with 4.1. And now, in 1955, he had won as the fourth-most valuable Yankee, behind Mantle (7.2 WAA), Bauer and McDougald (4.2 WAA each.) His 1.8 WAA were the lowest for an MVP since Roger Peckinpaugh in 1925, when repeat winners were not allowed. In none of these years could it be argued that Berra's role as a catcher gave him enough extra value to make him the MVP, and if he helped the Yankees' pitching staff, he never managed to get them much above average. We shall find that Berra's Brooklyn counterpart, Roy Campanella, was benefitting from a similar prejudice in the National League.

The Yankees team of 1956 regained their status as a superior pennant winner with 97 wins thanks to three superstar performances. Mantle, still only 24, won the Triple Crown and the MVP Award he deserved the year before with a .353 average (beating out Williams narrowly), 54 homers, and 8.8 WAA, and Yogi Berra had his greatest season with 4.1 WAA, only the second time a catcher broke the superstar barrier. McDougald and Skowron (now a regular) contributed about 5 WAA between them, and those four players more than accounted for the +16 WAA earned by the Yankees line-up, almost all of them at the plate. Meanwhile, Whitey Ford had his first starring season and the second-best season of his career with 3.6 WAA in just 226 innings. Ford was the Lefty Gomez of Stengel's and Ralph Houk's Yankees. In his whole career he broke the superstar barrier only once, in 1964, and the 3 WAA barrier only twice more, but his team won the pennant in 11 or his first 13 seasons (a much better record than in Gomez's time) and he finished his career with one of the highest winning percentages in history.[22] The rest of the 1956 Yankees staff was essentially average, but the line-up enabled Johnny Kucks to go 18–9 (with -0.9 WAA), Don Larsen 11–5 (1.5), and Tom Sturdivant 16–8 (1.2). In his book on managers, Bill James cited Kucks and Sturdivant as two of Stengel's pitchers, along with Bob Grim in 1954 and Tommy Byrne in 1955, who posted impressive won-lost records but did not win a regular place in the starting rotation. There was really no mystery about this. As Stengel seems to have understood, most of his pitchers were pretty average, interchangeable parts, and that those won-lost records simply reflected their good fortune in their teammates and in the games in which they happened to pitch.

Berra eventually finished his catching career with one superstar season (1956), three more seasons over 3 WAA, and four more seasons over 2 WAA. That record is almost identical to Mickey Cochrane's, slightly superior to Bill Dickey's, and definitely superior to Roy Campanella's. His remarkable consistency from 1950 through 1956 contributed a great deal to the Yankees' success, but we have seen that he was never their best player. As of 1960 Berra, Cochrane and Dickey were the greatest catchers of all time, but a greater catcher than they had already been born.

The Yankees in 1956 prevailed quite easily over a Cleveland team that completed perhaps the best three-year pitching run of any team in baseball history. Having earned 14 WAA in 1954 and 15 WAA in 1955, they earned 14 again. Only ten teams in the whole 1946–1966 era, in both leagues, had pitching staffs that posted as many as 14 WAA, and the 1954 Indians were the only one to win a pennant. The 1956 team had Cleveland's greatest big three starters: Wynn (5.6 WAA with a 20–9 record), second-year man Herb Score (5.1 WAA, also 20–9) and Lemon (3.2 WAA, his best season, and a 20–14 record). Relievers Mossi and Narleski earned nearly 3 WAA between them. Although Lemon at the time had the reputation as the Indians' ace, Wynn was the better pitcher at his peak, with two superstar seasons to Lemon's none. Still, that leaves Wynn in the second tier of GI Generation pitchers, behind Newhouser, Wes Ferrell, Hubbell, Dean, Feller, and Warren Spahn. No one will ever know how great Herb Score might have been. Early in the 1957 season, Score was struck in the face by a line drive and missed the rest of the year. When he returned in 1958, he hurt his arm and tried to pitch through the injury, and he never regained his original form. There is every reason to think that he, rather than Sandy Koufax, could have been the best left-handed pitcher of his generation.

Nineteen fifty six marks a convenient dividing line within the 1946–1966 era, both because it splits it in half and because it was the last of six times that the dominating Yankees met their National League counterparts, the Brooklyn Dodgers, in the World Series. During that period, the National League had surpassed the American in overall quality for the first time since about 1909, largely because of integration. It is time to look at the parallel Dodgers

---

22. It has been pointed out by Bill James and others that Ford, unlike other "great" Yankees pitchers like Gomez and Ruffing, had a winning percentage significantly higher than his team's. Yet it should be obvious that any pitcher who allows fewer than average runs *should* have a better winning percentage than his team, unless luck is very much against him.

dynasty and at the teams that competed with it and, in the case of the Milwaukee Braves, were about to succeed it.

Crippled by a dearth of superstars, the National League hit one of its worst troughs from 1946 through 1948. While Greenberg, DiMaggio, Feller, Williams, Gordon and Boudreau among prewar stars continued posting superstar seasons in the American League, only Johnny Mize managed to do the same in the National, with 6.1, 5.5 and 4.9 WAA in 1946–1948 for the mediocre New York Giants. Stan Musial, who had broken in spectacularly with the Cardinals in 1942 with 5.9 WAA and averaged 10 WAA in each of the next two wartime seasons, was one of the other two dominant hitters in the league in the late 1940s, with 6.7 WAA to lead the Cardinals to the pennant in 1946, 9.1 in 1948, probably his greatest season, and 5.7 in 1949. The only other dominant hitter in the league was Ralph Kiner, whose career was evidently delayed by the war, and who crashed through in 1947 at age 24, after a very mediocre rookie season, with 51 home runs, 98 walks, and 6.9 WAA for the awful Pittsburgh Pirates. Kiner added 5.4 WAA in 1948, 5.3 in 1949, and 6.8 in 1951. After an off-year in 1952, when he was still only 29, he missed much of the next two years with injuries and quickly fell below average. With 4 superstar seasons, Kiner was a solid Hall of Fame candidate, but like Charlie Keller, he fell quickly from a very high plateau. Given the lack of outstanding players, it is not surprising that no NL team reached the level of a superior pennant winner until the Dodgers of 1949.

In 1946 the Dodgers, now run by Branch Rickey, and the Cardinals picked up right where they had left off in 1942, albeit with less dominant teams, and finished the season tied at 96–58. The Cardinals were substantially superior, but Brooklyn won six games through Pythagorean luck. St. Louis deservedly swept the best-of-three playoff and went on to win the World Series for the third time in five years. The whole league had only four superstars, and the Cardinals had two of them—Stan Musial (6.7 WAA, the fourth consecutive superstar season, with 1945 lost to war, of his young career), and pitcher Howie Pollet (4.6 WAA). Only Enos Slaughter (2.5 WAA) and third baseman Whitey Kurowski (2.2) joined Musial as significant assets in the lineup, while second baseman Red Schoendienst (-3.4) and veteran Terry Moore (-1.3) were disastrous. Their pitching accounted for their superior run differential, as left-hander Harry Brecheen earned 3.8 WAA, and the staff totaled +11. Most of their regulars were veterans from before the war. The same was true of the Dodgers, whose lineup included Reese, prewar third baseman Cookie Lavagetto, and Pete Reiser and Dixie Walker in the outfield. Neither they nor newcomer Eddie Stanky at second base earned more than 2 WAA. A fine young outfielder, 24-year-old Carl Furillo, played more center field than Reiser did and earned 1.2 WAA in just 117 games. The pitching staff was generally mediocre.

The Dodgers team that edged out a superior Cardinals squad in 1947 had no superstars. Their MVP, 21-year-old pitcher Ralph Branca, went 21–12 in 1947 with 3.8 WAA, but evidently hurt his arm doing so and was never anywhere near that level of effectiveness again. The Dodgers were lucky to have him—despite Branca, their pitching staff overall earned just +1 WAA. Their line-up was not much better. Pee Wee Reese led it with 2.9 WAA, with outfielder Carl Furillo at 1.7 thanks to +15 runs saved in the field. Furillo had signed with the Dodgers in 1940, moved up through the minors for two years, but missed 1943–1945 in the war. The team's +11 WAA overall was one of the lowest totals for a pennant winner ever, and only six games' worth of Pythagorean luck enabled them to win a mediocre 94 games.

Nineteen forty seven was, of course, Jackie Robinson's rookie year as well. The story of his selection by Branch Rickey has been told many times, but one aspect of it has never received much attention. Robinson, who was 26 when Rickey signed him in late 1945 and 28 when he reached the majors, was a very accomplished young man with four years of college and service as an army officer under his belt. He had proven himself a great athlete in college, but he had played relatively little baseball when Rickey signed him after just one season with the Negro Leagues Kansas City Monarchs in 1945. He spent just one year in the minors. Rickey, however, loved great athletes, which the Cardinals farm system he created had always sought. Given Robinson's inexperience and the abuse he had to endure, his 1.6 WAA in 1947 was a promising start, and we shall find that he improved quickly. Fortunately for the Dodgers, the Cardinals, whose run differential was +35 better than Brooklyn's, had an even weaker lineup, although their remarkable pitching staff earned +14 WAA. They lacked even a single superstar, but Murray Dickson, Harry Brecheen, Red Munger, Al Brazle and Jim Hearn each earned between 2 and 3 WAA.

The Dodgers slumped in 1948 at bat and on the mound, and the Boston Braves won their second and last pennant in roughly the same way that they had won their first one 34 years earlier: with excellent pitching in a very mediocre league. Winning just 91 games, they still finished comfortably ahead of the Dodgers and Cardinals. Their one superstar was pitcher Johnny Sain, who posted 4.9 WAA. Warren Spahn, who had begun his career in 1946 at the age of 25 after military service, had had an even better season in 1947, with 6.5 WAA, but he seems to have hurt his arm doing so, and finished 1948 just one win above average. With Bill Voiselle and Vern Bickford also adding 1 WAA each, the staff as a whole earned +7 WAA. A very balanced lineup added 9 more, led by third baseman Bob Elliott and outfielder Jeff Heath. The Cardinals lost the pennant because their legendary farm system had evidently dried up during the war. Stan Musial hit .376 with 39 home runs, posting 9.1 WAA in his greatest season,[23] Enos Slaughter had the second and last superstar season of his career with 4.8 WAA, and pitcher Harry Brecheen had 7.4 more. But the entire rest of the Cardinals' lineup was composed of significantly below-average players, led by Marty Marion and outfielder Nippy Jones, with -2.8 WAA each. Overall, despite Musial and Slaughter, the lineup was average.

The same pattern was destined to repeat itself during the next 15 years and keep Stan Musial from ever reaching a World Series again. Musial ranks with Ted Williams as the greatest hitter of the GI Generation, each with 13 superstar seasons. Musial posted superstar seasons again in 1949 (when the Cardinals lost the pennant on the last day of the season), consecutively from 1951 through 1954, and again from 1956 through 1958, when he was 37 years old. Largely because he missed only one year in the war, Stan Musial was luckier than Williams and played in four World Series, but a team with such an asset should have been

---

23. Musial had 11 WAA in 1943, but that figure clearly owed a lot to the weakness of the wartime league.

able to do better. They finished second in 1957 and again in 1963, when Musial, like Williams, finished his career at the age of 42, but by then, he, unlike Williams, had become a liability.

The Cardinals resisted integration and developed only one other superstar in all that time. That was Ken Boyer, who started his career in 1949 at age 18 but spent 1952–1953 in the military and did not reach the majors until 1955, when he was 25. After a poor rookie season, he earned 2.7 WAA in 1956, but unfortunately spent more than half of 1957 in center field and slumped badly during Musial's great 1957 season. Boyer and Musial both exceeded 4 WAA in 1958, but the rest of the lineup featured dreadful performances by Wally Moon, Del Ennis, and shortstop Eddie Kasko, who cost the team a total of -8 WAA. Incredibly, the rest of the lineup—without Musial and Boyer—was about -12 WAA. Helped by fine fielding, Boyer put up four consecutive superstar seasons in 1958–1961. While he had nowhere near the power of Eddie Mathews, he was much better in the field, and if he, like Mathews, had been able to start his career in 1952 at the age of 21, his overall record might easily have been just as good. As it is, Boyer, like most hitters with only four WAA, has not been chosen for the Hall of Fame.

In 1949, the Brooklyn Dodgers fielded the lineup that became famous as the Boys of Summer, including Roy Campanella behind the plate, Gil Hodges at first base, Jackie Robinson at second (where he had been moved in 1948), Reese at shortstop, Billy Cox at third, Duke Snider in center, Carl Furillo in right, and a cast of changing characters in left. Their pitching staff already included Don Newcombe—the first black star from the Silent Generation—Preacher Roe, and Ralph Branca. This team was nearly as dominant as the Yankees for the next seven years, posting the league's best run differential in every year from 1949 through 1953 and again in 1955, even though they managed to lose the pennant on the next-to-last and last day of the season in 1950 and 1951. They were a superior pennant winner in 1949, 1953, and 1955. They also won the pennant on the last day of the season in 1956, even though the Milwaukee Braves had by then surpassed them in run differential. Since this team consistently fielded a set lineup, we may look one by one at the players who were truly responsible for their success.

Jackie Robinson, Rickey's great experiment in more ways than one, was the team leader on and off the field. Rickey "turned him loose" in 1949, allowing him to shed his superhuman self-control on the field and play like the fierce competitor he was, and the 30-year-old Robinson responded with 6.5 WAA, the league MVP in fact as well as in name. He added 4.2 in 1950 and then, with the help of a fantastic year in the field at second base, 7.5 WAA in 1951, when he deserved the MVP again. He followed with 5.0 and 5.5 in 1952 and 1953, even though he was switched to third base in the latter year and played only 124 games. His playing time fell still further in his last three years but he finished with a solid 2.6 WAA in 1956. His five superstar seasons tie him with Charlie Gehringer and Joe Gordon as the greatest second baseman of the GI Generation, even though he did not reach the majors until he was 28.

The man who eventually supplanted Robinson as the team MVP was Duke Snider, a great player from the Silent Generation who could have been considerably greater had he played left field instead of center. Snider did not reach his peak as a power hitter until 1952, when he was 26, but from then through 1956 he earned 5.4, 4.8, 5.4 and 4.6 WAA in four straight seasons. Yet he would have been a far greater asset from 1949 onward had he not been a very poor center fielder, costing his team -16 runs in 1949, -8 in 1950, -19 in 1951 (reducing his overall value below average), -7 in 1952, -8 in 1953, -14 in 1954, and -4 in 1955. This was all the more distressing, from the Dodgers' point of view, since a much better outfielder was readily available. Because of his fielding problems, Snider was, as the BBWAA concluded in their voting, significantly inferior to his New York contemporaries Mantle and Mays, but with four superstar seasons in four years he was not an unworthy selection to the Hall of Fame.

Equally as valuable as Snider, it turns out, was first baseman Gil Hodges, whose career was extraordinary in ways that have only recently come to light. Hodges, like Warren Spahn, was from the GI Generation, but the war had interrupted his career in 1944–1945. He came up as a catcher but was switched to first base in 1948, when Robinson moved to second. He was a good hitter with power, and an asset to the team in 1949–1950. But he blossomed further as a hitter in 1951, when he was 27, and remained a superstar for the next five years (1951–1955) because he emerged as one of the great fielding first basemen of all time, saving the team +13, +18, +26, +29 and +14 runs. With five consecutive superstar seasons, there is no doubt that Hodges belongs in the Hall of Fame.[24]

Carl Furillo was undoubtedly the unluckiest of the Boys of Summer. Known today as a good-hitting outfielder with an extraordinary arm, he was actually one of the greatest outfielders of his generation—one who could have helped his team a lot more than he did. Born in 1922, he spent 1940–1942 in the minors and then went into the military for three years. From 1946–1948, he had to split playing time with the aging Dixie Walker and Pete Reiser, even though he was good enough in the outfield to save +37, +15 and +29 runs in the field in those years in just 117, 124 and 108 games. In 1949 he finally became a regular in right and turned in his only superstar season with 4.2 WAA. He slumped badly in 1950 and continued an odd-even career pattern through 1955, but he had 3.2 WAA in 1951, 3.5 in 1953, and 2.2 in 1955. These figures scream that Furillo, not Duke Snider, should have been the center fielder on this team, and if he had been, the Dodgers probably would have won at least one of the 1950–1951 pennants, and quite possibly additional World Series as well.

Roy Campanella, the Dodgers' catcher, had been signed in 1946 and reached the team in the middle of 1948 at the age of 26. In contrast to Robinson, he had had a nine-year career in the Negro Leagues, beginning at the age of 15 in 1937. Perhaps in part because of his age, Campanella was very injury-prone and caught 130 or more games just three times from 1949 through 1957, the last year of his career before an auto accident left him a paraplegic. In four of those seasons, he was only an average player. But he was a fine hitter when healthy, and he earned 3.6 WAA in 1951, 3.6 in 1953, and 2.5 in 1955—a very good, but far from overwhelming peak value for a catcher. Popular with the writers, he was awarded the MVP in each of those three seasons—even though he was far less valuable than Robinson or Hodges in 1951, well behind Robinson, Hodges and Snider in 1953, and behind Snider

---

24. I apologize for having argued the opposite, based on inadequate statistical analysis, on the SABR listserv.

and Hodges in 1955. In 1953, Junior Gilliam replaced Robinson at second base, and he hit, fielded and walked well enough to be the team's MVP in 1956, edging out Snider with 4.7 WAA to 4.6, his only superstar season.

With these players, it is easy to see how the Dodgers' lineup earned +12 WAA in 1949 (despite giving up -4 in the field), +7 in 1950 (when they lost -3 in the field), +19 in 1951 (+4 of them in the field), +12 in 1952, +22 in 1953, +16 in 1955, and +12 in 1956. Pee Wee Reese at shortstop had star seasons in 1949 (2.3 WAA) and 1954 (2.6), but was average between those and below average in 1955–1956. Third baseman Billy Cox did have fine years in the field in 1949–1950, saving +13 and +16 runs respectively, but he hit too poorly even then to make his performance above average overall, and his defense regressed to average in 1951–1952. A series of left fielders contributed relatively little.[25] The team had a terrible off-year in 1954 both in the lineup and on the mound, and only 11 wins' worth of Pythagorean luck enabled them to finish second with 92 wins.

Dodgers pitching in most of this era was far more erratic and contributed very little to the team's success. The Brooklyn moundsmen were outstanding in 1949, earning +10 WAA. Preacher Roe was the ace in 1949 with 3.5 WAA, and Don Newcombe, just 23, was nearly as good with 2.9. Roe earned 4.1 and Newcombe 2.4 in 1950, and the staff totaled +5. Roe's 1950 season was the only superstar performance by a Dodgers pitcher in this period. Roe and Newcombe earned 3.7 WAA between them in 1951, but the Dodgers had no less than five pitchers, including Carl Erskine, who were more than one win *below* average each, and the team's pitching overall was a liability. In 1952 Newcombe went into the army for two years, but three youngsters—Carl Erskine (2.4 WAA), reliever Joe Black (2.6), and Billy Loes (2.6)—allowed the staff to bring home +6 WAA. But in 1953, the dynasty's strongest single season, Erskine was the only starter of any value with about 2 WAA—the total positive value of the staff. Things got even worse when Erskine regressed to average in 1954, and the pitching staff cost the team -4 WAA. They got only a little better in 1955, when Newcombe led the starting staff with a 20–5 record with only 1.4 WAA and the whole staff earned 4 WAA. Johnny Podres, the hero of the World Series, was below average in 159⅓ innings during the season. But the slide continued in 1956, when the team was lucky to beat the Braves. Thirty-nine-year-old Sal Maglie, acquired in mid-season, was the hero of the staff, with 3 WAA in 191 innings, and Don Newcombe added 1.9. Don Bessent, 19-year-old Don Drysdale, and Clem Labine combined for 3.1 WAA in 294 innings. At the bottom of the Dodgers table, six other pitchers, including Loes, Ed Roebuck, Erskine, and 20-year-old Sandy Koufax, combined for -5.7 WAA in 400 innings, and the staff as a whole, however, earned just 2 WAA.

Like Ruffing, Gomez, Pennock and Hoyt, Don Newcombe benefited from pitching for the right team. Like Ralph Branca in 1947, Newcombe in 1949 got his career off to a rollicking start, with a 17–8 record and an impressive 2.9 WAA. He continued strongly with a 19–11 record and 2.5 WAA in 1950, but may have hurt his arm, since he slipped to 1.2 WAA in 1951 despite a 20–9 record. He was ineffective in a short season in 1954, after his

---

25. That includes Andy Pafko, acquired in mid-1950 after an excellent, 3+ WAA season with the Cubs in 1950, but who immediately regressed to average and stayed there for the rest of his career.

return from the army, but went 20–8 with a very strong team behind him in 1955—with just 1.2 WAA, a slightly above-average pitcher. To top that off, he went 27–7 in 1956 and was named the first winner of the Cy Young Award *and* the National League's MVP—but he had earned just 1.9 WAA in 268 innings. Newcombe during his career took a great deal of heat for supposedly choking in big games, most notably in the 1956 World Series. The truth was very simple: after his stellar rookie season, he was never that good again until 1959, when he earned 3.6 WAA in 222 innings for the Cincinnati Reds.

Newcombe was a fine hitting pitcher, and the foregoing analysis does not do him complete justice with respect to his 1955 season. If one adds his remarkable +11 Runs Above Average at the plate in 1955 to his total, he emerges as much more valuable player, with 2.7 WAA. That, however, was incomparably his best year at the plate, and since this book has otherwise ignored the contributions—*both positive and negative*—of pitchers at the plate, it does not make sense to adjust Newcombe's figure.

All told, the Dodgers generated 16 superstar seasons from 1949 through 1956, while the Yankees had just eight. By the early 1950s, the National League was probably the stronger of the two. But the Yankees, of course, beat the Dodgers in four of the five World Series they played against each other, including three close ones in 1952, 1953, and 1956. Luck seems to have favored the Yankees. The Dodgers, overall, were surely the stronger team until 1955.

We must now look at the teams that broke the Dodgers' monopoly in 1950, 1951, and 1954, the Philadelphia Phillies and the New York Giants—both of whom relied on several superstars who became some of the greatest players of the Silent Generation.

Born in 1926, Robin Roberts had entered professional baseball in 1948 and reached the Philadelphia Phillies in that same year. Beginning in 1950, he had a run of six seasons that no other pitcher of the late 1940s and 1950s could come close to matching, earning 2.9, 4.1, 4.9, 7.1, 6, and 2.3 WAA. During those years he threw between 304 and 347 innings, his record ranged from 21–15 in 1951 to 28–7 in 1952. After 1955 he regressed to average, going 19–18 in 1956 and 10–22 in 1957, when the Phillies were simply awful, with 0.4 WAA each year. With four superstar seasons, Roberts is tied for third among Silent Generation hurlers with Sandy Koufax, Jim Bunning, Juan Marichal and Luis Tiant. He eventually had three more star seasons, in 1958 and with the Baltimore Orioles in 1962 and 1964, but he never cracked 4 WAA again.

It has taken many years to realize that Roberts's teammate, center fielder Richie Ashburn, was even more valuable than he was. Ashburn, bizarrely, had played most of a season in the minors in 1945 at the age of 18, but found himself in the military during 1946. After a quick discharge, he spent 1947 in the minors and reached the Phillies in 1948. Although Ashburn had little power as a hitter, he had a lifetime average of .308 and a lifetime on-base percentage of .396, topping .400 four times. And he was a superb fielder, fully comparable to Willie Mays, who saved more than +30 runs in a season twice and more than +20 four other times. Ashburn had not reached his peak in 1950, when he earned just 1.7 WAA, but he shot up to 7.6 WAA in 1951 (giving him and Roberts 13.8 WAA between them). After an off-year in 1952 during which Ashburn must have played hurt—his fielding fell to average—he had superstar seasons in five of the next six years. An exact contemporary of Duke Snider, Ashburn was a considerably more valuable player over his career.

The Phillies managed to win the pennant in 1950 with a very mediocre 91 actual and 87 projected victories, while the Dodgers matched their projection with 89. With Ashburn below 2 WAA and Roberts at 2.9, their MVP and only superstar was right fielder Del Ennis, who turns out to have had a truly extraordinary career. Born in 1925, the first year of the Silent Generation, he played the 1943 season in the minors but spent the next two years in the military. The Phillies brought him straight to the majors in 1946, and he hit .313 with 17 homers, saved 12 runs in left field, and earned 4.3 WAA, the first superstar of the Silent Generation, and the only such non-pitcher before 1950. He remained a good player for the next three years and then peaked in 1950 with 31 homers, 126 RBI (with thanks to Richie Ashburn), and 4.1 WAA. He had another good year in 1951, but in 1952, when he should have been at his peak at 27, his defense began to collapse. By 1956 he had surrendered an extra -35 runs in the field, costing the Phillies a full -4.3 WAA—in other words, essentially neutralizing the presence of Richie Ashburn. The Phillies wisely unloaded him, but he cost the Cardinals -5 WAA over the next two seasons, dealing a serious blow to their pennant chances. Catcher Andy Seminick earned 2 WAA in 1950, and most of the lineup was slightly above average, totaling 10 WAA, 6 of them, thanks to Ashburn and Ennis, in the field. Among the pitchers, reliever Jim Konstanty and Bubba Church made positive contributions, but there were enough weak spots to make the whole staff average. The team remained above .500 for several years thanks to Roberts and Ashburn, but the Phillies refused to integrate despite the presence of a well-established black community in Philadelphia, and they had sunk below .500 by 1955. Roberts's eclipse sent them far into the second division.

More interesting were the New York Giants, who transformed themselves under manager Leo Durocher, took advantage of integration, and won pennants in 1951, when they went 37–7 in their last 44 games to force a playoff with a superior Dodgers team and won it on Bobby Thomson's third-game, ninth-inning, three-run homer. Leo Durocher had managed the Dodgers from 1940 until 1946, sat out a year's suspension for suspicious associations in 1947, and returned the next year, only to switch to the Giants in mid-season when the Dodgers were doing badly and Branch Rickey evidently decided it was time for a change. The team he took over in 1948 was dominated by aging power hitters, including Johnny Mize, Sid Gordon, and Willard Marshall, and its pitching was mediocre. The Giants added two black players to the roster late in 1949. One, third baseman Hank Thompson, had played briefly for the St. Louis Browns in 1947. The second, Monte Irvin, had started in the Negro Leagues in 1938, when he was 19, missing 1943–1944 because of the war. An infielder and a fine hitter, he had been widely expected to be the man to break the color barrier, but Rickey had picked Irvin's contemporary Robinson instead, delaying Irvin's full-time entry into the majors for two years. According to Irvin himself, Rickey had wanted to sign him in 1948, but could not after he refused to pay Effa Manley, the owner of the Newark Eagles, a reasonable price.

There is every reason to think that if Irvin had joined the majors in 1947, as Robinson did, and if he had just a tiny bit more luck, he would have been at least as great a player as Robinson. In his first full year in 1950, he fielded brilliantly both at first base and in the outfield, hit .299 with 15 home runs, and earned 3.8 WAA in just 110 games. In 1951 he played the whole year, hit .312 with a .415 OBP and led the league in RBIs with 121, finishing third in the MVP voting, with 6.1 WAA. Certainly he seemed to have more superstar seasons ahead of him, but in early 1952 he suffered a severe ankle fracture and missed most of the season. He never returned to his top form again, even though he was still a star in 1953 and 1954, earning more than 3 WAA with the help of fine work in left field. Then his career faded. Irvin was eventually selected to the Hall of Fame based upon his performance in the Negro Leagues, but he certainly proved himself of Hall of Fame caliber in his brief major league career. Initially, Hank Thompson turned out to be nearly as valuable because of two relatively invisible skills. In 148 games in 1950, he walked 83 times and hit 20 homers, and he was an outstanding third baseman, saving the Giants +22 runs. He just missed superstar status with 3.9 WAA. Thompson, unfortunately, had a serious drinking problem, and he lost his job in 1951, performing poorly when he was in the lineup, and never approached his 1950 form again.

The Giants had been transformed by trades that unloaded their power hitters—mostly to the Boston Braves—in exchange for second baseman Eddie Stanky, a Durocher favorite who fielded well and walked more than 100 times a year, and Alvin Dark, who turns out to have been even more overrated than Pee Wee Reese or Phil Rizzuto. Helped by Thompson, Irvin, Stanky, and fast outfielder Bobby Thomson, the Giants' fielders in 1950 saved more than 100 runs, earning the lineup more than 10 WAA. But their pitching was dreadful, and the batting order still had too many weak spots. Some help arrived in the miracle year of 1951.

Irvin's 6.1 WAA—fifth in the league in a year of superstardom, behind Musial, Ashburn, Robinson and Ralph Kiner—were trailed on the Giants by two men, outfielder-third baseman Bobby Thomson (who performed adequately at both positions), and 20-year-old rookie center fielder Willie Mays, the greatest player of the Silent Generation, each of whom put up 2.9 WAA. Like so many great players, Mays had started his professional career young, at 17, in the Negro Leagues. He had spent only 116 games in the minors after the Giants signed him in 1949. Alvin Dark, who had a fine year at the plate, and Eddie Stanky followed with 2.6 and 2.2 WAA, catcher Wes Westrum had 1.6, and outfielder Don Mueller added 1 more in 122 games. Only first baseman Whitey Lockman among the regulars was average. The bench pulled the whole lineup down to +13 WAA—but the Dodgers, with Robinson, Campanella and Hodges all having great years, had +19.

The Giants were superior on the mound. Thirty-four-year-old Sal Maglie, who had lost four years of his career to a Major League blacklist after jumping to the Mexican League (1946–1949), had an 18–4 record with 3.3 WAA, and Larry Jansen earned 2.6. But the staff had its weak spots, too, and was only about +2 WAA overall, while the Dodgers were -1. According to their Pythagorean records, the Dodgers should have finished four games ahead of the Giants, but they won only one game through Pythagorean luck while the Giants won five. The three-game playoff told the story: the Giants won two games out of three, but the Dodgers outscored them, 15–8. Both teams had finished the season with 96 wins, one below the level of a superior pennant winner.

Any chance that the Giants might overtake the superior Dodgers again vanished in 1952 when Monte Irvin broke his ankle and Willie Mays was drafted into the U.S. Army. Helped again by six wins' worth of Pythagorean luck, the Giants finished just four games behind the Dodgers in 1952 without Irvin and Mays, but fell well below .500 in 1953. Then, in 1954, Mays returned.

The 23-year-old Mays hit .345 with 41 home runs, saved an extraordinary +30 runs in the field, and won a well-deserved MVP award with 9 WAA, the greatest season of his career. He was a one-man team, since that 9 WAA equaled the total contribution of the entire Giants lineup. While Irvin and Hank Thompson earned 2.4 and 2.3 WAA, Mueller (who had 212 hits but fielded very poorly) and Dark were average, and first baseman Whitey Lockman, second baseman Davey Williams, and the catching platoon of Wes Westrum and Ray Katt cost the team a dreadful -6.7 WAA. In contrast to the Dodgers, who combined Robinson and Campanella with Snider and Hodges, the Giants owed their pennant-quality lineup entirely to integration. The pitching staff, meanwhile, was nearly in the class of the Indians team they beat in the World Series, and allowed the team to win 97 games. Young lefty Johnny Antonelli put up 4.6 WAA, Maglie added 2.2 more in 218⅓ innings, Ruben Gomez had 1.9, and relievers Marv Grissom and Hoyt Wilhelm were as good as Mossi and Narleski, with 4.6 WAA between them in 233⅔ innings. All told they earned +11 WAA. Sadly, Antonelli fell below 2 WAA in 1955 and never reached 4 again. Although the Giants, a superior pennant winner with 97 victories, finished only five games ahead of the Dodgers, that was only because of Dodgers luck. The Dodgers projected to win only 81 games on the season (they won 92), and the Milwaukee Braves won 89, -1 off their projection. Unfortunately, the Giants got the idea that as long as they had Willie Mays, the pennant was within reach.

Although the Dodgers barely won the last pennant of the Boys of Summer era in 1956, that year began an era of relative mediocrity in the National League that lasted for a very long time. Not until 1970 did a National League team reach the level of a superior pennant winner, represented after 1962 by 102 wins out of 162 games. In 1949–1953 and 1955 the Dodgers had led the National League in adjusted run differential every year and averaged 97 wins; in 1956–1959, the Milwaukee Braves led in that category every year, with an average of just 91 wins. Before turning to that Braves team, however, let us take a look at another remarkable aggregation, the Cincinnati Reds of 1956, who finished just two games behind the Dodgers and one behind the Braves with one of the most bizarre collections of strengths and weaknesses of any team in baseball history.

The 1956 Reds tied the team record for home runs in a season, hitting 221 among them, 32 more that Brooklyn and 34 more than Milwaukee. Chief contributors were 20-year-old rookie Frank Robinson, with 39; right fielder Wally Post, with 36; first baseman Ted Kluszewski, with 35; center fielder Gus Bell, with 29; and catcher Ed Bailey, with 28. All these numbers, however, were somewhat inflated by Crosley Field, a hitters' park—and as a result, while the Reds comfortably led the Braves for the league in team runs scored, 775 to 709, when park adjustments were included, the Reds fell to 731 runs scored while the Braves climbed to 762.

That, however, was only the beginning of the Reds' problems. No team that we have encountered so clearly lost a pennant because of poor fielding. The worst offender, by far, was center fielder Gus Bell, who cost the team no less than -46 adjusted runs, or more than four full games. Despite his 29 homers, Bell's presence in the lineup cost the Reds -1.7 WAA because of his poor defensive performance—which was not at all unusual for him. This was all the more inexcusable because Bell was flanked by two relatively talented outfielders, rookie Frank Robinson, who saved the team +10 runs, and Wally Post, who saved +13. (While four National League teams—the Giants, Braves, Reds and Pirates—brought black superstar outfielders to the majors during the 1950s, only one of them, the Giants, played theirs in center field where he could do the most good. Incredibly, the bias against good-hitting black center fielders was still alive thirty years later, when the Pirates switched young Barry Bonds to left field in favor of Andy Van Slyke.) In the infield, Roy McMillan was an excellent shortstop, saving +21 runs, and big Ted Kluszewski was average at first, but second baseman Johnny Temple—who had a good reputation—cost the team -12 runs, costing the team -2.3 WAA overall, and third baseman Ray Jablonski cost them -19 more, totaling -2.1 WAA. Frank Robinson, who had started his minor league career at 17, had one of the greatest 20-year-old rookie seasons ever with 4.9 WAA, and Post and catchers Ed Bailey and Smokey Burgess added 4.1 WAA. But Kluszewski was such an entirely one-dimensional offensive player that he earned only 1.5 WAA.

The Reds' fielders had cost the team -46 park-adjusted runs; the team as a whole saved 39 park-adjusted runs. That leaves 85 runs, nearly nine wins, saved by the pitching staff. The pitchers did in fact allow significantly below-average numbers of home runs and walks, despite having to work 77 games in Crosley Field—although they fell well below the league average in strikeouts. The team did not have a single dominant pitcher, even though Brooks Lawrence went 12–0 during the first half of the season and finished at 19–10, albeit with just 1.1 WAA. Four men used mainly in relief—Tom Acker, Hershel Freeman, Don Gross and Hal Jeffcoat—were the team's most effective hurlers, earned 7 WAA in 431 innings, while the starters, including Lawrence, Johnny Klippstein, and Joe Nuxhall, earned about 1 WAA each in about 200 innings apiece. Universally regarded as the team's weak spot, the Reds' pitching staff was actually the best in the league. Since the Reds did not understand what their weaknesses were, they could not correct them, and they faded rapidly from contention after 1956.

The Braves, meanwhile, had decamped from Boston to Milwaukee in 1953 with one remarkable player, pitcher Warren Spahn, already on the roster, and had added two all-time greats in 1953 and 1954. Spahn began his career in 1942 at age 21, missed three years in the military, and finished it in 1965 as the winningest left-hander in history. His career fell into three distinct phases. In 1947, in his first season as a regular starter, he pitched 289⅔ innings and posted a 21–10 record, led the league in ERA with the help of Braves Field, and earned 6.5 WAA. That apparently took a toll on his arm, however, as he fell to 0.9 WAA in the Braves' pennant-winning year of 1948 and did not reach the superstar level again until 1951, with 4.7 WAA. He reached the superstar level for the last time with 5.3 WAA in 1953, the team's first year in Milwaukee. The second phase of Spahn's career lasted from 1954 through 1963. While he never added to his total of three superstar seasons—fifth within the GI Generation behind Newhouser, Ferrell, Feller and Hubbell—he was over 3 WAA twice, over 2 WAA twice, and fell below 1 WAA only once before 1964, when he was 43 years old. Meanwhile, the team made striking additions to the players behind him.

Eddie Mathews, a left-handed hitting third baseman born in 1931—an exact contemporary of Mickey Mantle—had started his career at the age of 17 in 1949 and reached the Braves in 1952. Unlike his contemporary Ken Boyer, his career was only very briefly interrupted by military service during the Korean War because he received a hardship discharge after the death of his father. After an average rookie season, he had one of his greatest seasons in 1953 at age 21, hitting 47 home runs with a .408 OBP and 5.3 WAA. That was the first of eight superstar seasons in the next 11 years—tying him with Mickey Mantle and Carl Yastrzemski—and by 1957 Mathews was clearly the greatest third baseman of all time, eclipsing Home Run Baker. Like so many power hitters at the hot corner, he had a poor defensive reputation, but his fielding statistics show him to have been perfectly average in the field for essentially the whole of his career. His on-base percentage consistently remained between .380 and .410, and he finished his career with more than 500 home runs despite playing all of it in pitchers' parks.

The Braves had signed Henry Aaron, meanwhile, in 1952 at the age of 18, when he played half a season in the Negro American League, and he had jumped from single-A to the majors in 1954, the team's second year in Milwaukee. Although his rookie season ended with a broken ankle in early September, he returned in 1955 and immediately broke the superstar barrier with 4.1 WAA. Although Aaron's on-base percentages were generally a little lower than Mathews's, his batting averages were higher, and he eclipsed Mathews as a home run hitter in the early 1960s. He was also a fine right fielder, saving between +10 and +23 runs on six occasions, and the Braves would probably have been well advised to put him in center, where Billy Bruton, a Negro Leagues veteran who had joined the club in 1953, was a very average player at bat and in the field. While Aaron's three best seasons were not quite the equal of his two slightly older contemporaries, Mickey Mantle and Willie Mays, he had an unmatched record for consistency. Beginning in 1955 through 1973, his WAA totaled 4.1, 5.4, 6.1, 6.2, 6.2, 6.2, 7.1, 5.9, 7.3, 6.0, 6.5, 5.7, 8.5, 6.7, 6.5, 3.7, 4.6, 3.5, and 3.7 (at the age of 39.) In 1966 he took advantage of his move to Fulton County Stadium to increase his home run output, and he eventually, of course, set an all-time record of 755 home runs, one which undoubtedly would still stand but for the advent of performance-enhancing drugs.

Mathews and Aaron simultaneously posted superstar seasons six times—in 1955, 1957, 1959, 1960, 1961, and 1963—only two fewer times than Ruth and Gehrig, who did so consecutively from 1926 through 1933. No other team in baseball had a comparable pair of players in the 1946–1966 era, raising the question of why the Braves never posted a run differential of +200 and why they won the pennant only twice. The answer has to do with their supporting cast on the one hand, and their much-ballyhooed pitching on the other.

The Braves, to repeat, led the league in adjusted run differential from 1956 through 1959, but never won more than 95 games and lost the pennant in the first and last of those years on the last day of the season. Their hitters in those four years earned WAA totals of +10, +16, +7 and +11, meaning that except in 1957, Mathews and Aaron contributed most or all of the positive value of Milwaukee batters. Essentially, during this whole four-year period the Braves lacked anyone else in the lineup who could be a real asset for more than one season at a time.

Thus, in 1956—when Mathews himself had a mildly off year, with 3.1 WAA—Johnny Logan at short and Billy Bruton in center field combined for 2.9 WAA between them, thanks to fine seasons in the field. The first base platoon of Joe Adcock, who earned about 3.5 WAA at the plate but gave half of them back at first base, and Frank Torre, who couldn't hit, earned .8 WAA. The rest of the team was essentially average. In 1957, by far the lineup's best year, Aaron and Mathews combined for 9.9 WAA. The Braves acquired second baseman Red Schoendienst early in the season. A veteran of the Cardinals (1945–1956) and Giants (1956–1957), Schoendienst had a reputation as a star, but he had been over 1 WAA only three times in his career, 3.4 WAA in 1952, 4.5 in 1953 (when he nearly won a batting title), and 2.3 in 1954. Apparently buoyed by a pennant race, Schoendienst earned 2.2 WAA for the Braves in 93 games in 1957 but was completely average the next year, when he had contracted tuberculosis.[26] Logan earned another 1.7 WAA, and outfielders Wes Covington and late-season call-up Bob Hazle added 3.2 WAA between them (1.5 from Hazle, who never did anything comparable again). Adcock earned 1.5 WAA in 231 plate appearances, while Torre was perfectly average in 411. Manager Fred Haney's preference for the left-handed Torre over the powerful Adcock against right-handed pitching cost the team at least a win. Catcher Del Crandall had a perfectly average season.

The hitters slumped badly in 1958, when Aaron and Mathews again combined for 10 WAA, but Logan and Schoendienst fell from a combined 3.9 WAA in 1957 to -2.2 WAA, while Adcock and Bruton fell to average. Del Crandall behind the plate and Wes Covington in the outfield combined for 4.7 WAA. Aaron and Mathews each had one of their greatest seasons in 1959, combining for nearly 12 WAA, and Adcock, given a chance with 444 plate appearances, earned 3.4 WAA more. But Crandall and Covington gave up nearly all the value they had earned in 1958; Logan and Bruton remained average; and a long string of second basemen, including Felix Mantilla and the aging Bobby Avila, cost the team several wins.

Aaron and Mathews in 1959 finished behind Cubs shortstop Ernie Banks as NL MVP, both in the BBWAA voting and in reality, as Banks had his greatest of three superstar seasons with 6.3 WAA. Born in 1931, Banks had spent two years in the Army during the Korean War, played briefly in the Negro Leagues, and reached the Cubs late in 1953. His other great seasons came in 1955 (4.7 WAA) and 1958 (4.8), when he won his first MVP award. He topped 3 WAA twice and 2 WAA on two other occasions. A fine fielder early in his career, he is the only Silent Generation shortstop whose impact was even close to that of Cronin, Appling, and Boudreau among the GIs, and the only one of his generation to have a real claim to the Hall of Fame. Alas, not until 1969–71, when Banks was a very mediocre first baseman, did his team even contend for the pennant.

Like the Yankees throughout much of the twentieth century, the Baltimore Orioles in the late 1960s and early 1970s, and the Oakland Athletics in several periods of their history, the Milwaukee Braves of 1956–1959 reputedly had a great pitching staff, but actually were a good (though not great) hitting team playing in a pitchers' park. Although Warren Spahn's

---

26. With just one superstar season and three others over 2 WAA (including his full 1957 season), Schoendienst does not rank with Charlie Gehringer, Joe Gordon, or even Bobby Doerr among second basemen of his generation, and the BBWAA never gave him as many as 45 percent of its votes for the Hall of Fame. The Veterans Committee selected him in 1989.

days as a dominant pitcher were now behind him, he averaged 2.3 WAA in about 280 innings a season over this four-year period. The much-esteemed number 2 of the staff was Lew Burdette, who had been signed by the Yankees, reached the Boston Braves in 1952, and established himself as a good pitcher in 1954, when he earned 2.3 WAA with a record of 15–14. He had also provoked a great deal of controversy about his supposed use of a spitball. After a bad off-year in 1955, Burdette had a 19–10 record in 1956 with 2.1 WAA—his second and last star season. He improved that record to 17–9 in 1957 as the Braves won the pennant—but his pitching was -1.3 WAA, hurting the team. In the 1957 World Series, however, Burdette became the first pitcher ever to win three games against the Yankees in a fall classic, shutting them out twice, and establishing himself in the public eye as a great pitcher.

In 1958, when the Braves' hitters slumped, Burdette earned 1.1 WAA, but emerged with a record of 20–10. His real ability level caught up with him in that fall's World Series, however, when he gave up an astonishing 18 runs against the Yankees in three games, winning Game 2, 13–5, losing Game 5, 7–0, and losing Game 7, 7–2. Despite the presence of a number of promising young pitchers on his staff, Fred Haney sent Burdette to the mound for a career-high 289⅔ innings in 1959. He posted -1 WAA but still managed a record of 21–15. He had records of 19–13 and 18–11 in the next two years although he remained average at best. He surely ranks as one of the luckiest and most overrated hurlers of all time.

After Spahn and Burdette, the Braves' pitching only got worse. In 1956, their next three starters—Bob Buhl, Ray Crone and Gene Conley—combined for -2.1 WAA, and the staff as a whole earned just +4 WAA. In 1957, only Spahn was above average, and the pennant-winning Braves finished with a pitching staff that cost them. In 1958, three youngsters, Carlton Willey, Joey Jay, and Juan Pizarro, combined for 3.1 WAA in 333⅓ innings, but the staff still accounted for just +3 WAA. But in 1959, Spahn and Buhl were the only above-average starters on the team, and the three youngsters pitched more innings but wound up below average overall. With dreadful fielders behind them, the staff still earned +4 WAA, 2.8 thanks to Spahn. The 1959 team lost partly from bad luck, but mostly because they simply had too many weak spots in the lineup and on the mound.[27] Despite one of the greatest 1–2 punches in the history of baseball, the Braves were never even close to being a great team. They were the first illustration of the phenomenon that would dominate baseball for most of the 1960s: a terrible shortage of talent created by the decline of the minor leagues.

The Braves' loss of a playoff to the Dodgers in 1959 ushered in three rather odd seasons in National League play. The Dodgers team that beat them after the two teams finished the season tied at 86–68 was, quite simply, the weakest team ever to win a pennant, let alone a world championship, between 1901 and 1968. Their .564 winning percentage was the lowest ever for a pennant winner, and even that exaggerated their ability. Their Pythagorean percentage would have given them a record of 81–73—and they tied the Braves with the help of six wins' worth of Pythagorean luck, while luck cost the Braves three games. They were

---

27. In *The Bill James Guide to Baseball Managers from 1870 to Today* (New York: Scribner, 1997), 202–205, Bill James blamed Haney for the loss of the 1959 pennant, but many of his arguments do not hold up. He argued that Jay, Willey and Pizarro should have pitched much more and Spahn and Burdette much less, but the three youngsters were in fact average at best.

also substantially inferior to the Giants, who were eliminated from the race on the next-to-last day of the season. (We shall look at the Giants a little later.) Not surprisingly, their roster did not include a single superstar. Their lineup earned just +1 WAA and their pitching staff +3. Those were entirely the work of Don Drysdale, the team MVP, who earned 2.8 WAA in 272 innings. The only above-average players in their lineup were left fielder Wally Moon, who had a knack for hitting home runs over the short screen in left field in the Los Angeles Coliseum, and second baseman Charlie Neal. Fortunately for them, they encountered another weak pennant winner, the Chicago White Sox, in the World Series, and managed to prevail.

The Pittsburgh Pirates team that succeeded the Dodgers in 1960 was resoundingly mediocre. Overall their line-up earned +11 WAA (+10 at bat) and their pitching staff +4, and their most valuable offensive player was third baseman Don Hoak, with a mere 2.3 WAA. Roberto Clemente, who had posted just one superstar season since joining the team at age 20 in 1955, and shortstop Dick Groat, who won the league MVP Award, finished with 2 WAA, and center fielder Bill Virdon had 1.8. (There were six superstars in the 1960 National League, led by Aaron and Mays at 6.2 WAA.). Long-time pitching ace Bob Friend earned 3.2 WAA, and two other starters and reliever Elroy Face all earned at least 1, but the rest of the staff was very weak. Clemente, as we shall see, blossomed very late. Second baseman Bill Mazeroski was only average in the field and below-average overall, the only Pirates regular in that category. Although Mazeroski became a consistently great fielder from 1961 through 1966, earning the Pirates from 1 to 3 WAA in the field every year, he was such a poor hitter that he had only two star seasons of 2 WAA in his whole career, and was below average overall in ten of his 17 seasons. Yet he is in the Hall of Fame.

The Pirates in turn were succeeded by a pennant winner even luckier and less worthy than the 1959 Dodgers. The Cincinnati Reds in 1961 won 93 games only with the help of ten wins' games worth of Pythagorean luck, the equivalent of two more superstars. Their lineup was the weakest in history for a National League pennant winner, about one game below average overall, and their pitchers contributed +7 WAA. Right fielder Frank Robinson had his fifth superstar season in six years and his best one yet, 6 WAA, and center fielder Vada Pinson, in only his third season, joined him with 4.3 WAA, his best year. But the supporting cast included shortstop Eddie Kasko (-2.6 WAA), second baseman Don Blasingame (-3.5), and the catching platoon of Jerry Zimmerman and Johnny Edwards (-5.3 combined). In an increasingly common National League pattern, the black players were superstars, the white players dreadful. The heroes of the pitching staff were Jim O'Toole and Joey Jay, who combined for 5.3 WAA.

The most likely pennant winners in 1961 had been the San Francisco Giants, led by the most dominant player of his era, Willie Mays. When we last met Willie, he had finished the 1954 season with an extraordinary 9.2 WAA, a batting title, a pennant and a world championship. Since then his career had been a study in unmatched individual brilliance and organizational incompetence. Just as in the 1930s, the Stoneham-led Giants could not complement great players with even an average supporting cast.

In 1955, Mays hit 51 home runs and finished with 7.1 WAA, easily the league's most valuable player. Hank Thompson added 1 WAA at third base, but the line-up also included

Don Mueller in right (-21 runs in the field and -3.2 WAA), first baseman Whitey Lockman (-0.7), catchers Ray Katt and Wes Westrum (-3.8 combined), shortstop Al Dark (-3.8), and second baseman Davey Williams (-2). The pitchers were only marginally above average as well, and the Giants finished the season at 80–74.

In 1956 Mays topped the National League again for the third year in a row (5.8 WAA), but the only other player in the lineup with positive value was 22-year-old black first baseman Bill White, with 1.6 WAA. Thanks to Mueller (-3.1), outfielder Daryl Spencer (-3), Dusty Rhodes (-1.5), and catchers Bill Sarni, Katt and Westrum (-1.5), he whole lineup surrendered -13 WAA, and the team finished at 67–87. In 1957, in their last year in New York, Mays was the best player in the league again with 6.6 WAA, but White had gone into the army and there were no other positive assets in an aging cast of Giants. Don Mueller and Dusty Rhodes, who seemed to have earned lifetime positions thanks to their contributions in the first half of the decade, combined for -5.8 WAA. The whole lineup earned -4 WAA, and the pitching was nearly as bad, leaving the team 69–85.

In 1958, the Giants arrived in San Francisco and Mays was again the league MVP with 8.2 WAA, his second-best season to date. The Giants had now discovered the Caribbean, and they added 20-year-old first baseman Orlando Cepeda, who had a fine rookie season with 2.1 WAA, but cost Bill White his job. The roster now featured some other good young players, including Leon Wagner and Felipe Alou, who earned 1.6 and 1 WAA in just 445 plate appearances between them, and the disastrous veterans were finally purged. The pitching improved somewhat, and the Giants finished at 80–74. That still left Willie Mays accounting for 3.2 WAA more than the team's positive value.

Helped by another spectacular acquisition, the Giants suddenly became contenders again in 1959, finishing with a better run differential than the Dodgers and staying in the three-way pennant race until the last weekend of the season. Not only did Cepeda improve to 3 WAA, but another first baseman, 21-year-old Willie McCovey, joined the team in August and hit .354 with 13 home runs and 3.3 WAA in just 52 games. The presence of McCovey and Cepeda—both natural first basemen—had already led the Giants to trade White, and still created a problem that lasted for six years. Cepeda spent the last two months of 1959 in the outfield. The rest of the Giants' line-up was, however, made up of players of average or marginal value. Together, Cepeda, McCovey, and Mays—who fell to fourth-most valuable National Leaguer with 5.3 WAA, behind Ernie Banks, Aaron, and Mathews—earned 11.6 WAA, but the only other asset in the lineup was outfielder Jackie Brandt (1.1 WAA), and the lineup overall earned only +9, and the pitchers just 1 more. The Giants' 83 wins left them three games behind Los Angeles and Milwaukee. Mays tied Aaron for tops in the NL in 1960 with 6.2 WAA, but McCovey and Cepeda fell to 4 WAA between them, and outfielder Willie Kirkland (.9 WAA) was the only other positive player in the lineup. Twenty-two-year-old pitcher Juan Marichal earned 1 WAA in just 81⅓ innings, but the staff as a whole gave up -2 WAA and the lineup earned just +6. This time the team finished 79–75.

In 1961 the Giants began what might have been—with a little more luck and one or two simple roster moves by management—a three-year stint at the top of the league. Although Mays fell back to the fourth-most valuable player in the league with 4.8 WAA, behind Aaron, Frank Robinson, and Ken Boyer, Cepeda joined him with 4.6, and McCovey added 1.8. Outfielder Felipe Alou, maturing at 26, hit .289 with 18 homers and earned 1.6 WAA, and third baseman Davenport had his first above-average season thanks to a fine year in the field. But four infielders and one outfielder contributed a combined -9 WAA. Even those players and four wins' worth of bad Pythagorean luck reduced the team to 85 victories, they had easily the best run differential in the league, but the Reds and Dodgers beat them out thanks to better luck. The lineup overall earned +9 WAA and the pitching staff +5, good for a league-leading adjusted run differential or +120, about 70 runs better than the pennant-winning Reds, but the Giants finished four wins below their Pythagorean projection while the Reds finished ten above theirs.

As the increasing mediocrity of one pennant winner after another showed, the Giants were falling victim to a dreadful shortage of even average talent in the major leagues. The problem reflected the drop in the birth rate in the 1930s, the bonus rule, the increasing availability of a college education, the growing popularity of other sports, and above all, the decline in the minor leagues. In 1939 the minor leagues included 24 AA teams (then the highest classification0, 24 class A teams, 38 class B teams, 54 class C teams, and 142 class D teams—the entry level into organized baseball. In 1959 there were 26 AAA teams, 14 AA, 16 A 20 B, 20 C, and 48 class D teams. Although minor league rosters may have been a little larger in 1959, more than twice as many young men were playing at the lowest level of organized baseball in 1939 than 20 years later. The next two steps up the ladder also seem to have been only about half as full in 1959. Integration, which had initially provided the majors with about ten new superstars, was doing much less by 1960 because a pipeline of young black talent had not been established. Caribbean players were only just beginning to have an impact. It was not, perhaps, a coincidence that baseball was suddenly losing ground to pro football among the nation's fandom.

It was paradoxically at this moment that the majors had decided to expand. Expansion came to the American League in 1961 and hit the National League in 1962. Its impact there was even greater than it had been in the American League, and deserves a look before we look at the pennant-winning San Francisco Giants and the mostly new Los Angeles Dodgers team that lost to them in a playoff.

The National League expansion, of course, introduced two new teams into the league: the New York Mets and the Houston Colt .45s. Houston performed surprisingly well, finishing in eighth place—ahead of the Chicago Cubs—because of a remarkable performance by their pitching staff, which earned +4 WAA overall while their lineup dropped -18 WAA. (The hero of Houston was pitcher Turk Farrell, who earned 3.5 WAA in 242 innings—yet finished with a record of 10–20.) Their -133 run differential led the Cubs, whose pitching was awful, by 53 runs. The Mets, however, were much, much worse, winning only 40 games and losing 120 (including nine losses' worth of bad Pythagorean luck), with an amazing adjusted run differential of -312. Essentially, the equivalent of 16 regular players who would not otherwise have been in the majors—most of them aged veterans—were playing full seasons, and the Mets' pitching staff was equally bad. The impact of all this has never been completely understood.

Three different factors helped the league's best players. To begin with, the season was now five percent longer, which in 1961 had enabled Roger Maris to hit 61 home runs and break Babe Ruth's single season record, and Tommy Davis in 1962 to top 150 RBIs, the first time anyone had done that since 1949. Secondly, especially when they faced the Mets, the league's best hitters feasted upon pitchers who in 1961 would not have been throwing nearly so many major league innings, if they had been in the major leagues at all. These changes meant that the best hitters and pitchers might be expected to put up higher totals in traditional statistics like home runs and won-lost record—as indeed they did. But lastly and most importantly for our purposes, the expansion teams included the equivalent of 16 below-average regular players and 16 pitchers in their lineups. The league average dropped significantly as a result, and the performance of most of the superstars in the league showed it.

Willie Mays in 1961 had had what amounted to an off-year for him, finishing with just 4.8 WAA. In 1962 he regained his status as the National League's MVP with 7.1 WAA. Frank Robinson, who had finished just behind Henry Aaron in 1961 with 6 WAA, finished just behind Mays in 1962 with 6.5. Aaron was an exception: he had a genuine off-year and dropped from 7.1 WAA in 1961 to 5.9 in 1962. Roberto Clemente also declined. Outfielder Tommy Davis of the Dodgers, who won the batting title and drove in 153 runs to lead the league, had 5.3 WAA, by far the best season of his career. Cubs shortstop Ernie Banks rebounded from 3.4 WAA in 1961 to 5.2. Among pitchers, Bob Gibson of the St. Louis Cardinals went from 2.9 WAA to 4.3, his first superstar season, and Sandy Koufax was on his way to 4 or 5 WAA when a finger ailment sidelined him in mid-season. He still finished with 2.4 WAA. Only three National Leaguers had topped 5 WAA in 1961, but five did in 1962. This made for an extremely exciting season. The trend continued in 1963, when the total number of National League superstars reached 11, with eight of them over 5 WAA.

The 1962 Giants needed a last-week collapse by the Dodgers to force a playoff, but they deservedly won the pennant with an adjusted run differential of +190, a full 40 runs better than the Dodgers. Their 101 wins and 64 losses (including a 3-game playoff) fell short of the definition of a superior pennant winner in a 162-game season. Except for Mays, whose 7.3 WAA represented one of his best seasons, their hitting stars had mediocre years: Cepeda slipped to 1.8 WAA and McCovey, platooned in left field, to 1.9. McCovey was foolishly platooned with Harvey Kuenn, who was inferior to him both at bat and in the field, where McCovey actually performed quite adequately despite his very large, lumbering physique. For once, however, nearly the whole Giants supporting cast contributed, and the lineup earned +13 WAA. Felipe Alou earned 2.8 WAA in right field, third baseman Davenport had his best season with 2.5 WAA, and second baseman Chuck Hiller and catchers Tom Haller and Ed Bailey were average. The one exception was shortstop Jose Pagan, an early example of a trend towards Latin shortstops, who gave up -2.7 WAA. The starting pitching corps was very good, as Marichal and Jack Sanford earned 2 WAA each while Billy O'Dell and Billy Pierce earned 1.5, although poor relieving pulled the staff down to +6 WAA.

Unfortunately, the Giants reverted to form in 1963. Remarkably, they became the first National League team ever to have four superstars: Mays (7 WAA), McCovey (5.5), Marichal (5.2 in 321⅓ innings, with a 25–8 record), and Cepeda (4.2, his second superstar season.) Felipe Alou added another 2.8, but the entire rest of the infield of Chuck Hiller (-2.3), Jose Pagan (-1.7), and Jim Davenport (-2) were awful. With Harvey Kuenn putting up another

-1.4 WAA, the lineup overall earned just +2 WAA. The pitchers, beyond the magnificent Marichal, were about average, and the Giants won only 88 games and finished third. Mays improved to a magnificent 8 WAA in 1964 at age 33, rookie third baseman Jim Ray Hart added 3.3 (and performed well in the field, despite a dreadful later reputation), and Cepeda had 3.5. Hart, the first great prospect developed by the Giants since McCovey, remained a star for four seasons, but his career apparently suffered from alcohol problems. But with even McCovey having an awful year, the infield was more than -6 WAA (with Pagan at -3.8), and the line-up as a whole was below average. The pitchers, led by Marichal (4.1 WAA) and 25-year-old Gaylord Perry (3.4), earned more than +10 WAA, but the team won only 90 games and finished fourth. The press often referred to the Giants of the early 1960s as not one team, but three: white, black, and Latin. It will not have escaped the reader's attention that while most of the black and Latin players were great or good, most of their white players were terrible—a pattern that went back all the way to 1954. Compounding the problem, the Giants after 1963 traded Felipe Alou, whose best years were ahead of him, to the Milwaukee Braves in exchange for three players, including pitcher Bob Shaw.

The last four years of the GI-Silent era in the National League, from 1963 through 1966, was a tale of two teams that won pennants—the Dodgers and the Cardinals—and three others, the Giants, the Phillies, and the Reds, that failed to do so. The 1962 Giants were the strongest team of this era, and none of the succeeding pennant winners had an adjusted run differential of more than +127, equal to a record of about 94–68. The Astros and the Mets—and in 1966, the Cubs—remained much worse than any team was good, their negative run differentials repeatedly averaging more than -200. Their inability to win turned teams with just one or two major assets into contenders, and the National League had an outstanding pennant race in every year from 1962 through 1966, often involving at least three teams.

The Dodgers teams that won the pennant in 1963, 1965 and 1966 were in no way comparable to the teams of 1949–1956. LA had one enormous asset: Sandy Koufax, who had four consecutive superstar seasons, with 7, 4.5, 4.9 and 6 WAA. Although Koufax broke Feller's all-time strikeout record in 1965 and posted lower ERAs than Feller had in 1939–1941 and 1946, his WAA were generally lower because of a general collapse in offense after the enlargement of the strike zone in 1963. The combination of Koufax, the Dodgers' new park, Chavez Ravine, a fine defensive ball club, and the sharp decline in offense around baseball that began in 1963 gave the impression that the Dodgers had an all-around great pitching staff. But they did not: the rest of the staff generally added only marginally to Koufax's value. Koufax's right-handed opposite number, of course, was Don Drysdale, who was usually at his worst when his teammates were at their best. Drysdale did post three superstar seasons with the Dodgers in 1957, 1960, and 1962, but he had just 1.7 WAA in 1963, .7 in 1965, and -.6 in 1966, when the team won pennants. (He rebounded with star seasons in 1967–1968, after Koufax retired.) But every year, the Dodgers gave hundreds of innings to below-average pitchers, including Johnny Podres, who had his last above-average season in 1961. Like other pennant winners from pitchers' parks, the Dodgers' pitching was nowhere near as good as it seemed, while their hitting was at least a little bit better.

Center fielder Willie Davis posted his only superstar season in the year the Dodgers missed the pennant—1964—but he was their most under-appreciated asset. A great athlete with tremendous speed, he saved the team +12 runs in the field in 1962, +15 in 1963, +27 in 1964, and +15 each in 1965 and 1966. Although his hitting earned only 1–2 WAA per season, his fielding made him a star, and undoubtedly was a huge help to the team's fastball pitchers. Tommy Davis had posted 5.1 WAA in 1962, when the Dodgers lost the playoff to the Giants, but faded rapidly after that and broke his ankle in 1965. Other modest offensive assets included Jim Gilliam, now switched to third base, outfielder Frank Howard in 1963, and one of the more overrated players in the history of baseball, shortstop Maury Wills.

Wills, a switch-hitter, had become a Dodgers regular during a bad rookie season in 1959. In the World Series his team beat the Chicago White Sox, whose shortstop, Luis Aparicio, had just revived the art of the stolen base with 56, the highest figure in decades. Picking up that ball and running with it, Wills stole 50 in 1960, and in 1962 set off after, and broke, Ty Cobb's single-season record of 96 with 104 of his own. Those 104 thefts, according to modern calculations, added +19 runs in the course of the season, but Wills's value as a hitter was negligible. Wills was also a very average fielder in every year but two, 1960 and 1965, and his best overall years were 1962 (2 WAA) and 1965 (2.6 WAA, the most valuable player in the Dodgers' lineup). But so enormous was the hype over his stolen base total in 1962 that he was voted the MVP in the National League, beating out not only his teammate Tommy Davis (who drove in 153 runs and earned 5.1 WAA), but also Mays (7.1 WAA), Frank Robinson (6.5 WAA), Aaron (5.9 WAA), and several dozen other superior players. Together, Wills and Willie Davis did more than anyone but Koufax (who won 26 games) to hold down the Dodgers' opposition runs in 1965. But Wills was never close to a great player.

What differentiated the Dodgers from the Giants' other contenders from 1963–1966 was their ability to fill their lineup with at least average players. The 1963 team won the pennant thanks to seven wins' worth of Pythagorean luck, allowing them to win 99 games. Their lineup—only +3 wins overall—included three stars: left fielder Frank Howard (2.9 WAA), Tommy Davis (2.8) and Jim Gilliam (2.7), even though five other players were about -1 WAA apiece. Koufax provided nearly all of the pitchers' +8 WAA. The lineup of the Cardinals, who had a better run differential, included Bill White (3.8 WAA), center fielder Curt Flood (2) and shortstop Dick Groat (3.5), and was similar in overall value, but their pitchers, including Curt Simmons (3.2) and Ernie Broglio (1.4), were superior overall. The Dodgers' lineup and the pitching staff beyond Koufax slipped a bit further in 1964 and their luck failed them, and they finished below .500 as the Cardinals won a close race. We shall return to them shortly.

The 1965 National League race was one of the most exciting in history, involving five contenders—the Dodgers, Giants, Reds, Pirates and Braves—for most of the season, and featuring fantastic performances by three of the league's greatest players. However, because talent was so rare and evenly distributed, none of these teams remotely approached the level of a superior pennant winner. The Giants in 1965 had one of the great one-two punches in baseball history: pitcher Juan Marichal, who despite his fight with John Roseboro and suspension posted 7.8 WAA, nearly 3 more than Koufax, and Willie Mays, who hit 52 homers and recovered most of his magic in the field at age 34, with 8.5 WAA. This was the eighth time in 12 years that Willie had been the most valuable performer in the National League, and the writers graciously awarded him his second MVP Award. Cepeda missed the entire season with a knee injury, but McCovey added 3.1 WAA and Jim Ray Hart added 2. The rest of the lineup, however, included second basemen Dick Schofield and Tito Fuentes (-3.5 WAA between them), shortstop Hal Lanier (-4), Jim Davenport, who unaccountably shared third base with Hart (-2.2), and outfielders Jesus Alou, Matty Alou, and Len Gabrielson (-1.5 WAA among them)—*dropping the lineup overall to -6 WAA.*[28] Giants pitchers, on the other hand, were easily the best in the league, earning at least +14 WAA, as Bob Shaw (3.6 WAA), Bob Bolin (3.2 WAA) and reliever Frank Linzy (2.2 WAA) complemented the great Marichal. Still, the Giants needed four games of Pythagorean luck to win 95 games. The Dodgers' contrast with the Giants was remarkable and was completely misunderstood at the time. No one in their line-up was remotely close to being a superstar: their best players were shortstop Wills (2.6 WAA) and rookie second baseman Jim Lefebvre (2.3), both of whom excelled in the field. But the only negative factor in their lineup was catcher John Roseboro (-2.3 WAA), while outfielders Ron Fairly, Willie Davis, and Lou Johnson, first baseman Wes Parker, and third baseman Gilliam (now 36) earned between .3 and 1.4 WAA each. All of those players but Johnson had come through the Dodgers' farm system. Meanwhile, with Koufax slipping (by his own standards!) to 4.9 WAA, reliever Ron Perranoski (1.5 WAA), and Claude Osteen (1.6) were the only other significant assets on the pitching staff. Overall, with a better lineup and inferior pitching, the Dodgers were marginally superior to the Giants, but they also needed five games of Pythagorean luck to win the pennant. The Reds and the Pirates had the best run differentials.

In 1966, Koufax, finishing his career with a 27–9 record and 6 WAA, got some help from rookie Don Sutton (.8 WAA) and an excellent performance from Phil Regan, 2.4 WAA in 117 innings. Drysdale fell below average. All told, the rest of the staff managed to add +5 WAA to Koufax's total. The Dodgers' line-up excelled in the field, and although Wills fell below average overall, Willie Davis, Lefebvre, Parker and Johnson earned 3.3, 3.3, 3.4 and 2.2 WAA, while Roseboro rebounded to 1.5. The Giants by contrast had three superstars, with Mays once again the true league MVP with 7.7 WAA and Marichal (25–6) only slightly behind Koufax with 5.7. McCovey, finally the regular first baseman for good, was the third superstar with 5 more; and Jim Ray Hart, continuing to improve, had 3.7. Bu the next best player in the lineup was catcher Tom Haller (0.2 WAA), and infielders Tito Fuentes, Lanier, and Davenport subtracted –5.3 WAA while outfielders Jesus Alou, Ollie Brown, Len Gabrielson and Cap Peterson took away another -8.2. On the mound, although Gaylord Perry (2.8 WAA) and Bob Bolin (2) complemented Marichal beautifully, Ray Sadecki, a hugely overrated pitcher acquired in a trade for Orlando Cepeda, gave up more than -2 WAA, and the rest of the staff was very weak. With a lineup worth +2 WAA and a staff worth +3, the Giants finished second to the Dodgers, 1.5 games back, thanks only to seven games' worth of Pythagorean luck. Their all-time greats deserved a better fate.

No one knew it, but in 1966, Willie Mays had been at least the NL's most valuable

---

28. Hart, as mentioned, had a reputation as a poor fielder, but he was superior defensively to Davenport, as well as massively superior offensively, in 1965.

offensive player—and usually the overall MVP—in nine of the last 13 years, never once falling below the superstar level. Not even Ruth, Cobb or Speaker could match that record. Although Mays declined significantly from his own stratospheric level in 1967, he still earned 4.3 WAA in that year and 4.4 in 1968, and after a real off-year in 1969, another round of expansion enabled him to get back to 3.1 WAA in 139 games in 1970 and 4.8 WAA in 136 games in 1971, when he reached post-season play for only the fourth time with the help of Marichal and Bobby Bonds. Not even Ted Williams, who won the 1958 batting championship when he was also 40, could match Mays' performance at that age. Mays, not Joe DiMaggio, should have been named baseball's greatest living player in 1969, Even though he missed nearly two full seasons in the military when he was 21 and 22, his 16 superstar seasons tie him for third all-time with Henry Aaron, behind Ruth (18, including 2 as a pitcher) and Barry Bonds (17). Undoubtedly the great players of the early Silent Generation, including Mays, Aaron, Mantle, Frank Robinson, and Roberto Clemente, all benefited from living through one or two rounds of expansion, which maintained their superiority relative to the league despite their advancing age. Yet that does not diminish their greatness, and it was sad that the Giants, blessed with perhaps the greatest single asset of all time, failed to take more advantage of it by providing him with an adequate supporting cast.

Although Juan Marichal outpitched Sandy Koufax only once, in 1965, his career was longer. Both finished with four superstar seasons, tied for third among Silent Generation pitchers with Robin Roberts, Jim Bunning, and Luis Tiant. McCovey, who reached his peak in 1969, finished with six superstar seasons and is very deservedly in the Hall of Fame. Even more than the Giants of Terry, Ott, and Hubbell, these Giants should surely have won more pennants than they did, but like those Giants, they kept a crew of the same dreadful players in the lineup year after year.

Much the same, it turns out, could be said of the Philadelphia Phillies, who led the National League for most of the 1964 season before a spectacular September collapse, and never came close to a pennant again. While the Giants had three superstars for much of the mid–1960s, the Phillies had four players who reached that level more than once. Outfielder Johnny Callison, a tremendous fielder, had four superstar seasons from 1962, when he was 23, through 1965; pitcher Chris Short had two from 1962 through 1965; pitcher Jim Bunning had 3.2 WAA in 1964 and superstar seasons in the next three years; and infielder Richie Allen, as he was then known, had four superstar seasons in six years, 1964–69, just missing a fifth. Of these players, Allen and Short had come through the Phillies' system, while Callison and Bunning had been acquired in very clever trades. Yet the Phillies suffered from Stoneham's disease. In 1964, Allen had one of the greatest rookie seasons in history (7.3 WAA), Callison and Short joined him at the superstar level with 4.3 and 4.2, and Bunning added 3.6. But Callison, Allen and center fielder Tony Gonzalez (0.5 WAA) were the only positive factors in the lineup, and the rest of the hitters that played at least 100 games totaled -8 WAA, with second baseman Tony Taylor (-3.4 WAA) the worst. On the mound, nearly all the other pitchers were modestly negative. Overall the lineup earned just +1 WAA and the pitchers +6, and only four games of Pythagorean luck allowed the Phillies to win 92 games, missing the pennant by one. Their late-season collapse reflected their actual ability level.

That was the only time the Phillies contended in this era. In 1965, Allen (3.8 WAA) and Callison (5) were again the only real assets in the lineup, with Taylor, who could play badly almost anywhere on the field, giving back -2.1. On the mound, Bunning and Short earned 8.6 WAA between them (4.8 for Bunning), but the staff overall earned +5 WAA while the lineup added +1, giving the team 85 wins. In 1966, Allen had 5.7 WAA, but Callison, who should have been at his peak at age 27, slipped to 1.5. The Phillies had traded young Alex Johnson (who eventually became a great hitter, but whose career was shattered by emotional problems) to acquire 32-year-old first baseman Bill White, who earned 3.2 WAA, and 35-year-old shortstop Dick Groat, who earned -0.6 because he could no longer hit. On the mound, Bunning had a fantastic season with 5.9 WAA, but Short fell all the way to average and the rest of the staff was below average. Early in 1966, the Phillies had given Ferguson Jenkins, destined to become one of the greatest pitchers of the Silent Generation, and Adolfo Phillips, who briefly became a superstar, to the Chicago Cubs in exchange for aging hurlers Larry Jackson, who earned +2.7 WAA, and Bob Buhl, who surrendered -1.5. This time the Phillies won 87 games. In 1967, Allen, who missed the last six weeks of the season after cutting his hand, had 4.6 WAA in 122 games, and center fielder Tony Gonzalez, usually a below average player, had a great year in the field and put up 3.9 WAA as well. But Callison was average now, having lost all his positive value in right field, and infielders Cookie Rojas and Bobby Wine and utility (?) man Taylor combined for -6.6 WAA. Bunning (4.8 WAA) was the best pitcher in the league, and Short returned to superstardom (4.1), allowing the staff as a whole to earn +8 WAA—but the team still won only 82 games, and declined much further in 1968. The weak lineup and bad luck kept Jim Bunning, one of the great pitchers of his generation, out of the Hall of Fame for decades, simply because he failed ever to win 20 games for the Phillies, with 19, 19, 19 and 17 in 1964–1967.

Yet the strangest, least understood team of the mid–1960s was the Cincinnati Reds, who finished second in the league by one game in 1964 and fell out of contention in the last week of the season in 1965. Although Frank Robinson remained a superstar with 6.3 WAA in 1964, the lineup as a whole was -6 WAA in 1964, partly because Vada Pinson had become a very poor center fielder. The entire strength of the team was in its pitching staff. Pitcher Jim O'Toole led the staff in 1964 with 4.1 WAA, and his teammate, Jim Maloney, had 3.4 in 216 innings. With nearly every other pitcher contributing at least 1 WAA, the staff led the league with +14 WAA. Although Frank Robinson fell all the way to 2.3 WAA in 1965—leading to a disastrous decision to trade him—the lineup did much better at the plate, with nearly every regular at 1–2 WAA, including Pete Rose (2.3) at second base. (First baseman Deron Johnson led the NL in RBIs with 130—but earned 1 WAA.) Despite dreadful fielding, the lineup earned +4 WAA, with by far the best hitting in the league. Maloney was the team MVP in 1965 with 5.9 WAA, second in the league behind Marichal among pitchers, and roughly equal to the contribution of Reds' pitching staff as a whole. The unlucky Reds led the league in run differential by 21 runs in 1964 and 17 in 1965, but came up empty. As in 1956, Crosley Field remained a hitters' park, and no one realized that the Reds easily had the best pitching staff in the league in 1964 and the second-best, behind the Giants, in 1965. Those pitchers, like so many others, were not destined to maintain their form for long. But by 1966, the Reds had added two players destined to play a role in a new dynasty: second baseman Rose and a young third baseman named Tony Perez. Another even more critical player, from the Boom Generation, arrived one year later.

The National League was deservedly known as the stronger league in the early 1960s and won four out of seven World Series and almost every All-Star Game from 1960–1966. With the exceptions of Mickey Mantle, Al Kaline, and a young Carl Yastrzemski, the NL had all the all-time greats now playing—Mays, Aaron, Frank Robinson, Clemente, Mathews, McCovey, Dick Allen, and Jim Wynn—on its rosters. But beyond those superstars, the NL seems to have been almost equally struck by the dearth of young talent during these years. The early Silent Generation cohorts (born about 1925–1929) had had careers wrecked by the Second World War and Korea; the later ones (born about 1936–1942) were severely impacted by low numbers at birth, and by the collapse of the minor leagues. That was why none of these great players had ever played on a truly great team. But starting in 1967, the far more numerous Boom Generation was about to arrive with a bang.

We left the American League in 1956, when Mickey Mantle had established himself as the dominant player for two seasons. He remained so, for the most part, through 1962, and the Yankees lost only one pennant from 1955 through 1964, in 1959. Like the National League, the American League trended towards mediocrity in the last years of the 1950s, only to undergo the profound shock of expansion, with striking consequences, in 1961. By the early 1960s, however, the shortage of superstars in the AL had become critical.

The Yankees comfortably won the pennant in 1957 and 1958, winning 98 games in 1957 but falling to a mediocre pennant winner with 92 in 1958. Mantle was the team's only superstar in 1957, peaking at 9.4 WAA (while Ted Williams hit .388 and had 8.3 of his own). But his supporting cast was slipping, and Skowron (2.6) and Gil McDougald (2.1) were the only other stars in the lineup, while Berra and rookie Tony Kubek were only average. Bobby Richardson, who took over from the traded Billy Martin at second, and Elston Howard, the regular left fielder, cost the team -3.5 WAA. The lineup earned +16 WAA and the pitchers +5. Tom Sturdivant topped the staff with 201⅔ innings pitched and 2.1 WAA, and veteran Bobby Shantz was second, while Whitey Ford pitched only 129⅓ innings. The lineup earned +17 WAA but the pitchers dropped to 2 in 1958. Mantle slipped to 5.7 WAA, dropping behind Al Kaline (6.8), largely because he fell from average in the field in 1957 to -16 runs in 1958. Young Norm Siebern hit well and picked up +17 runs in left field, cancelling out Mantle's problems, and giving him his only superstar season with 4.2 WAA. Ironically, Siebern's poor fielding cost the Yankees all three runs in a 3–0 defeat in the fourth game of the 1958 World Series. The lineup featured eight other players with at least 262 plate appearances, all of whom—veterans like Berra, Bauer, McDougald and Skowron, and younger additions like Kubek, Howard, and Jerry Lumpe—earned between 0 and 1.7 WAA. On the mound, Ford rebounded to 2.9 WAA in 1958, and Bob Turley and reliever Ryne Duren added 2.3 and 1.4. The rest of the staff was below average. Turley pitched 245⅓ innings to Ford's 219⅓, and luck allowed him to post a 21–7 record compared to 14–7 for Ford, whose ERA was nearly a run lower. He emerged from that season and a great World Series (winning Games 5 and 7) with the Cy Young Award and a greatly enhanced reputation, but he was never more than a good pitcher.

3. The GI and Silent Generation Era, 1946–1966

Closing the Books on the GI Generation, 1926–1959

In 1959, 36-year knuckleballer Hoyt Wilhelm, in his only season as primarily a starting pitcher, posted 4.4 WAA. This was not only his only superstar season, but the last one posted by a member of the GI Generation. This book, to repeat, defines greatness as at least five seasons of 4 WAA or more. Amazingly, the Lost and GI Generations, both of whom played their entire careers in the era of two eight-team leagues, had almost exactly the same number of men who achieved this, a total of 15 for the Lost and 16 for the GIs. The game, however, changed significantly from 1901–1925 to 1925–1946. Four of the Lost Generation greats were pitchers, but only two of the GI generation greats, Hal Newhouser and Wes Ferrell, made their living on the mound. Although Newhouser had two spectacular superstar seasons during the war, he proved in 1946–1948 that he could pitch at the superstar level in normal times as well. The most unfortunate Ferrell, as we have seen, toiled in obscurity for mediocre clubs and has never received any recognition for his greatness. Right behind Newhouser, with four superstar seasons each, came Carl Hubbell and Bob Feller. Feller would almost surely have added to his total had he not gone into the Navy from 1942 until late 1945. Warren Spahn had only three superstar seasons, but he had nine seasons of at least 2 WAA, second only to Hubbell's 11 among his generation. Clearly, however, this was an era largely ruled by hitters.

It is a principal finding of this book that pitching has been overrated by nearly everyone since the beginning of baseball time. Measured by their peak value—that is, the seasons in which they made an important contribution to getting their team over .500—the careers of many Hall of Fame pitchers are more similar to those of Hall of Fame catchers and middle infielders than to those of truly great hitters. Thus, GI Generation pitchers in the Hall of Fame include Red Ruffing, who had only one superstar season and three more of at least 2 WAA; Lefty Gomez, who had two superstar seasons and two more over two WAA; Dizzy Dean, who had two superstar seasons and four more over 2 WAA in his short career; Bob Lemon, who had three seasons over 2 WAA but no superstar seasons; and Early Wynn, who had two superstar seasons and two more over 2 WAA. It is most unlikely that Gomez, Ruffing, Lemon or Wynn would have gotten anywhere near the Hall had they not played most of their careers for very successful teams.

Among the hitters, Williams and Musial top the field with 13 superstar seasons each. War probably cost Musial one such season in 1945, but Williams, who missed almost five full years (1943–1945 and 1952–1953), would surely have equaled and possibly surpassed the leaders of the Silent Generation, Mays and Aaron, who finished with 16 superstar seasons each, had it not been for his military service. Next come Lou Gehrig, with 12; Mel Ott with 11; Jimmy Foxx with nine; and Johnny Mize, who missed three wartime seasons, with eight. Then come Greenberg, who missed most of five seasons in the war, and Joe DiMaggio, who missed three, with seven; Paul Waner, with six, and Joe Gordon, Charlie Keller, Jackie Robinson and Gil Hodges, with five each. Gordon lost three years to the war and Keller two.

Great hitters of this generation almost always found their way to the outfield (six out of 14) or first base (five out of 14). The remaining three all-timers were second basemen: Gordon, Gehringer, and Robinson, with five superstar seasons each. Under different circumstances, Gordon and Robinson (who played other positions but spent four of his superstar seasons at second) would surely have had more. All of them are now in the Hall of Fame, but so are Tony Lazzeri, who had two superstar seasons, and Bobby Doerr, who just missed having any, although he topped 3 WAA four times.

Three GI Generation shortstops—Arky Vaughan, Luke Appling, and Lou Boudreau—turned in four superstar seasons apiece. Just behind them came Joe Cronin, with three. No other generation remotely approaches that record at the most critical defensive position. Unfortunately, while all of them eventually found their way to Cooperstown—two via the Veterans Committee—the Hall has been unable to distinguish them from much lesser players who had the good fortune to play for pennant-winning teams in New York. The Hall has also admitted Phil Rizzuto, who topped 4 just once, in 1942, and 3 on one other occasion; Travis Jackson, who topped 3 twice; and Pee Wee Reese, who topped 3 WAA only once. Vern Stephens of the Browns and Red Sox, whose best four seasons were almost exactly the same as Rizzuto's, never received a single vote. Another chapter in this long history will be written in 2019.

Yet on the other hand, for reasons that would be very hard to uncover today, the GI Generation never developed anyone even close to greatness at third base. Incredibly, the leading GI performers at this position, based on superstar seasons, are Harland Clift of the St. Louis Browns in the 1930s and Al Rosen, a truly great player whose career was cut short on one end by the Second World War and on the other by injuries. Each of them posted exactly two superstar seasons, while Bob Elliott and Ken Keltner had one each. It was evidently easier for a great hitter to find a home at second base or shortstop than at third during this era. By the end of the 1950s, Eddie Mathews of the Silent Generation was clearly the greatest third baseman of all time.

Mickey Cochrane and Bill Dickey were by far the greatest catchers of the GI Generation. Cochrane had the first superstar season ever for a catcher (and the last one until 1956) in 1933, and topped 3 WAA on three other occasions; Dickey never broke that barrier, but also topped 3 WAA four times. Roy Campanella, whose career began late and who had several injury-plagued seasons, topped 3 WAA just twice. Ernie Lombardi, who earned 3.8 WAA in 1938, was never over 3 WAA again, but was posthumously elected to the Hall of Fame. Gabby Hartnett's peak years were extremely similar to Campanella's.

Even before integration, the production of great players, as we have seen, was reaching a peak in the late 1930s and early 1940s, when the war intervened. Had it not been for the war, the list of GI Generation players with five superstar seasons would surely include Bob Feller and Ralph Kiner, and probably Al Rosen as well. Johnny Pesky, who had superstar seasons at shortstop in 1942 and 1946 but missed the intervening years, might have equaled Boudreau, Vaughan and Appling. Monte Irvin might also be on the list if he had been signed a couple of years earlier. In my opinion, the GI Generation was the greatest baseball-playing generation of all time, simply because the highest number of young men among it went into professional baseball, it seems, around the age of 18—both absolutely and as a percentage of the population.

Although Mantle was the only hitting superstar in the AL in 1959, with 5.2 WAA, the only other asset in the lineup was Berra, who rebounded to 2.7 WAA after two average years, and Mantle contributed the lineup's total above-average value. The only other superstars in the league were two pitchers, Hoyt Wilhelm of the Orioles and Camilo Pascual of the lowly Washington Senators. The Yankees' collapse plunged the league into an unusual depth of mediocrity and opened up the way for the Yankees' perennial rivals, the Chicago White Sox and the Cleveland Indians. The Go-Go Sox, with a projected total of just 90 wins. beat out the Indians, who had a slightly better adjusted run differential, by five games, thanks to eight wins' worth of Pythagorean luck. In an astonishing, Don Newcombe-style performance, 39-year-old Early Wynn posted a 22–10 record for the offensively weak White Sox despite earning just 1.2 WAA in 255⅔ innings. Bob Shaw, who went 18–6 with 3.3 WAA, was a far superior pitcher. Second baseman Nellie Fox hit .306 with no power, but was completely average in the field and finished with 1.5 WAA—and the American League's MVP award. Shortstop Luis Aparicio, who generally saved 10–15 runs during his good seasons, had an off-year in the field as well, and was a below-average player despite his 56 stolen bases, worth +10 runs. The real star of the team was center fielder Jim Landis, who saved 25 runs in the field and just missed superstar status with 3.9 WAA.

White Sox owner Bill Veeck knew his team was not really very good, and he made a series of disastrous trades in the off-season, sending first baseman Don Mincher and catcher Earl Battey to Washington for aging power hitter Roy Sievers; first baseman Norm Cash and catcher John Romano to Cleveland for once-great Minnie Minoso; and young outfielder John Callison—who had four superstar seasons ahead of him—to the Phillies for Gene Freese. In the long run, those trades surely cost the White Sox pennants, but in the short run, remarkably, they did what Veeck had hoped they would do, raising the team's adjusted run differential by 43 runs to +127 in 1960, essentially as good as the rebounding Yankees. This time, however, Chicago's Pythagorean luck ran out, losing them three games, and they finished third behind the Yankees and the very lucky Baltimore Orioles.

The 1960 Yankees were transitioning from Stengel's teams, which used so many players at so many different positions, to the set lineup that Ralph Houk employed from 1961 through 1963. That lineup included homegrown second baseman Bobby Richardson and shortstop Tony Kubek, plus left and right fielders Hector Lopez and Roger Maris, and third baseman Clete Boyer, all acquired in trades from Kansas City. With the exception of the disastrous Richardson, who cost the team -3.3 WAA, all these younger players fielded brilliantly in 1960. Kubek and Boyer earned 1.8 and 1.6 WAA, and Lopez added another 1.8. Maris hit 39 home runs, saved 19 runs in right field, and emerged as the only offensive superstar in the wretched league with 6.4 WAA. Mantle missed superstardom for the first time since 1954, with 3.7 WAA, but veterans McDougald and Skowron chipped in with 2.4 and 3.5 WAA (Skowron's best year). All in all the lineup earned +20 WAA, a full nine of them in the field, but the pitching staff was one of the worst ever on a pennant-winner, costing the team -8 WAA. Art Ditmar, Ford and Turley pitched 566 essentially average innings, but the rest of the staff was dreadful. The team reached the 97-victory level of a superior pennant winner with the help of eight games of Pythagorean luck. It appropriately lost the seventh game of the World Series to the Pirates by the score of 10–9.

Expansion hit the American League in 1961, adding new franchises in Washington to replace the one that became the Minnesota Twins, and in Los Angeles. It also added eight games to the American League schedule. Thanks to an excellent pitching staff, the Los Angeles Angels achieved respectability in their very first season (and contended for much of their second one), and neither team was nearly as bad as the Mets in 1962. But the 25 percent increase in players that resulted from expansion from eight to ten teams had a very measurable effect on the average performance of both pitchers and hitters, drastically improving the relative performance of better players and the teams that were lucky enough to have them. In 1960, the AL had had just two superstars, Maris and Detroit pitcher Jim Bunning. In 1961, it had eight, all hitters. Mantle, still only 29, returned to peak performance with 54 homers and 8.8 WAA. Detroit first baseman Norm Cash hit .361 with 41 home runs and 8.3 WAA. Tigers great Al Kaline had 6.7 WAA, Orioles first baseman Jim Gentile earned 5.7, Tigers outfielder Rocky Colavito had 4.6, and Minnesota first baseman Harmon Killebrew had 4.3. Roger Maris suffered a decline in the field, where he saved about two games' worth of runs in 1960 but cost them about a game and a half in 1961, but set an all-time record with 61 home runs and won a dubious MVP Award with just 4 WAA. At the team level, the Yankees' pennant-winning percentage of .673 was the highest since the 1946 Red Sox, even though they won 109 games only with the help of six wins' worth of Pythagorean luck.

Bill James argued at length in his *Historical Abstract* that the 1961 Yankees were not really a great team despite their record-setting 240 home runs. Overall, these Yankees were roughly equal to Stengel's teams of 1953–1954 and 1956 and inferior to the best teams of the 1920s, and 1930s and early 1940s. When one examines their lineup in detail, however, James's argument looks very strong. After Mantle and Maris, the only star on the team Elston Howard, finally promoted to first-string catcher, who earned a superb 3.2 WAA. Kubek was average, Skowron and Boyer earned 1 WAA apiece, and second baseman Richardson—whom the Yankees should have let go in the expansion draft—surrendered an astonishing -4.2 WAA, making the infield as a whole a negative quantity.[29] The lineup earned +17 WAA, +12 of them at bat, compared to +20 WAA in 1960. The improvement was in the pitching staff, which added +4. Whitey Ford, used far more frequently by new manager Ralph Houk than by Stengel, set new personal records for starts and innings pitched (283) and had a 25–4 record—but earned only 2.1 WAA, suggesting that he received extraordinary run support. Bill Stafford and reliever Luis Arroyo actually pitched more effectively during their combined 314 innings than Ford did in his 283, earning a total of 4.0 WAA.

Among the second-place Tigers, Al Kaline was, along with Mantle, the only other all-time great to emerge in the American League in the entire decade of the 1950s. (Both of them, of course, were white; the National League could boast of Mays, Aaron, Frank Robinson, Clemente, and McCovey,[30] in addition to its two white all-timers, Eddie Mathews and Richie Ashburn.) Kaline, a bonus baby, had had his best season in 1955 at the age of 20 with 6.5 WAA. A great hitter and right fielder, he finished with six such seasons. Rocky Colavito,

---

29. As it happens, there was not the slightest chance of Richardson being left unprotected, since he had been named the MVP of the World Series thanks to an astonishing hitting performance against the Pirates, totally anomalous within the context of his whole career.
30. Ashburn, of course, had begun his career in 1948.

who had begun his career with the Indians and had a superstar season with them in 1958, had 4.6 WAA in 1961 and reached that level once more, in 1962. Cash had another superstar season in 1965 with 5.2 WAA, when he was the AL's most valuable offensive player. The Tigers hit just as well as the Yankees in 1961 but their fielding and pitching were only slightly above average.

Only a very few new superstars emerged during the next four years, and the league regressed rapidly towards mediocrity in the last three years of the Mickey Mantle dynasty, 1962–1964. The Yankees were a mediocre but comfortable pennant winner in 1962 with 96 wins (the Minnesota Twins were second with 91) but recovered to the superior level with 104 wins in 1963 and beat an essentially equal Minnesota team thanks to five wins' worth of Pythagorean luck. In 1964, the Yankees squeaked through in a three-way race with the White Sox and Orioles with 99 victories. Mantle remained one of the league's two offensive superstars in 1962 with 4.8 WAA, earned 2.3 in 1963 in less than 70 games after sustaining his second major knee injury, and recovered to 3.7 in 1964 despite other injuries. In 1962, Mantle's terminal decline in center field began, as he surrendered nearly ⅓ of the 6 WAA he earned as a hitter there. The only other star in the lineup was Clete Boyer, whose 2.8 WAA came almost entirely in the field, and Maris and rookie Tom Tresh added just 2.7 WAA between them in the outfield. Richardson, Kubek and Howard were all about average. The situation among the pitchers was similar: Ford earned 3.8 WAA and Ralph Terry 1.9, but the rest of the staff gave them all back.

The 1963 team achieved its improvement without a single superstar. Major injuries held Maris to 3.4 WAA in 90 games and Mantle to 2.4 in 65, but Tresh added 3 and Howard rebounded from an average season to 2.4. The lineup earned only 10 WAA but the pitchers added 8, one of the best Yankees staffs ever. Second-year man Jim Bouton was the actual ace of the staff with 2.9 WAA, and Al Downing added 2.5. Whitey Ford worked his customary magic again: he earned only 2.5 WAA, but finished with a record of 24–7 (Bouton was 21–7.) The Minnesota Twins team that lost to the Yankees because of worse Pythagorean luck began with the league's genuine MVP, Bob Allison, who hit .271 with 90 walks and 35 home runs, good for 6 WAA. The Twins also had Harmon Killebrew, a great power hitter, who had cracked the superstar barrier in 1961 but earned just .8 WAA in 1962, 1.8 in 1963 and 1.9 in 1964 because the Twins unwisely put him in the outfield, where he surrendered -12 to -23 runs. Another fine young player, outfielder Jimmie Hall, earned 3.3 WA, and catcher Earl Battey had 2.3. Hall's career was eventually wrecked by a beaning. Despite the presence of second baseman Bernie Allen (-2.6 WAA), the lineup earned +6 WAA. The pitching staff had a remarkable year with +12 WAA, led by the second-most valuable player in the league, Camilo Pascual (5 WAA), Bill Dailey (2.7), and Lee Stange (3.1). Because Metropolitan Stadium was a hitters' park, their pitching was unappreciated. Twins rookie outfielder Tony Oliva, although already 25, took over the league MVP from Allison in 1964 with 5.9 WAA, although he had to settle for "Rookie of the Year" honors instead.

The Yankees' victory in 1964 was nothing short of miraculous. While the hitters earned a total of 51 runs above average, the team benefitted from 44 runs' worth of run luck. The individual statistics told the story. Mantle, Maris, and Howard remained stars, with 3.3, 2.6 and 2.7 WAA. But Joe Pepitone at first (-0.6 WAA), Richardson at second (-5.8 WAA, one of the worst performances in history), Kubek at short (-0.6) and Boyer at third (-2.9 thanks to a dreadful year at the plate), the Yankees had the worst infield ever seen on a pennant winner.[31] Once again the pitchers helped save the day with +7 WAA, led by a remarkable 4.3 WAA from 35-year-old Whitey Ford, his second and last superstar season, 1.9 from Bouton, and 1.8 from Mel Stottlemyre, a late-season call-up who pitched just 96 innings. With 99 victories, the Yankees won the pennant by one game.

Under the circumstances, the Yankees' collapse in 1965–1966 was not surprising. Mantle in 1967 was shifted to first base, where he spent the remaining two years of his career. Although Bill James wrote in his *Historical Abstract* that Mantle was a substantially superior player to Willie Mays at their peaks, that turns out not to be correct once accurate fielding statistics are taken into account. Mantle's three best seasons earned his team 9.4 (1957), 8.8 (1956), and 8.8 (1961) WAA; Mays's best seasons were worth 9.2 WAA (1954), 8.2 (1958), and 8.1 (1964), and he also had 8.0 in 1965. Mantle's superiority was only marginal, and he played in a weaker league. Over their careers, Mays and Henry Aaron both had twice as many superstar seasons as Mantle, 16–8. Mantle was very unlucky that the designated hitter rule did not come in sooner. In his last year, 1968—the "year of the pitcher"—his hitting earned the Yankees 4 WAA thanks to his power and on-base-percentage, and even with -16 runs at first base pulling him down to 2.4 WAA, he was still a star.

The Orioles contended for the pennant into the last week in 1964 thanks to third baseman Brooks Robinson, who posted his first superstar season with 4.3 WAA, and first baseman Boog Powell, with 5.1 Thanks to his great numbers at third base, where he saved 37 runs in 1964 and at least 12 for four years after that, Robinson posted two other superstar seasons during the 1960s, and ties with Ron Santo as the third-most valuable third baseman of his generation, behind Eddie Mathews and Ken Boyer. Remarkably, the greatest strength both of the 1964 Orioles, who finished two games behind the Yankees, and of the White Sox, who finished just one game back, was their fielding. Led by center fielder Jackie Brandt (+25 runs saved), third baseman Robinson, shortstop Luis Aparicio—just acquired from the White Sox—and second baseman Jerry Adair, the fielders as a whole earned +7 WAA compared to just +2 for the hitters and +4 for the pitchers. The White Sox fielders were even better, earning +9 WAA compared to -2 for their hitters and +7 for their pitchers. Their glove men were led by shortstop Ron Hansen (+25 runs saved), third baseman Pete Ward (+14), and outfielder Gene Stephens (+11). Their pitching star was Joel Horlen, who earned 3.4 WAA in just 211 innings, with a 13–9 record and a 1.88 ERA.

In 1965, the Minnesota Twins reached the level of a superior pennant winner with 102 wins, led by right fielder Tony Oliva, who remained at the superstar level for the second of three consecutive seasons with 4.3 WAA. Bob Allison, still very much a star and a great fielder, added 3.8 in left, Killebrew earned 2.7 (and fielded quite adequately at third and first) in only 113 games, and shortstop Zoilo Versalles, who won the MVP that Oliva deserved, had 3.1. Oddly, both Oliva and Allison were clearly much better fielders than Jimmie Hall, the regular center fielder, who earned only 1.4 WAA. An excellent Twins lineup

---

31. Utility man Phil Linz helped a bit with 1.6 WAA in 112 games.

earned +17 WAA—the same as the 1961 Yankees—and the pitching staff just +2. No player has more clearly been kept out of the Hall of Fame by bad luck and injury than Tony Oliva. To begin with, thanks in part to the Castro revolution in Cuba, he was 25 by the time he played his first full season in the big leagues. Then, after four superstar seasons and four star seasons in eight years, he was stricken with terrible knee injuries. Although the DH rule allowed him to continue, he was so crippled that he was a below-average player for the last five years of his career. His peak, however, is very comparable to Minnie Minoso's, and superior to Orlando Cepeda's or Tony Perez's—though not as good as Jim Wynn's.

In 1966, the last year of the GI-Silent era, the Baltimore Orioles were transformed by the addition of the first Silent Generation all-timer to move from the National League to the American, Frank Robinson, and the addition of some excellent younger players. That 1966 team, however, inaugurated a new dynasty, and we shall postpone discussing it until the next chapter, to which it properly belongs.

Because of the general and steadily worsening shortage of talent, the best teams of the 1946–1966 era were substantially less dominant than those of 1926–1945. While 63 percent of the pennant winners in the earlier era had been superior, only 40 percent of the new era's pennant winners reached the .630 threshold. Stengel and Houk's Yankees won more often not because they were better than Huggins' and McCarthy's, but because their league was worse. As 1967 dawned, baseball was on the verge of momentous changes. To begin with, thanks to the drought in hitting superstars and rule changes favoring the pitchers, offense was about to fall to an all-time low during the next two years. A new round of expansion was also only two years away. Meanwhile, in 1965, the major leagues had instituted amateur drafts. No longer would they bid tens of thousands of dollars for untested prospects just out of high school. And as luck would have it, in 1967 the first of the massive Baby Boomer postwar cohorts, those born in 1946, was turning 21. The nation's colleges were also emerging as an alternative route to the major leagues, which they had rarely been for the last 40 years. Helped by expansion, a new supply of superstars was about to create two new great dynasties, and to revive interest in the national pastime, which in the mid–1960s had been dramatically losing ground to professional football.

4

The Silent and Boom Generation Era, 1967–1983

The Boom Generation (b. 1943–1960) made its entrance onto the superstar stage in 1967, led by center fielder Paul Blair of the Orioles (4.8 WAA), 19-year-old pitcher Gary Nolan of the Reds (4.1), and pitcher Jim Merritt of the Twins (4.3). Gary Nolan and Jim Merritt, like so many young pitchers, never reached that level again, but Paul Blair would undoubtedly have wound up in the Hall of Fame had he not been beaned in 1970. Partly because of the expansion that took place in 1969 and partly because of the trough in talent in the late Silent Generation, the impact of the Boom Generation was unprecedented. Beginning in 1907, when Ty Cobb had his first great season, the Lost Generation had 18 superstar seasons in four years. Beginning in 1926, the GI Generation contributed 15 such season in four years. The Silent Generation, as we have seen, was the slowest to get going, with only one superstar season in 1946–1949. From 1967 through 1970, the Boom Generation put up 21 superstar seasons. They arrived at a propitious moment.

By 1967, a new war was well underway, and draft calls had substantially increased to fill the ranks of units on their way to Vietnam. This time, baseball's response—like that of the draft-age population—was more nuanced than during the Second World War or the Korean War. Six years' service in the military reserve or National Guard—usually with only about six months' of full-time duty for training—was now an alternative to being drafted, and during the Vietnam era, major league organizations proved remarkably adept at getting their top prospects into reserve or guard units. Undoubtedly, as in the early 1940s and early 1950s, a great many possible careers were aborted or pre-empted by military service among the Boom Generation as well, but the impact of Vietnam on baseball seems to have been much less than that of the two earlier wars, even though it drew far more young men into the military than Korea had.

Of the three Boomer superstars of 1967, only Jim Merritt was a major player in the great drama of the season, the American League pennant race, in which Boston, Minnesota, and Detroit went into the last day in a virtual tie, having eliminated the White Sox from the race only two days before. The main actor in that drama, of course, was the Red Sox's left fielder, Carl Yastrzemski, who won the Triple Crown with an average of .326, 44 homers

4. The Silent and Boom Generation Era, 1967–1983

and 121 RBIs. In a year of low offense, even those figures were considerably more impressive than they looked.

As usual in four-team pennant races, none of the contenders could be reckoned even a superior team. Winning just 92 games, the Red Sox had the second-lowest winning percentage of any pennant winner in the pre-playoff era. Yastrzemski, now 27, had already posted superstar seasons of 5 WAA or more in 1963 and 1966, but in 1967 his performance, at bat and in the field, accounted singlehandedly for 10 of their 11 WAA—the greatest single season ever put up by a hitter from the Silent Generation, marginally better even than the best seasons of Mickey Mantle and Willie Mays. Tony Conigliaro, who was on his way to a superstar season at age 22 when he was beaned in August, earned 3.2 WAA in just 92 games, and first baseman George Scott also starred with 3.4 more. Unfortunately outfielder Jose Tartabull and three catchers surrendered -8.6 WAA among them, and the lineup was only +7 overall. The team's pitchers earned +6 WAA, contributed mainly by Jim Lonborg, who went 22–9 while earning 2.6 WAA, and Lee Stange, who added 2.4.

Yastrzemski, astonishingly, had nearly as dominant a season in 1968, the Year of the Pitcher, as he had in 1967. With offense at an all-time low, his .301 average, 121 walks, 23 homers and 74 RBIs once again made him the batting champion and the league MVP (in fact, if not on the writers' ballots), with 9 WAA. But the rest of the team's hitters plummeted, the pitching fell below average, and Boston was lucky to finish five wins above .500, 17 games behind the pennant-winning Tigers. Although Yaz had another fantastic season with 7.9 WAA in 1970, barely missing a fourth batting title, the team suffered in 1969–1970 from very poor fielding and never managed to contend for the pennant. Injuries cut into Yaz's production substantially in 1971–1972, but he returned to superstar form with 4.3 and 4.1 WAA in 1973–1974. He did much less well in 1975, but new teammates, as we shall see, picked up the slack. He had one more great year, in 1977, and finished his career with eight seasons of 4 or more WAA, well behind Mays, Aaron, Clemente and Frank Robinson, but even with Mickey Mantle and Eddie Mathews among the Silent Generation. He was the first all-time great to play his whole career in the post-expansion era.

The big story of 1968 in the American League was the Detroit Tigers, a superior pennant winner with 103 victories. *Their* big story, in turn, was Denny McLain, who by dint of effort, a league-leading (for pitchers) 5.5 WAA, his teammates' batting prowess, and luck, posted an extraordinary 31–6 record with a 1.96 ERA. Starter Earl Wilson and relievers John Hiller and Pat Dobson contributed the rest of the staff's +9 WAA, while Mickey Lolich, the hero of the World Series, was average during the season. McLain was actually just as valuable in 1969, when he went 24–9 in a much bigger hitting year and earned 5.9 WAA. McLain was still only 25 with three superstar seasons to his credit, but his career came a cropper after 1969, when he was suspended for half a season for involvement with illegal gamblers. He was never effective again. Although the Tigers in 1968 lacked a single .300 hitter (as did every American League team except Yaz's Red Sox), they fielded a strong lineup, with two remarkable exceptions. Center fielder Jim Northrup was a superstar with 4.3 WAA, while catcher Bill Freehan (3.3), first baseman Norm Cash (2.8), Al Kaline (2.6 WAA in 102 games) and Willie Horton (2.2 despite dreadful fielding), were stars. Unfortunately, infielders Don Wert (who hit .200), Ray Oyler (who hit .135) and Dick Tracewski surrendered a combined -8.5 WAA, leaving the lineup +12 WAA. The team was aging, however, and after 1968 they were no match for one of the greatest dynasties of the twentieth century: the Baltimore Orioles of 1969–1975.

In 1969, as in 1961–1962, expansion widened the gap between the league's best and worst players and teams. The Orioles won their first pennant in 1966 with only 97 wins, but from 1969, the year of MLB's second expansion to 12 teams and two divisions in each league, through 1971, they had one of the most dominant runs in baseball history. There had been 22 superstar performances in the two leagues in 1968; there were 29 in 1969. Winning 109, 108 and 101 games, the Orioles were great in 1969–1970 and superior in 1971, when they missed four games and finished with a 101–57 record. After a severe slump in 1972, they won the American League East again in 1973–1974 and remained the best in the American League East in run differential in 1975. Unfortunately for their reputation, they lost close playoff series to the Oakland As in 1973–1974, and lost the division to a somewhat inferior Red Sox team in 1975. One would have to go back to McCarthy's Yankees (1936–1943) to find comparable dominance; Stengel and Houk's Yankees won more often, but against weaker leagues, and with a smaller margin of superiority. But just how the Orioles managed to accomplish this has never really been understood, not even, perhaps, by general manager Harry Dalton and manager Earl Weaver, who put the team together.

The Orioles had won their first pennant in 1966 with only 97 wins, after acquiring Frank Robinson—one of the three greatest players in the National League, along with Mays and Aaron—from Cincinnati in exchange for Milt Pappas, a slightly above average pitcher, and two undistinguished players. Robinson had slumped from 6.3 WAA in 1964 to 2.6 in 1965, prompting the Reds to trade him before he reached 30, but he dominated the American League in 1966, winning the Triple Crown and posting 6.4 WAA. (Given that that was almost identical to his 1964 mark, it suggests that the average strength of the leagues may have been pretty close to the same.) Thanks to first baseman Boog Powell (2.1 WAA), left fielder Curt Blefary (2), and third baseman Brooks Robinson (just 1.7 thanks to an off-year in the field), the 1966 lineup earned +12 WAA. Veteran shortstop Luis Aparicio and rookie center fielder Paul Blair were average. Manager Hank Bauer handled his young pitching staff like his mentor Casey Stengel. Twenty-three-year-old Dave McNally and 20-year-old Jim Palmer each pitched about 200 average innings, while older relievers contributed most of the staff's +6 WAA. During the next two years, Brooks Robinson returned to the superstar level and Paul Blair reached it, but pitching problems and an injury to Frank Robinson in 1967 kept the team out of contention that year, and poor hitting left them 12 games behind the Tigers in 1968.

The 1969–1971 Orioles rank with the Yankees of the late 1930s as one of the most dominant dynasties in history. While their hitting was their greatest single strength, they showed the most extraordinary balance of any such team. In 1969, when they took advantage of a new round of expansion to win 109 games, their hitters earned +14, WAA, their fielders +9, and their pitchers +7. Thirty-three-year-old Frank Robinson topped the team with 5.5 WAA, and 25-year-old Paul Blair had his second superstar year in three seasons with 4.7, saving 23 runs in center field. Boog Powell was the team's third superstar with 4.5 WAA, and the rest of the lineup was at least average. Among the pitchers, 23-year-old Jim Palmer, who had missed almost all of the previous two seasons, threw 181 superb innings and wound up with a 16–4 record and exactly 2.8 WAA. Mike Cuellar, acquired by trade, was right behind with 2.5, and as so often happens on such dominant teams, Dave McNally managed to put up a 20–7 record with just 0.7 WAA. Still, this team, one of the greatest of all time, lost the World Series to the miracle Mets.

The 1970 team slipped somewhat but won only one less game (108) with the help of four wins' worth of Pythagorean luck. This time Powell (4 WAA) was the only superstar in the lineup, but Blair added 3.8 WAA in 133 games before he was beaned, Frank Robinson had 3, and left fielder Don Buford improved to 2.5. Twenty-seven-year-old Merv Rettenmund, who had taken much too long to find a place in the majors, earned 3.6 WAA in just 106 games. For the second straight year, shortstop Mark Belanger was a big liability at the plate but made up for it with +17 runs saved in the field. This year Jim Palmer pitched 305 innings and wound up with 3.4 WAA, nearly the entire positive value of the staff. Cuellar was average and McNally earned 1.2 WAA, but they finished with a combined 48–17 record. The fielders contributed +4 wins.

The 1971 team remained a superior pennant winter and won their third straight AL pennant with help from other players. Frank Robinson and Powell slipped to 2.4 and 2.3 WAA, and Paul Blair, sadly, fell to average after his 1970 beaning and was never the same player again. Rettenmund, however, showed his 1970 performance was no fluke with an outstanding 4.8 WAA, and Don Buford added 4.2, the only superstar season of his career. Brooks Robinson regained his mastery in the field and added 2.5 WAA, second baseman Davey Johnson improved from about average to 2.1, and Belanger created an average number of runs at bat and finished with 1.1 WAA overall. The big story of the 1971 Orioles was that they became the second team in history (the 1920 White Sox were the first) with four 20-game winners: Palmer, Cuellar, McNally, and Pat Dobson. The pitching staff was the best of the dynasty, with +10 WAA overall, thanks to Palmer (2.9 WAA), McNally (2.1), Dobson (2) and Cuellar (1.7).

The aging Orioles suddenly fell to a record of 80–74 in 1972, but new players allowed them to rebound smartly in 1973, easily winning their division with a 203-run differential that should have been worth 102 wins (they won 97). The team's most valuable player was its new superstar, second baseman Bobby Grich, who followed up an excellent rookie season with 6 WAA, a shade behind George Scott, now of the Milwaukee Brewers, who had his greatest season and was the genuine AL MVP of 1973. Although Grich hit only .251, he walked 116 times, hit 12 homers, and saved an astonishing +34 runs in the field, leading Orioles fielders in one of the greatest defensive performances in the history of major league baseball. While a series of Orioles first basemen and catchers turned in average performances, Mark Belanger saved +22 runs and an aging Brooks Robinson still saved +19. The outfield featured average performances in left and right field, but Paul Blair saved +23 more runs in center. All told the Orioles' defense saved 115 adjusted runs, worth +12 wins, trailing only the 1940 Cincinnati Reds. Their pitchers earned only +2 WAA but that hardly mattered. In 1974 the Orioles' fielders did only half as well, and their pitching slipped into negative numbers, but luck gave them five extra wins and they nosed out the resurgent New York Yankees with just 91 victories. In 1975 the Orioles fielders, led by Belanger (+33 runs), Grich (+25), and Blair (+19), earned the team ten extra wins. Jim Palmer broke the superstar barrier for the first time with 4.2 WAA, Grich was even better with 5.5. and despite average pitching, their run differential was 56 runs better than the pennant-winning Red Sox, whom we shall look at later. The Orioles, however, fell four wins short of their Pythagorean projection while the Red Sox beat theirs by six and won the pennant. Grich had also had 4.7 WAA in 1974. He finished 14th, 19th and 9th in the MVP voting in those three years.

The Orioles were the first great dynasty of the divisional era, and no subsequent team has matched their 1969–1970 record in games won. But their post-season fate established another critical fact about baseball after 1969: that being a dynasty was not worth as much as it had previously been. The Orioles had a superior run differential to every team but one that they met in the playoffs and World Series from 1969 through 1974, but they reached the World Series only three times in five attempts. It has only become harder to translate real greatness into World Series victories in subsequent decades.

In 1969 and 1970, the Orioles had defeated the Western Division champion Minnesota Twins in the playoffs, each time in three games. They beat the Oakland A's in 1971, but lost to them in 1973 and 1974 in five and then four games, several of them decided by a single run.

We have seen that from the time of the late 1950s, when they were still the original Washington Senators, the Minnesota Twins under Calvin Griffith's ownership had had a remarkable record of player development. After reaching the World Series in 1965, the Twins slumped in 1966, but added Rod Carew at second base and fought the Red Sox and the Tigers down to the final day of the season in 1967. Two Twins, Killebrew and pitcher Jim Merritt, turned in superstar seasons of 5 and 4.3 WAA, respectively, but the team lost the pennant in the field. Their league-leading pitching staff and their hitters earned +10 and +5 WAA, respectively, but the same players gave up more in the field than they earned at the plate, 60 runs' worth a full -7 WAA. Their many infielders, including Killebrew, Carew (who would improve), Rich Rollins and Cesar Tovar, gave up -43 runs, and center fielder Ted Uhlaender (surely one of the worst players in the league) and an aging Allison were nearly as bad in the outfield. In 1968 roughly the same cast cost the team -5 WAA in the field, and both Killebrew and Oliva went down with injuries as the team plummeted. In the off-season, Griffith let go manager Cal Ermer, and the extraordinary managerial career of Billy Martin began with a bang.

In the first of a long series of astonishing managerial achievements, Martin in 1969 improved the Twins' record from 79–83 to a division-winning 97–65. Only by improving across the board could a team do so much. Their only superstar (4.5 WAA) was ace pitcher Jim Perry, although Carew, who won the first of many batting titles in only 123 games, and Killebrew, who won the league's MVP Award with 49 homers and 140 RBI, each had more than 3 WAA. The fielders, however, improved all the way to average. Cesar Tovar, previously an infielder, eventually replaced Uhlaender in center field and saved +12 runs, Oliva saved +2 more in right, and shortstop Leo Cardenas, acquired from Cincinnati in a trade, turned a liability into a +14 run asset. Billy Martin had been a Twins coach for some years, and subsequent events proved beyond a doubt that he could recognize good and bad fielders and replace the latter with the former. The Twins' lineup was +12 and their pitching staff +7. Unfortunately, Martin's first year as a manager was a preview of things to come in other ways. He had frequent conflicts with management, he beat up one of his best pitchers, Dave Boswell, in a fight outside a bar, and Calvin Griffith fired him in the off-season and replaced him with Bill Rigney. But the Twins managed to repeat in 1970 with 98 wins, helped by a tremendous season at bat and in the field by Tony Oliva (5.1 WAA), and their fielding became a modest asset. But for the second year in a row, the great Orioles team eliminated them in the playoffs in three straight games.

The Twins in 1971 gave way to the second budding dynasty of the era, the Oakland A's. The A's won five consecutive division championships in the next five years, and three World Series in 1972–1974. They had moved to Oakland in 1968, and the Oakland-Alameda County Coliseum, a round Bauhaus edifice with huge foul territory, favored pitching at the expense of hitting. And thus, like their great rivals the Baltimore Orioles, they were destined to be misunderstood and celebrated for their pitching staff, which was in fact the weakest part of their team.

The overall strength of the A's was more comparable to Casey Stengel's Yankees than to the Orioles, whom they supplanted as pennant winners. Only once, with the help of six wins' worth of luck, did they win even 100 games. Their eccentric owner, Charlie Finley, had evidently been blessed during the 1960s with a fine staff of scouts, and they were the first team to win pennants with the help of several superstars from the Boom Generation. The most important of these, born in 1946, became one of the two greatest outfielders of the Boom Generation: Reginald Martinez Jackson. Jackson reached post-season play 11 times for three different teams in his 21-year career, and he turned in eight seasons of at least 4 WAA. Yet without questioning his greatness, it is hard to look at his record and not conclude that he might have done even better and become what he seemed likely to become in 1969: the Willie Mays or Henry Aaron of his generation.

Drafted out of college in 1966, where he had played football, Jackson was taller than Mays and longer-limbed than Aaron. The young Jackson had an extraordinary body, combining slimness and muscles, speed and power. After a superstar rookie season in 1968 (4.2 WAA), Jackson in 1969 outperformed the entire American League, hitting just .275 but drawing 114 walks, with 36 doubles and 47 home runs. Together with the +11 runs—a full win's worth—that he saved in right field, that gave him a league-leading total of 8 WAA—almost exactly the same total as that turned in by Willie Mays in 1954, when Mays was also just 23 years old. But in sharp contrast to Mays, Jackson, who had hit only ⅓ of his 1969 homers in the second half of the season, became embroiled in a lengthy contract dispute with Charlie Finley, slumped all through 1970 and finished only slightly above average, and was thus largely responsible for the A's failure to contend seriously that year.

During the next five years, Jackson was usually the best player on the division-winning A's, with seasons of 5.3, 3.8, 5.7, 6.2 and 5.3 WAA from 1971–1975—seasons that would be right at home in the career records of Mays and Aaron. He was not, however, the team MVP in 1971. That honor fell to one of the truly tragic figures of the Boom Generation, 22-year-old Vida Blue, who went 24–8 with an ERA of 1.82 in 312 innings pitched, good for 5.4 WAA. No other Oakland pitcher came within a whole run of Blue's ERA, and despite his fantastic season, the pitching staff as a whole was only average. Blue, like Jackson and so many other Boomers, did not believe that he should have to wait any longer to be paid what he was worth, and he held out into the strike-delayed 1972 season. He succeeded in more than quadrupling is salary to $63,000 for 1972, but pitched only 151 mediocre innings and started only one of the A's 12 post-season games that year. Blue, like so many other young phenoms, seems to have hurt himself during his 1971 season, and he remained a completely mediocre pitcher in 1973–1974 before rebounding to 1.8 WAA in 1975 and 4.4 in 1976, when the A's had fallen out of contention. Yet he was the most dominant starting pitcher that the A's ever had during their dynasty.

The A's were, in fact, another dynasty playing in a pitchers' park whose pitchers were never nearly as good as they appeared to be. Their pitching staffs, which included Catfish Hunter, Ken Holtzman, Blue Moon Odom, and reliever Rollie Fingers, earned -1, +5, -7, +4, +5, and 0 WAA in 1971–1975. The only two seasons of more than 2 WAA turned in by Oakland pitchers during these years were Blue's in 1971 and Hunter's 3.6 WAA in 1972. Few pitchers have had more deceptive records than Hunter. From 1967 through 1976, he was extraordinarily durable, pitching between 234 and 328 innings a season. But he was above average in only four of those ten years: 1967, 1972, 1974, and 1975, and he had only two seasons over 4 WAA. In 1975, the 29-year-old Hunter rewarded George Steinbrenner, who had signed him to the first free-agent contract in modern history, with 5 WAA in 328 innings. (An arbitrator had declared Hunter a free agent after Finley had refused to make annuity payments called for by his contract. The Messersmith-McNally decision that ushered in the era of free agency followed the next year.) But like Lefty Gomez, Red Ruffing, and Whitey Ford before him, Hunter was pitching for dynasties, and he won between 20 and 25 games every year from 1971 to 1975. His post-season record of 9–6 was no better than his regular season stats, but he played on very good teams, had high visibility, a catchy nickname, and 224 career wins, and he is now in the Hall of Fame.

Charlie Finley, the A's owner, continually acquired new veterans, and Dick Williams, the manager in 1971–1973, liked to use the whole roster. The A's lineup had fewer stars than the Orioles but generally managed to avoid playing a severely below average player. In 1971, Jackson (5.1 WAA) and Sal Bando (2) were the only stars, with Joe Rudi and Bert Campaneris adding 2.6 WAA. The lineup as a whole earned +15 WAA. In 1972 Jackson slumped to 3.8 WAA, but Bando had 2.5 and first baseman Mike Epstein had a great year with 3.8, as the team won without a superstar. Finley promptly traded Epstein (whose career immediately collapsed) in 1973 to make room for Gene Tenace at first, and Tenace responded with 2.3 WAA in 1973, the lineup's best year, while Bando added 2.5. Jackson had a great year with 5.6 WAA (and won the league MVP Award), and a new center fielder, fleet Billy North, saved +29 runs in the field and nearly equaled Jackson with 5.4 WAA. Second basemen Dick Green and Ted Kubiak saved +32 runs, shortstop Bert Campaneris—whose fielding was consistently worth at least one win per year—saved +21, and left fielder Joe Rudi saved +11. All told, the team's fielders balanced the wretched pitchers, earning the team +8 WAA, while the hitters added +15 and the lineup totaled an outstanding +24. The same Oakland fielders earned the team +4 extra WAA in 1974 and +3 in 1975. In 1974, the line-up's biggest stars were Jackson (6.2 WAA), North (3.7), Tenace (3.2) and Campaneris (2.2), although this year the second basemen and catchers were liabilities and the line-up slumped to +10 overall. In 1975, the line-up rebounded to +17 WAA with three superstars: Jackson (5.2 WAA), North (4.3), and Tenace (4.1), while nearly everyone else was at least average.

Luck, surely, played a huge role in the record that the A's established in 1971–1975. They won six out of eight post-season series, but nearly all of them were extremely close, and two of the three teams they beat in the World Series—the 1972 Reds and the 1974 Dodgers—had much better records than they did. Their luck ran out in 1975, when they lost three straight to a decidedly inferior Red Sox team. But they were the first Boomer dynasty, symbolized, in this respect, by their garish uniforms, long hair, and mustaches, which Finley encouraged the entire team to grow in 1972. Finley, who understood what free agency meant, began breaking up the team in 1976, trading Jackson to the Orioles with one year left on his contract. Jackson had his last great year with the Orioles that season, with 6 WAA. The next year, George Steinbrenner signed him to the Yankees. There Reggie won new fame and fortune, but he had gained at least 20 pounds and lost much of his athleticism, and he was never the same player again. Jackson was only 31 when he reached the Yankees, but only once in his Yankees career, in 1980, did he reach 4 WAA. In a famous incident in the summer of 1977, Yankees manager Billy Martin pulled Jackson from a game at Fenway Park and nearly engaged him in a televised fist fight in the dugout because he thought Jackson had loafed in the field. Martin had a point: Jackson was now a mediocre fielder and got worse. In his late 30s, when Mays and Aaron were still putting up superstar seasons, Jackson became a below-average player for his last team, the California Angels. With eight superstar seasons in his career, he was very great. He could have been even better.

Jackson was the first all-time great to sign a free agent contract, and his subsequent career illustrates the great pitfall of the free-agent era. He was already a ten-year veteran when the Yankees signed him, and for the rest of his career with them he was almost always a star, not a superstar. Even though players could now become free agents after only six seasons, that pattern was destined to be repeated by other players and teams again and again. While expensive free agents could provide 1–3 WAA per year, they very rarely provided the superstar performance that nearly every pennant winner needs. Those, in the vast majority of cases, had to be developed at home or acquired very young in trades.

Three new teams dominated the American League from 1975 through 1980: the Yankees and the Red Sox in the East, and the Kansas City Royals in the West. After several years of contention, the Yankees won the pennant in 1976 with a mediocre 97 wins. The team featured three superstars in the field. Their MVP was left fielder Roy White, now 33, who had been one of the top players in baseball in 1970–1971, with 6.4 and 7.4 WAA, and who added 4.8 in 1976. His strengths as a hitter were somewhat obscured by Yankee Stadium, and his brilliance in the field, where he was one of the best left fielders of all time, was largely unrecognized. Right behind in 1976 was third baseman Graig Nettles, now 31, who earned 4.5 WAA. Although Nettles batted only .254, he had 29 doubles, 32 homers, and 62 walks. More importantly, he was a great third baseman, and this was also his third superstar season (the other two having come with the Cleveland Indians.) Fleet center fielder Mickey Rivers, another big defensive asset, was right behind with 4.1 WAA, and 21-year-old rookie second baseman Willie Randolph, a tremendous fielder, just missed being the fourth superstar with 3.9 WAA in just 125 games. Following in the footsteps of Berra and Campanella, catcher Thurman Munson was voted the league MVP by the writers even though his 2.5 WAA ranked him fifth on the team.

Billy Martin, in his first year as Yankees manager, had worked his particular magic at once—magic that has never been understood until now. When we last met Martin, he had quickly moved the Minnesota Twins from sub-.500 to the playoffs in 1969, largely by improving their defense. Between then and 1976, he had already transformed two other teams in similar fashion, only to be let loose by frustrated owners. In 1971, Martin had taken over the Detroit Tigers, whose fielders had cost them -8 WAA in 1970. They improved to -3 WAA in 1971, whereupon they acquired two fine infielders, shortstop Eddie Brinkman and third baseman Aurelio Rodriquez, from the Washington Senators, in exchange for now-worthless pitcher Denny McLain. In 1972 their fielding improved to average, and they won their division. As usual, Martin failed to last out the next season, but was hired almost immediately by the Texas Rangers (formerly the Senators.) The Rangers finished 1973 at –9 WAA in the field, but Martin improved them to -6 in 1974. Their fielding was above average in 1975 when Martin was fired in mid-season.

The 1975 Yankees, who had finished third, were already a fine defensive ball club, whose fielders were worth +5 WAA. The additions of Randolph at second and Rivers in center field in off-season trades improved them +4 WAA, and their line-up was now worth +9 games over .500 in the field and +11 more at the plate. Randolph had been acquired essentially as a throw-in in a swap of established pitchers (the Yankees received Doc Ellis for Doc Medich), while Rivers and pitcher Ed Figueroa came from the Angels for Bobby Bonds, who had produced 4.6 WAA for the Yankees in 1975. The trade worked out well for the Yankees; Rivers managed to match that figure, and Bonds was never nearly that good again. But while the Yankees line-up was good enough to have won 101 games, their pitchers, led by starters Catfish Hunter, Ed Figueroa, Doyle Alexander, and an aging Ken Holtzman, were uniformly below average, and together cost the team -4 WAA. It is no wonder that the Yankees fell rather easily to the overpowering Cincinnati Reds in their first return to the World Series in a dozen years, and no surprise that Martin was not particularly happy at Steinbrenner's decision to sign a slowing Reggie Jackson for the next year.

The Yankees now fought out two year-long pennant races with the Red Sox, who had won a fortuitous pennant, and nearly a World Series, in 1975. They won only 95 games, and their projected win total was four wins lower than the Orioles' and essentially tied with the Yankees'. The big story on that Red Sox team, of course, was the arrival of what looked like one of the finest pairs of rookies in history, Fred Lynn and Jim Rice. Rice was destined for greatness, but as a rookie he hit only 22 homers, walked just 36 times, and cost the team ten runs in the outfield, earning under +1 WAA. Lynn took the nation by storm, hitting .331 with 21 homers and 105 RBI to Rice's 102. But he was only average in the field—despite a number of memorable catches—and his 4.2 WAA ranked him 13th in the league. Publicity, the luck of the Red Sox, and his handsome face nonetheless won him a near-unanimous MVP Award. The Red Sox's true most valuable player was their third outfielder, Dwight Evans, who saved an astonishing 30 runs in right field and nosed out Lynn with 4.6 WAA. Another asset was catcher Carlton Fisk. An exact contemporary of Bench and Munson, Fisk had begun his career as well as either of them, with 4.8 WAA in 1972, and despite injuries he was still worth 1.7 WAA in 79 games 1975. Unfortunately, Yastrzemski had a mediocre year, and three infielders—Rico Petrocelli at third, Rick Burleson at short, and Doug Griffin at second—combined for -6.9 WAA. First basemen Cecil Cooper and outfielder Bernie Carbo, however, combined for 3.4 WAA in a little more than a season's worth of at-bats. The team's six wins' worth of Pythagorean luck was its single biggest asset, beating out the +5 WAA of the lineup and the +4 of the pitching staff, where Luis Tiant, Bill Lee and Roger Moret were all modest assets. The Sox came astonishingly close, of course, to beating a great Cincinnati Reds club in the World Series, but it should not have been surprising that they fell out of contention in 1976 when the hitters slumped.

In 1977, the Yankees eliminated the Red Sox and the Orioles from the division race on the next-to-last day of the season. In 1978, the Red Sox roared off to a big lead while turmoil amidst the Yankees once again led to the mid-season firing of Billy Martin. But New York roared back in the second half of the season, the Red Sox swooned, and the race was eventually won by the Yankees in a one-game playoff. These were expansion years for the American League, marked by the advent of the Toronto Blue Jays and Seattle Mariners, and superstar seasons increased accordingly.

Just as in 1948–1950, the real strengths and weaknesses of these Red Sox and Yankees teams were completely misunderstood. Once again, and despite the illusions created by Fenway Park and Yankee Stadium, the Yankees had the better lineup and the Red Sox the better pitching. The Yankees did not have a single offensive superstar in either 1977 or 1978, but their line-up posted +16 WAA 1977 and +15 in 1978. Rivers led the team with 3.5 WAA in 1977, and Jackson, Randolph, White, Munson and Nettles remained stars. On the mound, rookie Ron Guidry and reliever Sparky Lyle combined for 4.2 WAA, but starters Ken Holtzman and Catfish Hunter gave them back, and the pitchers were barely above average. Munson and White fell out of the star category in 1978, but Randolph was the best player in the lineup with 3.5 WAA and outfielder Lou Piniella added 3.2 in 130 games. Ron Guidry had one of the most amazing seasons of the era on the mound, going 25–3 and earning 6.2 WAA, but starter Ed Figueroa and reliever Rich Gossage were the only other assets on the staff, earning 2.5 WAA between them, and the pitchers as a whole were worth just 2 WAA. With 100 wins in both 1977 and 1978, the Yankees did not rank as superior pennant winners.

Don Zimmer, who managed the Red Sox during these years, was known for his antipathy towards pitchers, but ironically, he came as close as he did to two pennants because of them. In an early, privately published *Baseball Abstract,* Bill James described the 1977 Red Sox pitching staff as the best in the league. That, it turns out, was an understatement. The great Ferguson Jenkins, acquired from the National League at the age of 34 (2.1 WAA), Reggie Cleveland (1.9), Luis Tiant (1.6), Don Aase (1.9), and relievers Bill Campbell (3.1 in 140 innings) and Bob Stanley (1.3 in 151 innings) earned an astonishing +13 WAA, the highest total in the American League during this whole era. Astonishingly, although the pitching staff's personnel changed drastically the next year, Dennis Eckersley (a superstar with 4.8 WAA), Tiant (3.6), Stanley (2.2), Jim Wright 1.3), and newly acquired Mike Torrez (1.2) did nearly as well in 1978, earning +10 WAA. But despite some outstanding individual performances, pitching was the *only* pennant-worthy part of the Red Sox in those years.

The Red Sox's lineup was only average in 1977, and earned +5 WAA in 1978. Jim Rice became a superstar in 1977 with 4.2 WAA, and Yastrzemski had his last great year at age 37 with 4 WAA. Carlton Fisk added 2 WAA behind the plate, but second baseman Denny Doyle and rookie third baseman Butch Hobson—a favorite with the press—surrendered a combined -7.8 WAA. Lynn was below average in his second consecutive poor season.

The Red Sox's offense was almost exactly as good in 1978, while their dreadful fielding improved all the way to -2 WAA. The biggest offensive hero in 1978 was Jim Rice, who had his greatest season with more than 400 total bases, 46 homers, 139 RBI, and 6.1 WAA. Fisk, with 2.9 WAA, was the only other star in the lineup. Yaz and Lynn were both average, and infielders George Scott, Jerry Remy, Rick Burleson and Hobson combined for -5.6 WAA. Man for man, the Red Sox in 1977–1978 were simply no match for Steinbrenner's Yankees.

A very heated MVP controversy erupted in 1978 between Rice, indisputably the league's best hitter, and Yankees left-hander Ron Guidry, who went 25–3 with an era of 1.74. Remarkably enough, their value turns out to have been identical: Guidry's 6.2 WAA edged out Rice's 6.1 by the equivalent of a single run. Rice eventually proved himself one of the best players of his generation. He became a good Fenway Park left fielder, and while he never came close to his 1978 figures and his production declined after roof boxes were added to Fenway Park, he finished his career with five seasons over 4 WAA, the last of those in 1986, when the Red Sox finally won the pennant again. The vast majority of players with five such seasons, as we have seen, are in the Hall of Fame—and so is he. Dwight Evans, with only three seasons over 4 WAA, was not as good and is not a strong Hall of Fame candidate now. Lynn had only one other superstar season after 1975—in 1979.

Luis Tiant—no longer the ace on the Red Sox teams of 1977–1978—of all the Silent Generation pitchers has been by far the most unfairly treated by the Hall of Fame. Tiant had four superstar seasons over his long career: 5.1 WAA in 1968 when he led the AL in ERA, 5.3 WAA in 1972 when he nearly pitched the Red Sox to the pennant, and 6.9 and 4.7 in 1974 and 1976 for two mediocre Red Sox clubs. Those four seasons tie him with Koufax, Robin Roberts, Jim Bunning, and Juan Marichal for third among his generation. Tiant, however, also had three more seasons over 3 WAA, while Marichal and Roberts had only one such season each and Koufax none. Tiant's peak value is far superior to that of Whitey Ford, Don Drysdale, and Gaylord Perry, all of whom are in the Hall of Fame. He is, sadly, the Wes Ferrell of his generation, but he is still very much alive and the Veterans Committee could redeem some of its mistakes by voting him in.

The Yankees' hitters were getting older, and in 1979 they lost nearly all of their edge at the plate and fell to fourth place, even though their fielders still were worth +6 WAA. The winners were the Baltimore Orioles, who just missed the level of a superior pennant winner with 102 wins. They did it with extraordinary balance. An entirely new offensive cast included outfielder Ken Singleton, young first baseman Eddie Murray, and outfielder Gary Roenicke, each of whom earned more than 3 WAA. The lineup earned +10 WAA and the pitchers 8, even though Mike Flanagan led them with 2.2. Even though Brooks Robinson had retired and Bobby Grich had signed with California (helping them win the AL West that year), a new generation of fielders earned them +5 wins. In 1980, the Orioles' run differential was marginally superior to the Yankees again, but the Yankees had better luck and beat them out by three games with 103 wins, reaching the superior level for the first time since 1963 with the help of six wins' worth of Pythagorean luck. Reggie Jackson, having his last great year at the age of 34, turned in 4.7 WAA, and Willie Randolph had 3.5. The team had aged and their fielders were now only average, but the pitchers, led by two aging hurlers, Rudy May and Tommy John, earned +6 wins. But this time the Yankees could not get by the new power in the AL West, the Kansas City Royals, whom they had beaten in three consecutive playoffs from 1976 through 1978.

The Kansas City Royals were the most successful expansion team in baseball history, taking only three years (1969–1971) to post a positive run differential, and only eight years to win their first division championship. They did it, as their no. 1 fan Bill James pointed out, by trading older players from promising young ones and developing some brilliant talent of their own. But never during their division-leading run did the Royals reach the level of a superior pennant winner, peaking in 1977 with 102 wins. The Royals played on artificial turf and looked like a highly athletic team with unusual speed. Except in 1977, however, when their pitchers had a banner year worth +8 WAA, their strength was almost entirely at the plate. It began with the great George Brett, one of the two greatest third basemen of the Boom Generation (and surely one of the five best of all time), who had 5.7 WAA in 1976, 5.6 in 1977, 3.6 in 1978, 6.7 in 1979 (when the team's pitching collapsed completely and they missed the playoffs), and 7.4 in 1980, when he missed almost a quarter of the season but finished the year with an average of .390, even now the best since Ted Williams in 1941. He generally hit well over .300 during this phase of his career, with about 20 homers and 45 walks a season, and until the early 1980s he was also an excellent third baseman. His supporting cast, however, was consistently uneven. Thus, in 1977, the team's best year, while Hal McRae joined Brett with 4.5 WAA and right fielder Al Cowens had 3.5, center fielder Amos Otis was perfectly average, and infielders John Mayberry at first, Frank White at second, and Freddie Patek at short combined for -4.3 WAA.

In 1978, the Royals added one of the most unique players in baseball history to their line-up. Willie Wilson, then 22 years old, was a switch-hitter from Montgomery, Alabama, and one of the fastest men ever to play the game. As such he was perfectly suited to the Astroturf of Royals Stadium both as a hitter and an outfielder. Wilson's game suffered at the plate because he refused to learn the strike zone and averaged only about 30 walks a year, but he hit .300 in five out of six years from 1979 through 1984, stealing between 34 and 87 bases in each of those years. Last but hardly least, he was in those years one of the greatest outfielders in the history of baseball. Playing mostly left field and occasionally filling in for Amos Otis in center in 1979–1980, Wilson saved +33 and +35 runs in those two years. He saved +26 in strike-shortened 1981, and +32 in 1982. As a result, Wilson posted 5.5 WAA in 1979 and an astonishing 7.9 WAA in 1980, edging out George Brett for team MVP. While Wilson and Brett combined for 15.3 WAA in 1980, when the Royals reached the World Series, the lineup as a whole earned just +10. Wilson was nearly as valuable in 1981 and had 6 WAA in 1982, when he won the batting title. Wilson apparently became addicted to cocaine during the next season, and although he played a major role in the Royals' 1985 world championship team, he never achieved the level of his early years again. But with four consecutive superstar seasons, he had more peak value than many players who are in the Hall of Fame.

The Royals' pitchers, meanwhile, were almost uniformly mediocre. They did not have one significantly above-average starter in 1976. Led by Dennis Leonard (3.2 WAA), their pitchers improved in 1977, winning +6 WAA (far more than their fielders), but slumped to -4 WAA in 1979, when they failed to win the pennant. They were essentially average in 1980–1981. In 1980 Larry Gura turned in their best season on the mound in this period, with 3.8 WAA, but the rest of the staff was below average. The Royals of 1976–1981 played in six post-season series and lost five of them, winning only the playoffs against the Yankees in 1980. Only in the World Series of 1980, however, do they appear to have lost to a lesser team. When the Royals finally won the World Series in 1985 over the Cardinals, they had become a completely different team with different strengths and weaknesses.

In 1977, their best year, the Royals had to deal with one of the more extraordinary teams of modern history, the Chicago White Sox, who contended for much of the season but finished in third place with 90 wins. Bill Veeck, who had previously owned the Indians (1945–1949), the Browns (1951–1953), and the White Sox (1959–1961), had bought the club again in 1975. The team was dreadful in 1976, winning only 64 games, and Veeck signed a series of aging veterans, none of them ever a superstar, to short-term contracts for 1977. He also had one genuine star, center fielder Chet Lemon. The most noteworthy feature of the team was its outfield. Lemon in center field hit well enough to earn about 1 WAA and saved an astonishing +31 runs in the outfield, making him nearly a superstar for the year. Left-fielder Ralph Garr hit .300, as he had often done in the past, but gave back -22 runs in the field. Right fielder Richie Zisk had 30 homers and 101 RBIs, but gave back 13 of his 20 offensive runs above average in the field. Shortstop Alan Bannister surrendered -22 extra runs, and second baseman Jorge Orta gave up a full -36. All told, the line-up in the field was average, earning +10 WAA at the plate and surrendering -10 WAA in the field. The pitchers, led by Francisco Barrios and Lerrin LaGrow (4.2 WAA between them), earned +7 WAA overall, the real strength of this most unusual team.

Four other teams played significant roles in American League pennant races in the late 1970s and early 1980s. The California Angels, owned by Gene Autry, were among the first teams to try to buy their way to the World Series by signing free agents, and won division titles in 1979 with 88 wins and 1982 with 93. The problem with this strategy, which was not thoroughly recognized at the time, was that most players were past their prime by the time they became eligible after six years of service. The great Bobby Grich had joined them from the Orioles in 1977 but promptly lost most of that season to injury and did poorly in 1978. He rebounded to 3.9 WAA in 1979, making him the team MVP. Rod Carew, now a first baseman, rivaled Reggie Jackson as the top American Leaguer of the 1970s at Minnesota, with seasons of 7.8 WAA in 1977 (when he hit .388), 6 WAA in both 1975 and 1976, and 4.7 in 1973. Acquired by California in 1979, he posted just 1.3 WAA, although he reached 3.5 in 1982, when the Angels won the division again. Carew, who became a more than adequate second baseman after his first few years, finished his career with six seasons over 4

WAA, one more than Joe Morgan.[32] Brian Downing added 2.4 WAA in 1979. The oddest performance came from a veteran outfielder acquired from the Orioles organization, Don Baylor. Baylor hit .296 with 71 walks and 36 homers. His offensive value—about 4 WAA—nosed out Grich and Downing to lead the team, but he was a defensive liability and earned 3.2 WAA overall. Thanks to the on-base percentages of the players in front of him and some excellent hitting with men on base, however, Baylor led the league with 139 RBIs, and the writers voted him the MVP Award, one of the worst choices in history. The Orioles beat the Angels in the 1979 playoffs in four games.

The Angels continued acquiring more high-priced free agents, and in 1982 they fielded a better playoff team, winning 93 games despite three losses' worth of bad Pythagorean luck. The lineup, +15 WAA, accounted for all their superiority. Their MVP was Doug DeCinces, a fine third baseman acquired from Baltimore in a trade, who posted his only superstar season with 5.9 WAA. Seven of the eight regulars were over 30, but Brian Downing (4.7 WAA), Fred Lynn (3.2), Rod Carew (3.4) and Reggie Jackson (3.5) turned in remarkable seasons. Unfortunately, 31-year-old shortstop Tim Foli cost them -3 WAA. Their pitching was average, but they took a 2–0 lead in the playoffs against Milwaukee before losing three straight. The flaw in the Angels' long-term strategy emerged immediately, as most of them fell back to earth and they regressed to below .500 the next year.

The Milwaukee Brewers team that beat them in the playoffs had been contending for several years thanks to a hitting corps that included first baseman Cecil Cooper, shortstop Robin Yount, and third baseman Paul Molitor. In 1982 their lineup was +22 WAA, good enough to have won 103 games with average pitching—which, as it happened, they did not have. Only the 1969 Orioles—who of course did not have a DH—had as good a lineup in the whole 1967–1983 era. Yount, the league MVP in fact as well as on the writers' ballots, had 6.7 WAA, Cooper had his best of three superstar seasons with 4.2, and Molitor and second baseman Jim Gantner rounded out one of the best infields in history with 3.9 and 1.2. The outfield featured Gorman Thomas in center and Ben Oglivie in left, each earning 2.4 more WAA. Yount, who had reached the majors at 18 in 1974, eventually posted four seasons of at least 4 WAA, and although he rapidly became a defensive liability both at shortstop and later at center field, he finished his career with more than 3,000 hits and became a Hall of Famer, arguably the most valuable shortstop of his era. The Brewers' pitchers in 1982 cost them -4 WAA, and they won only 95 games.

The third team of interest was the resurgent Oakland A's. Owner Charlie Finley, who had done much to bring about free agency by failing to meet the terms of Catfish Hunter's contract in 1974, was not about to pay his stars what they could command on the open market. In 1976, he traded Reggie Jackson and Ken Holtzman to the Orioles, and tried to sell Vida Blue, Joe Rudi, and reliever Rollie Fingers to the Red Sox and Orioles, sales that Commissioner Bowie Kuhn blocked. Sal Bando also departed as a free agent. In 1979, the A's had a record of 54–108. At the end of that year, Finley hired Billy Martin, who had just finished

---

32. In one of his annual Abstracts, Bill James in effect credited manager Gene Mauch's decision to move Carew to first base in 1977 for Carew's greatest season that year. The expansion of the American League was surely at least as responsible for it.

a second stint as manager of the Yankees, as both manager and general manager. Martin worked his magic again. The A's in 1980 improved from -8 WAA to + 11 WAA in the field, from -14 WAA to -1 WAA at bat, and from −9 WAA to -5 WAA on the mound. Largely because of their fielding, the entire outfield of young Rickey Henderson, Duane Murphy and Tony Armas performed at a superstar level, with 7.8, 4.9 and 4.8 WAA respectively. (Their total of 17.5 WAA did not equal the 18 WAA of DiMaggio, Keller and Heinrich on the 1941 Yankees, however.) This was the first of 12 such seasons for Henderson, who by this measurement was the greatest player of the Boom Generation. Pitcher Mike Norris also had 3.2 WAA. The team's infield, obviously, was very weak, and both their hitting and pitching was below average overall. Typically, the media attributed most of the A's success to their pitching staff, which was actually well below average. Henderson did even better during the shortened 1981 season, and the A's made the expanded playoffs that year, swept the Royals, but failed to win a game against the Yankees. Martin typically was fired halfway into the 1982 season. The team's pitching collapsed completely in 1982–1983, and the A's did not rebound until late in the decade. The rapid decline of their pitching staff should not have been such a big surprise.

Nineteen eighty three was the first year of the post–Earl Weaver era in Baltimore, and the team rewarded successor George Bamberger with a world championship. First baseman Eddie Murray, by far the best at his position in the Boom Generation, had the third of eight consecutive superstar seasons, with 4.7 WAA. The team and league MVP, however, was 23-year-old shortstop Cal Ripken, with 5.3. This was a true two-man team—the rest of the lineup was below average. Even more than Reggie Jackson, Ripken looks in retrospect as if he could have had a considerably more valuable career than he did. 1983 was the first of only three superstar seasons that he posted, although the other two were truly phenomenal, 7.4 in 1984 and 6.9 in 1991. He remained at least an adequate shortstop for the whole of his career. But his three next-best seasons were all in the low 2 WAA range, and he was a below-average player overall for the last ten years of his career, from 1992 through 2001. His successful quest for Lou Gehrig's consecutive game record, in my opinion, cost him and his team a great many wins above average. Robin Yount was more valuable to his team overall. The strength of the 1983 Orioles was quite evenly divided between hitting and pitching, with Scott McGregor and Mike Boddicker posting 6 WAA between them. The American League was now in the midst of a stretch in which eight different teams would win pennants in eight years, seven of them without reaching the level of a superior pennant winner.

The St. Louis Cardinals won the first two National League pennants of the Silent/Boomer era in 1967–1968, winning 101 and 97 games. They had two superstars in 1967, first baseman Orlando Cepeda, who was awarded the league MVP with 5.7 WAA, his greatest year, and Lou Brock, with 4.1. Brock had replaced Maury Wills as the National League's stolen base king, but his 52 thefts (in 70 attempts) were worth only five extra runs to the Cardinals. Despite his great speed, Brock was only average in left field, and with only three superstar seasons apiece in their careers, he and Cepeda are most fortunate members of the Hall of Fame. The 1967 lineup also included center fielder Curt Flood (3.9 WAA) and catcher Tim McCarver (3.2 in 134 games, the only above-average season of his long career.) The pitching staff earned +4 WAA.

4. The Silent and Boom Generation Era, 1967–1983

In 1968, the year of the pitcher, the Cardinals won 97 games with the help of five wins' worth of Pythagorean luck. Bob Gibson, who had missed much of 1967 with an injury, led the Cardinals to the pennant with the most extraordinary pitching performance of the modern era. In 305 innings, Gibson posted a 22–9 record and a 1.12 ERA. That was enough to earn him a well-deserved league MVP, and the outstanding 6.7 WAA added up to almost half the team's projected wins over .500. Left fielder Lou Brock joined Gibson with his third and last superstar season, at 4.6 WAA. Flood repeated his near-superstar performance (3.8 WAA), but Cepeda fell to average and McCarver fell way below it. The lineup earned only +9 WAA, and the pitchers—despite Gibson's 6.7 WAA—only +5. As it turns out, their highly touted double play combination of Julian Javier and Dal Maxvill was overrated. Javier, an average hitter, was only an average fielder in 1967 and cost the team a game at second base in 1968. Maxvill won the team about two games in the field in 1967 and one in 1968, but he was the worst hitter in the league in 1967, costing the team nearly three wins at the plate, before improving almost to average in 1968. Converted outfielder Mike Shannon was an average third baseman and a modest offensive asset in 1968. Balance allowed the Cardinals to prevail over the second-place Giants, where McCovey and Mays each had 4.3 WAA in 1967 and improved to 6.3 and 4.4 in 1968, and whose pitching was very comparable to the Cardinals in both of those years. Again their supporting cast let them down.

Gibson's 1968 season is heavy with irony. On the one hand, because the league ERA was so low—2.99—the 6.7 WAA that he earned with his ERA of 1.12, while very impressive, was not unprecedented in his era. Koufax and Marichal had topped it with 7.1 and 7.8 in 1963 and 1965, respectively, and the best single season for a Silent Generation pitcher was Dean Chance's 8.4 WAA for the Los Angeles Angels in 1964. But Gibson is now remembered primarily for that 1968 season—when he deserves to be remembered as by far the most dominant pitcher of his generation. While Koufax and Marichal each finished his career with four superstar seasons, Gibson had eight, the most since Lefty Grove, and a figure that was not topped until the 21st century. He had topped 4 WAA four times in five years from 1962 through 1966. Like Denny McLain in the AL, Gibson followed up his 1968 season with one almost exactly as good in 1969, with 6.6 WAA, even though the increase in offense left him with less impressive traditional stats. He reached the superstar level again in 1970 and 1972. No other pitcher from the GI, Silent or Boom Generations was so dominant for so long.

The best hitter in the National League in 1967 was Henry Aaron, who adjusted his hitting stroke to take advantage of the high altitude in Atlanta's Fulton County Stadium and topped the league with a career-best 8.5 WAA—very close to Mantle's and Mays's best marks. Aaron chalked up another 6.7 WAA in 1968, but Roberto Clemente, who won the batting title at .357 and saved 24 runs in the field, had 8.1 WAA in that year, the third consecutive season in which he had topped 7. The rest of the Braves and Pirates, alas, were well below average in those years. Aaron hit just .307 with 39 homers in 1967 and .287 with 29 homers in 1968, but these were two of the worst offensive seasons in the history of baseball, and he was never more dominant within his league. As we saw in the last chapter, the National League was in the midst of a severe drought of young talent.

Nineteen sixty nine was the year of one of the most celebrated, mythologized and misunderstood teams in the history of baseball, the Miracle Mets. The nature of baseball changed in both leagues, partly because of rule changes designed to increase offense, such as lowering the height of the pitching mound, but partly because of expansion, whose effect was once again dramatic. In the National League, the new Expos and Padres were a combined 57 wins below average—the negative equivalent of three 100-victory teams. So bad were their records that every other team in the National League but one, the Philadelphia Phillies, scored more runs that they allowed. The impact of expansion was much less in the AL, where Seattle's run differential was only -17 wins below 500 and Kansas City's just -12, better than either Cleveland or California. As in 1962, the NL expansion contributed to a very exciting two-team race, this time between the Chicago Cubs under Leo Durocher, who had moved them into contention in 1967, and the Mets, in the new National League Eastern Division. As so often happens in pennant races, the strengths and weaknesses of the two teams were completely misunderstood.

Shea Stadium was a pitchers' park—though hardly an extreme one—and the Mets in the last three years had come up with a superb arm from the new Boom generation. Tom Seaver had joined them in 1967 at age 22 and promptly turned in seasons of 2.5 and 3.8, WAA, although the rest of the team was so bad that he won only 16 games in each of those two seasons. Jerry Koosman had been nearly as good in 1968, with 3.4 WAA, although the team had won just 73 games. With the help of expansion, Seaver improved to 3.8 WAA (and a record of 25–7) and Koosman posted 3 WAA (17–9) in 1969. But the rest of the pitching staff, including 22-year-old Nolan Ryan, was mediocre—and the great strength of the 1969 Mets was *not* on the mound.

Overall the 1969 Mets pitching staff won +4 WAA, leaving no doubt that all of them except Seaver and Koosman were below average as a group. Despite a tremendous season at the plate by left fielder Cleon Jones, their hitters were -2 games WAA. But their fielders saved a remarkable 87 runs, worth nine wins, lowering the pitchers' ERAs by half a run a game. That was part of the reason that Seaver went 25–7 without reaching the superstar level. The team's fielding heroes were center fielder Tommy Agee, who saved +12 runs; Jones, a former center fielder himself, who saved +20; and shortstops Bud Harrelson and Al Weis, who saved +16 between them. Jones's combined hitting and fielding gave him 6.8 WAA, second-best in the league behind Willie McCovey (7.7), who did win the MVP Award. Interestingly enough, the Mets' fielding also did a great deal to win the World Series as well, especially in Game 3, when Gary Gentry was the winning pitcher with the help of two catches by Agee that may have saved five runs between them. Given that the team's fielding fell to +6 games in 1970, it does seem that luck, in the form of a lot of balls hit just within reach of the Mets' fielders, also played a role. Beyond Jones the only star in the lineup was center fielder Tommie Agee (3.2 WAA), but everyone else in the lineup was average except for Wayne Garrett at third (-2.3 WAA.) The Mets earned +8 WAA in the field, surrendered -2 WAA at the plate, earned +4 on the mound—and won 100 games, three wins shy of a superior pennant winner, thanks to eight wins' worth of Pythagorean luck.

The Mets won the NL East, of course, by overhauling the Chicago Cubs, who had led the division for most of the year. The Cubs in 1967 had finished third, and in 1968 they had been exactly average in every phase of the game, pitching, hitting, and fielding. Because they played their home games in daylight in Wrigley Field, the best hitters' park in the league,

4. The Silent and Boom Generation Era, 1967–1983

and because their line-up featured third baseman Ron Santo, shortstop-turned-first baseman Ernie Banks, and left fielder Billy Williams, the nation thought of them as an offensive powerhouse. But they were not, even in 1969. Although Santo had been a tremendous hitter in the mid–1960s, posting seasons of 6.2, 6.6 and 7.4 WAA in 1964 and 1966–1967, he had fallen to 3.0 in 1969 and fell rapidly thereafter. With only three superstar seasons, he was only a marginal Hall of Fame candidate. Billy Williams had 4 WAA in 1969, the first of five consecutive superstar seasons and seven overall, expansion having turned him from a star into a superstar. But Banks had not been a superstar since 1959, and in 1969 he was the worst player in the lineup, with -1.7 WAA. Everyone else was average; the line-up as a whole earned one win.

The real story of the 1969 Cubs was their pitching. Ferguson Jenkins and Bill Hands, who went 21–15 and 20–14, respectively, earned the Cubs 3.8 and 5.0 WAA, respectively, and Ken Holtzman and Dick Selma combined for 3 more. Jenkins eventually finished his long career with three superstar seasons (peaking at 5.9 in 1971), three more seasons over 3 WAA, and four more seasons of more than 2 WAA—ten star or superstar seasons, far more than many of his fellow Hall of Famers. The Cubs' pitchers earned the team +10 WAA, +6 more than the Mets'. And in fact, the Cubs' adjusted run differential was essentially the same as the Mets, but while the Mets exceeded their Pythagorean won-lost percentage by eight wins, the Cubs missed theirs by two. In that sense the Mets' victory was miraculous, and it is not in the least surprising that they did not become a dynasty. They swept the Atlanta Braves, who won the very evenly divided NL West with only 93 wins, and won four straight from the great Orioles team after losing the opening game of the World Series.

Tom Seaver finished his long and distinguished career with four superstar seasons, third among the Boom Generation. His best year was 1973, when he singlehandedly won the Mets the NL East with 8 WAA while the team finished with a record of 82–79. Seaver, however, was the unluckiest player that we shall encounter within the framework of this book, since he also had three seasons with 3.8 WAA and one with 3.9. His 11 seasons of 3 WAA or more top Bert Blyleven by one, even though Blyleven had six superstar seasons to Seaver's four. Both of them, of course, pitched most of their careers with mediocre clubs.

Four teams dominated the National League for the remainder of the 1970s: the Cincinnati Reds and the Los Angeles Dodgers in the West, and the Pittsburgh Pirates and Philadelphia Phillies in the East. Of the four, the Reds were easily the strongest, reaching their peak in 1975 with 108 wins. While they did not enjoy a three-year peak comparable to the 1969–1971 Orioles, they averaged one additional win more from 1970–1976 than the Orioles did from 1969–1975. They won the National League pennant in 1970, 1972, and 1975–1976, and the NL West in 1973, when they were beaten by the Mets, who won the NL East with a record of 82–79. Their four superstars were divided between the Silent and the Boom Generations, and all of them were offensive players whose value came mainly from their hitting.

The 1970 Reds went 102–60, but that record was 11 games better than their run differential would have indicated. Their line-up contributed their entire +10 WAA. They were clearly a team of both strengths and weaknesses. They had three offensive superstars that year: catcher Johnny Bench, the official MVP (5 WAA), third baseman Tony Perez (5.1), and rookie left fielder Bernie Carbo (4 WAA in just 126 games.). Right fielder Pete Rose (3.8 WAA) and center fielder Bobby Tolan (3.5) were also stars. But the lineup also included first baseman Lee May, who combined 34 homers with a .297 OBP and was perfectly average; shortstops Woody Woodward and Dave Concepcion, who cost the team -2.3 WAA between them; and second baseman Tommy Helms, probably the worst player in baseball, who cost the team -5.1 WAA, just as many as Perez earned. 1970 was Tony Perez's greatest season, although he topped 4 WAA again in 1972–1973. Although a high error total gave him a poor reputation as a third baseman, he was actually quite adequate at the position. Johnny Bench, meanwhile, was establishing himself as the greatest catcher in the history of baseball. As a 20-year-old rookie in 1968, he had broken in with a very impressive 3.2 WAA, improved to 3.7 in 1969 and won the league MVP Award in 1970 with 5, the highest total ever posted by a catcher to that date. As we saw in Chapter 3, it has been impossible for catchers to sustain superstar levels of hitting for more than a few years, and their defensive value was limited in the first half of the century for the simple reason that there are so few ways for them to save runs. But stolen bases were way up by 1970, and Bench saved the team +15 runs in the field thanks to his great arm. He eventually topped 4 WAA three times (1970, 1972, and 1974), and was over 3 WAA in two other seasons. His three seasons over 4 WAA are the all-time record for a catcher, and his overall record is far superior to any previous man behind the plate.

Not surprisingly given their lack of any distinguished pitchers, the Reds in 1970 were beaten by the great Orioles in five high-scoring games. Almost everything went wrong for the Reds in 1970, when Tolan missed the entire season and Bench, Rose and Perez all slumped badly. General Manager Bob Howsam responded with one of the greatest trades in the history of baseball, sending Tommy Helms, first baseman Lee May (who had just had his best season), and throw-in Jimmy Stewart to the Houston Astros for pitcher Jack Billingham, young outfielder Cesar Geronimo, infielder Denis Menke, throw-in Ed Armbrister, and one of the five greatest players of the Boom Generation, second baseman Joe Morgan.

In retrospect, the Houston Astros, rather than the Kansas City Royals, clearly should have become the first expansion team to create a genuine dynasty. By 1967, their roster included three Hall of Fame-caliber players in their early twenties: Joe Morgan, Rusty Staub, and Jim Wynn. In 1972, when only Wynn of those three players was even 30, they also added Cesar Cedeno, who posted 6.7 WAA as a rookie—the most valuable offensive player, in fact, in the NL—and 4.6 WAA in 1973, but faded rapidly after that. Unfortunately, no one seemed to understand how badly both that low-hitting era and the Astrodome, where it was very difficult to hit, hurt these players' statistics.

No modern player has been treated more unfairly by Hall of Fame voters than Jim Wynn. Wynn posted seven seasons over 4 WAA, peaking at 6.6 in 1965. There is not one other player in the history of major league baseball, including Joe Jackson and Wynn's contemporary Dick Allen, who has seven such seasons and is not in the Hall of Fame. He had very good power—obscured until 1974 by the Astrodome—and excellent on-base percentages, and he was a very adequate center fielder. But he never received a single Hall of Fame vote from the BBWAA, and he did not appear on the most recent Veterans Committee ballot for his era, even though he had more than twice as many superstar seasons as Ron

Santo, Orlando Cepeda or Tony Perez, who have been elected. Such was the impact of playing in the worst hitters' park in the league during a low-offense era.

It took expansion to turn Rusty Staub into a superstar in 1969, but by that time the Astros had traded him to the new Montreal Expos, where he proceeded to top 4 WAA for three years in a row. Joe Morgan, to be fair, had not shown his greatness for Houston. He had posted 3.6 WAA in 133 games in 1967, but a knee injury cost him his 1968 season, and it took him until 1971, the year of the trade, to recover to 2.9 WAA. Then, suddenly, at the age of 28, he became one of the greatest second basemen of all time, the key to the Reds' mid-decade dynasty. His value was almost entirely offensive, based on his tremendous on-base percentage (short in stature, he had more than 100 walks eight times), his base running skill (although it never won his team more than one win in a year), and his considerable power. He was never more than an average fielder.

The 1972 Reds were the second National League team, after the 1963 Giants, to field four superstars: Morgan (5.8 WAA), Rose (5.5), Bench (5.1), and Perez—now switched to first base (4.2). The lineup as a whole was +20 WAA, but their pitchers cost them -3 WAA, and they won only 95 games, one less than the NL East-winning Pittsburgh Pirates, who came within three outs of beating the Reds in the NL championship series. Bobby Tolan earned another 2.8 WAA in center after returning from injury, but Menke at third, young Dave Concepcion at short, and Cesar Geronimo in right were average at best. Bench, Perez and Tolan all slumped in 1973, although Concepcion and Geronimo improved, and the team won 99 games thanks to five wins' worth of Pythagorean luck, losing to the 82–79 Mets in the playoffs. (The Mets were at least somewhat better than their record indicated; they had suffered numerous injuries during the season.) Rose had his greatest season with 6.8 WAA in 1973, although Seaver was better with 8. In 1974, Morgan, Rose and Bench all turned in superstar seasons again and the Reds won 98 games, but they lost to a superior Dodgers team, the best Dodgers team since 1955.

Nineteen seventy four marked the end of the superstar phase of the extraordinary career of Pete Rose. Although Rose had consistently been a very good hitter during his career, fielding reduced his value. Although he played every position on the diamond except catcher and shortstop at one time or another, he was below average in all of them except left and right field. He had posted his first superstar season in 1968, when he won the batting title, with 4.1 WAA, but he lost his second one in 1969 because he spent a good deal of the season in center field and cost the Reds a full -28 runs as an outfielder. As a corner outfielder from 1972–1974, he posted three more superstar seasons in a row, but after moving back to the infield in 1975—initially at third base—he never broke the superstar barrier again. We shall evaluate his whole career a little later.

The 1975–1976 Reds made several key changes, and they were rewarded with 108 and 102 wins, and two successive World Series victories. Morgan was now their only superstar, with fantastic seasons of 7.9 and 5.6 WAA, good for two deserved MVP Awards. Bench, though now past his peak, still accounted for 3.6 WAA in 1975, while a new power hitter, George Foster, fielded very well in left and added 3.8. Perez earned 1.4, shortstop Concepcion and center fielder Geronimo fielded brilliantly and earned 3.1 between them, and a new right fielder, Ken Griffey, added 1.1 despite poor fielding. Because Rose gave up -20 runs at third base, he was the worst player in the lineup, with 0.9 WAA. Morgan, Foster and Geronimo had come to the Reds by trades; the rest were homegrown. The lineup earned +22 WAA, the pitchers +4. Although the Reds lacked a dominant pitcher, injury-prone Don Gullett earned 2.0 WAA in 159⅔ innings, Gary Nolan had 1.4, and relievers Will McEnaney and Rawley Eastwick added 1.7 in 181 innings.

Every member of the Reds' lineup was again above average in 1976: Morgan (5.6 WAA despite dreadful fielding), Foster (5), Rose (3.5 thanks to better fielding), Griffey (3.3), Geronimo (1.5), and Bench (0.8 in an injury-plagued year.) The lineup fell from +22 WAA to +18 because of poor fielding, but the pitchers added +5. Pat Zachry had 2.5 WAA and four pitchers had more than 1. Foster had 5.9 WAA in 1977, when he became the only player of the 1970s to hit more than 50 home runs, but the rest of the team was now in decline. The Reds swept the NCLS in both 1975 and 1976, beat the Red Sox in seven extraordinary games in 1975, and swept the Yankees in 1976.

The 1970s Reds, as Bill James pointed out many years ago, were extremely similar, player for player, to the Dodgers of the early 1950s. Joe Morgan and Jackie Robinson, Johnny Bench and Roy Campanella, Pee Wee Reese and Dave Concepcion, and Tony Perez and Gil Hodges were similar players. The two teams were similar in this as well, that they put up remarkable numbers without ever developing an outstanding pitching staff. The Reds were—and remain—the best National League dynasty since the Dodgers of 1949–1956.

The Pittsburgh Pirates were even more successful in the NL East in the early 1970s than the Reds were in the West, winning the division five times in six years from 1970 through 1975. Their division was weak and they won in 1970 and 1974 with 89 and 88 wins—figures that would never have allowed a team to reach postseason play before 1969. Even in 1971–1972, when they won one World Series and came within three outs of reaching another, they won only 97 and 96 games, although the 1971 team projected to win 102. Their fielding was generally mediocre overall, and their hitting was their biggest asset. The great Roberto Clemente put up seasons of 5.1 and 4.4 WAA in 1971–1972, the last before his untimely death, giving him a total of 12 such seasons, third in the Silent Generation behind Mays and Aaron. Michael Humphreys found Clemente to be the greatest right fielder of all time, and his fielding was still worth more than +1 WAA in his last season. Almost alone among all-time greats, Clemente seems to have thrived on limited playing time. He averaged only 122 games played in his last five seasons, but averaged more than 5 WAA during those years all the same.

Outfielder Willie Stargell trailed Clemente with 4.7 WAA in 1971, when he hit 48 homers in 141 games, even though he cost the team -14 runs in left field. He later moved to first base. He slipped to 2 WAA in 1972, and 1973 was his only other superstar season, also with 4.7 WAA. He topped 3 WAA on five other occasions. Longevity, visibility and popularity largely account for his election to the Hall of Fame. Playing first base, he reached 1 WAA only once in the last six years of his career. (Jim Wynn, to repeat, had seven seasons over 4 WAA, and his best was better than Stargell's.) The 1971 team's line-up was excellent, worth +19 WAA thanks to Clemente, Stargell, first baseman Bob Robertson (3.2 WAA) and catcher Manny Sanguillen (2.6). Only the double play combination was below average. Steve Blass was their only pitching asset of note, with 2 WAA, and he won two games when the Pirates defeated the Orioles in the World Series. With Clemente and Stargell both slipping in 1972, the lineup fell to +14, although the pitchers added +6.

The Pirates won 88 games and their division again in 1974 without a superstar, but in 1975 they added a new one, 24-year-old Boomer Dave Parker, who had replaced Clemente in right field and put up 5.3 WAA. They won the division with 92 victories. Overall their offense slipped badly despite the emergence of Parker, but they finally put a strong pitching staff on the mound, led by left-hander Jerry Reuss (3.7 WAA), and rookie John Candelaria. They were, however, no match for either the Dodgers in 1974 or the Reds in 1975, and they were overtaken by the Philadelphia Phillies for the next three years.

Parker had a most unfortunate career, somewhat parallel, in fact, to his exact contemporary Cesar Cedeno, who had broken in sensationally with the Houston Astros in 1972 with 6.4 WAA. Parker slumped somewhat in 1976, but then put up 6.1, 4.9 and 5.1 WAA in 1977–1979. He was only 28 in 1979, when the Pirates won the World Series, but he became addicted to cocaine and was a below-average player, overall, for the remainder of his career. Of all the players with exactly four seasons over 4 WAA, he has one of the weakest cases for entrance into the Hall of Fame. The Pirates won the 1979 pennant with 98 wins, sweeping a much less impressive Reds team in the NLCS and beating the Orioles once again in seven games. Their lineup had a mere +10 WAA and their pitchers +4. The National League had fallen into a mediocre state.

The 1979 Pirates pitching staff included Bert Blyleven, who reached the majors with the Minnesota Twins in 1970 at the age of 19. No pitcher's greatness has been more obscured by the teams he played for than Blyleven. Of the three qualifications that get pitchers into the Hall of Fame—dominant stuff, durability, and the right teammates—he had the first two in spades. He pitched well over 200 innings in every year from 1971 through 1980, and five times more after 1984. He had an extraordinary six seasons of at least 4 WAA, tied for first in his generation and well ahead of Jim Palmer, Nolan Ryan, and Steve Carlton. But with very rare exceptions, the teams for which he pitched—the Twins (1970–1976 and again in 1985–1988), the Rangers (1976–1977), the Pirates (1977–1980), the Indians (1981–1986), and the Angels (1989–1990) were mediocre or worse. He won 20 games only once, going 20–17 for the 1973 Twins, when he posted a career-high 6.5 WAA, and finished with an amazing lifetime record of 287 wins and 250 losses. He never came close to a Cy Young Award, receiving *any* votes for it only four times during his career, and it took him 14 ballots, from 1998 until 2011, to be elected to the Hall of Fame. By any reasonable measure, he is surely one of the 20 best pitchers in Cooperstown.

Two new teams became the dominant powers in the National League in the late 1970s: the Dodgers in the West, who had already won the 1974 pennant, and the Phillies in the East. The Dodgers of the mid–1970s, it turns out, were significantly better than the Dodgers of 1963–1966. Their pennant winners of 1974 and 1977–1978 won 102, 98 and 95 games (despite about three games' worth of bad luck every year), compared to 92, 93 and 98 in 1963 and 1965–1966. But because they lost all three World Series, and because they lacked one commanding star like Sandy Koufax, they are not so fondly remembered.

The 1974 Dodgers won 102 games and took the pennant from the Reds by four games, but they were actually good enough to have won 106, and had exactly the same adjusted run differential as the 1975 Reds. Their hitting was just as strong as that of the 1975 Reds, worth 18 wins. How they did this was rather interesting. Beginning in 1973, the Dodgers had fielded a new infield, composed entirely of Boomers: Steve Garvey at first, Davey Lopes at second, shortstop Bill Russell, and third baseman Ron Cey. All of them occupied their positions for nearly a decade. Of the four, only Cey ever posted superstar seasons—two of them, in 1975–1976, when the team could not beat the Reds. But all performed consistently well, rather like Parker, Lefebvre, Wills and Gilliam in the mid–1960s. Garvey and Cey combined for 4.6 WAA in 1974, and Lopes and Russell added 1 more. Catcher-outfielder Joe Ferguson and catcher Steve Yeager combined for 3 WAA, and outfielders Bill Buckner and Willie Crawford combined for 3.1. But the team MVP, by a wide margin, was 32-year-old Jim Wynn, acquired from Houston in a trade. Dodger Stadium was another poor hitters' park—although not as bad as the Astrodome—but Wynn responded with a .387 on-base average, 32 home runs, and 5.2 WAA—more than twice as many as Garvey, whose good looks won him the MVP Award. This excellent lineup contributed +19 WAA. Their pitching contributed eight more wins, led by Andy Messersmith, who threw more than 300 innings and earned 3.1 WAA, Tommy John (1.5), and reliever Mike Marshall (1.4), who threw more than 200 innings in a record 106 games.

Cey had his best seasons in 1975 and 1976, with 4.4 and 4 WAA. Garvey and Lopes did well too, but Wynn played only 130 games in 1975, finishing with 3.3 WAA. He was traded to Atlanta the next season and never performed at a high level again. Overall the team's hitters slumped all the way to average in 1975–1976, while the pitchers earned six and three wins, and the team never challenged the Reds. In 1977–1978, however, when the aging Reds slumped, the Dodgers fielded a new outfield, composed of Dusty Baker—acquired from Atlanta in exchange for Wynn—Reggie Smith, who came from St. Louis, and Rick Monday. Smith had a tremendous year with 5.2 WAA, his second superstar season, but Baker earned just 1.5 and Monday gave up -2.5, largely because of dreadful defense. Catcher Steve Yeager, who earned 2.8 WAA with his defense, and Lopes, with 2.4, added the rest of the positive value, and the lineup was +10 WAA. A superb pitching staff also contributed +10 WAA, led by Burt Hooton (3.2 WAA), Don Sutton (2.2), and Tommy John (2.4). The lineup earned +10 WAA again in 1978, but the pitchers slipped to +6. Smith, Garvey, Cey and Lopes were all stars, but Yeager was as bad in 1978 as he had been good the previous year. On the mound, Hooton (3 WAA) and young Bob Welch (2.2 in 111⅓ innings) contributed the positive value while John and Sutton fell to average.

Don Sutton, remarkably, was, along with Tom Seaver and Steve Carlton, one of three 300-game winners born in 1944. He was the least distinguished of the three, having posted no superstar seasons (just missing with 3.9 in 1980), and only five star seasons of 2 WAA or more. That record is quite comparable to those of Early Wynn (another 300-game winner), Red Ruffing, and Lefty Gomez, although all three of them broke the superstar barrier at least once. The Dodgers beat the surging Philadelphia Phillies in the NLCS in 1977–1978, but lost to the Yankees in two six-game series. In 1981, they won the two rounds of playoffs that concluded the strike-shortened season, reached the World Series against the Yankees again, and beat them. While truly superior only in 1974, and lacking as many superstars as the Reds, these Dodgers teams had so many assets that they reliably performed at a high level.

4. The Silent and Boom Generation Era, 1967–1983

Closing the Books on the Silent Generation

In 1979, knuckleballer Phil Niekro, who turned 40 that year, posted the last superstar season of the Silent Generation, with 5.1 WAA. The Silent Generation drew on 18 birth years, from 1925 through 1942, compared to 19 for the Lost Generation (1883–1902), 20 for the GI Generation (1903–1922) and another 18 for the Boom Generation that followed (1943–60). It produced 16 players who met this book's standard for all-time greatness of at least five seasons of 4 or more WAA, compared to 15 for the Lost, 16 for the GIs, and 16 for the Boom. The reasons for this will become apparent in just a moment.

The Silent Generation produced the same number of great hitters as the GIs, 14. Its four greatest hitters, all black, were Mays and Aaron with 16 superstar seasons each, Roberto Clemente with 12, and Frank Robinson with 11. Mays and Aaron tied for third on the all-time list, behind only Babe Ruth and Barry Bonds. Then come Mickey Mantle, Eddie Mathews, and Carl Yastrzemski with eight each—clearly in the second rank—and Billy Williams and Jim Wynn with seven. Richie Ashburn, Al Kaline, Willie McCovey, and Dick Allen had six superstar seasons apiece, and no Silent hitter had five.

As we have seen, the oldest stars in the Silent generation reached the majors in the midst of a severe dearth of talent in the 1950s, and most of their stars clearly benefited from living through two rounds of expansion. That surely added superstar seasons to their careers. This list is quite astonishingly one-dimensional, including only three infielders: Mathews, McCovey (the only career first baseman), and Allen, who played third and then first base. Some all-time greats had played second base and shortstop among the GI Generation and would again in the Boom, but the best-hitting member of the Silent Generation at those positions was Ernie Banks, with three superstar seasons at short. Eddie Mathews, by the time he finished his career, was easily the best third baseman of all time, and his contemporaries also included Ken Boyer, who had four superstar seasons, and Ron Santo, who had three. The Hall of Fame has seen fit to admit second basemen Nellie Fox, who had one superstar season, and second baseman Bill Mazeroski and shortstop Luis Aparicio, who had none at all. Among the all-timers, Allen never came close to election by the BBWWA, for reasons unrelated to his performance on the field.

Jim Wynn has been treated more unfairly than any player in the history of the game. His whole career, most of which took place in the Astrodome—one of the worst hitters' parks of all time—and in the low-hitting era of 1965–1968, seems almost to have been designed to obscure his greatness. He became eligible for the BBWAA ballot in 1983 and immediately dropped off of it *without receiving a single vote*. Wynn is an exact contemporary of Dick Allen, who was nearly elected by the Veterans Committee last year. Although Allen's very best seasons were slightly superior to Wynn's, Wynn had seven superstar seasons to Allen's six. He played more games than Allen and scored more runs than he did. He drew far more walks. He played center field, one of the most demanding defensive positions, well. The difference in their batting averages and home run totals can be traced largely (although not entirely) to the parks they played in. And while Allen's presence was a continual source of turmoil to his teams, leading to frequent changes of scenery when he should have been in his prime, Wynn never caused any trouble for anyone. There is still time to remedy this huge injustice and put him in the Hall where he belongs, before Allen goes in.

The best pitchers of the Silent Generation were superior, as a group, to the GIs. Both generations had only two all-time greats with five or more seasons of 4 WAA: Hal Newhouser (5) and Wes Ferrell (5) among the GIs, and Bob Gibson (8) and Phil Niekro (5)—incomparably the greatest knuckleballer of all time. Niekro undoubtedly ranks as the most unique all-time great in the history of baseball. The only other knuckleballers who *ever* broke 4 WAA in a season were Hoyt Wilhelm, in 1959, Wilbur Wood on two occasions in the early 1970s, Tom Candiotti in 1991, and Tim Wakefield in 1995. But while only Bob Feller and Carl Hubbell had four such seasons among the GIs, Koufax, Roberts, Bunning, Marichal and Tiant had four each The main reason these men probably had more impact than their GI counterparts was that they tended to pitch more innings, but there is also evidence that the best pitchers began throwing harder in the 1960s. The unluckiest pitcher of the Silent Generation—aside from Herb Score, who might have been the greatest but for injuries—was Billy Pierce, who had three superstar seasons and just missed a fourth, but never had one for a pennant winner and has never gotten any serious Hall of Fame consideration. Don Drysdale also had three superstar seasons and Whitey Ford two, but they pitched on many pennant winners and both secured election. Gaylord Perry had a career quite similar to Warren Spahn's. He had no less than 12 seasons of 2 WAA or more, but only two of them, in 1972 and 1974, topped 4 WAA, reaching 6.9 and 6.1 WAA, respectively. As in the case of Walter Johnson, the statistics for his 1970 and 1973 seasons suggest that numerical anomalies may have cost him a couple of additional years of 4 WAA or more.

Silent Generation hitters with only four superstar seasons include Minnie Minoso, Duke Snider, Ken Boyer, Johnny Callison—and Pete Rose. Of those five, Minoso, the one great Latin player of the 1950s, peaked at 21 percent of the BBWAA ballots in 1988; Snider, who would have had more superstar seasons had he never played center field, was elected in 1980 in his 11th year of eligibility; Boyer peaked at 26 percent in 1997; and Callison appears to have received one vote before dropping off the ballot after 1979. It is surely not a coincidence that Minoso, Boyer and Callison played in a total of one World Series among them, while Snider played in six. Rose, of course, is ineligible, but since he still has a part to play in our story we shall defer the evaluation of his career for a few more pages.

A few other Silent Generation pitchers should be noted. Two of them pitched for the same team and manager, the Chicago White Sox in the early 1970s under Chuck Tanner. From 1971 through 1975, knuckleballer Wilbur Wood started between 42 and 49 games a season and pitched from 320 to 377 innings. He posted won-lost records reminiscent of the dead ball era, 22–13, 24–17, 24–20, 20–19, and 16–20, even though the rest of the team, with the exception of Dick Allen, was largely mediocre. But because Wood pitched so much, and with considerable effectiveness, he posted 6.2 WAA in 1971, 6.1 in 1972, and 3 in 1973. (Wood and Dick Allen combined for nearly 14 WAA in 1972, but the rest of the team was 10 wins *under* .500.) The veteran Jim Kaat joined the team in 1974, pitched 277⅓ and 303⅔ innings in the next two years, and posted the only two superstar seasons of his career, with 4.8 and 5.4 WAA. With five other seasons in the 2–3 WAA range, Kaat has a clearly superior record to Ruffing, Gomez, Bob Lemon and Early Wynn. His extraordinary durability allowed him to retire in 1983, at the age of 44, with 283 wins and 237 losses. He did not play for enough good teams to reach the magic 300 number of wins and win election to Cooperstown.

While the Silent Generation exited from the top rung of the ladder, a newly dominant team emerged in the NL East: the Philadelphia Phillies. They won divisional titles in 1976–1978, losing in the playoffs every time; the World Series in 1980; and the National League pennant in 1983. Their dynasty, which declined steadily in overall value from 1976 onward, was built around two all-time greats: Mike Schmidt, the greatest third baseman of all time and the second-greatest Boomer offensive player, with 11 seasons of more than 4 WAA, and Steve Carlton, one of that generation's top six pitchers. As the experience of the Pirates showed in the early 1990s, the presence of one all-time great in the era of divisional play generally sufficed to keep a team in or very near to post-season competition in the divisional era—and even more, after 1994, in the Wild Card era.

Mike Schmidt spent his first full season with the Phillies in 1973. He hit less than .200, but his power and superb fielding, which saved the team +16 runs that year, still earned the team 1 WAA. In the next year, at age 24, Schmidt revealed his greatness, hitting .282 with 106 walks, 36 home runs, and 36 runs saved in the field, all good for a remarkable 8.5 WAA, easily the best in the National League. This was the first of four seasons in which Schmidt was the genuine NL MVP. He continued with 5.8 WAA in 1975, 5.7 in 1976, 6.8 in 1977, 3 (an off year!) in 1978, 6.1 in 1979, and 7.9 in 1980. He performed at a level that would have given him his greatest season ever during strike-shortened 1981, and had 6, 5.1, 4.4 and 4.8 WAA in 1982–1985. With no expansion in his later years to help him, he did not sustain superstar performance for quite as long as Mays or Aaron, but he was just as valuable as they had been for a dozen years. And because the Phillies were not playing in a very strong division, it generally took only one other superstar to get them into the playoffs.

In 1976, the Phillies' second-best player was center fielder Gary Maddux, who earned 4.5 WAA, while outfielder Jay Johnstone, with 3.3 WAA, was the third. The team's hitters contributed +11 WAA with the help of Greg Luzinski, the left fielder, whose hitting was worth +3 WAA. Unfortunately Luzinski, who really ought to have been traded to the AL where he could have become a DH or shifted to first base, was one of the worst fielders in history, and gave back in left field 18 of the 29 runs above average that he earned at the plate, leaving him average overall.[33] The lineup also included shortstop Larry Bowa (-3.4 WAA), first baseman Dick Allen—now average at 34 years old—and disastrous first baseman Bobby Tolan (-2.8 WAA at 30.). Led by Steve Carlton (2.9 WAA), Ron Reed (1.9), Jim Lonborg (1.8), and Jim Kaat (1.4), the pitchers were outstanding, earning a combined 13 WAA, and the team won 101 games despite three games' worth of bad Pythagorean luck. In 1977, Schmidt (6.9 WAA) paced the lineup again, and although Ted Sizemore and Bowa cost the team -4.1 WAA in the middle of the infield, Luzinski reached 1.9 WAA overall, and new acquisitions at first base and in the outfield allowed the line-up to improve to +17 WAA. Unfortunately, although Carlton had 3.9 WAA, the rest of the staff was below average, and

---

33. Dick Cramer has pointed out to me that Luzinski had played first base in the minor leagues.

the team won 101 games again before losing to the Dodgers in the playoffs. In 1978 the whole team, including Schmidt and Carlton, regressed towards the mean, and the team squeaked through to another division title with just 90 wins, before losing to the Dodgers in the playoffs for the second straight time. The pitching collapsed in 1979, and the Phillies were barely over .500.

The 1980 Phillies were one of the more astonishing World Champions in baseball history. The entire National League was rapidly leveling off, and the Phillies won the NL East by one game over Montreal. Despite sensational performances from Schmidt (7.8 WAA) and Carlton (6.8, the second-greatest season of his career), the line-up earned just +6 WAA and the pitchers +4, as the team won just 91 games. In the line-up, Bake McBride (2.5 WAA) and new second baseman Manny Trillo (2.4, nearly all in the field) were more than counterbalanced by Bowa (-3.8), Luzinski (-2.1), and a new first baseman, 39-year-old Pete Rose (-1.9). Therein lay a tale.

We have seen that although Pete Rose had been a genuinely great hitter for most of the period 1967–1976, his overall performance had suffered for much of that time because of problems in the field. Only in 1972–1974, when he played corner outfield positions, had Rose been a positive force defensively. And as a result, Rose in 1968–1974 had posted just four superstar seasons, the only ones of his career—a number which historically would make him a marginal Hall of Fame candidate, and far from a certainty. The Reds wisely let Rose go after the 1978 season, when he had been a completely average performer for two years. At that time Rose, age 37, had 3,164 career hits and an announced ambition to get more than 1,000 more and break Ty Cobb's all-time record.

During the next eight years, Rose, now exclusively a first baseman—always in theory one of the premier offensive positions on the field—accomplished that feat with WAA totals of 1.4, -1.9, 2.7 in the shortened 1981 season (a figure it seems unlikely he would have maintained without the strike), -2.6, -2.5, 0.6, 0.4, -0.9, and -1.1 (the last three figures as his own manager with the Reds.) Three teams—the Phillies, the Expos (for one year), and the Reds, allowed Rose to hurt their record badly simply to allow him to break an all-time record. The same thing, as we shall see, happened during the next decade, when the Orioles promoted Cal Ripken's successful run at Lou Gehrig's consecutive game record even though his performances were hurting their team. Both Cobb and Gehrig, let it be noted, were significant assets to their teams to the very end of their careers (or in Gehrig's case, until his last full half-season when he was stricken with illness). These episodes were not a credit to baseball or to the players involved, and it is interesting that Rose, even leaving aside his suspension for gambling as a manager, is not an overwhelming candidate for the Hall of Fame based upon his peak value.

The pitching staff of the 1980 Phillies showed a similar pattern. Beyond Carlton, its only asset was reliever Tug McGraw, with a remarkable 2.7 WAA in just 92⅓ innings, while nearly every other pitcher was below average. Having won their mediocre division by one game, the Phillies managed to eke out a dramatic victory in the NLCS over the Houston Astros, who had projected to win just 86 games but tied the Dodgers thanks to six wins' worth of Pythagorean luck. They then defeated the Kansas City Royals, who were also well past their dynastic peak, in the World Series. These Phillies, featuring two tremendous assets and several major liabilities, were obviously somewhat similar to (although not as good) the Giants of the mid–1960s. But while those Giants consistently fell short of the pennant, the Phillies managed not only to make it to the World Series, but to win it. Times had changed.

The Phillies had prevailed by one game over a Montreal Expos team that had similar problems. They also had two superstars: catcher Gary Carter, with a tremendous 4.3 WAA, the best at his position since Johnny Bench, and center fielder Andre Dawson, with 4.2. Pitcher Steve Rogers had 3.4, but the rest of their pitching staff was perfectly average. Worse, the rest of the lineup was about five wins below average, leaving Carter, Dawson, and right fielder Ellis Valentine high and dry as the only real assets among them. Dawson posted superstar figures for three seasons in a row in 1980–1982 but declined rapidly after that. He won the NL MVP Award for the Chicago Cubs in 1987 when he hit 49 homers and drove in 137 runs, but he earned only 1.9 WAA that year. In a bitter essay in his last annual *Baseball Abstract*, Bill James stated that Dawson had not been one of the 30 best players in the National League in 1987; actually, he ranked in the low 20s. His Hall of Fame selection ranks with those of Cepeda, Santo, and Perez as one of the more dubious of the last 30 years. Once again baseball seemed to be in the midst of a talent shortage, and superior pennant winners had vanished from the scene.

In 1983, the Phillies made it into the World Series with an even more mediocre club, whose run differential suggested that they should have won only 88 games (they in fact won 90.) Schmidt had 5 WAA; the rest of the lineup had –7 WAA. The pitchers won the team the pennant with +10 WAA. Two of them provided most of them: 30-year-old John Denny (19–6), who posted a 4.9 WAA, and Carlton, with 2.8. Carlton had come up with the Cardinals, who had foolishly traded him to the Phillies in 1972 over a contract dispute. In that season, he posted one of the most extraordinary seasons ever turned in by a Boomer pitcher, winning 27 games for a last-place team and earning them 8 WAA, the exact same figure as Tom Seaver in the previous year. Carlton finished with three superstar seasons and five more of more than 2 WAA, ranking him just behind Seaver as the fourth-most dominant pitcher of his generation, based on their best years.

The late 1970s and early 1980s were a transitional era in major league baseball, one most unfavorable to greatness. The impact of free agency was being felt, although teams had not grasped some of the essential principles of the new era, which we shall discuss in due course. Joe Morgan remarked in the late 1970s that he did not expect to see many more teams like the great Reds dynasty, because no one would be able to afford them. The wisdom of this remark was already very apparent by the early 1980s, as one team after another made it into the World Series with run differentials that left them well short of 100 wins. The trend was destined to accelerate during the rest of that decade.

And while the major leagues had continued to grow, the minors, relatively speaking, had continued to shrink. In 1965, there had been six full-season minor league teams operating for each major league team. By 1983 there were only four, plus two part-time summer leagues. While more and more players were coming into the majors after playing in major college programs, the base of the talent pyramid seems to have been at least as small, relative to the size of the major leagues, as it had been 20 years earlier, and many times smaller than it had been at its peak around 1940.

The era of 1967–1983 was one of the more eventful and, in retrospect, one of the more exciting periods of baseball history. It was bracketed by two disastrous events: the dismal "Year of the Pitcher" in 1968, when the NFL began to eclipse baseball as the nation's leading sport and the death of baseball was freely discussed, and the strike of 1981, the first of two seasons which could not be completed as planned. In between, however, expansion, which prolonged the greatness of players like Aaron, Mays, and Clemente, the emergence of the new stars of the Boom Generation such as Seaver, Morgan, Jackson, Carew, Schmidt, and Carlton, and the creation of real dynasties in Baltimore, Cincinnati, Oakland, New York, Pittsburgh, and Los Angeles, produced some of the most exciting baseball since the early 1950s. The Orioles of 1966–1975, the Reds of 1970–1976, the Yankees of 1976–1981 and the Dodgers of 1974–1981 rank among the great dynasties of all time. And after falling significantly during the GI-Silent era to .69 per team per year, the number of superstars had recovered somewhat to .73 per team per year. Such dynasties, alas, have nearly ceased to exist in subsequent eras.

5

The Boom and Gen X Era, 1984–2004

Generation X posted its first superstar seasons in 1984 thanks to 23-year-old first baseman Don Mattingly of the Yankees, who batted .343 to lead the league and earned 5 WAA. The Boomer and Xer era produced more superior pennant winners and great teams than the previous era. In the Silent-Boomer era (1967–1983), there had been only three great teams, winning at least 108 games—the 1969–1970 Orioles and the 1975 Reds—and 8 more superior teams, winning 102–107 games. The Boomer-Xer era included 13 superior pennant winners and four great teams.[34] Those were the 1986 Mets; the 1995 Indians; the 1998 Yankees who won 114 games; and the 2001 Mariners who won 116, just missing the Indians' 1954 record for American League winning percentage, while leaving the 1906 Cubs all-time record comfortably intact.

Nothing is more remarkable during the first two-thirds of the twentieth century than the extraordinarily consistent number of superstar performances. The average number of superstar performances per year was 12.5 from 1901–1925, 12.1 from 1926–1945, and 12.8 from 1946–1966. During the Silent/Boomer era of 1967–1983, it increased to 18.4 per year, evidently because the Boom generation produced enough outstanding athletes to fill in the six new teams that took the field during those years. The average number of superstar seasons per team in each year had fallen from .76 in 1926–1945 to .69 in 1946–1966, reflecting the shortage of top-level talent that we identified as a result of the Second World War and the Korean War. But despite the addition of ten new teams from 1961 through 1977, the average number of superstars per year recovered to .74 from 1967–1983. Four more teams took the field during the 1990s, but the number of superstar seasons kept pace, averaging 20.6 per year and holding steady at .74 per team per year in 1984–2004. It is now clear, however, that only PEDs kept the percentage of superstar seasons that high. In the last 12 years, as we shall see in the next chapter, drug testing has coincided with an unprecedented drop in the number of superstar seasons, and a corresponding further increase in the mediocrity of teams.

The Boomer-Xer era was both the age of steroids and an era of high offense generally. This has confused our view of it. Measured against their league averages, the top *hitters* of Generation X, we shall find, were no more numerous nor higher in quality than the all-time

---

34. These figures do not include any teams from the very short 1981 and 1994 seasons.

greats of earlier years. The pitchers, however, were an entirely different story. Not only did annual superstar seasons by pitchers increase about 20 percent during this period, but the number and quality of all-time mound greats in Generation X was completely unprecedented. The Silent and Boom generations had only two pitchers each—Bob Gibson, Phil Niekro, Bert Blyleven and Dave Stieb—with at least five seasons of 4 WAA. Generation X had eight such pitchers. This trend also came of an abrupt halt in the middle of the last decade.

Unfortunately, we will never know exactly who among the greats of this era did and did not take performance-enhancing drugs. While a few users have confessed and others have been identified publicly through tests, the practices of many will remain a mystery. We can, however, say with certainty that several hitters *became* great at much more advanced ages than almost anyone in the past, and that a number of pitchers sustained superstar performance for longer, and at much older ages, than anyone in history. Clearly both of those developments bear some relation to drug use, although they cannot be regarded as absolute proof in any individual case.

We begin with the American League, where a superior team, the Detroit Tigers, got off to an extraordinary start and coasted to the 1984 pennant. They won 104 games—four of them through Pythagorean luck—with only one superstar, center fielder Chet Lemon, who saved 20 runs in the field and earned 4.4 WAA. Other assets in the lineup included right fielder Kirk Gibson (2.7 WAA despite -11 runs in the field), shortstop Alan Trammell (3.3 WAA), second baseman Lou Whitaker (1.3 WAA), catcher Lance Parrish (1 WAA), and four extraordinary bench players—Dave Bergman, Tom Brookens, Ruppert Jones and Johnny Grubb—who combined for 5.9 WAA. The Tigers' pitching staff contributed only 2 WAA, but featured one of the most amazing relief performances in history. Willie Hernandez, a journeyman reliever, pitched 140⅓ innings, but had an ERA of 1.92 and earned 3 WAA. The writers voted him the league's MVP, although his total value was far behind that of Cal Ripken, who had his best season with 7.4 WAA. No one could know that Lemon was the real Tigers MVP, and Ripken's performance may have cost his fellow shortstop Trammell the prize.

Although Chet Lemon had been an outstanding center fielder for years, he never repeated his superstar performance. Trammell, however, had not yet reached his peak, and he eventually concluded his career in 1996 with three seasons of 4 to 4.9 WAA, two more over 3 WAA, and two more over 2.5 WAA. While his three best seasons were not as good as Cal Ripken's, his next two were, and his overall record is quite similar to Robin Yount's, as well. While none of these shortstops maintained the peak level of Arky Vaughan, Lou Boudreau, or Luke Appling, they are *far* superior to Reese, Rizzuto, Aparicio, and their contemporary Ozzie Smith, who are all in Cooperstown, and to Derek Jeter, who soon will be. Ripken, Yount and Trammell are most similar to Joe Cronin. Thus, while Trammell does not meet the standard for greatness of this book—five superstar seasons—he would be one of the better shortstops in the Hall of Fame. (Trammell was elected to the Hall by the Veterans Committee in December 2017.) Second baseman Lou Whitaker, Trammell's exact contemporary, had a remarkable career as well. A superb fielder who saved 20 runs or more in three different years, he never quite had a superstar season, but topped 3 WAA six times. He cannot be compared to Rod Carew, Joe Morgan, Bobby Grich (who is not in the

5. The Boom and Gen X Era, 1984–2004

Hall), or Ryne Sandberg, but he ranks above Willie Randolph. All five of these second basemen were far superior to anyone at that position from the Silent Generation.

With the help of Trammell, the Tigers also posted the best record (though not the best run differential) in the American League three years later, in 1987, with 98 wins, despite a totally mediocre pitching staff. Unfortunately they lost the league championship series to a record-setting Minnesota Twins club: the first team to reach the World Series with a negative run differential. The Tigers' other 1987 superstar, in addition to Trammell, was one of the most remarkable and unappreciated players of his generation, Darrell Evans, who topped 4 WAA for the third time at the age of 40 at first base, with 4.2. Although Evans entered professional baseball at age 20, he did not become a regular third baseman for the Atlanta Braves until 1972, when he was 25. A power hitter and excellent fielder, he earned 6.1 and 5.1 WAA in the next two seasons. He slumped badly from 1975 through 1979, when he would normally have been at his peak, but posted three seasons over 3 WAA through 1985 before breaking the superstar barrier again in 1987, this time as a first baseman. Not only did he have the same number of superstar seasons as Cal Ripken, Jr.—three—but the average value of all his full seasons was significantly higher than Ripken's, 2.3 to 1.5. Had the Tigers had more pitching, they might easily have been the dynasty of the 1980s. Their lineup was consistently of pennant-winning caliber, but their pitchers cost them -9 WAA in 1982 and -6 in 1983, earned just 2 and 1 WAA in 1984–1985, and fell to -6 in 1986 and -2 in 1988. The Tigers' durable ace, Jack Morris, never had a single superstar season. He topped 3 WAA just once, in 1979, and 2 WAA on only three other occasions. But durability allowed him to win 254 games while losing 186, and he has now been elected to the Hall of Fame.

The Toronto Blue Jays, a 1977 expansion team that first reached the .500 mark in 1983, succeeded the Tigers as Eastern Division champions in 1985, finishing as a mediocre pennant winner with 99 wins. The Blue Jays' lineup had one great player, right fielder Jesse Barfield, peaking in 1985 at age 26 with 6.7 WAA. Second-best was left fielder George Bell with 2.3, but his presence was entirely balanced by a dreadful second baseman, Damaso Garcia, who cost the team more than -2 WAA at bat and in the field. Their fielders, led by Barfield and Fernandez, earned +6 WAA and their pitchers +11, including 4.6 from Dave Stieb, 3.3 from Jimmy Key, and 2.8 from Doyle Alexander. Their run differential was almost identical to the Yankees, who displayed an exactly opposite pattern. Led by Rickey Henderson (6.7 WAA), Don Mattingly (5.3), and Willie Randolph (2.3), the Yankees' line-up earned +15 WAA—+13 at the plate—to the Blue Jays' 8, but their pitchers earned only +3. The Blue Jays lost the LCS to a Kansas City Royals team that won 91 games with the help of five wins' worth of Pythagorean luck.

Toronto pitcher Dave Stieb was the Boom Generation's counterpart of Wes Ferrell and Billy Pierce: a truly great pitcher who pitched for the wrong teams and will never reach the Hall of Fame because of bad luck. Beginning in 1980, when he was 22, Stieb earned 2.2 WAA; pitched at a superstar level that projected to 4.5 WAA in the strike-shortened 1981 season; and showed it was no fluke with 5.6, 4.6, 5.5 and 4.6 WAA in the next four years, pitching more than 260 innings every time. Alas, those performances earned him won-lost records of just 12–15, 11–10, 17–14, 17–12, 16–8, and 14–13 (in the year the team won their division). Stieb turned in his sixth superstar season in 1990 (4.0 WAA), but never won 20 games in a season. His five superstar seasons rank second behind Bert Blyleven among Boomer hurlers, but he was eliminated from the Hall of Fame ballot after getting just seven votes in his first year of eligibility in 2004. Dennis Eckersley, who had three superstar seasons, was elected in that same year.

After slumping in 1986, the Blue Jays won 96 games in 1987 and had the run differential to win 100, but were nosed out by the Tigers on the last weekend of the season. Once again Barfield was their best player, this time with 4 WAA, and once again their pitching contributed 10 WAA while their line-up contributed 9. Jimmy Key, with 4.9 WAA, replaced Stieb as the ace of the staff, and Lloyd Moseby and George Bell in the outfield and Tony Fernandez at short were the other stars. Continuing their odd-even pattern, they slumped again in 1988 but won a very cheap division title in 1989 with just 89 wins, losing to Oakland in the playoffs. Jesse Barfield—who by then had left the team—was a tremendous player whose four superstar seasons make him a legitimate Hall of Fame candidate. His value was not appreciated because so much of it was in the field, where he saved between 25 and 29 runs for four consecutive seasons in 1985–1988. The Blue Jays probably would have been well advised to put him in center field, where Lloyd Moseby was roughly average. But his career ended when he was only 33, and he will never get serious consideration. When the Blue Jays returned to the top of the league in 1991–1993, they had a very different team.

The last team of the 80s in the AL East was the Boston Red Sox, who won the pennant in 1986 and division titles in 1988 and 1990. They were mediocre at best, winning 95, 89, and 88 games in those years in a very balanced division, and they had a bizarre mixture of strengths and weaknesses. Their fielding was bad and got steadily worse, costing them -2 WAA in 1986, -4 WAA in 1988, and -5 WAA in 1990. Tony Armas and a host of shortstops in 1986; Marty Barrett and Dwight Evans (who played most of the year at first base) in 1988; and Barrett, Wade Boggs (in an unusually bad year), two shortstops, and center fielder Ellis Burks in 1990, were very poor fielders. (Red Sox fans will be interested to learn that Bill Bucker *saved* +12 runs during the 1986 season.) Their hitting was a bizarre mixture of strengths and weaknesses. Wade Boggs (5.5 WAA) and Jim Rice (4.2 WAA) had superstar seasons in 1986, and Boggs (5.3) and Rice's replacement Mike Greenwell (4.6) did the same in 1988. But in 1986, Buckner at first and DH Don Baylor were average at best at the plate, and center fielder Tony Armas (replaced late in the season by Dave Henderson) was much worse. Three regulars were well below average in 1988, and the line-up lacked a single player with as many as 2 WAA in 1990. All told, the lineup contributed +1 WAA in 1986, +4 in 1988, and -9 in 1990.

Red Sox third baseman Wade Boggs tied for fourth with Eddie Murray among the great offensive players of the Boom Generation with eight superstar seasons, behind Henderson, Schmidt, and Reggie Jackson. He might well have rivaled Mike Schmidt as the greatest third baseman of all time had the Red Sox organization rated him at his true value. Boggs, like so many greats, began his professional career in 1976 at the age of 18, but spent five and a half seasons in the minors—two of them in AAA—while Butch Hobson, Glenn Hoffmann and Carney Lansford played in Fenway. He hit .349 with an OBP of .406 in 104 games in 1982, when he was already 24, and followed that up with seven consecutive superstar seasons, peaking at 6 WAA in 1985. He averaged over .360 overall for four seasons, from 1985 through

1988, and was consistently a slightly above-average third baseman as well. He clearly might have had more such seasons had he reached the majors sooner. Boggs had an off-year in 1990, but remained an asset through 1995, when he was 37. Like so many other recent players, he remained in the majors a full four seasons after falling to average or below, enabling him reach 3,000 hits, but not adding to his indisputable greatness.

The strength of this Red Sox team—as in 1977–1978, when they had a stronger team but lost their division—was their pitching. And the key to the pitching was the greatest pitcher of Generation X, and *the most dominant pitcher of all time*, Roger Clemens.

Born in 1962, Clemens began his professional career at age 20 and reached the Red Sox a year and a half later. After starting 35 games in 1984–1985, he blossomed in 1986 with a record of 24–4 and 6.9 WAA in 281⅔ innings. That was the beginning of a seven-year run without parallel since the end of the dead ball era, in which Clemens earned 6.9, 8.2, 5.8, 3.6, 8.3, 5.9. and 5.7 WAA. Clemens in 1990 was essentially a one-man team, supplying 8.3 WAA on a team that won only 88 games. By the time he turned 30, in other words, Clemens had seven superstar seasons, more than any pitcher from the GI, Silent or Boom Generations except Blyleven. He was, however, far from finished. After an off-year in 1993, he had already earned 4.6 WAA in 1994 when the season was interrupted. He slumped badly in 1995 but recovered to 5.4 WAA in 242⅔ innings in 1996. At that point, the Red Sox decided to let him go, and he signed with the Toronto Blue Jays. In 1997, at the age of 34, he tied his personal best with 8.3 WAA. Clemens' two top seasons made him the first pitcher in the history of baseball with two seasons of 8 WAA or more, and he followed them up in 1998 with 5.7 WAA. In the "decline" phase of his career, which began in 1999 and lasted through 2007, Clemens never pitched more than 220⅓ innings in a campaign. He had three star seasons with the Yankees from 1999–2003, and then, after a strategic move to Houston in the weaker National League, earned 4.5 and 5.4 WAA in 214⅓ and 211⅓ innings in 2004–2005, when he was 42 and 43. His 12 beat Lefty Grove's record, and no other pitcher has had such a season at the age of 41 or more. No other human being, needless to say, has ever come remotely close to what he achieved relative to his contemporaries. And we shall find that he was only the best of a number of Generation X pitchers who maintained a level of superstar performance for an unprecedented length of time.

Baseball was changing rapidly in the course of Clemens's career. The American League averaged 747 runs per team in 1986. That figure fell for the next few years, but jumped to 761 runs in 1993 and to 870 in 1996, the next full, 162-game season. It remained at or near 800 until 2010. In the National League, where the lack of a DH resulted in far fewer runs, the average went from 673 in 1986 and 640 in 1992 to 711 in 1993 and 758 in 1996. It rose again to 805 in 1999 and 816 in 2000. What this meant, obviously, was that the average hitter, in both leagues, was generating substantially higher numbers of runs. But what was not realized at the time was that it also *increased* the impact of an exceptional pitcher.

In 1968, the year of the pitcher, when Bob Gibson posted an ERA of 1.12, the National League averaged 558 runs per team, and the league ERA was 2.99. In 1997, when Roger Clemens posted a 2.05 ERA for Toronto, an average team scored 797 runs and the league ERA was 4.56. That is why Clemens earned 8.3 WAA to Gibson's 6.7. And that is why the five greatest *pitchers* of Generation X—Clemens, Randy Johnson, Greg Maddux, Pedro

Martinez, and Roy Halladay—were more dominant relative to earlier generations than the five greatest hitters, Barry Bonds, Albert Pujols, Jeff Bagwell, Frank Thomas, and Edgar Martinez. It is also the reason why pitching became more important to team success during the Boomer-Xer era than it had ever been in the past, or than it has been for the last ten years. Two dynasties—the Braves from 1991 into the next decade, and the Yankees from 1996 through 2003—built themselves around starting pitchers who sustained extraordinary performance levels year after year. In that sense, the undistinguished Red Sox of 1986–1990 represented a new trend.

While the Tigers, Blue Jays and Red Sox traded titles in the AL East, the AL West eventually produced a genuine dynasty. The division hit a real trough in the mid–1980s. The Kansas City Royals became the first division winner with a negative run differential in 1984, winning only 84 games, and won 91 in 1985 only with the help of five wins' worth of Pythagorean luck. Their pitching in 1985 featured two superstars, young Brett Saberhagen (5.6 WAA) and Charlie Leibrandt (4.9 WAA), and accounted for 13 WAA overall, enough to have won 95 games with an average lineup. As it happened, however, even with George Brett turning in his last superstar season with 5.3 WAA, the lineup overall was -8 WAA, the worst performance ever by a World Series winner. Hal McRae, Frank White, and Willie Wilson—who had aged quickly—were all average, and everyone else in the line-up was significantly worse. They were the first example of a new kind of world champion, one destined to become much more common in the years ahead.

The California Angels team of 1986 that came within one out of beating the Red Sox in five games won just 92 games. They had one superstar, center fielder Gary Pettis, whose five-year run as one of the greatest ever at that position peaked at +36 runs saved and who earned 4.5 WAA. Helped by Pettis, catcher Bob Boone, and shortstop Dick Schofield, their line-up earned +9 WAA in the field and +16 overall, even though aging veterans like Reggie Jackson, Bobby Grich and Doug DeCinces contributed little. Despite 3.9 WAA from Mike Witt, however, their pitching staff lost them -5 WAA. The 1987 Twins, as we have noted, went two steps further than the 1984 Royals, and won not only their division but the pennant and the World Series with a negative run differential, winning just 85 games with a Pythagorean record worth just 79. They lineup was -4 WAA, and their pitchers were +2 WAA thanks to Frank Viola, who posted the first of three superstar seasons with 6 WAA. The team, in short, was quite reminiscent of the 1940 Indians—but those Indians could not win the pennant.

Two rounds of expansion in the American League, one in the National, and a decade of free agency—which the owners were about to try to defeat with collusion—had reduced the leagues to an unprecedented level of mediocrity, and the playoff system had made it possible for perfectly average teams to win pennants and World Series. We shall see that this trend was reversed to some extent in the late 1990s after new rounds of expansion, but that it returned with a vengeance in the first decade of the new century and has now become the norm. Meanwhile, in the AL West, a genuine dynasty managed to emerge in the late 1980s.

From 1988 through 1990, the Oakland A's won three consecutive pennants for the second time in their history, outperforming the 1972–1974 team with 104, 99, and 103 wins, making two superior pennant winners out of three with the help of several wins a season of Pythagorean luck. Their lineup earned +17 WAA in 1988, +13 in 1989, and +20 in 1990. Their manager, Tony LaRussa—the greatest manager of the Boom Generation—demonstrated great adaptability and emerged as a manager who, like Billy Martin, understood fielding.

These A's were most closely associated with the "Bash Brothers," Mark McGwire and Jose Canseco, who had become regulars in 1986 and 1987, respectively. Their careers had some bizarre similarities whose cause eventually came to light. Neither was ever nearly as good as his reputation. Canseco had started his career at the age of 17 in 1982 and spent most of four years in the minors. Never more than an average outfielder, he earned about 1 WAA in year in each of his first two seasons, 1986–1987. In 1988, he shot up to a remarkable 6.5 WAA with the help of 42 homers, and he was the team MVP. But he missed more than half the 1989 season, earning 2 WAA in 65 games, and the 5.2 WAA he earned in 1990 represented the last superstar season of his career. He remained a star, earning more than 2 WAA in five of his next ten seasons, but his career line looks more like that of a pitcher than a hitter.

McGwire was an even more interesting case. He had started his career at 20 and spent two seasons in the minors. In 1987, he had a sensational rookie year with 49 home runs. This, however, was highly deceptive. American Leaguers hit 2,290 home runs in the previous year 1986, 2,634 in the fluke year of 1987, and only 1,901 in 1988. Something was evidently different about the baseballs in 1987, and it was a very long time before young McGwire approached 49 home runs again. Meanwhile, he was such a dreadful liability at first base, costing the team -17 runs in each of his first two seasons, that even with 49 home runs, he earned only 2.8 WAA in 1987 and contributed just .3, 1.4, and 2.7 WAA in the next three years. He remained at about that level through 1994, when he was 30. Then, suddenly, in 1995–1996, he became a new man, earning 5.2 WAA in just 104 games in 1995 and another 5.5 in 130 games in 1996. He remained at that level in 1997 and then increased all the way to 6.9 WAA in 1998, when he hit 70 home runs. His 65 home runs the next year were worth only 4.8 WAA, because his entire league was hitting so many. McGwire effectively confessed to using steroids in 2004, although the Congressmen before whom he testified allowed him to avoid giving any details. Although McGwire ended his career with five superstar seasons (1995–1999), he has in my opinion the weakest case of the players of the steroid era for election to Cooperstown, simply because his career line suggests that he never was a superstar until he began taking them, presumably in 1995, when he was 31.

The A's did field another superstar in 1988, center fielder Dave Henderson, who earned 4.1 WAA with the help of a fine year in the field. But what turned them into a dynasty was the reacquisition, in 1989, of the greatest player of the Boom Generation, Rickey Henderson. Henderson is undoubtedly one of the most unique players in the history of baseball. Although he is in the Hall of Fame, the nature of his contributions is widely misunderstood and deserves a close look here.

Henderson will always be best known as the holder of the single-season and all-time records for stolen bases. The list of all-time stolen base leaders illustrates what a random skill large numbers of stolen bases represents: it includes Ty Cobb and Rickey Henderson, two of the top ten players of all time, and Lou Brock, who had only three superstar seasons.

Maury Wills showed that one can steal more than 100 bases in a season without coming close to being a superstar. Henderson, like Cobb, was repeatedly a superstar—in 12 seasons, in his case, one more than his fellow Boomer Mike Schmidt. But according to the calculations of baseball-reference.com, only twice in Henderson's career—in 1985 and 1988—did his stolen bases earn about 2 WAA for his team. In 1982, when he stole 130 bases but was caught 42 times, they earned only 11 runs, about 1 WAA. Henderson's stolen bases may also have been responsible for his tendency to miss 15 to 30 games a season. Only four times in his long career did he play 150 games or more.

Like every great everyday player, Henderson helped his team the most at the plate, and specifically by getting on base, posting OBPs of .400 or more no less than 15 times. Meanwhile, he was slightly more valuable in the field, where he was an excellent outfielder, than he was on the bases. Like Roberto Clemente and Henry Aaron, Henderson had the ability to play center field, and he saved the New York Yankees nearly a game's worth of runs a year there in the mid–1980s. But he was far more valuable in left field, where average performance is much lower, and where he played both from 1979–1984 and 1989–1993 for Oakland. Henderson posted ten superstar seasons in 12 years from 1980 through 1991, missing the 4 WAA mark only in 1986 (3.5) and in 1987, when he earned 3.9 in just 95 games. He reached his peak in 1990, the last year of the A's dynasty, when he had 9.3 WAA in just 136 games, proportionately perhaps the greatest performance in history.

Two other aspects of Henderson's career deserve our attention. First, he was traded twice at the height of his powers, both times without earning his team anyone of remotely the same value in return. After 1984, when he was about to become eligible for free agency, the A's traded him to the Yankees for four players, including Stan Javier, a slightly above-average outfielder, and Jose Rijo, a young pitcher who had two terrible years with Oakland but became a superb pitcher with Cincinnati in the early 1990s. After 1987, the Yankees traded Henderson back to Oakland for outfielder Luis Polonia, who had earned 1 WAA, and two journeymen pitchers. Secondly, he played the last nine years of his career—which concluded when he was 44—without ever reaching 2 WAA in a season, and his last six years without ever reaching 1. Like Pete Rose—a *much* lesser player—Henderson owes his lifetime totals to the value of his name.

The A's hitters slumped significantly in 1989, when Henderson was their only superstar with 4.1 WAA in just 85 games, but had their best year, as we have seen, in 1990, when Henderson peaked at 9.3 WAA, Canseco had 4.3, Dave Henderson had another fine season with 3, and McGwire had 2.8. Meanwhile, their fielding improved steadily, saving +24 runs in 1988 thanks to shortstop Walt Weiss (+25); +61 runs in 1989, thanks to second basemen Glenn Hubbard and Tony Phillips (+28 between them), left fielders Henderson and Polonia (+21 runs saved), and shortstop Mike Gallego (+14); and a truly great +93 runs in 1990, including +25 by Gallego at three infield positions, +12 and +23 by Dave and Rickey Henderson, and +14 by Weiss.

Given their hitting and fielding, the A's would have been one of the great teams of all time had they had pitching to match. They didn't. In these three years, their pitchers earned 2, 2, and -2 WAA. Their ace was Dave Stewart, the kind of pitcher who benefits most from playing for a great team: large, imposing, and durable, rather like Early Wynn. Stewart went

20–13, 21–12, and 21–9 during these three years, but earned just 1.4, 0.6, and 2.5 WAA. Bob Welch in 1990 had one of the most fortunate seasons in history, going 27–6 in 238 innings while earning just .7 WAA. Like Don Newcombe, who had exactly the same won-lost record in 1956 with 1.9 WAA, Welch won the Cy Young Award. Meanwhile, the A's invariably had a couple of pitchers at the bottom of their rotation who cost them a few games a year.

Reliever Dennis Eckersley, who had had two superstar seasons as a starting pitcher much earlier in his career, drew a great deal of attention during these years as the A's closer. Eckersley pitched 73, 58, and 73⅓ innings in 1988–90, earned 1, 1.3 and 1.8 WAA. That, we shall find, is not far from the upper limit of what a closer can mean to his team.

The Minnesota Twins, who had won the 1987 World Series with a negative run differential, won the 1991 one with a respectable, if undistinguished, 95 victories. Although their lineup lacked a superstar, they had excellent balance. They earned +10 WAA, led by outfielders Shane Mack (3.6 WAA) and Kirby Puckett (2 WAA), DH Chili Davis (3.1) and second baseman Chuck Knoblauch, who had a fine year in the field (2.1). Puckett, a very popular player and a World Series hero, had only two superstar seasons in his career, 1988 and 1992, and was a very questionable selection to Cooperstown by the BBWAA. Pitcher Kevin Tapani had a 16–9 record and just missed superstardom with 3.9 WAA. Scott Erikson had 2.2 WAA and Jack Morris 1.6, but the staff totaled only +3.

The Twins had deservedly beaten the Toronto Blue Jays in the 1991 ALCS, but the Blue Jays—an almost entirely new team from the contender of the mid–1980s—took the World Series during the next two years. They were mediocre pennant winners, with 96 and 95 wins in 1992 and 1993. The lineup earned +9 WAA in 1992 but fell to +4 in 1993 thanks to terrible fielding. The constants in the lineup were Devon White, a good-fielding center fielder who earned 2.3 and 2.8 WAA in those two years; second baseman Roberto Alomar, whose poor fielding cost him two superstar seasons but who nonetheless brought home 3.8 and 3.6 WAA; first baseman John Olerud, who had 2.9 WAA in 1992 and a tremendous 6.5 in 1993, when he won the batting title; and left fielder Joe Carter, who was totally average. Two aging stars, Dave Winfield in 1992 and Paul Molitor in 1993, filled the DH role very ably, with 3.2 and 4.4 WAA, respectively.

Alomar, Winfield and Molitor are now in the Hall of Fame. Although Alomar cost his teams -38 runs as a second baseman, suggesting that he should have played a different position, he had three superstar seasons in his career, peaking at 5.9 WAA for Baltimore in 1996, and earned at least 2 WAA in seven other seasons. Olerud's statistics are very similar, and his two best seasons were better, but he was a good first baseman instead of a bad second baseman, and he has never gotten any serious consideration. Molitor had an absolutely unique career, posting six superstar seasons without ever reaching 5 WAA.[35] Winfield, a fine athlete who kept himself in shape into his 40s, represented a new breed of Hall of Famer. While he certainly did not ride into Cooperstown on the backs of his teammates like Tony Lazzeri and Earle Combs, he had only three superstar seasons and six more star seasons, but with the help of the DH rule, he played long enough to accumulate 3,110 hits and 465 home

---

35. This includes a projected figure for the shortened 1994 season.

runs. His nine seasons of 2 WAA or more were balanced by six seasons in which he was of less than average value. The Blue Jays' pitchers were average in 1992 but earned +6 WAA in 1993, thanks to reliever Duane Ward (2.0 WAA) and starters Juan Guzman and Pat Hentgen (nearly 2 each). The 1993 season, coming in the middle of another round of expansion and just before two strike-shortened seasons, breaks the Boomer and Xer era conveniently in half, and gives us a good opportunity to turn to the National League.

In 1984, the Chicago Cubs returned to post-season play for the first time in 39 years with a mediocre 96 wins, achieved with the help of five wins' worth of Pythagorean luck—only to lose the NLCS in five games to the San Diego Padres, who had won only 92 games with the same degree of luck. Second baseman Ryne Sandberg, with 4.4 WAA, accounted for most of the Cubs' lineup WAA and was the league MVP. Sandberg had spent three and a half years in the minors after being signed by the Phillies at the age of 18. After bringing Sandberg briefly to the majors in 1981, the Phillies made one of the worst trades in history, giving him to the Cubs in exchange for Ivan DeJesus, who earned about -2 WAA for the next two years. Although Sandberg never managed to combine great hitting and fielding seasons, he had five superstar years, peaking at 4.8 WAA in 1991. The Boom Generation was as strong at second base as the Silent Generation had been weak, and Sandberg joins Rod Carew and Joe Morgan as second sackers exceeding this book's standard of greatness with five or six superstar seasons apiece. The 1984 Cubs were as strong on the mound as in the lineup, thanks to Rick Sutcliffe, Steve Trout, Dennis Eckersley (still a starter), and Scott Sanderson, each of whom earned 2–2.9 WAA. Sutcliffe had an extraordinarily fortunate season. Joining the team in mid-year, he started 20 games and finished with a record of 16–1, rather than the 11–6 that would have been expected from his 2.4 WAA. Sandberg once again accounted for nearly all the line-up's positive value in 1989, when the Cubs again won the division and lost the NLCS, this time with just 93 wins.

The weaker San Diego team that beat the Cubs in 1984 also featured a future Hall of Famer, right fielder Tony Gwynn. The Padres drafted and signed Gwynn after he had spent several years in college. They wisely brought him to the majors in 1982 after only one year, but an injury slowed his career. 1984 was his first full season, and he won the first of eight batting titles, hitting .351 at age 24. Gwynn had an odd career path. He began with three superstar seasons in four years, peaking at a remarkable 7.5 WAA in 1987, partly because he was initially a very good right fielder. His value was suddenly cut at least in half during the next six years, however. His hitting recovered somewhat beginning in 1993, but by that time he had become injury-prone and such a liability in the field that he never crossed the superstar barrier again, except in strike-shortened 1994.[36] He could have been much more valuable as an American League DH in the latter part of his career.

The St. Louis Cardinals won the world championship in 1982 with only 92 victories; won a close pennant race with the Mets in 1985 with 101 wins; and managed to do it again two years later with a mediocre 95. The 1982 team, which was very fortunate to beat the strong Brewers club in the World Series, owed its success mainly to three players: outfielder

---

36. Gwynn projected to earn more than 5 WAA in 1994.

Lonnie Smith (4.9 WAA), first baseman Keith Hernandez (3.9 WAA in an off-year), and pitcher Joaquin Andujar (3.2). The very different team of 1985 and 1987 appeared at the time to have a line-up of remarkable athletes, including five switch-hitters: Tommy Herr at second base, Ozzie Smith at shortstop, Terry Pendleton at third base, and Vince Coleman and Willie McGee in the outfield. It turns out, however, that none of their players were very consistent, that their base stealing, as usual, contributed only marginally to the team's success, and that they had very surprising weaknesses in the field. In 1985, when the lineup earned +11 WAA, half of those came from center fielder McGee, who hit .353, but who turns out to have been a mediocre center fielder. Second most valuable was shortstop Ozzie Smith, who saved 13 runs in the field and earned 2.3 WAA overall. Herr hit .302 but was a very poor second baseman and earned just 1.4 WAA. Coleman, who stole 110 bases, saved 15 runs in left field, but earned just 1.6 WAA overall. Right fielder Andy Van Slyke earned 1.9 WAA, evenly divided between the plate and the field, while Pendleton was below average, and a catching platoon cost the team about two games. Power-hitting first baseman Jack Clark, a major defensive liability, hit well in 126 games but earned just 1 WAA. The team, in short, was consistently just a little above average. Two years later, the line-up earned only +8 WAA. Clark had a tremendous year at the plate and broke the superstar barrier with 4.3 WAA in 131 games, but McGee cost the team -16 runs in the field, hit poorly, and cost the team -2 WAA. Smith once again earned 2.1 WAA, but Herr was -2.4, Pendleton was average, and Coleman, despite 109 stolen bases, earned only 1.1 and was average in the field. The catcher, Tony Pena, was a major liability.

The MVP of the 1985 team was pitcher John Tudor, who went 21–8 with a 1.93 ERA in 275 innings and earned a remarkable 5.5 WAA. The rest of the staff was slightly below average, and Joaquin Andujar, 21–12, was a perfectly average pitcher over 269⅔ innings. The 1987 staff did somewhat better overall, but without a single pitcher who threw more than 200 innings or earned much more than 2 WAA.

Ozzie Smith's career at shortstop was parallel to Bill Mazeroski's at second base, insofar as he established a reputation as the greatest fielding shortstop in baseball and eventually rode it into the Hall of Fame. As Michael Humphreys pointed out in an extensive analysis, Smith began his career as if he might indeed turn out to be the greatest shortstop of all time, saving 12, 28, 18 and 19 runs for the San Diego Padres in 1979–1982. At that point, however, those figures were cut approximately in half by injury.[37] Unfortunately, Smith was a dreadful hitter during those same years, costing his team between -1.5 and -3.5 runs a season, and his overall value was low. He improved as a hitter later, while his fielding declined. Essentially, his overall career numbers resemble those of Pee Wee Reese or Phil Rizzuto, *but with their best years taken away*. Smith's overall value peaked at 2.8 WAA in 1988, and he had four other seasons over 2 WAA. Among Boom Generation shortstops, he did not remotely compare in overall value to Robin Yount, Cal Ripken, Jr., or Alan Trammell—who are now all in the Hall of Fame.

The 1986 Mets were the best team of the 1980s, winning 108 games with the help of

---

37. Humphreys wrote in *Wizardry* that Smith tore his right rotator cuff in 1985, but Smith's numbers suggest that he did so in 1983.

five wins' worth of Pythagorean luck. A fascinating mix of young, homegrown talent and great players acquired in mid-career, they won another division title in 1988 with 100 wins, but could not become a real dynasty because their young stars did not, as initially seemed almost certain, become all-time greats.

The team MVP was first baseman Keith Hernandez, the most underrated player of the Boom Generation. Following the pattern of most great players, Hernandez had started his career at 18 in 1972 and became a regular at 21 in the second half of 1975 for the St. Louis Cardinals. He was a fine hitter and one of the greatest fielding first basemen of all time, saving an average of 15 runs per season from 1976 through 1987. From 1977 through 1986, this combination allowed Hernandez to post eight superstar seasons in ten years, including three over 6 WAA. Hernandez was a key figure in the Cardinals' pennant winner of 1982—even though he barely missed another superstar season with 3.9 WAA—but manager Whitey Herzog unloaded him to the Mets in the middle of the next season in exchange for two useless relievers. The reason, reportedly, was that Herzog would not tolerate Hernandez's addiction to cocaine. Whatever the facts, Hernandez finished the 1983 season with 5.3 WAA and earned the Mets 6.1, 4.8 and 4.1 WAA in the next three seasons. No other superstar has ever been traded for so little—and without any additional cash—in the middle of his career. Hernandez's total of eight superstar seasons ranks fourth among all the hitters in the Boom Generation, and it is shocking that he never got as many as 11 percent of the BBWAA vote for the Hall of Fame. This is another huge mistake the Veterans Committee can still correct.

Two outfielders essentially tied for the next-most-valuable Met, and many will be surprised to learn that they were Lenny Dykstra, a fine all-around player, and Mookie Wilson, whose main value was in the field, with 3.4 and 3.3 WAA each. Dykstra remained a star for his next three seasons, earning about 2 WAA a year despite injuries, fell to -1.5 in 1989, and then displayed a new physique and new capabilities in 1990 with the Phillies, earning 6.7 WAA. Right fielder Darryl Strawberry had signed with the Mets at 18 and reached the club three years later amidst enormous fanfare. Only three times in his major league career, however, did he hit more than 29 home runs, and he never posted an OBP of as much as .400. He was never above average in the field, and he finished his long career with just two superstar seasons, in 1987 and 1988. He was average at best in the long decline phase of his career. He earned 2 WAA in 1986.

By the time he reached the Mets via trade in 1985, catcher Gary Carter already had a very solid case for the Hall of Fame. His two superstar seasons (in 1980 and 1982), two more of better than 3 WAA, and four more of 2, put him in the top tier of catchers all-time, although somewhat below Johnny Bench. A tremendous record in the field, where his arm consistently saved at least a game's worth of runs per season, was largely responsible. But unfortunately for the Mets, Carter had only one more good year left in him when they acquired him. He earned 3.1 WAA in 1985 but fell to average in 1986 and stayed well below average for the next two years before becoming a part-timer in 1989. The Mets made a dreadful mistake playing Ray Knight, nearly -1 WAA overall thanks to dreadful fielding, at third base in place of young Kevin Mitchell, who fielded quite adequately and earned 1.2 WAA in just 108 games. Tim Teufel, who platooned with Wally Backman at second, cost the team

-21 runs—two whole games—in the field, leaving their platoon one full game below average. Since Teufel was normally average, he may well have been hurt. Shortstop Rafael Santana cost the team another -1.8 WAA because he could not hit. The line-up overall earned +8 WAA.

The Mets' pitchers were much better, earning an outstanding +14 WAA. Dwight Gooden, still only 20 years old in 1985, had just turned in two outstanding seasons, earning 3.5 WAA as a rookie in 1984 and 8.5 WAA in 1985, when he went 24–4 with a 1.53 ERA in 276⅔ innings. That 8.5 was the best mark since Walter Johnson's 9.9 in 1913. Gooden has now admitted becoming seriously addicted to cocaine in 1986. He also seems to have hurt himself in 1985, however, because he was never remotely the same pitcher again. In 1986, he went 17–6 but earned only 2.7 WAA. Both Bob Ojeda (3.1) and Ron Darling (3.0) topped him, while Sid Fernandez and reliever Jesse Orosco earned 2.5 WAA between them. For the remainder of his career, Gooden was generally worth between 1 and 2 WAA per year.

Luck caught up to the Mets in 1987, and they won just 92 games and lost to the Cardinals despite a better run differential, as their pitching fell below average. In 1988, however, they won 100 games, again with an amazing combination of strengths and weaknesses. The team's fielding cost them more than -4 WAA. Strawberry had his second-best season with 5 WAA, and the rest of the outfield, Kevin McReynolds and Dykstra, added 4.9 between them. Unfortunately, Carter, now 34, and new shortstop Kevin Elster each cost the team -2 WAA. Hernandez, also 34, played only 98 games and earned 1.8 WAA. Poor fielding held the lineup to just +8 WAA, but the pitchers contributed +12. The team's new ace, 25-year-old David Cone, earned 3.5 WAA in his rookie season, three starters from 1985—Gooden, Darling and Fernandez—earned 1–2 each, and reliever Randy Myers earned 1.3 in just 68 innings. Cone was launched on a great career that eventually included two superstar seasons and six star seasons. The Mets could not prevail, however, against the Los Angeles Dodgers in the NLCS.

Mediocrity ruled the NL West throughout the 1980s. Five teams won the division with poor playoff-era records of 92 wins or less. The Dodgers won the division in 1985 and the World Series in 1988 with the help of two key men in each year: outfielder Pedro Guerrero (5.5 WAA) and pitcher Orel Hershiser (3.7) in 1985, and Hershiser (5.2 WAA) and outfielder Kirk Gibson (5.6) in 1988. (Gibson, although famously crippled by the time of the World Series, had had a tremendous season in 150 games.) Since those Dodgers teams won 95 and 94 games, their two superstars accounted for most of their wins over .500 in both cases. Hershiser's 1988 season, in which he set a new record for consecutive scoreless innings, was his only superstar season, although he also had 3.7 WAA in 1985, 1987, and 1989. He tore his rotator cuff in 1990 and was average for the rest of his career. The 1986 Houston Astros were very close to a one-man team: their Pythagorean projection was worth 91 wins, and pitcher Mike Scott earned 5.8 WAA, leaving just 4 for the rest of the line-up. (Good luck secured five more wins for a total of 96.) The 1989 Giants won 92 games thanks to sensational performances from first baseman Will Clark (7.3 WAA) and left fielder Kevin Mitchell (6.4 WAA). The team earned six full games in the field thanks to shortstop Jose Uribe, center fielder Brett Butler, and Clark, but their pitching had -4 WAA.

The 1990 Cincinnati Reds, who swept the A's in the World Series, showed a similar pattern of mediocrity, winning 92 games. They owed their success to two players. Shortstop Barry Larkin was nothing less than the second-greatest shortstop of all time, behind only Honus Wagner. Larkin is one of the first recent all-time greats to have spent as many as three years in college, attending the University of Michigan, but the Reds then kept him in the minors for parts of only two seasons, and he was a regular by the time he was 23, in 1987. A good hitter and a brilliant fielder who saved more than +20 runs in four consecutive seasons, he had his first of five consecutive superstar seasons in 1988 and earned 4.1 WAA in 1990. Several of his seasons were shortened by injury, beginning in 1993, but his hitting improved while his fielding declined during the 1990s, and he added one more great season in 1996. With six superstar seasons, *he is the only shortstop since Honus Wagner to have more than four.* While Robin Yount and Cal Ripken had better peak seasons, neither came close to Larkin's period of extended greatness, largely because neither was anywhere near as good a fielder. Although Alex Rodriguez now has more superstar seasons than Larkin, he did not have as many at shortstop. Had Larkin played in New York, he would deservedly be hailed as the greatest shortstop of the modern era. The Reds' second-best player was pitcher Jose Rijo, who had had three disastrous years with Oakland in 1985–1987 after the A's acquired him for Rickey Henderson. After blossoming with two good seasons for the Reds in 1988–1989, Rijo had 3 WAA in 1990, following that with 3.9 in 1991, 3.4 in 1992, and 5.6 in 257⅓ innings in 1993. He was on his way to a good season in strike-shortened 1994, but injuries wrecked his career after that.

The pattern of the National League changed suddenly as the decade of the 1990s opened. After a full decade in which one mediocre pennant winner succeeded another, dynasties emerged in both divisions. The first one, based upon the greatest player of Generation X, took the Pittsburgh Pirates to the playoffs three years in a row. The second, in Atlanta, lasted well over a decade and became the only long-term dynasty based primarily upon its pitching staff.

Barry Bonds, whose father Bobby had posted six superstar seasons in the late 1960s and early 1970s, spent two years in college but joined the Pittsburgh Pirates' system at the age of 21 in 1986. He immediately earned 2.4 WAA in just 113 games, hitting just .223 but walking 65 times and fielding brilliantly in center field. In his second season, 1987, the Pirates had acquired Andy Van Slyke from the St. Louis Cardinals, and General Manager Syd Thrift put Van Slyke in center field and shifted Bonds to left. This seems to have been a serious mistake, and one that Bonds—who wore the number 24 of his father's teammate, Willie Mays, whom he had known from earliest childhood—understandably resented. Although Bonds did not have a strong arm, his speed was a tremendous asset on the artificial turf of Three Rivers Stadium, and he had saved +14 runs in 113 games in 1986 in center. Van Slyke equaled that figure in a full season in 1987 but quickly fell to average after that, while Bonds saved +20 runs or more in left field. In the early 1980s, when the Pirates were just coming off their 1979 World Championship, scout Howie Haak had remarked publicly that the team did not draw enough fans because it had too many black players. General Manager Syd Thrift apparently wanted Van Slyke, who was white, in the marquee position of center field, but this decision undoubtedly cost the team some runs in later years.

Helped by his outstanding figures in left field, Bonds broke the superstar barrier for the first of 12 consecutive seasons in 1987, with 5.4 WAA. He earned more than 4 in each of the next two seasons and really blossomed in 1990 at the age of 25, hitting .301 with an OBP of .406 and 33 home runs, adding up to 8.3 WAA. Although Bonds was now stealing 30–50 bases a year, his stolen base percentages were not outstanding, and his base-running never added as much as a game to his WAA. Not coincidentally, the Pirates in 1990 won the first of three consecutive division titles. They were never, however, more than a mediocre division winner, winning 95, 98 and 96 games.

Only once, in 1991, did the Pirates' pitching staff contribute significantly to their victory. The 1990 lineup earned +15 WAA, only about half of them from Bonds, while the pitching staff cost them -2. Center fielder Van Slyke, third baseman Bobby Bonilla (one of many large, power-hitting third basemen who turns out to have been quite an adequate fielder), and good-fielding first baseman Sid Bream all starred with more than 2 WAA, and the rest of the line-up was average. Second baseman Jose Lind, a remarkable player, saved +22 runs in the field but gave them all back at the plate. The line-up slumped from +15 WAA to +9 in 1991, when Van Slyke had a dreadful year in the field and Bonds (6 WAA) and Bonilla (2.5 WAA after being switched to the outfield) were its only significant assets. The pitchers did not include one remotely dominant player, but all were at least average, and a strong bullpen did much to earn the team a total of +6 WAA. Bonds rebounded to 8.8 WAA in 1992 and won his second very deserved MVP Award, and Van Slyke had the year of his life with 4.9 WAA. Unfortunately, Lind, who had lost his magic in the field, cost the team -2.7 WAA, utility man Jeff King was nearly as bad, and Bonilla was gone to free agency. Although Bonds and Van Slyke earned nearly 15 WAA between them, the line-up as a whole earned only 10, and the pitchers regressed to average. Bonds left for San Francisco via free agency after 1992, and the Pirates' dynasty was over. Not once had they reached the World Series, missing out in Game 7 of the NLCS in both 1991 and 1992.

The Pirates lost in those years to an emerging dynasty, the Atlanta Braves. From 1991 through 2005, the Braves won their division 14 times, missing out only in the strike-shortened season of 1994, when no post-season play took place. This remarkable record was in many ways a reflection of the huge change that took place in major league baseball in 1995, when both leagues expanded to three divisions instead of two, and four teams per league, instead of two, now reached the post-season. They achieved this record even though they were a superior team, winning 103 games or more, in only two of these 14 seasons, making them mediocre winners in 11 of them. Winning the pennant, however, left teams much further from a World Series victory in the era of three rounds of post-season that began in 1995. Although the Braves had the best record in the National League in nine of those seasons, they reached the World Series only five times, and only three times from 1995–2005, when they had to win two playoff series to do so. Suddenly it had become impossible for a league's best team to be assured of having anywhere near a 50 percent chance of reaching the World Series, much less winning it. Meanwhile, the average winning percentage of a playoff team dropped substantially.

Pitching played an unprecedented role in this dynasty. From 1991 through 2002, the Braves' pitching staff contributed an average of +10 WAA to the team's fortunes, and only in 1998, when the team had its best season with 106 wins, did the lineup contribute as much as the pitching staff to the team's success. From 1991 through 2000—the heyday of the pitching staff—the Braves got a total of 14 superstar seasons from their pitchers: seven from Greg Maddux from 1993–2001; five from Tom Glavine (1991–1997); one from John Smoltz, and one from Kevin Millwood. In 1992, in his sixth season with the Chicago Cubs, Maddux had posted 6 WAA, more than four times as many as in his previous two seasons, and the Braves then signed him at age 26, one of greatest free agent acquisitions ever. His eight superstar seasons tie him for third among Generation X, behind Clemens (14) and Randy Johnson (10). The Braves' line-up, meanwhile—and especially their hitting—was remarkably mediocre. The line-up earned as many as +10 WAA for the team only once from 1991 through 2002, in 1998. Beginning in 2003, the pitching suddenly regressed to average and the team assumed a more normal pattern for a pennant winner.

Led by Glavine's 4.1 WAA, the four starters on the 1991 Braves—Glavine, Smoltz, Steve Avery and Charlie Leibrandt—accounted for more than the +7 WAA earned by the pitching staff overall. Meanwhile, third baseman Terry Pendleton, just acquired as a free agent after a long career with the Cardinals, supplied the total positive value in the lineup with 4.3 WAA. Only one other player, speedy outfielder Otis Nixon, earned more than +1 WAA. The total value of the lineup was unchanged in 1992, and with Smoltz (2.5 WAA) and Glavine (2.8) leading the way, the pitching staff as a whole improved to +9 WAA, with the same starters all over 1. This time Pendleton, Nixon and outfielder David Justice each earned more than 2 WAA, but were balanced out by catcher Damon Berryhill, second baseman Mark Lemke, and shortstop Rafael Belliard, who combined for -7.3 WAA. Highly regarded outfielder Ron Gant was average. The 1993 team was much improved. Thanks to much better fielding by Gant, Justice (who earned 3.5 WAA) and Lemke, and the midseason acquisition of first baseman Fred McGriff (2.4 WAA), the lineup was +9 WAA overall. Meanwhile, with Maddux adding 4.8 WAA and Glavine, Avery and Smoltz combining for 6.7 WAA more, the pitchers earned a total of +14. The team roughly doubled its run differential and won 104 games, by far its best showing yet, but lost the NLCS to a significantly weaker Philadelphia Phillies team.

The Braves' pitchers were on their way to another amazing season in strike-shortened 1994, and in 1995 they had their best year of all, with a remarkable +18 WAA in only 144 games, one of the greatest pitching performances in history. It was a good thing they did. Although the team now included 24-year-old catcher Javy Lopez and 23-year-old third baseman Chipper Jones, David Justice, with 2.5 WAA, was the only significant asset in the lineup, which as a whole was -6 WAA. The pitching, then, was totally responsible for their fine record of 90–54 in the shortened season, and they managed to win two rounds of playoffs and beat a truly great Cleveland Indians team in the World Series. Maddux had his greatest season, going 19–2 with 8.7 WAA and passing Clemens on the all-time single-season list, where he ranks behind only Pete Alexander (10.2 WAA in 1920), Walter Johnson (9.9 in 1913), and Ed Walsh (9 in 1912). Glavine had 4.1, and Smoltz added 3.5

The situation remained the same in 1996, when the Braves reached the World Series again but lost to the Yankees. Once again their line-up was average because their above-average fielders (Mark Lemke and various part-time infielders) could not hit, while their best hitters could not field. The most striking example was 24-year-old, switch-hitting third baseman Chipper Jones, who earned about 4 WAA at bat, but gave away -36 runs at third base and at shortstop. This was only the first of a number of dreadful fielding seasons for Jones, whose deficits kept him out of the superstar range for seven of eight seasons, 1996–2003, including in 1999, when he won the MVP Award with 3.3 WAA. Remarkably, Jones managed to improve his fielding up to average beginning in 2005, when he was 33, and he posted two of the three superstar seasons in his career in 2007–2008, at the ages of 35 and 36, playing about 130 games a year. He is not a strong candidate for the Hall of Fame. Although the 1996 pitching staff was not quite as great as the 1995 one, earning 14 WAA overall, it was the only staff of all time to include three superstars: Smoltz (5.5 WAA), Maddux (5.4 WAA), and Glavine (4.3). The rest of the hurlers were average.

The Braves' line-up improved dramatically in 1997 and 1998, helping the team win 101 and 106 games. The best player in the 1997 lineup was 20-year-old Andruw Jones, from Curaçao in the Caribbean, who had reached the team late in the previous season after spending parts of three seasons in the minors. He saved an amazing +33 runs in right and center field in 1997, and although his hitting was slightly below average, he led the team's lineup with 2.7 WAA. Kenny Lofton, the regular center fielder, aged 30, had 2.2 WAA thanks to +9 runs in the field, and second baseman Mark Lemke and shortstop Tony Graffanino saved +38 runs in the filed while giving up -16 at the plate. Although catcher Javy Lopez hit .295 with 23 home runs and first baseman Fred McGriff hit .277 with 22, they were both only very modest offensive assets, as major league hitting approached a new peak. The lineup as a whole earned +10 WAA, but the pitchers had another extraordinary season with +12, all of them coming from the starting corps of Maddux (5.8 WAA), Glavine (3.9), Smoltz (3.1) and Denny Neagle (3).

In 1998, Chipper Jones had an excellent year at the plate and a somewhat better one in the field (-10 runs), and earned 3.5 WAA. Thirty-seven-year-old first baseman Andres Galarraga had a very similar season with 3.1. But the biggest difference in the lineup came from Andruw Jones, who replaced Kenny Lofton in center field and saved an amazing +33 runs in his first full season there, earning 4.9 WAA, the first lineup superstar the Braves had had since Terry Pendleton in 1991. Jones is deservedly rated by Michael Humphreys as the greatest fielding center fielder of all time, and he saved an average of +29 runs a season in his first six years, posting four superstar seasons during that period. But he was never a great hitter, and his hitting declined sharply after age 26, when most hitters reach their peak. He topped 3 WAA on only one other occasion, and in the end his career looks similar to Willie Wilson's, with a much longer decline phase. He is a marginal candidate for the Hall of Fame. The 1998 Braves' pitching staff tied the line-up with +13 WAA, including 5.3 from Maddux, 5 from Glavine, and 2.6 from Smoltz. With 106 victories (despite -1 games of bad luck), this was the best team of the Atlanta dynasty, but it lost the World Series to the Yankees.

The Braves' lineup slipped to +7 WAA in 1999 and to 0 in 2000, when the team finally failed to post the best record in the National League. The Jones boys were the only assets in the lineup in 1999. MVP Chipper earned 3.3 WAA despite giving up -26 runs in the field, while Andruw saved +48 runs in center—the all-time record at that position, beating out Tris Speaker in 1914 by 1—and hit well enough to earn 5.8. The 1999 pitchers still earned

+11 WAA, led this time by Kevin Millwood with 4.2 WAA and Smoltz with 2.9 in just 186⅓ innings, as Glavine slumped to 1.2 and Maddux to 1.7. Chipper (2.4 WAA) and Andruw (5.2) were joined by rookie shortstop Rafael Furcal (1) in 2000, but outfielder Bobby Bonilla, now 37, cost the team -2 WAA and Andres Galarraga, a -20-run liability at first base, cost them another. But the pitching staff still earned about 10 WAA, nearly all from Maddux (5.4) and Glavine (4), both of whom were now 34 years old.

Atlanta showed an interesting new pattern in 2001 and 2002. While their hitting cost them -3 WAA in 2001 and -1 in 2002, their fielding suddenly improved to +4 WAA and +7 WAA, making their line-up a very modest asset. Two outfielders, Andruw Jones (+26) and Brian Jordan (+18), were largely responsible in 2001, and in 2002 Chipper Jones did what Derek Jeter never managed to do, improving his defense to +8 runs, while Andruw saved +21 more, Furcal reached +10, and second baseman Keith Lockhart saved +14. The pitchers were +8 WAA in 2001, led by Maddux (3.5 WAA), Glavine (2.2), and 36-year-old John Burkett, who posted a career-high 3.4 WAA. Burkett was a below-average pitcher for most of his 15-year career and had posted .7 WAA in his next-best season. His salary had reached $4 million a year by 1999, but the Braves had signed him in 2000 for $750,000. After his 3.5 WAA in 2001, he signed a two-year contract with the Red Sox for $5.5 million a year. He was below average in less than 200 innings in both the next two seasons. In 2002, the pitchers posted another +10 WAA, led by Maddux (2.9), Glavine (2.5), and Kevin Millwood (2.1), who returned to form after two very poor seasons.

After 13 outstanding seasons, the Braves' pitching staff finally regressed to average in 2003, but two new acquisitions gave them a lineup that earned +16 WAA at the plate, almost twice as many as in any previous year of the dynasty. Gary Sheffield had come to the Milwaukee Brewers in 1989 at 20, after three years in the minors, as a shortstop and third baseman. For the first 11 years of his career, he averaged 1.5 WAA per season, even though he had outlier superstar years of 4.8 WAA in 1992 and 4.2 in 1996. He was a mediocre fielder both at third base and in the outfield, to which he was eventually shifted. But beginning in 2000, when he was with the Dodgers, Sheffield averaged 4.1 WAA over his next six seasons, from ages 31 through 36, and broke the superstar barrier three times. He had joined the Braves in 2002, when he had 3.6 WAA, and in 2003 he was their MVP with 5.8, his career high. Close behind him was second baseman Marcus Giles, who became a regular for the first time at the age of 25, went from below average at bat to +31 runs at the plate and +19 in the field, and earned 5.6 WAA. Giles followed that up with two star seasons, two poor ones, and ended his career before he was 30. Andruw Jones, still only 26, earned 3.5 WAA, most of them in center field, and Chipper hit well enough to earn 0.6 WAA despite surrendering -24 runs at third base.

In 2004, the Braves won 96 games with a far more typical pattern, a lineup that earned +9 WAA and a pitching staff worth +6. Andruw and Chipper Jones both slumped and earned only 1.7 WAA between them, and Giles slipped to 1.6, but right fielder J. D. Drew, acquired from St. Louis for a young pitcher named Adam Wainwright and two other players, had the second and last superstar season of his career with 6 WAA. The well-balanced pitching staff included no stars, and the team lost the first round of the playoffs to Houston. The Braves allowed Drew to depart as a free agent before 2005, and not surprisingly slipped to only 91 wins, losing to the Astros in the NLDS once again. They did not return to postseason play for five more years.

From 1926 through 1932—seven seasons—the Philadelphia Athletics' pitching staff earned an average of +12 WAA per year, thanks largely to Lefty Grove. For three years, 1954–1956, the Cleveland Indians' pitchers averaged +14 WAA. From 1907 through 1913, the New York Giants' pitchers averaged +10 WAA per season. In 1935–1938, the Chicago Cubs' pitchers averaged +10 WAA per season. In nine years, from 1942 through 1950, the St. Louis Cardinals' pitching staff averaged +11 WAA per season, although they clearly had some help from the weakness of their opposition during the Second World War. Those were the most remarkable, sustained performances by pitching staffs before the Boomer/Xer era. None of them remotely compares in sustained peak performance to that of the Atlanta Braves from 1991 through 2002, who averaged +12 WAA over those 12 seasons.[38] Several other contemporary dynasties, including the Yankees and Red Sox in the late 1990s, the A's in the early 2000s, and the Phillies late in that decade, also got most of their WAA from their pitching staffs. None of them, however, put up a long-term record remotely comparable to the Braves. One reason, perhaps, was the high standing of their great pitchers with National League umpires, who, it seems, tended to give Maddux, Glavine and Smoltz strikes on pitches that seemed clearly to have missed the outside corner.

The importance of pitching was related, oddly enough, to the explosion of offense in the 1990s. American League teams had averaged 553 runs scored in 1968, 729 in 1980, and 696 in 1990. They averaged between 788 and 872 from 1996 through 2003. The National League had registered 558 runs per team in 1968, 654 in 1980, and 681 in 1990. The total went up to between 759 and 811 between 1996 and 2003. The ERAs posted by Maddux and Glavine (and by Roger Clemens, Pedro Martinez, Randy Johnson, and many more) were lower relative to the league average than the leaders in any other period. They therefore managed to post one superstar season after another, even though they frequently pitched well under 250 innings a season, much less than top starters in earlier eras. Clearly, however, something else may have helped at least some of these men to sustain such extraordinary levels of performance for so long. We shall find that there is no comparable crop of pitchers doing the same among the Millennial generation.

The Braves also stood out for the first half of their dynastic reign because of the remarkable mediocrity of the rest of the National League, but several other teams performed well enough to deserve analysis. The San Francisco Giants lost to the Braves by a single game in the last genuine pennant race in the history of major league baseball in 1993, and returned to contention late in the decade. The Houston Astros put together a strong team in the late 1990s. The Arizona Diamondbacks became contenders in 1999, the second year of their existence, and won the World Series two years later. That broke a record set in 1997 by the Florida Marlins, who won only 92 games but beat an even less dominant Cleveland Indians team to win the World Series. The Mets challenged the Braves for several consecutive years and reached one World Series. And the St. Louis Cardinals began a long run at or near the

---

38. The Braves' staff earned +9 WAA in the very shortened 1994 season and clearly would have exceeded that average had it run its full course.

top of the league in 2001 thanks largely to the emergence of the second-greatest hitter of Generation X, Albert Pujols.

The 1993 Giants were surely the last team that will ever win 103 games and fail to reach post-season play. They were the converse of the Braves team that beat them by a single game, with a line-up worth +19 WAA, a pitching staff worth -1, and four wins' worth of Pythagorean luck. Their biggest asset was the best player in baseball, Barry Bonds, whom they had signed as a free agent and who rewarded them with 8 WAA. Second baseman Robby Thompson, who saved +23 runs in the field, earned 5.5 WAA in only 128 games. Third baseman Matt Williams earned 2.8 WAA, all of them at the plate, and shortstop Royce Clayton and center fielder Darren Lewis made major contributions in the field. First baseman Will Clark, a superstar when the Giants reached the playoffs in 1987, earned 1.6 WAA. The Giants' record for the next six years resembled their record in the late 1950s, with Barry Bonds cast in the role of Willie Mays. Bonds had another great season in strike-shortened 1994 and earned 6, 7.1, 5.5, 7.4 and 3.3 WAA in 1995–1999. He had been the true NL MVP in 1990, 1992, 1993, and 1998, and the most valuable offensive player in 1991, 1995, and 1996. Yet the rest of the Giants were simply awful. Until 1998, the lineup without Bonds was well below average, while the pitching staff posted extraordinary figures of -15 WAA (1995), -10 WAA (1996), -8 (1997), -4 (1998), and -6 (1999). Although the line-up improved and the Giants broke the .500 barrier in 1998–1999, they still failed to make the playoffs. But in 2000, a new phase in the career of Barry Bonds and the fortunes of the San Francisco Giants began.

Bonds had still performed at a superstar level in 1999, although injury limited him to 102 games, and he finished with 3.3 WAA. He had had 12 consecutive superstar seasons from 1987 through 1998,[39] an unequalled record of excellence. Although he had now lost his defensive value, he could presumably have had at least a couple more such seasons. Now, however, a new factor intervened. Mark McGwire—whom as we have seen had not been a superstar before the age of 30—had hit 70 home runs in 1998, and Bonds evidently knew he had done it with the help of performance-enhancing drugs. He decided to find out what they could do for him, and with the help of Greg Anderson and Victor Conte of BALCO, a sports supplement company, he did.

We have seen that Willie Mays and Henry Aaron, with the help of two rounds of expansion, had performed at a superstar level into their late thirties. Bonds—who in the late 1990s was also benefitting from two more rounds of expansion—went them one better. From 2000 through 2004, aged 35 through 39, he rewrote the record books and posted seasons of 6.9, 10.1, 9.8, 8.4, and 9.6 WAA. He was the true NL MVP in 2001–2002, but narrowly trailed Todd Helton of Denver in 2000 and 2003. We must note that while Bonds's traditional statistics in some of those years broke all-time records—73 home runs in 2001, and 198 and 232 walks in 2002 and 2004—these figures in part reflected the overall expansion of offense in those years, and thus, his overall value measured in WAA was not unprecedented. His 17 superstar seasons tie him with Ruth for the most ever (and Ruth just missed

---

39. This includes 1994, when Bonds was on a pace to earn 7 WAA over a full season.

an 18th with 3.9 WAA in 1933). His peak 10.1 WAA of 2001 trails the best single-season marks of Ruth (11.6), Speaker (11.4), Cobb (11.3), and Hornsby (10.4), and ties Ted Williams. Williams also managed to post four consecutive seasons (in 1941–1947, on both sides of the Second World War) that were very comparable to Bonds's in 2001–2004. But no one else, obviously, has come remotely close to posting a string of such seasons in their late thirties, and Bonds, although he had already established himself by 1999 as one of the greatest players of all time, clearly could not have been expected to do anything remotely comparable without his well-documented and acknowledged use of PEDs.[40]

And despite Bonds's remarkable record, the Giants never became a great team in 2000–2004. Only once, in 2002, was their pitching significantly above average (+4 WAA.) Only in 2000 and 2002 did their line-up contribute significant positive value in addition to Bonds's. They did get superstar performances from second baseman Jeff Kent (4.8 WAA) and outfielder Ellis Burks (4.2) in 2000 and again from Kent (4.9) in 2002, and from pitcher Jason Schmidt in 2003. These contributions allowed them to reach the level of a mediocre pennant winner, with 97 and 95 wins in 2000 and 2002, when they nearly won the World Series but lost to the Angels, but that was all. They won 100 games in 2003 with seven wins' worth of Pythagorean luck.

With the help of a remarkably mediocre NL Central Division, the Houston Astros reached the postseason six times in nine years from 1997 through 2005, losing in the first round of the playoffs on the first four of these occasions. (We shall look at 2004–2005, when they reached the NLCS and the World Series, in the next chapter.) In the midst of this era, the team moved from the Astrodome, the worst hitters' park in baseball, to a new stadium, originally named Enron Field, which was a relatively good hitters' park. Their most important player by far was first baseman Jeff Bagwell. The Boston Red Sox had signed Bagwell out of college in 1989 at the age of 21, and in his one full year in the minors in 1990 he had hit .333 with four home runs. Boston traded him to the Astros during the 1990 season for 37-year-old reliever Larry Anderson, who had one save for them that year and whose contract they did not renew. Playing in the worst hitters' park in baseball, the Astrodome, Bagwell immediately established himself as a superstar, earning 3.4, 4.3 and 5 WAA in 1991–1993. Bagwell in 1994—the expansion year that was well on its way to being the biggest offensive year in baseball history when it was interrupted by a strike—was in the midst of one of the greatest seasons in the history of baseball, with 104 runs scored, 116 RBI, 39 home runs and a .368 batting average in 110 games. At it happened, he was seriously injured after 110 games, just as the strike ended the season, but not before he had earned an incredible 8.3 WAA in a little more than ⅔ of a season. He missed about 30 games in strike-shortened 1995 as well, but still finished with 4.8 WAA, and followed that up with 6.6 in 1996, 6 in 1997, 5.5 in 1998, 5 in 1999, 4.2 in 2000, and 5.8 in 2001. He remained a star in 2002–2003, earned 1 more WAA in 2004, and retired after a partial season in 2005 at the relatively early (for this era) age of 37. Bagwell had posted ten consecutive superstar seasons. That gives him the third-highest total of such seasons in Generation X, behind Bonds (17) and Albert

---

40. Bonds admitted using two steroids known as "the cream" and "the clear" given him by Conte, although he denied *knowing* that they were steroids.

Pujols (11). Bagwell's 2017 election to the Hall of Fame is clearly more than warranted by his record.

If one had to choose one player whose career best illustrates the different evaluations that grow out of traditional statistics on the one hand, and yearly WAA on the other, Bagwell's teammate Craig Biggio would be a leading candidate. Biggio was signed by the Astros in 1987 at the age of 21 and reached the team as a catcher in 1988. He spent three full seasons behind the plate, hitting .295 once and 13 homers on another occasion, and earning -0.9, .3, and .4 WAA—a completely average player. In 1992, the Astros and Biggio created a sensation by switching him from behind the plate to second base, where he remained through 2002. Biggio now blossomed as a base stealer, swiping between 33 and 50 bases on five occasions from 1992 through 1998, but only once, in 1998, did his base-running add a full 1 WAA to his overall total. Biggio's power improved markedly in 1993, when he was 27, and he became more of an asset as a hitter, but his overall value suffered because he was more often than not a dreadful second basemen, five times costing the Astros -15 runs or more in a season. Thus, beginning in 1993, he earned 2.3, 2.2 (in strike-shortened 1994), 2.4, and 1.6 WAA in the next four years—a star, but not close to a superstar.

In 1997, at the age of 32, Craig Biggio had perhaps the greatest fluke season in the history of baseball. He hit .325 with 51 doubles and 20 home runs, stole 50 bases and was caught just eight times, and, most astonishing of all, *saved* +18 runs at second base, the only time he was ever significantly above average at this position. All this added up to an extraordinary 8.5 WAA. That is slightly more than Norm Cash's 8.3 WAA in 1961—a season that always comes to mind when flukes are discussed—but Cash had another superstar season later in his career, while Biggio never did. In the next year, Biggio had his second-best season with 3.8 WAA. Extraordinarily durable, he played regularly for eight more years, shifting to center field and then to left field after 2002. In those last eight years, he never earned as much as 1 WAA, and he had two of the worst seasons in baseball history with -4.3 WAA in 2002 and -5.7 in 2007. The switch to Enron Field concealed how bad his hitting had become.

Craig Biggio over the whole of his career was an almost perfectly average player, earning an average of 0.3 WAA per season. Yet he played 19 full seasons in one of the highest-offense eras in baseball history, averaging 143 games a season over all that time. Biggio caught the country's imagination by switching from catcher (where he was mediocre) to second base (where he was much worse), and, critically, his long career enabled him to accumulate 3,060 hits. Like the last few teams Pete Rose played for, the Astros surrendered a number of games to allow Biggio to reach that milestone. And it secured him his election to the Hall of Fame in 2015, while his teammate Jeff Bagwell remained outside it. A number of other Gen X players have suffered badly in Hall of Fame voting because of suspicions of steroids use, but it is at least equally important for the BBWAA voters to realize that career milestones like 3,000 hits and 500 home runs simply do not have the same meaning for players who played through the 1990s and into the 2000s that they had in earlier eras. One no longer had to be a great player for a sustained period of time to reach them.

The Astros squeaked into the playoffs for the first time in the Bagwell-Biggio era in 1997, Biggio's fluke year, when they earned 14.5 WAA between them, but the pitching was mediocre and the rest of the line-up below average. Because of -8 games' worth of bad Pythagorean luck, they won only 84 games. In 1998 the lineup included Bagwell (5.5 WAA), Biggio (3.8), outfielders Moises Alou (2.9), Carl Everett (2.3) and Derek Bell (1.9), and the lineup earned +15 WAA. Among the pitchers, mid-season acquisition Randy Johnson (of whom more later) was almost unhittable, earning 3.3 WAA over his entire season and posting a 10–1 record in just 84⅓ innings, while Jose Lima, Shane Reynolds and Mike Hampton earned 2 WAA apiece. Those pitchers added +10 WAA to the line-up's +15, and the Astros reached the level of a superior pennant winner with 102 victories, despite -4 games of bad Pythagorean luck. This was also Atlanta's best year, however—they were almost exactly as good, although their pitching was better and their hitting a little worse—and they defeated the Astros in the playoffs.

The free agent market was now very active, and things could happen very quickly as a result. Although Bagwell and Everett were nearly as good in 1999 as in 1998, Moises Alou missed the whole season with an injury, Biggio regressed to average, and Derek Bell had a dreadful season at bat and in the field, totaling -4.9 WAA. The lineup as a whole fell from +15 WAA to +1. The pitching staff lost Randy Johnson, but Mike Hampton had a 5.4 WAA superstar season, Lima earned 3.5, reliever Billy Wagner had a remarkable 2.4 WAA in 75 innings, and the staff as a whole was +14 WAA, making up for some dreadful fielding. The team won 97 games but was quickly eliminated in the playoffs again. The hitting was strong in 2000 but the fielding was even worse, costing the team -9 WAA, and the pitching staff lost Hampton to free agency and collapsed as well, as the team won just 72 games. They got their fielding back on track in 2001 and reached the playoffs luckily with 93 wins, but slumped again for the next two years.

The free agency market was very impactful to the standings in the late 1990s, when *something* was allowing far more players to maintain superstar performance well into their thirties. This among other things enabled expansion teams to break the Mets' 1969 record of winning a world championship in eight seasons. The first to do so was the Florida Marlins in 1997, the fifth year of their existence. The Marlins and the Colorado Rockies debuted in 1993; the Tampa Bay Devil Rays and the Arizona Diamondbacks followed in 1998. To be sure, the Marlins owed their 1997 victory mainly to luck. They had the fifth-best run differential in the National League and won only 92 games with the help of three wins' worth of Pythagorean luck, and they defeated a superior Cleveland Indians club in the World Series. The line-up showed the problem of relying upon free agents. Although Gary Sheffield, in his prime at 28, earned 2.4 WAA, Bobby Bonilla, now 34, cost the team enough runs at third base and on the bases to more than make up for a decent performance at bat, and Moises Alou (30) cost the team the same -23 runs in the field that he earned at the plate. Thirty-four-year-old Devon White, who had been a great center fielder earlier in his career, was an average player in 308 at-bats. The worst player on the team, ironically, was 20-year-old shortstop Edgar Renteria, with -2.9 WAA, and the whole line-up was just average. But pitcher Kevin Brown, acquired through free agency, earned a whopping 5.1 WAA, and another such acquisition, Alex Fernandez, added 2.3, accounting for more than the 7 WAA earned by the staff overall. This was Brown's second of four superstar seasons, a tremendous record, but his career bears a suspicious similarity to Mark McGwire's. Brown had been a slightly above average pitcher in the first six years of his career, peaking at 2.4 WAA in 1992. After five years with the Texas Rangers, he signed a one-year contract with the Orioles for 1995, but did not improve. The Marlins signed him for three years, beginning at a reduced $3.35 million in 1996, and it was in that year, at age 31, that he became a new pitcher, posting 7.6 WAA. The Marlins traded him to San Diego after 1997—failing to receive anything like his value—and in 1999, after finishing his contract with 3.8 WAA for the Padres—a figure which helped them reach the World Series—he signed a seven-year contract with the Dodgers for $105 million. In the history of baseball, only Dazzy Vance began a series of dominant performances at a comparable age.

Owner Wayne Huizenga was satisfied with his one world championship, and by the end of 1998, Brown, Alex Fernandez, Moises Alou, Sheffield, and Bonilla were gone from the Marlins, who finished that season with a record of 54–108. The Arizona Diamondbacks made their debut in that year with a record of 65–97, but went heavily into the free agent market themselves and reached the playoffs the next year with 100 victories. Their 1999 line-up was led by 31-year-old outfielder Luis Gonzalez, who earned 3.2 WAA, and included second baseman Jay Bell (1 WAA), third baseman Matt Williams (1.7), and outfielder Steve Finley (1.5), for a total of +10 WAA. The pitching was better.

Giant 6'10" left-hander Randy Johnson had become a starter with the Seattle Mariners in 1989 at age 25, and pitched four totally mediocre seasons for them, largely because he led the league in walks for three years running. In 1993, now 29, he cut his walks significantly, suddenly jumped from 0.4 WAA to 4.9 WAA, and followed that up with 4.0 WAA and 7.2 WAA in two strike-shortened seasons. Johnson missed most of 1996 with injury, but rebounded to 5.6 WAA in 213 innings in 1997. In 1998, as his contract was running out, he pitched at a totally average level for Seattle through July 31, but then became unhittable in the last two months of the year for Houston, with a 10–1 record and 3.3 WAA. The Diamondbacks signed him as a free agent before 1999, and in the next four years, at the ages of 35–38, he earned them 6.6, 6.5, 7.2 and 8.2 WAA. Just as Ted Williams in 1941–47 roughly equaled what Barry Bonds did in 2000–2003. Bob Feller had four almost identical years in 1939–46 (again, interrupted by war), but Feller was only 27 in 1946. Randy Johnson was that rare aging hurler signed as a free agent who was worth every penny he got, at least for four years.

Johnson's 6.6 WAA in 1999 was complemented handsomely by 3 more from Omar Daal, whom the team had acquired in the free agent draft. The staff as a whole earned +12 WAA, and the team's run differential was good enough to have won 102 games instead of 100. They were, however, quickly eliminated in the playoffs. In the next season, Johnson's 6.5 WAA enabled the pitching staff to earn +9 WAA overall, but the aging line-up collapsed almost completely, costing the team -5 WAA and they won only 87 games. In 2001, however, everything worked.

The 2001 Diamondbacks fielded three superstars: Johnson (7.2 WAA); pitcher Curt Schilling, acquired in mid-2000 for Omar Daal (6.1 WAA); and outfielder Luis Gonzalez, with 6.1 WAA. Johnson and Schilling—who fittingly won all four games of the World Series against the Yankees—were the most dominant pair of pitchers fielded by one team since McGinnity and Mathewson on the 1903 Giants, and these three players allowed the Diamondbacks to win 92 games even though the rest of their teammates were -7 WAA overall. Gonzalez, 33 years old in 2001, had become a regular outfielder for Houston in 1991. For five years he was a mediocre hitter but an absolutely brilliant left fielder, posting 5.7 WAA in 1993 thanks to +38 runs saved in the outfield. He had never earned more than 1 WAA at bat until 1999, when he joined the Diamondbacks, established dramatic new career highs of 206 hits, 45 doubles, and 26 home runs (in a neutral park), and earned 3.2 WAA. In the next two years, he improved his home run totals to 31 in 2000 and 57 in 2001, good for 2.3 and 6.1 WAA. He fell below 30 home runs and down to 2.2 WAA the next year and never came close to his 2001 figures again. Schilling and Johnson combined for 14.5 WAA in 2002, breaking McGinnity's and Mathewson's record, but the rest of the pitching staff cost the team -3 WAA, and the line-up was only +3 WAA thanks to very poor fielding. The team slipped to 98 victories. The pitching staff was still good for +10 wins in 2003, but the line-up fell all the way to -7 WAA and the team fell out of contention.

The New York Mets returned to the playoffs in 1999 and reached the World Series in 2000 with a team composed almost entirely of free agents. Even in their best year, 1999, they were only a mediocre pennant winner with 97 wins, thanks to a +10 WAA line-up and a +5 pitching staff. The line-up mixed great strengths with alarming weaknesses. John Olerud, still an excellent hitter and a fine fielder at 30, earned 4.4 WAA at first base in 1999. It was the last of three superstar seasons for Olerud, who had had 6.4 WAA for the Mets the year before. Robin Ventura, who was even better at third, earned 3.6, and second baseman Edgardo Alfonzo, whom they had developed themselves, earned 3.1. Two other great veterans were now only slightly above average: catcher Mike Piazza, who had a dreadful year behind the plate, and left fielder Rickey Henderson, who earned about 1 WAA at the age of 40. Shortstop Rey Ordonez turns out to have been wildly overrated in the field, where he was only average and cost the team -2.3 WAA overall, and center fielder Roger Cedeno was even worse. Ordonez had saved the Mets +12 runs in his rookie season in 1996, but he was completely average for the remainder of his career. Their rotation of aging, high-priced starting pitchers earned less than 2 WAA among them, and three relievers—Turk Wendell, Armando Benitez, and John Franco—earned 3 WAA more.

The 2000 team had an adjusted run differential of just +73 and won 94 games only with the help of six wins' worth of Pythagorean luck. Because of poor fielding, its lineup was perfectly average, while the pitchers improved to +7 WAA. This time Edgardo Alfonzo was the team's only superstar with 4.2 WAA. The Mets had failed to resign Olerud—who remained a major star for three more years for Seattle—but 34-year-old Todd Zeile, who replaced him at first base, fielded brilliantly and earned 1.9 WAA. Piazza, who had a tremendous year at the plate and another very poor one behind it, added another 1.9 WAA. But Ventura and Henderson regressed to average and below, and outfielder Derek Bell cost the team a game. This time the starting pitching was much better, with Al Leiter earning 3.7 WAA and new acquisition Mike Hampton 3.5. Glendon Rusch and Rick Reed combined for 3.5 more, and Benitez had another great year in the bullpen with 1.5 WAA in just 76 innings.

Piazza, who was elected to the Hall of Fame in 2016, ranks just behind Johnny Bench as one of the two greatest catchers of all time. Bench's three best seasons (5.2, 5 and 4.7

WAA) top Piazza's (5.6, 4.1, and 3.7), but they each had nine seasons of 2 WAA or more. Though Bench saved far more runs behind the plate with his arm, Piazza probably deserves the title of greatest hitting catcher of all time. Although Piazza's career was longer, Bench was somewhat more durable, catching more than 140 games in nine different seasons, compared to six for Piazza. No other catcher, however, ever did nearly as much as these two to help their teams win games.

The St. Louis Cardinals returned to post-season play for three consecutive seasons beginning in 2000. They never won more than 97 games and their pitching was entirely mediocre for all three seasons, but their lineup earned them between +12 and +16 WAA each year. The only superstar on the team was center fielder Jim Edmonds, who at 30 suddenly mutated from a star (an average of 2.8 WAA from 1995 through 1998 with the California Angels) to a superstar (4.2 WAA in 2000 and four more superstar seasons in the next five years.) Some of Edmonds' improvement undoubtedly stemmed from his movement from the American League to the National. Because far above-average DHs batted in the American League in place of the pitchers who batted in the National, average hitting in the American League was significantly higher, so that any hitter who changed leagues could expect to see his runs above average and WAA shift accordingly. That, however, was not all. Edmonds also had his four best consecutive years in center field with the Cardinals, saving +11, +18, +9 and +22 runs from 2002–2005. His five superstar seasons would normally qualify him for the Hall of Fame, but he is another Gen X player like Mark McGwire and Kevin Brown, who bloomed remarkably late. The Cardinals' second-strongest position in 2000 was first base, where two aging veterans, Mark McGwire and Will Clark, combined for 4.7 WAA, and third-best was right field, where 24-year-old J. D. Drew earned 2.4 WAA. Second baseman Fernando Vina had a remarkable year in the field and earned 1.8 WAA.

Edmonds slipped to 2.9 WAA in 2001, but Drew improved to 4.2 WAA in just 109 games. Meanwhile, 21-year-old Albert Pujols earned 5.5 WAA in his rookie season while splitting his time between third, first, and the outfield, and fielding quite well overall. A Dominican, Pujols had spent just one year in the minors after briefly attending community college in the U.S. This was the first of 12 consecutive superstar seasons for Pujols, who became a full-time first baseman in his third season. Not until he moved to the American League in 2012 at 33 did he fall below the superstar level, and he has not been able to regain it since. Yet he seems certain to finish his career as the second-greatest hitter of Generation X, behind Bonds. Versatile infielder Placido Polanco earned another 2 WAA in 2001, but shortstop Edgar Renteria and catcher Mike Matheny—whose great fielding did not nearly make up for his dreadful hitting—cost them a combined -4.8 WAA. McGwire and 38-year-old Bobby Bonilla cost them -2 WAA more in limited playing time. The lineup earned +12 WAA and the team won 94 games. Having reached the LCS in 2000, they were eliminated by the Diamondbacks in the first round this year.

The 2002 lineup earned +12 WAA again, half in the field and half at bat. Pujols, shifted to left field, did poorly there and fell to 4 WAA, but Edmonds had a fine year in center and had 4.8, giving the Cardinals two superstars. Pujols gave way at first to 34-year-old free agent Tino Martinez, whose hitting was average (despite coming from the American League) but who saved +10 runs in the field. And third baseman Scott Rolen, acquired from the Phillies in a trade, earned 2.1 WAA in 55 games. Drew, however, slipped to 1.2 WAA, and Vina had become a major liability. This time the Cardinals got revenge on the Diamondbacks in the NLDS, but lost to Bonds and the Giants in the NLCS. The team slumped badly in 2003 but came back stronger than ever from 2004–2006 thanks to new acquisitions. We shall look at that team in the next chapter.

Our survey of the National League has touched upon the great majority of its playoff teams from 1995 through 2003, but three other teams from this era deserve a mention. The 2003 Florida Marlins won both the pennant and the World Series with a team that was almost exactly as strong—or as weak—as the 1997 version. They did not have any superstars, and they won 91 games only with the help of four wins' worth of Pythagorean luck. The Marlins reached the World Series with a famous seven-game victory over the Chicago Cubs, who appeared on the verge of their first trip to the fall classic since 1945 in the eighth inning of the sixth game of the NLCS, which they began leading, 3–0, and exited trailing, 8–3. However painful that loss may have been, it is difficult to feel too much sympathy for a team that had won its division with 88 victories. The miracle was that the Marlins and the Cubs were playing each other in the NLCS, having beaten the Giants and the Braves, who had won 100 and 101 games, respectively.

On the other side of the coin, the 1994 Montreal Expos lost their chance for a truly great season because of the strike. They were 74–40 when the season ended, a pace that left them eight games ahead of the second-place Braves and that would have given them 105 wins. Their outfield of Moises Alou, Marques Grissom and Larry Walker—all 27 years old, at their peak—were all contributing at a superstar pace, and their pitching staff figured to earn +8 WAA. Had their four top starters—Ken Hill, 22-year-old Pedro Martinez, Jeff Fassero and Butch Henry—maintained their pace, they would have averaged almost 3 WAA apiece.

Closing the Books on the Boom Generation

In 1993, Rickey Henderson, Paul Molitor, and pitcher Mark Langston posted the last three superstar seasons put up by members of the Boom Generation.[41] The generation that had now played through two rounds of expansion, the coming of free agency, and a huge increase in player salaries now left center stage.

The Boom Generation featured almost exactly the same number of great offensive players as the Silent Generation, besting them 14 to 13 overall. Leading the way, as we have seen, were Rickey Henderson and Mike Schmidt, with 11 each—the lowest total by a considerable margin of any generation's leaders. The Boomers were also the only generation without a single hitter to post a season of 10 WAA or more—Henderson's 9.3 in 1990 was their best. Schmidt and Henderson were followed by Reggie Jackson with eight superstar seasons, and Wade Boggs, Eddie Murray, and Keith Hernandez with seven. Then come Bobby Bonds and

---

41. Several Boomers, including Tony Gwynn, Henderson, Wade Boggs, and Tony Phillips, were on the pace to reach the superstar level in 1994, but we will never know if they would have done so.

Paul Molitor with six, and Rod Carew, Joe Morgan, Jim Rice, Tim Raines, and Ryne Sandberg with five each. Raines was deservedly elected to the Hall of Fame in 2015, but Hernandez is more deserving—a better version of his GI counterpart Gil Hodges. While the Silent Generation's greats were almost entirely confined to the outfield, the Boomers were much more versatile. Their list of all-timers includes three second basemen—Carew, Morgan, and Sandberg—and three third basemen, Schmidt—the greatest ever by far—Boggs, and Brett. The Boomers also boast the greatest catcher of all time, Johnny Bench, but lack a shortstop quite in the same class, since Cal Ripken and Alan Trammell had only three superstar seasons each.

The Boom Generation also boasts a long list of players with four superstar seasons, including Jose Cruz, who toiled obscurely for the Houston Astros during the 1980s; Bobby Grich, another great second baseman who certainly deserved much more consideration for the Hall of Fame; and Buddy Bell, a third baseman whose value is very similar to Ken Boyer's. While Bell's hitting was generally worth only 1 or 2 WAA a year, he was easily the best-fielding third baseman of his generation, better even than Graig Nettles or Mike Schmidt. Michael Humphreys, indeed, ranks him as the second-best fielder at third base *of all time*, behind only Brooks Robinson—something of an irony, since as we have seen his father, Gus Bell, was one of the *worst* fielders of all time. Other Boomers with four seasons over 4 WAA include outfielders Dave Parker, Willie Wilson, Jesse Barfield, and Tony Gwynn. Only Gwynn of those players posted eye-catching career totals, and he alone is in the Hall of Fame.

Among hitters, the least appreciated great hitter is Bobby Bonds. Born in 1946, Bonds seemed for the first seven seasons of his career to be almost as good as his contemporary Reggie Jackson. He earned the Giants, and then the Yankees, more than 4 WAA in six of those seasons, combining speed, power, and good annual walk numbers, and performing well in both right and center field. He too reached the post-season just once, in 1971, when the Giants' roster included not only Bonds, but future Hall of Famers Gaylord Perry, Juan Marichal, Willie McCovey, and Willie Mays. Astonishingly, Mays, then 40 years old, was the team MVP with 4.8 WAA, easily a record for his age. The team had weaknesses as well, clearly, and lost to the Pirates in four games in the NLCS. Bonds, like Dick Allen, had a drinking problem, was traded from the team that signed him after six years, bounced from team to team repeatedly after that, and declined early and sharply. He will never get serious consideration for the Hall, but he was a dominant player for half a decade.

Bench ranks as history's greatest catcher thanks to his three superstar seasons, to which he added three more over 3 WAA and another three over 2 WAA. Gary Carter ranks just behind him with two superstar seasons, two more over 3 WAA, and four over 2, Both Thurman Munson and Carlton Fisk had one superstar season and four star seasons, but Fisk's long career took him into the Hall of Fame.

Boomer pitchers' records are quite similar to those of the two next-older generations, the GIs and Silents. Just as Bob Gibson and Phil Niekro were the only two Silents pitchers to reach the standard of greatness of five seasons of 4 WAA or more, the only two Boomers to do so were Bert Blyleven and Dave Stieb, with six. Although Blyleven spent most of his career with very mediocre teams, he eventually reached the Hall, but Stieb, despite his dominance in the 1980s, never received any support because of his relatively short career and his failure to win 20 games in a season. Below Blyleven and Stieb, the peak value of Boomers hurlers falls off fast. None of them had four seasons of 4 WAA or more, and only two of them—Tom Seaver and Steve Carlton—had three. Seaver in particular was very unlucky in this respect—he had four seasons of 3.8 or 3.9 WAA as well. The careers of Seaver, Carlton, Jim Palmer, Nolan Ryan, and Don Sutton are very similar to those of GI pitchers Warren Spahn and Early Wynn. While Carlton and Seaver had three superstar seasons each, Palmer had two, and neither Sutton nor Ryan had any. Taking a broader view, we find that Seaver had 14 seasons of at least 2 WAA; Blyleven 13; Palmer ten; Carlton, Ryan, and Stieb eight; and Sutton five. Sutton could be not unfairly described as the Craig Biggio of pitchers. A mediocre player for most of his career, he played for enough good teams to pass the magic marker of 300 wins and reach Cooperstown. Catfish Hunter, as we have seen, had even weaker credentials overall (although he did top 4 WAA twice), but reached Cooperstown thanks to his teammates.

The National League in the first ten years of the new era of expansion playoffs had produced only one genuine dynasty, the Atlanta Braves. The American League, to which we now turn, had produced several. It also produced the 1998 Yankees and the 2001 Mariners, the best teams since at least the 1954 Indians, and the last truly great teams that major league baseball would see for many years to come.

The first of the AL dynasties were the Cleveland Indians, who had been enjoying a fine season in strike-shortened 1994 and reached the World Series in 1995 with a truly great winning percentage of .694, albeit with six wins' worth of Pythagorean luck. That turned out to be their best season, but they won 99 games in 1996, reached the World Series again with just 86 wins in 1997, and made post-season play in 1999 and 2001 with 97 and 91 wins, respectively. They were a home-grown dynasty, featuring left fielder Albert Belle, right fielder Manny Ramirez, and third baseman Jim Thome, all of whom posted a number of superstar seasons. Belle's career is difficult to evaluate. Signed at age 20 in 1987, he played only partial seasons through 1990, in part perhaps because of serious alcohol problems which he eventually overcame. He was a mediocre player in his first two full seasons in 1991–1992 and became a star in 1993, at the age of 26, when he earned 3.1 WAA. Then he had superstar seasons in four of the next five years before fading badly in 2000, his last season. Belle posted 6.2 WAA in the 144-game 1995 season, making him the league's most valuable hitter. The impressive Cleveland lineup, good for +14 WAA overall, included four other stars: 24-year-old Thome (3.3 WAA), 23-year-old Ramirez (2.6 WAA), second baseman Carlos Baerga (2.3 WAA, most of them in the field), and 39-year-old DH Eddie Murray (2.1 WAA). Shortstop Omar Vizquel turns out to have been as overrated as his National League contemporary, Rey Ordonez. With the exception of two remarkable seasons at opposite ends of his career (1991 for Seattle and 2007 for San Francisco), DRA shows that he was consistently slightly below average in the field, and he was a very poor hitter. The pitching staff won an additional +8 WAA for this fine team, featuring 41-year-old Dennis Martinez with 4.2 WAA in just 187 innings, 36-year-old Orel Hershiser with 2.2, young Chad Ogea with 2.5 in 106⅓ innings, and fine relief performances from Jose Mesa and Eric Plunk, who earned about 4 WAA in 128 innings between them.

The 1996 Indians very nearly had four superstars. Their lineup showed an extraordinary mix of triumph and disaster. Belle (6.2 WAA), Thome (6) and Ramirez (4) all had superstar seasons, and center fielder Kenny Lofton—whose defense was very overrated—added 3.3. Thirty-seven-year-old Julio Franco took over at first base and earned 3 WAA with the help of +12 runs in the field. But Baerga and his substitute, Jose Vizcaino, both had dreadful seasons, catchers Tony Pena and Sandy Alomar cost the team -2.6 WAA between them, and Murray fell into below-average territory as well. Amazingly, while the five best players earned +22.5 WAA among them, the lineup as a whole earned just +9. The pitching staff added +7 WAA thanks mainly to Charles Nagy (3.9 in just 222 innings, just missing being the team's fourth superstar), and relievers Eric Plunk, Jose Mesa, and Paul Shuey (3.2 WAA in 203⅔ innings). The Indians lost the division series.

What had looked like a potentially dominant, long-term dynasty began to evaporate in 1997. The Indians decided not to resign 30-year-old Albert Belle, who as it turned out slumped to mediocrity for the White Sox that year and posted only one more superstar season in his short career. Kenny Lofton and Carlos Baerga also left the team. Jim Thome, now switched to first base, and Ramirez slipped to 3.8 and 3.5 WAA, respectively. Brian Giles and 30-year-old Marquis Grissom combined for 1.0 WAA in left and center, compared to 9.5 for Belle and Lofton, whom they had replaced, in 1996. Franco regressed to average, and 35-year-old Tony Fernandez, acquired to play second base, cost the Indians about a game. Thirty-one-year-old Matt Williams, signed to play third base, earned 1.4 WAA. The lineup as a whole regressed to +5 WAA, and the pitching staff dropped all the way to average. Fittingly, the Indians, winners of just 86 games, lost to the Marlins, who won only 92, in extra innings in the seventh game of the World Series.

Ramirez (3.5 WAA) and Thome (3.1) remained stars in 1998, but Sandy Alomar and Pat Borders cost the team -4.3 WAA behind the plate, Vizquel cost them another game, and the lineup as a whole was only slightly above average. +8 WAA from the pitching staff, led by reliever Michael Jackson and 25-year-old starter Bartolo Colon, allowed the team to win 88 games and reach the ALCS. But the team rebounded very smartly in 1999, with 97 wins thanks to a lineup worth +15 WAA. Ramirez returned to the superstar level with 5.8 WAA, his greatest season, and 31-year-old second baseman Roberto Alomar, acquired from the Orioles as a free agent, added 4.5. This was the second of Alomar's three superstar seasons, and with another over 3 WAA and six more over 2, he beats out Chase Utley as the greatest second baseman of Generation X, while ranking behind Boomers Morgan, Carew, and Grich and Millennial Robinson Cano. Thome turned in 3.5 WAA, and Lofton and Justice combined for 3.6. Amazingly, Vizquel had a good year at the plate, earning 1.4 WAA overall, and Sandy Alomar became average at age 33. In 2000, Alomar, an injured Ramirez (who played just 118 games), Thome and Lofton combined for 11.2 WAA. The lineup and the pitching staff each earned 6, but the team finished second in its division with just 91 wins and missed the post-season. The lineup earned another +6 WAA in 2001, replacing Ramirez, who had decamped to the Red Sox, with Juan Gonzalez, late of the Rangers, who earned 3.1 WAA. Alomar and Thome had great years, with 4.9 and 4.1 WAA, but Vizquel, third baseman Travis Fryman, and outfielder Will Cordero cost the team -8.3 WAA. The team was now mostly over 30, and poor fielding reduced the lineup's contribution from +10 WAA to +6. The pitching staff was average. Neither Gonzalez nor Alomar returned in 2002, and the Indians slumped to 72–90. Thome, in his walk year, had his greatest season at age 31, with 6.5 WAA, and left the next year. He eventually added two more superstar seasons with the Phillies in 2003 and the White Sox in 2006, when he was 35, giving him five in his 19-year career—normally enough for the Hall of Fame. After their one year of greatness in 1995, the Indians had become a fairly typical post-season team in the post–1993 era, relying on a few stars to get them between 90 and 95 wins.

This book defines a great player as one with at least five seasons of 4 WAA or more. Generation X has produced 21 such players, and will not produce any more. Three of those 21—Ken Griffey, Jr., Edgar Martinez, and Alex Rodriguez—signed with the Seattle Mariners and reached the majors during the 1990s, and a fourth, pitcher Randy Johnson, joined the Mariners in 1989, when he was 25 years old and had pitched just 55⅔ major league innings for Montreal. Two of these four players are already in the Hall of Fame, and the other two have records that would normally assure them of entering it as well. Although two other teams—the 1929–1931 Athletics (Grove, Foxx and Simmons) and the 1962–1971 Giants (Mays, McCovey and Marichal) have brought three such players to the majors, no other has had four at such early stages of their careers. Yet from 1995 through 1999, when the Mariners had at least three of these players in their lineup every year, they won just 79, 85, 90, 76, and 99 games, making the playoffs only twice. Like the Giants of the early 1960s, they nearly always balanced their great players with several dreadful ones.

Ken Griffey, Jr., had signed right out of high school at 17 and spent just two years in the minors. A fine hitter with power whom the Mariners put in center field, Griffey had his first superstar season (4.3 WAA) in 1991 at age 21, and followed it up with two comparable seasons in 1993–1994.[42] In 1995, Griffey broke his wrist making a leaping catch against the fence in late May and missed 71 games. He earned only 1.4 WAA in half of the strike-shortened season, but the team won their division with a .545 percentage (79–66). Griffey, DH Edgar Martinez (6.1 WAA), and first baseman Tino Martinez (2.6 WAA) were the only above-average players in the line-up. Right fielder Jay Buhner (-26 runs in the field), second baseman Joey Cora (-22 fielding runs), and shortstop Luis Sojo (-13) were so terrible that team fielding cost the team -6 WAA, making the line-up completely average. Pitcher Randy Johnson, with a remarkable 7.2 WAA, provided most of the +9 WAA earned by the pitching staff. The Mariners reached the ALCS for the only time in the 1990s, losing to the Indians.

Edgar Martinez, the greatest DH of all time, finished his long career with seven superstar seasons, but his record shows the same unusual feature as Mark McGwire's. Entering organized baseball at age 20 in 1983, Martinez did not become a major league regular until 1990, when he was 27, and earned 1.9 WAA in that year. He improved to 3.1 in 1991 and 5.1 in 1992, but missed most of 1993 with an injury and posted 1.1 WAA in 1994. Then, starting in 1995, when he was 32, he had six superstar seasons in seven years.

Every generation includes one or two relatively late bloomers among its all-time greats. Among the Lost Generation, these include Harry Heilmann, who did not break 4 WAA until he was 28 and did so in four of the next five years, and Bill Terry, who also debuted in

---

42. Griffey is one of the players who definitely deserves to be credited with a projected 4.8 WAA in 1994—he had had 4.9 in a full season the year before.

the superstar column at 28 in his third full season, and remained there for seven out of nine years. Among GIs, Charlie Gehringer had his five superstar seasons from ages 30 through 34. Neither Terry nor Gehringer were power hitters. Among the Silent Generation, both Roberto Clemente and Billy Williams had most of their greatest seasons in their 30s, but Clemente had three superstar seasons in his 20s and Williams had two. Among Boomers, Joe Morgan and Rod Carew did not become superstars until ages 28 and 27 respectively, but then remained solidly in that category for five consecutive seasons. Generation X, however, included late bloomers of a different kind. We have seen that Mark McGwire, who became a regular at age 23, did not break the superstar barrier until he was 31, but then did so four times in five years. Martinez had broken that barrier at age 28—when most players reach their peak—but it was in 1995, when he was 32, that he became a superstar for six of the next seven years. That pattern, like McGwire's, was without precedent.

The 1996 Mariners once again had three superstars totaling 15.9 WAA: Edgar Martinez (5.6 WAA), Griffey (4.8), and 20-year-old shortstop Alex Rodriguez, the second-greatest Generation Xer at that position, who posted 5.5 WAA in his first full season. Thanks to Buhner, Joey Cora, and Louis Sojo, however, the lineup as a whole was only +10 WAA. Meanwhile, Randy Johnson missed most of the season and the Mariners barely missed the playoffs. In 1997, Johnson (6.9 WAA), Martinez (5.4) Griffey (5.2) and Rodriguez (3.1) combined for 20.5 WAA, but the rest of the team was about 11 wins below average, and they made the playoffs with just 90 wins, losing in the first round.

In 1998, Martinez, Griffey, Rodriguez and first baseman David Segui earned 16.4 WAA among them, but Cora, third baseman Russ Davis, catcher Dan Wilson, and the bench were so bad that the line-up was only average as a whole. So was the pitching staff—Johnson was dealt to Houston in mid-season—and bad luck left the team with a 76–85 record. In 1999, the team moved from the neutral Kingdome to Safeco Field, a pitchers' park. Martinez, Griffey and Rodriguez all slumped, earning only 8.4 WAA among them, while new second baseman David Bell, third baseman Davis, catcher Wilson and outfielders Brian Hunter and Buhner cost the team -9.2 WAA. The pitching was -3 WAA and the team won 79 games. The Mariners traded Griffey to Cincinnati after 1999 and received center fielder Mike Cameron in return.

Cameron outperformed Griffey for the next few seasons. Handsome, graceful, and athletic, Griffey won the hearts of America's writers and fans, and no suspicion of steroids was ever attached to him. While his six superstar seasons certainly entitled him to his place in the Hall of Fame, it turns out that he was never significantly more than an average center fielder, and he became a major liability in the field during the second half of his career. He suffered from numerous injuries beginning in 2001, when he was only 31, and he was below average in three of his last ten seasons, and barely average in the other seven. One could certainly argue that Charlie Keller, whose peak was more impressive, deserves to be in the Hall at least as much as Griffey. On the other hand, if Griffey in fact never used PEDs—and the extensive time he lost to injuries suggests that he did not—then he was in fact a significantly greater player than his performance relative to the drug-improved league average would suggest. His lifetime totals benefited enormously from the era he played in. Griffey hit 630 home runs, just 30 less than Willie Mays, but he needed only six superstar seasons to do so, while Mays had 16. During the last nine years of his career, Griffey never exceeded 0.8 WAA. He hit 210 of his home runs during that period. Several of his contemporaries are likely to reach the Hall by a similar route.

In 2000–2003, a new Mariners team won 90 games or more in four consecutive seasons, making the playoffs three times. In 2000, Rodriguez hit 41 home runs, walked 100 times, saved +11 runs in the field, and posted a remarkable 6.9 WAA. Edgar Martinez tacked on 4.7 WAA more, matching his age with 37 home runs and walking 96 times, and John Olerud, signed from the Mets, added 3.1 WAA. Mike Cameron was good for 2. The pitching staff cost them two wins, but the team won 91 games, losing in the ALCS to the Yankees. Then followed the most amazing season of the post-expansion era.

The 2001 Mariners broke the American League record with 116 wins, besting the season record of 114 wins that the Yankees had established in 1998, but just missing the winning percentage of the 1954 Cleveland Indians, .721 to .716. Like the Indians, they benefited from six wins' worth of Pythagorean luck, but this remained one of the greatest seasons in history by any measure. Alex Rodriguez was gone, signed by the Texas Rangers as a free agent, but the Mariners had a new right fielder, Japanese superstar Ichiro Suzuki, whom they acquired at his 27-year-old peak. A throwback to the dead ball era, Ichiro hit .350 with 242 base hits and 34 doubles, fielded brilliantly, and made up for Rodriguez's departure with 6.8 WAA. The team had three other superstars. Second baseman Bret Boone, 32 years old, had been average or below average for eight of his ten major league seasons. Now, in the walk year of his contract, he hit .331 with 37 homers and earned 5 WAA. The Mariners promptly resigned him, roughly doubling his salary to more than $8 million a year. Mike Cameron fielded brilliantly in center field and earned 4.2 WAA, and Martinez had 4 WAA in just 132 games. Olerud was right behind with 3.4. And for the first time in this whole era, the Mariners did not field a single significantly below average player. Like nearly every other great team, the Marines had outstanding fielding," worth +8 WAA, and their line-up accounted for +26 wins above .500.

Like most other great teams, the Mariners had outstanding fielding. Led by starters Freddy Garcia and Jamie Moyer and reliever Arthur Rhodes, the pitching staff added +3 WAA. The Mariners beat the Indians in the Division Series, but lost to the Yankees—winners of just 95 games—in the ALCS. While the Mariners were a great team, only a change in the major league schedules enabled them to win 116 games. 2001 was the first year of the unbalanced schedule, in which teams played their division rivals twice as often as teams from other divisions. Both Seattle and Oakland (who won 102 games) played 19 or 20 games each against Anaheim and Texas, but only nine and seven games each against New York and Cleveland. Seattle went 30–9 against its two weakest division rivals, but 11–5 against the Indians and Yankees. The schedule evidently added a few wins to their total.

The Mariners declined as spectacularly as the 1939–1940 Yankees, winning only 93 games the next year and missing the playoffs. The gods of baseball appeared to have commanded the whole line-up to return to earth. Ichiro slipped to 3.9 WAA, Cameron to 1.7, Martinez to 2.2 (in just 97 games), and Boone all the way to perfectly average. Olerud held steady at 3.3, but shortstop Carlos Guillen, aging outfielder Ruben Sierra, and third baseman Jeff Cirillo each cost the team a game. The pitching staff added +3 WAA, thanks largely to Jamie Moyer, now 39 years old. In 2003, the Mariners had a significantly better team but won just 93 games thanks to five games' worth of bad Pythagorean luck. Although Ichiro slipped to 3.5 WAA, Boone and Cameron both had extraordinary years in the field and returned to superstardom at 4.5 and 4.8 WAA, respectively. (Boone never had a remotely comparable season again.) Martinez managed 2.6 WAA at age 40, but Olerud fell to 1.6. Overall the team's fielding was remarkable, earning +8 WAA, and the pitchers, led again by Moyer, earned +5 more. They missed the playoffs again. With three trips to the ALCS from 1995 through 2001, the Mariners were unlucky not to have reached the World Series, and they remain one of only two MLB franchises never to do so. Had they been able to develop average players as well as superstars, they would have done much better.

In 1995, the New York Yankees made post-season play for the first time since 1981, with a mediocre percentage of .545. In 1996, they began an extraordinary streak in which they reached the World Series six times in eight years, winning it four times from 1996 through 2000. This achievement was all the more astonishing since only three times in the 1995–2003 period did they reach the level of a superior pennant winner. This Yankees dynasty, moreover, was utterly unlike those of 1921–1932, 1936–1942, 1949–1964, and 1976–1980. In most of these seasons, the pitchers accounted for the majority of the team's wins, while the lineup began strongly and declined quite steadily.

The 1996 Yankees had loaded up with aging stars whom the team had acquired via trade (first baseman Tino Martinez, outfielders Paul O'Neill, Ruben Sierra, and Tim Raines, and DH Cecil Fielder) or free agency (third baseman Wade Boggs, catcher Joe Girardi, second baseman Mariano Duncan). Such acquisitions tend to be liabilities in the field, and these were no exception. O'Neill, whom the Yankees had acquired in 1992 for a much lesser player, was the lineup's MVP with 3.3 WAA, but Martinez, Duncan, Boggs, Raines, Darryl Strawberry, and Fielder were all roughly average, and Sierra was worse. Center fielder Bernie Williams, a homegrown Yankee, was in the fifth full season of a very good career. Williams had enjoyed his finest season yet in 1995, earning 3.9 WAA. He had been a good fielder through that season, but unfortunately, starting in 1996, when he was 27, his fielding slipped to average at best, and eventually, in 2002, fell to dreadful. Williams was the other major asset in the 1996 lineup, with 2.4 WAA. Twenty-two-year-old rookie shortstop Derek Jeter, whom the Yankees had signed at age 18, had a season that was a portent of things to come. Jeter hit .314 with 48 walks and 10 homers, earning the team about 13 runs above average on offense, but he gave -10 of those runs back at shortstop. Against a weak field, he was selected AL Rookie of the Year. The line-up as a whole cost the Yankees -2 WAA, including -4 WAA in the field. The pitching staff got the team into postseason, led by 24-year-old, homegrown left-hander Andy Pettitte, who earned 3.2 WAA in 221 innings, and 26-year-old, second-year reliever Mariano Rivera. Not yet the closer, Rivera saved only five games in 1996, but posted an ERA of 2.09 (the league average was 4.99) in 107⅔ innings and earned a remarkable 3.4 WAA. He was the team MVP. Two ex-Mets, 33-year-old David Cone and 31-year-old Dwight Godden, added 2 and 1 WAA respectively, and the pitching staff as a whole earned +10 WAA. Still, it had taken three wins' worth of Pythagorean luck to get the team up to 92 wins, and their run differential was far inferior to that of the Cleveland Indians in their own league and the Braves they beat in the World Series.

As so often has happened since 1995, the 1997 Yankees improved their performance substantially but did much worse in the post-season. Tino Martinez had the year of his life at bat and in the field, finishing with 4.9 WAA, and O'Neill and Williams (who missed 33 games) added 4.9 and 2 WAA, respectively. Jeter—who once again gave away as many runs in the field as he earned in a poorer second year at the plate—Fielder, Boggs, Raines, Mark Whiten, and new acquisition Luis Sojo were average, and Joe Gerardi, third baseman Charlie Hayes, and Duncan cost the team -4.5 WAA. Overall the line-up earned +10 WAA (despite -2 WAA of poor fielding), and the pitchers added +10 more. Pettitte cracked the superstar barrier with 4.7 WAA in 240⅓ innings, going 18–7, and 34-year-old David Cone had 3.8 more. David Wells added 1.4 and Rivera, now the closer, had 1.8. Thanks to bad Pythagorean luck, the Yankees won only 92 games and made the playoffs as a wild card even though they had the best run differential in the league. The Indians beat them in the Division Series.

The 1998 Yankees broke the 1954 Indians' record of 111 wins with 114—although their winning percentage was slightly lower, since they played 162 games—and their percentage of .704 ranks just ahead of their 1939 counterparts (.702), though behind the 1927 team (.714). They owed their extraordinary improvement of 22 wins partly to four wins' worth of good Pythagorean luck, but also to a revamped lineup which turned their fielding from a -3 WAA weakness to a +6 WAA strength, and they improved their hitting substantially as well. Veterans Paul O'Neill and Bernie Williams had superstar seasons (4.2 and 4.4 WAA), and Tino Martinez added 3 WAA with the help of a great year in the field. Although Jeter surrendered -12 runs at short, he had his best year yet at the plate and finished with 3.2 WAA as well. Key to the team's improvement were second baseman Chuck Knoblauch, acquired from Minnesota in exchange for four prospects, and 31-year-old free agent Scott Brosius at third. Knoblauch, who saved +8 runs at second, earned 1.5 WAA compared to -.6 for the three players who shared the position in 1997, and Brosius, replacing Charlie Hayes and Boggs (-1.7 WAA in 1997), saved +18 runs at third and earned 3.6 WAA. Darryl Strawberry earned 1.7 WAA in 101 games at DH, new catcher Jorge Posada got the catching position slightly above average, and outfielder Chad Curtis earned 2.2 WAA more. The line-up earned +22 WAA overall. The pitchers did not repeat their dazzling 1997 performance but earned a solid +7 WAA. Pettitte, apparently injured, threw 216⅓ average innings, but Wells and Cone earned 2.1 and 1.5 WAA, and another new acquisition, Orlando Hernandez, earned 1.8. Closer Rivera earned 1.4 in just 61⅓ innings. No great team has ever had better balance through the line-up and pitching staff. The Yankees performed like a great team in the post-season, sweeping the Division and World Series and losing just twice in the ALCS. As it turned out, however, the age of the line-up did not bode well for the future, especially in the field.

The Yankees line-up lost half its positive value, from +22 WAA to +11, in 1999. Paul O'Neill, Scott Brosius and Tino Martinez fell from a combined 8.7 WAA to 3 WAA, and catchers Posada and Girardi cost the team -2.6 WAA behind the plate. Williams had his second and last superstar season with 4.6 WAA, and Jeter, despite a tremendous year at the plate, just missed the superstar line with 3.9 WAA because he surrendered -21 runs in the field. This was his greatest season. The pitchers stayed at the same level (+6 WAA), mainly because Pettitte had another off-year and remained average. Cone and Hernandez had about

4 WAA between them, and Roger Clemens, acquired from the Blue Jays for David Wells at age 36, earned just .5 WAA in 187⅔ innings. Rivera added 1.8 WAA 69 innings. The team won 98 games—a mediocre pennant winner—but swept through the post-season even more easily, losing only one game in the ALCS. The decline of the team continued in 2000, when the Yankees won just 87 games and emerged as one of the weakest World Series winners in history. Martinez, O'Neill, Brosius and Knoblauch—who suddenly became a liability in the field—cost the team a combined -3.5 WAA. Jeter had his worst year yet in the field, with -28 runs, and earned only 1.1 WAA, and Williams slipped to 2.5. Bright spots included catcher Posada, who suddenly blossomed as a hitter and earned 2.8 WAA, and another aging outfielder, David Justice, who earned 2.7 WAA in just 78 games. The whole, high-priced lineup was perfectly average, and the pitchers earned just +5 WAA. Roger Clemens, in his second year with the club, improved to 2.8 WAA at age 37, Pettitte rebounded to 1.8, and Rivera and Hernandez each had 1.5. This time the Yankees survived a scare against the Oakland Athletics in the Division Series, beat a better Mariners team in the ALCS, and prevailed four games to one against a Mets team that also ranked well below the top of its league in games won.

The team was only marginally better in 2001, but won 95 games with the help of six wins' worth of Pythagorean luck. The 2001 Yankees had one of the worst line-ups—and probably the worst-ever fielding—of any team to reach the World Series, -3 WAA overall and -8 WAA in the field. Bernie Williams was the only star in the lineup, with 2.7 WAA. Jeter surrendered -29 runs in the field and earned 0.9 WAA overall. Knoblauch, who had been struck with a mysterious affliction that prevented him from throwing to first base from second, was moved to left field, where he surrendered -11 runs while hitting poorly and cost the team -1.4 WAA. He was replaced at second by 25-year-old Alfonso Soriano, whose hitting was below average and who gave up -19 runs in the field, costing the Yankees -2.8 WAA overall. Posada, Brosius and David Justice were average, and O'Neill, 38, dropped to -1.4 WAA. The pitchers managed to earn +12 WAA and save the team, led by 32-year-old free agent Mike Mussina, the team's only superstar, with 4.9 WAA, and 38-year-old Clemens, with 3.6. Pettitte had 1.8 WAA, Rivera 1.8, and reliever Mike Stanton 1.9. The Yankees managed to beat the Mariners, who had just won 116 games, in the ALCS, but lost the World Series in the ninth inning of the seventh game to Arizona.

In 2002, the hitting improved substantially to +13 WAA, but the fielding cost the team -8 WAA for the second of three consecutive seasons. Free agent acquisition Jason Giambi, 31, was the first superstar in the lineup since 1999, with 41 homers, 109 walks, a .314 average, and 6 WAA. Soriano had 39 homers but walked just 23 times, surrendered -18 runs in the field, and finished with just 1.5 WAA overall. Williams, now 33, had a dreadful year in center, giving up -22 runs, and finished with just 1.6 WAA. Jeter slipped at the plate and had one of the worst years of any shortstop in the history of baseball, -42 runs, making him -1.9 WAA overall. Posada, who had become a good hitter, had 2.1 WAA, and 34-year-old Robin Ventura, another free agent, earned 1.9 WAA. The lineup earned +5 WAA overall but the pitchers added +13 WAA. Mike Mussina earned 2.5 in 216 innings at age 31, 39-year-old Wells—reacquired as a free agent—earned 1.9, and his contemporary, Clemens, earned 1.1. Orlando Hernandez, 36, earned 2.3, Pettitte 1.9, and Rivera earned 0.8 in just 46 innings.

This time playoff luck caught up to the Yankees, who had won 103 games, their most since 1998, but who won just one game against the Anaheim Angels in the Division Series.

2003 was the last year that the Yankees reached the World Series until 2008. They did so with 101 wins, four of them earned through Pythagorean luck, and a wretched defensive lineup that cost them -8 WAA runs in the field yet again and earned only +2 WAA overall. Jorge Posada, hitting his peak at 31, was the only superstar in the lineup, with 4 WAA. Giambi continued to hit well, but caught the virus that had infected the middle of the Yankees' infield, surrendered -12 runs at first base, and wound up with just 2.7 WAA. Soriano improved his defense substantially to just -6 runs and earned 2.2 WAA, but Jeter improved only to -32 runs and cost the team -.8 WAA in 119 games. Bernie Williams, also a significant defensive liability at 34, was also barely in negative territory. Hideki Matsui, acquired from Japan at age 29, hit .287 with 16 home runs, but he earned the team only 9 runs with his bat and surrendered -16 in the outfield. The aged pitching staff carried the team for the fourth straight year, earning about 14 WAA. Mike Mussina, 34, was the team's second superstar, with 4.7 WAA, the fifth superstar season of his career. Wells and Clemens combined for 5 WAA at age 40, and Pettitte added another 1.6. Rivera, with a 1.91 ERA, earned 2.2 WAA in just 70⅔ innings. The Yankees unwisely let Clemens go after that season and paid a heavy price the next year. They lost to a mediocre Florida Marlins team in the 2003 World Series.

The Yankees, of course, remained at or near the top of the American League East for the better part of another decade, and we shall follow their evolution in the next chapter. The dynasty of 1995–2004, however, was unique in several respects. Leaving aside Bernie Williams, Derek Jeter, Mariano Rivera, and Jorge Posada, it was built and sustained almost entirely with the help of trades and free agents. Older hitters provided most of the team's positive value through 1999, and older pitchers provided even more of it from 2000 through 2003. The ability of Mussina, Clemens and Wells to continue performing at a high level in their mid- or late thirties was remarkable. Several of these players, of course, including Pettitte, Clemens, and Jason Giambi, have admitted to or been accused of using PEDs. We shall find that it has become impossible to field and maintain a dynasty using older free agents in the last decade, after PED testing began. Last but hardly least, the Yankees' post-season luck was as good as their National League contemporaries, the Braves', was bad. They repeatedly advanced to the World Series at the expense of American League teams that had a better record during the season.

Looming over this team, of course, were two iconic figures. Although Mariano Rivera never broke the superstar barrier, he was incomparably the greatest relief pitcher of all time. From 1996 through 2011, he topped 3 WAA once and 2 WAA four times. all without ever pitching as many as 81 innings from 1997–2011. That is the best record of star seasons among relievers that I have discovered. Bruce Sutter, Rollie Fingers, and Rich Gossage, who have all been elected to the Hall, had three, one, and three seasons of at least 2 WAA, respectively, compared to Rivera's seven.

The Yankees' second icon was shortstop Derek Jeter, who finished his 20-year career in 2014 with 3,465 base hits and will be inducted into the Hall of Fame with an overwhelming vote in 2020. But in 18 years as the regular Yankees shortstop, Jeter, according to Michael Humphreys's DRA metric, surrendered -345 runs at shortstop, equivalent to almost -2 wins per year. No other long-time player at any position as ever done his team so much harm in the field. Because he was especially dreadful in the field when he was at his peak as a hitter, he never managed to post a single superstar season. He did top 3 WAA four times, a better record than Phil Rizzuto, Pee Wee Reese, Dave Bancroft, or Travis Jackson—four other New York shortstops that are in the Hall of Fame—but he cannot reasonably be compared to Barry Larkin, Alan Trammell, or Alex Rodriguez. The Yankees had a chance to replace him with a better shortstop in 2004 when they signed Rodriguez, but they chose not to. At the end of the 2007 season, Jeter had 2,356 hits, and he was a below-average player overall in five of his last six full seasons, during which he accumulated 1,109 more. His farewell season in 2014 was one of the worst in the history of modern baseball—-4.1 WAA—and the decision to play him that year cost the Yankees at least an even chance at the post-season. Jeter appeared regularly and performed well in post-season and was the symbol of the last Yankees dynasty, but he should never have played as much as one game at shortstop in the major leagues, and he was never the critical factor in the success of his Yankees teams.

The Yankees dynasty got some intermittent intra-divisional competition from the Red Sox, who won the AL East in 1995 with a mediocre run differential, had the second-best record in the league (92–70) when the Yankees won 114 games in 1998, and earned the wild card again with 94 wins in 1999. Like the Boston teams of the previous decade, these Red Sox got most of their positive value from their pitching. More specifically, it came from one extraordinary hurler, Pedro Martinez, who had begun his career in the Dodgers' bullpen in 1993 at age 21 and spent 1994–1997 with Montreal. After three star seasons of at least 2 WAA, he broke through to the superstar level in 1997 with a 17–8 record, a league-leading 1.90 ERA in a high-scoring league in 241⅓ innings, and 6.8 WAA. After moving to the Red Sox, he followed that up with seasons of 5.2, 8.6 and 8.7 WAA—a four-year run superior to Sandy Koufax's in 1963–1966. And while Koufax hung up his spikes after his four-year run, Martinez followed his up with two superstar seasons and three more over 3 WAA five years, leaving him with seven superstar campaigns.

Unfortunately, Martinez had a very poor supporting cast. Thanks to the combination of Fenway Park—still a hitters' park, although by no means as much as in the past—and a very high-offense era, their hitting seemed at least adequate, but they lacked any offensive superstars. In 1995, before Martinez arrived, power-hitting first baseman Mo Vaughn hit .300 with 39 home runs, but earned only 2.6 WAA. Shortstop John Valentin had a great year at the plate but cost the team -10 runs in the field, leaving him with 2.4 WAA, and the entire outfield of Troy O'Leary, Lee Tinsley, and Mike Greenwell was average. With a weak bench, the line-up overall earned only 3 WAA. The team MVP was knuckleballer Tim Wakefield, who broke the superstar barrier for the only time in his long career with 4.2 WAA, and the rest of the pitching staff contributed +2 WAA more.

The lineup was a bit better in 1998, when the team returned to the playoffs, earning a modest +5 WAA. Vaughn's .337 average with 40 homers still couldn't get him over the superstar barrier—although he was an average fielding first baseman—but he earned 3.4 WAA. Second-year shortstop Nomar Garciaparra, an excellent hitter and an average fielder, added 3 WAA more at age 24. Garciaparra's career burned out at the age of 30 because of injuries, but because he was both a good hitter and an average shortstop, he was a substantially more valuable player than his exact contemporary, Derek Jeter, from 1997 through 2003, and he finished with two superstar seasons to Jeter's none. John Valentin remained an important asset at third base with 1.9 WAA, but the outfield was entirely average again. Pedro Martinez accounted for nearly all of the pitching staff's +6 WAA.

The team improved to 94 wins in 1999, making the playoffs yet again, with one of the most extraordinary patterns of talent in history. Although Garciaparra had the first of two consecutive superstar seasons with 4.1 WAA, his performance was more than balanced out by disastrous second baseman Jose Offerman (-1.7 WAA); 27-year-old catcher Jason Varitek (-1.1 WAA); outfielder Darren Lewis (-1.7 WAA); and John Valentin, -.5 WAA because of a disastrous year at the plate. The starting line-up and the bench players cost the team a staggering -4 WAA overall. The pitchers, on the other hand, led by Pedro's 8.6 WAA, earned an amazing +16 WAA overall. This was Pedro's greatest season, and he finished with a 23–4 record and a 2.07 ERA. Thirty-five-year-old Bret Saberhagen was still good enough to earn 3.6 WAA in just 119 innings, and reliever Derek Lowe added 2.8 WAA in 109⅓ innings. This time the Red Sox won the first round of the playoffs but won only one game against the Yankees in the ALCS. Despite the acquisition of Manny Ramirez, the line-up remained dreadful in 2000 and 2001, keeping the team out of the playoffs.

In 2003, new management took over, including owner John Henry, general manager Theo Epstein, and sabermetrician Bill James. They took over at a fortuitous moment: the 2002 team, winners of 93 games, were good enough to have won 100 but fell seven wins short of their Pythagorean projection. Manny Ramirez posted 4.8 WAA in just 120 games, Garciaparra had 3.5, and right fielder Trot Nixon earned 2.4 thanks to a superb year in the field. Johnny Damon remained average for the second consecutive year. The line-up was +11 WAA overall, and the pitchers added +8, led by Martinez's 5.4 WAA. As it turns out, Epstein and James did not improve the 2002 team at all in 2003. The 2003 team featured three new acquisitions. Third baseman Bill Mueller, a free agent, had a great year at the plate and earned 3.5 WAA, while 27-year-old David Ortiz, also a free agent who had never exceeded average performance in three seasons with Minnesota, earned 1.9. Unfortunately, new regular second baseman Todd Walker was disastrous in the field—as were the team's other second basemen—and he cost them -2.2 WAA. Nixon (3.3 WAA, all at bat) and Garciaparra (2.4) had star seasons again. Jason Varitek (1.7 WAA) also became an asset behind the plate. The overall value of the 2003 line-up was almost identical to 2002, but its hitting was much better and its fielding much worse. Meanwhile, Pedro Martinez earned 5.5 WAA in just 186⅔ innings, and Derek Lowe and Tim Wakefield added 2.7 WAA. The rest of the staff was weak, however, and overall the pitchers earned just +4 WAA. The Yankees overcame a deficit in the late innings of Game 7 of the ALCS to beat the Red Sox in extra innings.

The Red Sox were now relying on older players and fell into some of the pitfalls of this strategy in 2004. Ramirez, Mueller, Nixon, and Garciaparra, who had earned 14.2 WAA in 2003, put up just 3 WAA in 2004, as Nixon missed most of the year and Garciaparra was traded after playing just 38 games. Mueller's re-signing as a free agent was particularly unfortunate, since he was keeping 25-year-old Kevin Youkilis on the bench or in the minors. But Damon suddenly became a major star again with 3.5 WAA, and Ortiz matched him as a DH. Kevin Millar and Jason Varitek also became stars, earning more than 2 WAA each. But the most valuable change in the line-up was the advent of second baseman Mark Bellhorn, whose -5 runs in the field were more than 40 runs better than Todd Walker and the rest in the previous season. The team's fielding improved all the way to average, allowing the lineup to remain +10 WAA overall despite a hitting slump. The team improved more on the mound. Martinez, now 32, slipped to 3.7 WAA. But taking a leaf from the Yankees' book, Epstein signed 37-year-old Curt Schilling as a free agent from Arizona, and he became the new ace with a 21–6 record, a 3.26 ERA (the league average was 4.63), and 5 WAA. Reliever Keith Foulke added 2.2 WAA in just 83 innings, and the staff as a whole earned 7 WAA despite a dreadful year from Derek Lowe. With 98 wins, the Red Sox were a mediocre pennant-caliber team, but they prevailed over the Angels and Yankees in the playoffs and swept a substantially superior Cardinals team in four straight games. Relying on veteran acquisitions rather than homegrown talent, the Red Sox had acquired significant assets—led by Schilling—and had managed to keep any significantly below-average players out of the line-up. Unfortunately, such players quickly returned.

The 2004 Yankees, meanwhile, self-destructed thanks to bad off-season decisions, but nearly managed to compensate with a remarkable 12 wins of Pythagorean luck, giving them 101 victories. Wittingly or unwittingly, the team slightly improved their dreadful fielding, going from -8 WAA in 2003 to just -5 WAA. Jeter and Matsui, who had cost the team a combined -48 runs in 2003, improved all the way to -26. Miguel Cairo, at second base, was a vast improvement over Soriano, who had been traded, and new acquisition Alex Rodriguez—who should surely have been given Jeter's shortstop spot—fielded slightly above average at third base. The Yankees' roster was both older and more expensive than the Red Sox's, and Rodriguez, now 28, was the youngest man in the lineup. He and 35-year-old Gary Sheffield led the lineup with 3.9 and 3.4 WAA, and Matsui (who had a fine year at the plate) and Posada added 3 and 2.1 WAA. Unfortunately, Jeter was only barely above average, and first basemen Jason Giambi and Tony Clark, DH Ruben Sierra, and infielder Enrique Wilson cost the team a combined -4.7 WAA. The line-up as a whole earned only 4. The pitching staff declined even more.

The 2003 Yankees, we have seen, had compensated for their dreadful fielding with tremendous pitching In the off-season, the Yankees' front office allowed Wells, Clemens and Pettitte to depart—633 innings' worth 5.4 WAA. (Clemens and Pettitte both signed with Houston and became superstars again.) Their replacements were only marginally above average, and Mussina, now 35, fell from 4.5 WAA to 1. The staff as a whole earned just +4 WAA—10 less than the previous year. Only Pythagorean luck compensated for that self-inflicted wound. Curiously enough, although both the 2003 and 2004 ALCS were decided by the very narrowest of margins, the outcomes reflected the teams' true relative strength. The Yankees had a slightly better run differential than the Red Sox in 2003, but the Red Sox's Pythagorean percentage was a full nine wins better than the Yankees' in 2004, when the Yankees still won the division thanks to 12 wins' worth of luck. As we shall see, the Yankees-Red Sox rivalry continued well into the next era.

After nearly a decade of mediocrity, the Oakland A's returned to the playoffs for the first of four consecutive seasons in 2000 under the direction of 38-year-old general manager Billy Beane. Beane's ability to field a winning team on a very low budget became the subject of a best-selling book, *Moneyball*, by Michael Lewis, and a successful movie. Many observers felt that the film in particular had given a misleading sense of the sources of the A's success, and that turns out, indeed, to be the case. Still, the A's story—roughly the reverse of the Yankees' in the same period—makes interesting reading.

The A's returned to the post-season in 2000 with a very modest 91 wins, good enough to win a weak AL West. Their one superstar was first baseman Jason Giambi, who had been completely average in his first two years as a regular (1996–1997) and reached the star level (2.3 WAA) in 1998, at age 28. In 1999, Giambi—who eventually admitted he had begun using steroids some time before 2002—reached the superstar level with 4.5 WAA. In 2000, he improved to 7.3 WAA, hitting .333 with 43 homers and 137 walks. The young, homegrown players who made up much of the rest of the A's line-up, including shortstop Miguel Tejada, center fielder Terrence Long, and third basemen Eric Chavez, were essentially average, and the line-up as a whole was just +8 WAA, nearly all of it from Giambi. The pitching staff, featuring 24-year-old Tim Hudson (1.8 WAA in 202⅓ innings) and 22-year-old Barry Zito (2.1 WAA in just 92⅔ innings)—both homegrown—added +4 WAA.

The 2001 lineup improved by 6 games to +14 WAA—+4 of them in the field. Giambi was again the only superstar, with a tremendous 8 WAA. Terrence Long had performed poorly in center field in 2000, but now gave way to 27-year-old Johnny Damon. The A's had acquired Damon at little cost from Kansas City, where he had earned 4.2 WAA in 2000, the only superstar season of his career. Damon had a very poor year at the plate for Oakland in 2001 but did much better than Long in center field, while Long turned into a better-than-average left fielder. Eric Chavez suddenly blossomed into a star at third with 3.4 WAA, but the rest of the line-up remained average. The pitchers, meanwhile, improved all the way to +10 WAA thanks to Mark Mulder (3 WAA), Hudson (2) and Zito (2.2). These A's, whose run differential was worth 105 wins, the level of a superior pennant winner, had five home-grown young players—Giambi, Chavez, Mulder, Hudson and Zito—worth 18.6 WAA, as well as Tejada, who was average. Only the Indians of the mid–1990s had achieved anything similar in this era. The Oakland scouting staff had evidently done a tremendous job over the last decade. Somehow the Yankees, with 95 wins, beat the A's, with 102, and the Mariners, with 116, to reach the World Series.

Because Jason Giambi signed with the Yankees and Johnny Damon with the Red Sox after 2001, the 2002 season—the one featured in *Moneyball*—was the one that established Beane as a presumed baseball genius. What actually compensated for the loss of Giambi's 8 WAA was Pythagorean luck. The A's run differential was worth 105 wins in 2001 and only 96 wins in 2002, but they actually won 103 games in 2002 (helped by a famous 20-game win streak) compared to 102 in 2001. It is rather ironic that while Beane's As have been repeatedly criticized for failing in the playoffs, supposedly because they could not do the little things that win close games, the 2002 team earned him his reputation by doing just that. The line-up was only +3 WAA overall, but Tejada suddenly blossomed as a hitter at age 28, improving from average to 2.6 WAA, and Chavez had another fine season with 2.2. Free agent Scott Hatteberg, who replaced Giambi at first, was the most valuable player in the lineup with 2.8 WAA largely because of excellent fielding. An aging David Justice was only average. The pitchers earned +12 WAA once again, with Hudson and Zito turning in superstar performances of 4.2 and 4.6 WAA and Mulder right behind with 2.5. The pitching continued to improve (to +13 WAA) and the line-up to worsen (to average) in 2003. Tejada and Chavez again had fine years with 2.2 and 3.3 WAA, but Hatteberg regressed to average, and two dreadful part-time outfielders, Chris Singleton and Jermaine Dye, cost the team -4.1 WAA. But Hudson, Mulder and Zito got even better, with 4.9, 3.9 and 3.1 WAA. The next year, the A's slipped considerably and missed the playoffs.

Beane's predecessor, Sandy Alderson, and his scouting staff had come up with four players who became great—Giambi and the three starting pitchers—and Chavez, a star in his own right. Given these enormous assets, Beane managed to stock the rest of his lineup with mostly young, average players—something which, as we have seen, other organizations such as the Mariners, the Yankees, the Indians, the Red Sox, and several clubs in the National League had not been able to do. Beane proved that homegrown younger players could perform at least as well as many aging free agents at a fraction of the cost. We shall see that he continued to keep the A's in postseason play, but they still unluckily failed to reach a World Series under his leadership.

The 2002 Angels were the American League's only other World Series winner in the Boomer Xer area. Winning 99 games despite three games' worth of bad Pythagorean luck, they were quite extraordinary in that they virtually fielded their way to a World Championship. Their line-up earned +19 WAA, half of them in the field. Their MVP and only superstar was a fantastic center fielder, Darin Erstad, who owed his 4.1 WAA to +41 runs saved in the outfield, one of the highest figures of all time. (Andruw Jones set the record of 47 in 1999.) Second baseman Adam Kennedy saved another +20 runs in the field and earned 3.4 WAA, and with the exception of catcher Bengie Molina, the entire line-up earned at least 1. Their pitchers earned just +2 WAA. 2002 concluded an extraordinary four-year period in which Erstad saved about +32 runs a season in the outfield. After that, he regressed to average.

Although we will never know when baseball players began using steroids and other critical performance-enhancing drugs,[43] the Boomer-Xer era obviously includes the peak of the steroid era, which was at least severely cut back just three years later, in 2006, when MLB began a serious testing program. The effects of these drugs were complex. On the one hand, they helped raise the general level of offense in both leagues, as we have seen, enabling players to post single-season totals for home runs, RBIs and even walks that had not been seen in decades, and in a few cases, ever before. We shall find when we come to close the books on Generation X in the next chapter, however, that steroids did *not* create an unusually great number of all-time great hitters—but *did* apparently help create an unprecedented number of all-time great pitchers, who as a group sustained peak performance for much longer than any other generation. No one will ever know for sure which pitchers did or did not improve their performance with steroids or other drugs, but the figures leave little doubt that some new factor had a dramatic impact. The Boom Generation included only two pitchers with at least five seasons of 4 WAA or more, and they had six such seasons each. Generation X

---

43. Amphetamines, in my opinion, do not fall into that category.

has ten such pitchers, and they averaged almost seven such seasons each. So far, no pitcher from the Millennial Generation has reached that mark.

Drugs, however, were only part of the story. There was clearly another reason why the outstanding pitchers of the 1990s stood out so much—and no one, to my knowledge, has ever written about it.

The Boom and Xer era witnessed fundamental changes in how pitchers were used. First of all, it completed a transition from a four-man to a five-man starting rotation. Secondly, it instituted the tradition of allowing relievers to finish almost every game. The increasing emphasis on closers and set-up men meant that more talented pitchers began their careers as relievers, destined to throw fewer than 100 innings a year. Lastly, two more rounds of expansion added four more teams to major league baseball during the 1990s. These three factors had a simple effect: they added a great many pitchers to the major leagues. What jumps out from an analysis of starting pitchers, very simply, is that there were not enough good or even average ones to meet the new demand. This had already been happening during the 1970s and 1980s, but the process accelerated further in the 1990s. A few figures tell the story.

In 1965, near the end of the GI-Silent era, the American League had 55 pitchers who made at least ten starts. Eighteen of them—33 percent—were above average as defined by this book, that is, they earned at least 1 WAA. 49 percent of them were average, earning between 0.9 and -0.9 WAA. Only ten of them earned -1 WAA or less, just 18 percent. The National League had more bad pitchers: of the 58 pitchers with at least ten starts, 15 of them (26 percent) were above average, 34 were average, and 19 of them, 33 percent, were under -1 WAA. That helped account for the outstanding performances of Juan Marichal, Jim Maloney and Sandy Koufax in that year.

In 1982, near the end of the Boomer-Xer era, the American League had 78 pitchers with at least ten starts—an increase corresponding quite closely to the increase in teams from ten to 14. The bad ones now outweighed the good ones. Nineteen earned 1 WAA or more (24 percent), 38 were average, and 21 of them (27 percent) were at -1 WAA or less. The pattern in the National League was even more striking. It had 72 pitchers with ten starts or more, roughly matching its 20 percent increase in teams. Only 18 of them, or 25 percent, were above average; 27 were average; and 27 (38 percent) earned -1 WAA or less. Both leagues were using many more inferior hurlers.

By 2002, the American League still had only 14 teams, but now had 88 pitchers with ten starts or more. Thirty of them, 34 percent, earned 1 WAA or more—because 25 of them—28 percent—earned 1 WAA or less. The National League, with 16 teams, had 96 such pitchers, of whom 31 percent were above average and 30 percent were below average.

This change, combined with free agency, enabled the Atlanta Braves and the New York Yankees to create the longest-running dynasties of the Boomer-Xer era during the 1990s and early 2000s. They, unlike almost every previous dynasty—and certainly any dynasty that lasted that long—depended on their pitchers' continuing high level of performance. The situation also allowed teams like the Florida Marlins in 1997 and the Arizona Diamondbacks in the early 2000s to buy their way into the post-season by securing one or more great pitchers through free agency.

Meanwhile, despite the extraordinary performances of the 1998 Yankees and the 2001 Mariners, superior pennant winners have gotten rarer and rarer. During the Silent/Boomer era of 1967–1983, of the 34 best teams in the two leagues, 11 of them won at least 103 games (or had winning percentages of at least .636). From 1984 through 2004 (but omitting strike-shortened 1994), only 12 of the 40 best teams were that good. More and more teams, of course, reached post-season play and even won the World Series with far fewer wins than that. Data suggests that once again, talent had failed to keep up with the expansion of the leagues. With the help of PEDs, the number of superstars per team per year managed to keep pace with expansion, holding steady at .74 from the previous era. But what we have seen time and time again in our analysis of the best teams of the era is the frequency with which they tolerated strikingly below-average players in their lineup—those who posted at least -2 WAA, and sometimes even less. Although more and more players were coming into baseball out of college programs, the size of the minors had not increased relative to the majors. In 1983, there were about four full-season minor league teams and two short-season teams for each of 26 major league teams. In 2003, the ratio of full-time minor league teams to major league teams remained the same. As we shall see, this was not enough to maintain the customary supply of superstar-caliber players in the post-steroid era.

6

The Gen X and Millennial Era, 2005–2017

Perhaps because of the popularity of high-priced free agents from Generation X, the Millennial generation (born about 1982–2000) made the latest entry onto the stage of major league baseball of any modern generation. In 2005, pitcher Dontrelle Willis—born in 1982—was the first member of his generation to post a superstar season, with 5.1 WAA for the Florida Marlins at age 23, and not until 2007 did David Wright, also born in 1982, become the first Millennial hitter to break that barrier, with 5.8 WAA for the Mets at the age of 25. Sherry Magee and Ty Cobb had posted the first superstar seasons for the Lost Generation in 1906 and 1907, when they were 21 and 20; Lou Gehrig and Paul Waner were the first GI superstars in 1926, when they were both 23; Del Ennis put the Silent Generation on the superstar map in 1946, when he was only 21; Paul Blair, Jim Merritt, and Gary Nolan were the first Boomer superstars in 1967, when they were 23, 23, and 19, respectively; and Don Mattingly was 23 when he broke the barrier for Generation X in 1984.

Sadly, the late debut, we can now see, marked the start of a most unfortunate trend: an unprecedented decline in the number of superstar performances throughout baseball. The oldest Millennials were 35 at the end of the 2017 season. By the time the oldest Boomers were 35, in 1978, the Boom generation had put up 132 superstar seasons. During most of that time since Boomers first made their impact in 1967, MLB had included 24 teams. By the time the oldest Gen Xers were 35, at the end of 1996, they had put up 153 superstar seasons. During most of that time (1984–1994) there had been 26 teams. As of the end of 2017, the Millennial generation had posted 125 superstar seasons, a significant decline. Generation X was also much less productive of superstar seasons after 2004 than before. Meanwhile, the number of major league teams had increased from 24 teams in 1976 to 30 in 2015. Measured per major league team, superstars have been getting rarer over the last half-century. There were an average of .86 superstar seasons per major league team from 1967–1983; .82 per team from 1984–2004; but only .55 per major league team from 2005–2017. The development of top quality talent has not kept pace with the growth of the major leagues. It is quite possible that the decline really began in the 1990s, but that it was masked by the use of performance-enhancing drugs.

The lack of superstars has contributed to an even more striking phenomenon: the general mediocrity of the two leagues. Superior pennant winners are almost extinct. During the

Silent/Boomer era of 1967–1983, of the 34 best teams in the two leagues, 11 of them won at least 103 games (or had winning percentages of at least .636). From 1984 through 2004 (but omitting strike-shortened 1994), only 12 of the 40 best teams were that good. In the 13 years from 2005 through 2017, only the New York Yankees of 2009, the Chicago Cubs of 2016, and the Los Angeles Dodgers of 2017 reached 103 wins, our standard for a superior pennant winner. Thanks in part to rule changes that have made it more difficult for richer teams to make their wealth count, there has been nothing close to a great team in the Xer-Millennial era. A further reason for the increase in mediocre records may have been the unbalanced schedule that MLB introduced in 2001. While previously each team had played every other team in its league 11 or 12 times, now they played rivals inside their division 19 or 20 times, and other teams only nine times. For a good part of this era, the schedule probably held down the records of the best teams in the AL East, where strength was concentrated, and made it easier for teams in other divisions to post winning records.

In the wake of their first World Series victory in 86 years in 2004, the Boston Red Sox remained in contention for eight of the next nine years, winning the World Series twice more. Yet they hardly ranked as a dynasty. Only once in those years did they win more than 96 games, and their lineup generally included only one superstar per year. David Ortiz filled that bill from 2005 through 2007 (4.7, 4.8, and 5.5 WAA), and first baseman Kevin Youkilis had 4.8 and 4 WAA in 2008–2009, when Ortiz fell off somewhat. Although the farm system eventually produced some star players and pitchers, the team, like the Yankees a decade earlier, relied very heavily on the free agent market to try to fill gaps in the line-up. This strategy was only intermittently successful and failed completely to fill one perennial weakness at shortstop.

The 2005 lineup slipped slightly from 2004, earning only +9 WAA thanks to poor fielding. Ortiz was the only superstar, with 4.7 WAA, but Damon (in his walk year) and Ramirez each earned 2.7 WAA. Nixon, Millar and Varitek were more modest assets, but Mueller—most unwisely signed to another season while Youkilis languished in the minors—regressed to average. New shortstop Edgar Renteria, though only 28, had a disastrous year and cost the team -2 WAA. On the mound, Martinez was gone, signed by the Mets, and Schilling missed most of the season, leaving 38-year-old Tim Wakefield the ace of the staff with 2.4 WAA, more than the value of the whole staff, which earned just +1. The team somewhat luckily won 95 games and was quickly eliminated in the playoffs. In 2006, Kevin Youkilis, switched to first base, finally became a regular at the age of 27 and earned 2 WAA, but third baseman Mike Lowell, acquired from Miami in a big trade, earned only 1. Three other new acquisitions—34-year-old second baseman Mark Loretta, 26-year-old center fielder Coco Crisp, and 29-year-old Alex Gonzalez, who replaced Renteria at short—cost the team a combined -4.8 WAA, dropping the whole line-up slightly below average. Although Schilling returned to form with 2.8 WAA and new closer Jonathan Papelbon began brilliantly with 2.4, the pitching staff as a whole was only average, as was the entire record of the team, which missed post-season play.

The Red Sox's improvement in 2007, when they won 96 games despite -6 games' worth of bad Pythagorean luck, was remarkable, marking the real highlight of the Epstein era. While Ortiz had his finest season (5.6 WAA), two of the previous year's acquisitions, Mike

Lowell and Coco Crisp, blossomed, with 2.7 WAA each. Crisp hit poorly but had a fantastic year in the field, where the team finally performed well. Youkilis improved to 2.8 WAA, and two homegrown rookies, second baseman Dustin Pedroia and outfielder Jacoby Ellsbury, earned about 1 WAA each, Ellsbury in just 33 games. But the line-up as a whole earned only +6 WAA, thanks in part to the presence of another disastrous shortstop, 31-year-old Julio Lugo (-2.7 WAA), and to -28 runs' worth of bad run luck. More remarkable was the pitching. Josh Beckett, also acquired in 2007, earned 3.7 WAA in just 200⅔ innings. Daisuke Matsuzaka, acquired from Japan, earned another 1.6 WAA in 204⅔ innings, Schilling added 2 more, and relievers Papelbon and Hideki Okajima added 3.4 WAA in just 127⅓ innings. The staff as a whole earned +15 WAA, a remarkable figure, and the team's run differential ranked among the best of the whole Xer-Millennial era. They deservedly won the World Series.

The 2008 Red Sox were a remarkable mixture of strengths and weaknesses. Although Ortiz missed a third of the season and was below average for the rest, the team had two relatively young homegrown superstars and a star pitcher—Youkilis (4.8 WAA at age 28), Ellsbury, whose fielding and base running earned 4 WAA at age 24, and 24-year-old starting pitcher Jon Lester, with 3.5 WAA. Matsuzaka, with an 18–3 record in just 167⅔ innings, earned 3.1 more. Pedroia, only 24, added 3.1 WAA, Ramirez earned 2 before departing in mid-year, and outfielder J. D. Drew, only average the year before, had 1.9. A mid-season acquisition, outfielder Jason Bay, earned 1 WAA in 184 at-bats. Unfortunately, Ortiz, Varitek, Crisp, shortstops Lugo and Jed Lowrie, and a couple of bench players cost the team -7.5 WAA. Because of them, the lineup earned just +8 WAA, and the pitchers slipped from +15 to +7. Although Lester, Matsuzaka, Beckett and Wakefield combined for 8 WAA, the team's 13 worst pitchers combined for 280 innings and -6.4 WAA. The 2008 team matched its Pythagorean projection, equaling the 95 wins of the unlucky 2007 one, but lost the ALCS to an inferior Tampa Bay team in seven games. With a core of young stars, the team had every reason to hope for greater success in 2009 if it could simply fill in its weak spots.

Instead, 2009 featured a series of mostly unpleasant surprises. On the plus side, Jason Bay had an extraordinary year at bat and in the field, earning 5.4 WAA, the best performance by any position player in the American League. Youkilis turned in 4.1 more, and Drew added 1.9. Ortiz, Pedroia and Ellsbury, however, slipped to a combined -1.6 WAA among them.[44] Varitek had a bad year at catcher, and this year's shortstop disaster was shared among Nick Green, Alex Gonzalez, and Lugo, who surrendered -2.1 WAA. Thanks largely to poor fielding, the line-up as a whole was average. The pitching staff rebounded to +13 WAA, led by Lester's 4.1 WAA in 203⅓ innings (15–8) and Beckett's 3.1 WAA in 212⅓ innings (17–6). The team won 93 games thanks to its pitchers but was quickly eliminated in the Division Series.

2010 found the team pretty fully committed to a strategy of free agent acquisition. Thirty-one-year-old Adrian Beltre was excellent at third base, earning 3.9 WAA, and catcher

---

44. Ellsbury appears to have been playing hurt. Having saved the team about 30 runs in center field in 2008, he cost them -14 runs there in 2009. Meanwhile, Bay was 19 runs better than average in left field. It would appear that Bay caught a good many balls that Ellsbury would normally not have reached.

Victor Martinez, who had joined the team in 2009, added 1.7. Youkilis earned an impressive 3.5 WAA in just ⅔ of a season. Both Pedroia and Ellsbury, however, missed the bulk of the year with injuries, and their replacements were average at best. Worst of all, the shortstop of the year was 34-year-old Marco Scutaro, the worst yet, a full -3.6 WAA. Among the pitchers, 25-year-old Clay Buchholz turned in a 4.3 WAA superstar season in just 173⅔ innings and Lester had 3.8 WAA, but Okajima and Papelbon fell to below average. The line-up overall was only +3 WAA and the pitchers +4, and they won 89 games and missed the playoffs.

The 2011 team marked the end of the era of Theo Epstein, GM (with one brief break) since 2003, and Terry Francona, who had managed the team with a gentle hand since 2004. Epstein traded for first baseman Adrian Gonzalez from San Diego and signed free agent Carl Crawford from Tampa Bay, while foolishly allowing Beltre and the versatile Victor Martinez to depart. The team once again mixed great strengths with terrific weaknesses. Gonzalez had a fantastic season, earning 6.3 WAA, more than any offensive player had earned for the Red Sox since Wade Boggs. Ellsbury, now 27, returned from his year of injury and turned in his best season, featuring 212 hits, 32 homers, and 4.6 WAA. Pedroia returned to form with his best season, 3.6 WAA, and Ortiz rebounded to 3.3. Crawford, however, had a dreadful year both at bat and in the field, totaling -1.7 WAA, and Drew fell below average as well. Thirty-five-year-old Marco Scutaro and Jed Lowrie combined to get the shortstop position almost up to average. Youkilis, now 32, slipped to 1.4 WAA in 120 games. but overall the line-up was +12 WAA, by far the best performance of the era. Beckett earned 4.3 WAA on the mound but the pitching staff earned just +1 WAA overall, and the team missed the wild card spot on the last day of the season, winning only 90 games thanks to four games' worth of bad luck.

The team suffered through a disastrous 2012 season, unloading Beckett, Gonzales and Crawford to the Dodgers in August. The deal amounted to a sale of Gonzalez, a superstar in 2011, in exchange for the salaries of the other two. In 2013, everything went right. Pedroia and Ellsbury, both now 29, returned to form with 2.3 and 2.1 WAA, and Ortiz had another superstar season, his fourth with 4 WAA at age 37. More remarkably, 32-year-old outfielder Shane Victorino and 31-year-old first baseman Mike Napoli, both signed as free agents, earned 5.5 and 2.7 WAA, respectively, with most of Victorino's value coming in the field. Last but hardly least, two shortstops, Stephen Drew and Jose Iglesias, combined for 1.7 WAA. The line-up earned +14 WAA and the pitching staff added +6, half of them from Buchholz. Bad luck held them to 97 wins instead of their projected 101, but they won the World Series.

Live by the aging veteran, die by the aging veteran. In the next two years, Victorino hardly played, Ortiz slipped significantly, and Napoli's value evaporated. Ellsbury was allowed to leave for the Yankees—a decision that has been vindicated by his performance—Youkilis also departed, and Pedroia regressed towards average. The Red Sox finished last in their division in both 2014 and 2015.

In 2016, the Red Sox returned to the playoffs with 93 wins despite -6 games' worth of bad Pythagorean luck. Their two superstars were David Ortiz, who earned a remarkable 4.2 WAA at age 40—missing the record of Willie Mays, who had put up 4.8 WAA a the same age in 1971—and 23-year-old right fielder Mookie Betts, who posted his second consecutive superstar season at age 23 with 5.8 WAA, the second-highest in the league behind Mike Trout. Catcher Sandy Leon had a remarkable year in the field and earned 2.7 WAA, although his fellow catcher Ryan Hanigan gave -2.1 of them back. Two other young players, center fielder Jackie Bradley and 23-year-old shortstop Xander Bogaerts, posted some fine hitting statistics but finished with 1.4 and -0.8 WAA, respectively, because Fenway substantially inflated their hitting stats, and Bogaerts had a poor year in the field, surrendering -10 runs. Poor fielding also held 32-year-old Hanley Ramirez to 0.9 WAA, but Dustin Pedroia had 1.6 and part-timers Brock Holt and Chris Young combined for 2.2. The line-up earned 12 WAA, and the pitchers added 5, thanks to Rick Porcello (3.1), David Price (1.3), and Steven Wright (0.9 in 156⅔ innings.)

Although they could not make up for the loss of retired David Ortiz, the 2017 Red Sox managed to win the AL East with only 93 victories thanks to a strengthened pitching staff. Although Mookie Betts slumped somewhat at the plate and just missed his third consecutive superstar season, he still earned 3.9 WAA thanks to a tremendous year in the field. The lineup, however, did not contain a single additional star, and Jackie Bradley and Xander Bogaerts performed so badly in the field (-17 and -23 runs) that they totaled -5.7 WAA between them, dragging the whole lineup down to -3 WAA. Like Carl Furillo for the Boys of Summer, Mookie Betts clearly belongs in center field. Their pitching staff, however, turned in a remarkable +15 WAA. Signed as a free agent, starter Chris Sale earned a remarkable 4.9 WAA, and Drew Pomeranz (3.1), Eduardo Rodriguez (1.2), David Price (1.3 in just 75 innings), and closer Craig Kimbrel (2.8) all contributed more to the team's success than any offensive player except Betts and Andrew Benintendi. But the Red Sox' pitching failed them in the ALDS, and they lost to Houston in four games.

The Yankees remained the Red Sox's major rival in the AL East, reaching postseason play eight times in 12 years from 2005 through 2016. Having let several of their best pitchers depart as free agents after 2003, however, they reverted to a hitting-dominated team, in contrast to the pitching-heavy dynasty of the late 1990s and early 2000s. Their post-season luck—so noteworthy from 1996 through 2003—deserted them, and they reached, and won, the World Series just once in eight post-seasons. Only in that year, 2009, did they reach the level of a superior pennant winner.

The year 2005 marked the arrival of the first homegrown Yankees great since the 1990s, second baseman Robinson Cano. Reaching the team at age 22 after four years in the minors, Cano had a bad year in the field and ranked as an average player, but great things lay ahead. The rest of the team was now extraordinarily old—Alex Rodriguez, the team MVP with 5.7 WAA, was the second-youngest regular at 29—and predictably erratic. While Jeter (who was nearly average in the field), Matsui, Sheffield and Jason Giambi earned 3,2, 3.7 and 2.9 WAA respectively, Bernie Williams, second baseman Tony Womack, and Tino Martinez cost the team a combined -4 WAA. Hurt by -5 WAA in the field, the line-up earned just +6 WAA. Forty-one-year-old Randy Johnson led the pitching staff with 2.4 WAA in 225⅔ innings and Rivera added 2 more in only 78⅓, but the staff as a whole earned only +4 WAA. The team won a lucky 95 games but lost the ALDS. The lineup improved to +13 WAA in 2006, even though Rodriguez slipped to 2.7 WAA and the team lacked any superstars. Jeter had the second of three consecutive fine years with 3.1 WAA, Jason Giambi and mid-season acquisition Bobby Abreu added 2.1 and 2 more, and free agent Johnny Damon chipped in 1.1 at the age of 32. Another homegrown player, switch-hitting center fielder Melky Cabrera, had an average year as a 21-year-old rookie, while Cano improved to 1.8 WAA. The only negative quantity was 37-year-old Bernie Williams, -1.3 WAA in 131 games. Randy Johnson finally regressed to average at age 42, but 37-year-old Mike Mussina earned 2.4 WAA in 197⅓ innings and Taiwanese pitcher Chien-Ming Wang went 19–6 and earned 3 WAA in 218 innings. Rivera again earned a remarkable 2.1 WAA in just 75 innings, but the staff earned just +4 WAA overall. This time the team won 97 games but lost the ALDS again to a Detroit Tigers club that was nearly as good.

The line-up earned +14 WAA in 2007. Rodriguez, although something of a liability in the field (-11 runs), had a fantastic year at bat, with 54 homers and 95 walks, and earned 5.8 WAA, the seventh superstar season of his career. Cano had a great year at second base and became a genuine star with 3.2 WAA, but Cabrera remained average. Posada had the greatest year of his life at bat at 35 years old, earning 2.7 WAA overall, and Damon, Matsui (who had improved his fielding over the years), Jeter and Abreu added 2, 1.8, 1.8 and 1.4 respectively. Wang repeated as the ace of the staff with 2.9 WAA. The Yankees had re-acquired Andy Pettitte (35) and Roger Clemens (44), both of whom had had a massive impact with the Houston Astros in 2004–2006, and although Clemens was merely average in 99 innings, Pettitte, the only other major asset on the staff, earned 1.7 WAA in 215⅓. The staff as a whole was only +3 WAA, and bad luck limited the team to 94 wins. Once again they went down in the ALDS, as a far superior Red Sox team won the World Series.

Joe Girardi replaced Joe Torre as manager in 2008, and the team fell out of contention. Rodriguez (4.5 WAA), Abreu (3) and Damon (2.7) had fine seasons, but Jeter began the long decline phase of his career with -2.1 WAA, Cano slumped inexplicably to -1.1, and Cabrera had a dreadful year at the plate and cost the team -2.1. The bench was also disastrous, and although the pitching staff improved markedly to +8 WAA, the team won just 89 games and missed the post-season. Then, suddenly, a great deal went right in 2009. Although Rodriguez slipped to 2.8 WAA and Cabrera remained a liability, Jeter rebounded to 1.9 WAA, Cano improved back to 2.3, Matsui earned 2.1 WAA as a DH, and free-agent acquisition Mark Teixeira earned 3.4 WAA at first base. The team's fielding was average for the first time in many years, and the pitching staff added a modest +4 WAA. Two free agent pitchers, CC Sabathia and A. J. Burnett, earned 3.1 and 2 WAA—in Burnett's case, only the second time that he had ever been significantly above average at the age of 32. The staff as a whole earned +4 WAA, with Rivera having another remarkable year, and the line-up added +11 WAA. The team won 103 games with the help of seven wins' worth of Pythagorean luck, making them the only superior pennant winner in the AL during the Xer-Millennial era so far. They also beat the Angels and the defending champion Phillies in exciting ALCS and World Series competition.

The 2010 Yankees were just as good, but less lucky. Although Jeter and Posada were now liabilities and Rodriguez earned only 2.4 WAA, the line-up included three superstars. Thanks to terrific years in the field—where the team as a whole earned +6 WAA—Teixeira, Cano, and outfielder Nick Swisher earned 4.6, 4.9 and 4.2 WAA. Although a new center fielder, free agent Curtis Granderson, earned only .9 WAA, he represented a significant improvement over the departed Cabrera, and homegrown outfielder Brett Gardner earned 2.9 WAA in his first full season as a regular at age 26. Sheffield, Abreu (now departed) and Cabrera should never have been allowed to keep Gardner out of the line-up for so long. With +17 WAA, this was one of the best line-ups in recent Yankees history. Alas, while the line-up was now significantly younger than in recent years, the pitching staff was not, and although Sabathia and Pettitte remained assets, Burnett and Javier Vazquez surrendered as many WAA as Sabathia and Burnett saved, making the staff average. The team nearly matched its projected percentage with 95 wins, but lost the ALCS in six games to the Texas Rangers, who had won only 90 games in a much weaker division.

Cano slipped only slightly to 3.4 WAA in 2011, but Teixeira and Swisher—now 31 and 30—could not repeat their outstanding years in the field, and slipped to 2.2 and 1.1 WAA. Rodriguez fell to +1.3 WAA, but Granderson had a great year at the plate, posting 2.5 WAA overall, and Gardner's fielding and base running earned 1.9. The acquisition of free agents in their late twenties allowed the team to field seven above-average players in its line-up, the exceptions being Jeter (-1.7 WAA) and Posada, who unaccountably became the DH and cost the team -1 WAA. The line-up as a whole slipped slightly to +13 WAA, but the pitching improved to +8 thanks mostly to Sabathia, the team's only superstar with 4.5 WAA, and relievers Dave Robertson and Rivera, who earned 2.6 and 1.8 WAA in 66⅔ and 61⅓ innings. The team's run differential was worth 102 wins, but it posted only 97 and lost the ALCS again.

Robinson Cano posted another superstar season in 2012 with 5.3 WAA, and Swisher remained a star with 3.3 WAA while Teixeira added 2.2 in 123 games. Granderson, Jeter and Rodriguez, however, were all below average thanks to problems in the field, and Gardner missed the whole season with injury. The Yankees attempted to fill the gap with 40-year-old Raul Ibanez and 38-year-old Ichiro Suzuki, who were average, and 35-year-old Andruw Jones, who was -0.9 WAA. This year's DH was Eric Chavez, never a great hitter and average now at 34. Like the Red Sox, the Yankees were discovering that aging free agents only occasionally came through. This year the line-up earned only +10 WAA and the pitchers +4, and the team lost the ALCS again. That was the end of this Yankees dynasty. Injuries destroyed the team in 2013, when Rodriguez, Jeter and Teixeira missed nearly the entire season. Cano earned 3.2 WAA, but Gardner, back in the lineup, was average, as was Granderson in less than half a season. The front office's faith in former stars was becoming embarrassing. After Cano and Gardner, the Yankees' leaders in plate appearances were 39-year-old Ichiro Suzuki (-0.8 WAA), 36-year-old first baseman Lyle Overbay (-0.9 WAA), and 34-year-old center fielder Vernon Wells (-0.5 WAA). Although the pitching staff was +4 WAA, the team was lucky to win 85 games. The 2014 team added Jacoby Ellsbury from Boston (2.9 WAA), but Rodriguez missed the entire year, suspended for PED use, and Teixeira, returning from injury, was an average player at 34. The new DH was 37-year-old Carlos Beltran, who was below average. Two disastrous decisions probably kept them out of the playoffs. First, the front office allowed Cano to sign with the Seattle Mariners, replacing him with 36-year-old free agent Brian Roberts. Cano earned 5.6 WAA for the Mariners, while Roberts cost the Yankees -1.4, a difference of seven wins in the standings. Secondly, they allowed Jeter to return from injury and play a farewell season—in which he cost the team -31 runs in the field and -15 at the plate, leaving him with -4.2 WAA. Had they kept Cano and found a shortstop of average quality, they would almost surely have made it into postseason. Cano posted his fourth superstar season for the Mariners in 2016.

Alex Rodriguez's reputation will always be clouded by his now well-documented involvement with performance-enhancing drugs. Measured purely by his performance on the field, however, he is tied for fifth among the hitters of his generation with seven superstar performances, trailing only Barry Bonds, Albert Pujols, Jeff Bagwell, and Frank Thomas. More importantly, he posted five of those seasons at shortstop for Seattle and Texas. In the whole history of baseball since 1901, only Honus Wagner (ten such seasons, 1901–1912) and Rodriguez's fellow Gen Xer Barry Larkin (six) have had more such seasons at baseball's most demanding defensive position. Rodriguez, in sharp contrast to Derek Jeter, had been a slightly above average defensive performer over his career when the Yankees acquired him, and they should definitely have found a way to keep him at short. He was an extraordinary player.

After two barely winning seasons in 2015–16, the 2017 Yankees rebounded impressively, and only a full -10 games worth of bad luck held them to 91 wins and a wild card berth in the postseason. Sensational rookie right fielder Aaron Judge set a new rookie record with 52 home runs, fielded very well, and earned a league-leading 6 WAA. Unfortunately Judge had spent three years in the minors after joining organized baseball at 22, and was already 25. 24-year old Gary Sanchez earned an impressive 2.4 WAA behind the plate, and might easily have been rookie of the year himself in a normal season. Brett Gardner earned 2.2 WAA and shortstop Didi Gregorius, a fine fielder, 1.9, as the lineup earned +12 WAA overall Although no pitcher threw as many as 200 innings, the staff earned another +8 WAA thanks to Luis Severino (3.4), closer Chad Green (2.1), and starters Jordan Montgomery and C. C. Sabathia (2.7 between them.) The Yankees beat the favored Indians in the division series but lost to Houston in the ALCS in seven games. With Judge and Sanchez in their prime, the Yankees are positioned to contend for some time to come.

The Yankees from 2005 through 2014 had followed essentially the same strategy as those of 1996–2004, buying up the best available free agents year after year, even though such acquisitions only rarely matched their previous performances. Yet in 1996–2004 the team had averaged 99 wins a year, whereas in 2005–2012 (before the roof fell in), they averaged 96. That .593 average winning percentage had gotten them into the playoffs nearly every season, but they had reached the World Series only once. The difference in the two eras was the unavailability, in the latter era, of free agent superstar pitchers. Far fewer such pitchers were sustaining peak performance well into their thirties. The Yankees were still as successful as any other team, but that was not as successful as dynasties from earlier eras, including the immediately preceding one. Meanwhile, another team in the Yankees' and Red Sox's division proved that one could achieve comparable records in a completely different way.

The Tampa Bay Devil Rays had come into the American League in 1998, and through 2007, they had won as many as 70 games only once. In 2008, they improved from 66 wins to 97 and won the AL East, an extraordinary achievement even with the help of five wins' worth of Pythagorean luck. Although they had many injuries and had to use a line-up of 14 players with at least 152 plate appearances, only one of those players, Eric Hinske, was below average. Only three of them were 30 or older, and they were strongest where the Red Sox and Yankees were nearly always weakest—in the field, where they earned +7 WAA, to go with +3 from their hitters and +1 from their pitching staff. Their MVP was a 22-year-old rookie in his third year of organized baseball, third baseman Evan Longoria, who fielded well and earned 3.1 WAA. Veteran first baseman Carlos Pena added 2.8. Center fielder B. J. Upton, just 23, added 1.1 WAA, and left fielder Carl Crawford, 26, had 1.3. The pitching staff was even younger, and four of the five starters had modest positive value. None of the Rays' starting pitchers, and only three of their ten top position players, had joined the team via free agency, and Upton, Longoria and Crawford had all been drafted by the organization. The Devil Rays beat the Red Sox in the ALCS but lost the World Series to the Phillies.

The young team slipped to 84 wins in 2009, but in 2010 they won the AL East again with 96 deserved wins. This time, Crawford—now in the walk year of his contract—and Longoria were superstars, with 5.5 and 4.5 WAA, respectively, while the versatile Ben Zobrist added 1.8, allowing the line-up as a whole to finish +17 WAA. This time the team had 12 position players with more than 150 plate appearances, nine of them under 30 years old, and none of them significantly below average. This year, 24-year-old David Price, a home-grown product, was the pitching star with 2.7 WAA, but unfortunately James Shields, the ace in 2008, had a terrible season and the staff as a whole was slightly below average. Tampa lost the ALDS to the Texas Rangers. In 2011, the team survived Crawford's departure to the Red Sox (where he had a very poor season) thanks to Longoria (4 WAA), Zobrist, who brought home 3.8 WAA at second base, and the outfield of Upton, Sam Fuld, and Matthew Joyce, who earned 6.2 WAA among them. Treating themselves to a rare splurge, the team signed 37-year-old Johnny Damon as a DH, and he earned about 1 WAA as the highest-salaried player on the team. Although the pitching staff was average, the lineup was +10 WAA—+7 of them in the field—and the team won 91 games and a wild card berth, losing in the first round again. Longoria missed half the season and earned only 1.2 WAA in 2012, but Zobrist posted another 3.4 WAA, and the team again fielded ten at least average players with 200 plate appearances or more—exactly what the Red Sox and Yankees were consistently failing to do. The line-up posted just +6 WAA, but pitcher David Price had a great year with 4.6 WAA and reliever Fernando Rodney—nearly three runs an inning below average—added 3.5 in 74⅔ innings, as the staff added 8 WAA. Sadly, the Rays won 90 games, missing their projection by four, and missed the playoffs.

In 2013, the Rays' line-up included a genuine liability for the first time in many years: 38-year-old catcher Jose Molina, who cost the team -2.2 WAA. But Longoria just missed superstardom with 3.9 WAA and Zobrist was right behind with 3.3. First baseman James Loney, a cheap free agent pickup, added 2.2, and once again the team featured 13 players with 200 PA or more, only one of whom was significantly below average. The line-up earned +7 WAA, and although the pitching staff was only average, the team's 92 wins were good enough to make the playoffs. Their hitting fell off badly during the next two years, 2014–2015, and they finished around .500. They fell out of contention in 2016–17.

Although the Rays have never received the attention of Billy Beane's A's, their story is at least equally remarkable. From 2008 through 2013, they averaged 92 wins a season. During the same period, the Yankees averaged 94 wins and the Red Sox 89. The Rays made the playoffs five times, the Yankees four, and the Red Sox three. The teams' payrolls in those years were as follows.

	Yankees	Red Sox	Rays
2008	$209 million	$133 million	$44 million
2009	$201 million	$123 million	$63 million
2010	$206 million	$163 million	$72 million
2011	$201 million	$161 million	$42 million
2012	$198 million	$173 million	$64 million
2013	$229 million	$151 million	$58 million

Even more strikingly, the Red Sox during these six seasons benefited from 13 superstar seasons, the Yankees had six, and the Rays just four. This comparison proves three things. First, keeping dreadful players out of one's line-up is just as important as getting great ones into it—and this is exactly what the Yankees and Red Sox, year after year, were unable to do, in large part because of their reliance on aging free agents. Secondly, unless the Rays were extraordinarily lucky, they seem to have proven that there is a plentiful supply of young, athletic average players in organized baseball who perform very adequately if given a chance. Had the Red Sox or the Yankees during these years found such a young man to play shortstop, they would have won several more games every year. Because these players were young and athletic, the Rays' big advantage was in the field, where their fielders earned the team about +4 WAA a year while the Yankees and Red Sox were usually average at best. Thirdly, attempting to fill holes in the line-up with over-30 free agents whose great years, if they ever had any, were in the past, works very intermittently if at all.

AL Central Division teams have made the playoffs as division or wild card winners 13 times from 2005 through 2015, but not one of them won as many as 100 games. The Minnesota Twins had taken over from the Indians as the division leader in 2002 with 94 wins despite a below-average line-up, thanks to a well-balanced pitching staff and eight wins' worth of Pythagorean luck. They repeated the same trick in 2003 and 2004, as their lineup steadily deteriorated. A combination of a +5 WAA pitching staff and five wins' worth of Pythagorean luck gave them 90 wins and the division title in 2003, and in 2004 the pitchers improved to +10 thanks to the emergence of a truly great hurler, Johan Santana. Santana had his first and best superstar season in 2004, with a 20–6 record and 6.4 WAA in 228 innings. The team's line-up was so bad, however, that they needed five wins' worth of luck to win just 92 games, losing in the ALDS for the second year in a row. Santana added 4.4 WAA the next year, but the line-up deteriorated further and the team won just 83 games. The lineup was +3 WAA in 2006, and Santana's 4.6 WAA led a +9 WAA pitching staff, allowing the Twins to win the division and the ALDS with 96 wins before losing to the Tigers in the ALCS. The 2006 team featured the greatest catcher to date of the Millennial Generation, Joe Mauer, who put up the first of three superstar seasons in four years—an unequalled record for a catcher—with 4.1 WAA. Santana posted one more superstar season in 2008, his first year with the New York Mets, finishing his career with four. After a two-year hiatus, the Twins returned to the playoffs in 2009 with a record low 87 wins. They returned again in 2010 with 94, thanks both to Mauer (3.5 WAA) and a well-balanced pitching staff that earned +7 WAA. Then they faded below .500.

The Chicago White Sox of 2005 brought to mind their counterparts, the "Hitless Wonders" of 99 years earlier. While American League teams averaged 771 runs scored, the White Sox's park-adjusted total was just 719—but their fielders earned the team +4 WAA and the pitchers +12. The extraordinarily consistent staff featured starters Mark Buehrle (2.3 WAA), Freddy Garcia (1.3), Jon Garland (2.2) and Jose Contreras (1.4), and outstanding relievers Cliff Politte (1.5 in 67⅓ innings) and Neil Cotts (1.3 in 60⅓ innings.) Helped by eight wins' worth of Pythagorean luck, they won 99 games and the World Series. This kind of success never carries over from year to year, and the team did not return to the playoffs until 2008, with just 89 victories, again due entirely to the pitching staff.

The strongest team of the Central Division in the current era, however, has been the Detroit Tigers, who have fielded several great players and reached the World Series twice. The Tigers had kicked off the 21st century with three absolutely dreadful seasons, bottoming out at 43–119 in 2003, just missing the 1962 Mets' modern record of 120 losses. After two more losing seasons, a series of free agent acquisitions allowed them to rebound smartly in 2006 with 95 wins. Although the line-up was quite old and their hitting was worth just +2 WAA, their fielders, led by center fielder Curtis Granderson, third baseman Brandon Inge, and catcher Ivan Rodriguez, earned the team +5 WAA, and the pitchers, led by 23-year-old Justin Verlander (2 WAA) added +8 WAA, giving the team 95 wins. Their run differential only narrowly trailed the Yankees team they beat in the ALDS, and they reached the World Series, losing to the Cardinals. Continuing the pattern established by the Twins and Tigers, the Indians in 2007 won 96 games and the division despite a below-average line-up, as their pitchers, led by Roberto Hernandez and CC Sabathia (4 WAA each) earned +12 WAA. They beat the Yankees in the ALDS and nearly took out the Red Sox in the next round before losing the last three straight.

After mediocre White Sox and Twins teams took the division from 2008–2010, a rebuilt Tigers club won the division for four consecutive seasons thanks to three superb players from the Millennial Generation. The most important was Miguel Cabrera, who had been a good player, but no more, for five seasons beginning with the Florida Marlins at age 21 in 2004. The Tigers acquired him in a trade for prospects in 2008 without giving up anyone of value, and in 2009, when he was 26, Cabrera blossomed, earning 3.6 WAA, largely because he became an average third baseman after surrendering 1–2 games' worth of runs at that position over the previous three years. Over the next five years, he put up five consecutive superstar seasons, peaking at 5.5 WAA in 2011. He might have done much better in 2013, but his fielding slipped and he cost the Tigers -18 runs at third base. They wisely switched him to first base the next year, where he has performed quite adequately. He is already a very strong candidate for the Hall of Fame. Their second major asset was homegrown pitcher Justin Verlander. After starring for four of his first five seasons, Verlander pitched a remarkable (for his era) 251 innings in 2011, good for a 24–5 record and 6.2 WAA. He followed that up with 5.7 WAA in 2012 and 2.4 in 2013. He has subsequently slipped to average. Pitcher Max Scherzer, acquired in 2010, was actually average in 2011 despite a 15–9 record, but he posted 2.9, 4.3 and 4 WAA over the next three years, replacing Verlander as the team ace. Apparently believing that he too was likely to regress towards the mean, the Tigers allowed him to sign with Washington at age 30 in 2015, where he posted his best season yet with 4.9 WAA.

Unfortunately the Tigers' line-up and pitching staff also included important weaknesses, and only once, in 2013, did they win as many as 97 games. In 2011, 37-year-old Maglio Ordonez and 34-year-old Brandon Inge cost the lineup -3.3 WAA, and the team bench cost them about -3 more, making the whole line-up only +8 WAA despite Cabrera's 5.5 WAA. The pitchers were much worse, and the staff as a whole was average despite Verlander's 6.2 WAA. The 2012 team included first baseman Prince Fielder (2.9 WAA) and center fielder Austin Jackson (2.4), as well as Cabrera, but shortstop Jhonny Peralta, right fielder Brennan Boesch, and utility men Ramon Santiago and Ryan Raburn cost the Tigers a combined -11.8 WAA. Although Verlander, Scherzer and the rest of the pitching staff were truly great, earning +19 WAA, the team's fielders gave -11 of those WAA back, and the Tigers won only 88 games. They nonetheless found their way into the World Series, losing four straight to a mediocre San Francisco club.

The 2013 Tigers improved significantly but won only 93 games. After Cabrera (5 WAA), only two players in the line-up were above average at all, and the line-up as a whole earned just +4 WAA. Again the pitchers were outstanding, with Anibal Sanchez (4.3 WAA) joining Scherzer (4.3) and Verlander (2.3) in the starting corps, as the staff as a whole earned +14 WAA. But this team—about ten wins better than 2012—lost the ALCS to the superior Red Sox. Poor fielding reduced the Tigers lineup to average in 2014, and only luck allowed them to win 90 games and squeak into the playoffs, where they were quickly eliminated.

The Kansas City Royals reached the World Series via a wild card berth in 2014 and won the AL Central and the World Series the next year. They did it with a line-up of fine athletes who could not hit, a good pitching staff, and five wins' worth of Pythagorean luck in each of those two seasons, allowing them to win 89 and 95 games with adjusted run differentials of +26 and +83. The 2014 lineup had only two above-average players, left fielder Alex Gordon, who put up 3.9 WAA—half of them in the field—and center fielder Lorenzo Cain, whose 1.9 WAA also came mostly from his defense. But it also included second baseman Omar Infante, who had an historically dreadful season with -4.8 WAA, nearly a whole WAA worse than Derek Jeter's farewell season in the same year. Their pitching staff was quite remarkable. A well-balanced quintet of starting pitchers earned 5.6 WAA, but the Royals' much-ballyhooed trio of late-inning relievers—Wade Davis, Kelvin Herrera, and Greg Holland—earned another 6.1 WAA in 204⅓ innings. The rest of the staff was dreadful, and the hurlers totaled +7 WAA. In 2015, the line-up improved to +5 WAA overall thanks to better hitting. Lorenzo Cain broke the superstar barrier with 4.3 WAA, and DH Kendrys Morales, third baseman Mike Moustakas, and Gordon made modest positive contributions. The double-play combination of Omar Infante and Alcides Escobar, however, cost the team an incredible -8.1 WAA. Somehow, they returned for the 2016 season. The 2015 pitching staff also earned +7 WAA, although the starting pitching earned only +.0.7 WAA, largely because of a disastrous -3.2 WAA from 36-year-old Jeremy Guthrie. In 2015, the three leading lights in the bullpen—Herrera, Davis, and Ryan Madson—earned 4.4 WAA in in 200⅓ innings.

Despite their mediocre record, the Royals came within two runs of winning two consecutive World Series in 2014–2015. This inevitably raises the question of whether an overwhelming bullpen available in the seventh, eighth and ninth innings could indeed be the shortcut to beating a team's Pythagorean projection on a consistent basis. The question lies outside the scope of this book, but I suspect that the answer is no. To begin with, Pythagorean luck averages plus or minus four wins a season, and there is thus nothing remarkable about the Royals posting five wins' worth in two consecutive seasons. Secondly, as it is used today, such a bullpen only comes into play when the team is leading after six innings, and those leads depend on the performance of the starting line-up and the starting pitching. Like Mariano Rivera, Jonathan Papelbon, and many others, Herrera, Davis and Madson are obviously talented pitchers who significantly reduce their team's numbers of runs allowed. They might easily contribute more to their organizations if they were turned into starters. The Royals, like the San Francisco Giants, have shown that mediocre teams can repeatedly reach, and therefore win, the World Series in the era of three divisions and two wild cards. That unfortunately will continue to reduce teams' incentive to develop that increasing rarity, a superior pennant winner—much less a great team.

The Cleveland Indians returned to the top of the Central Division in 2016 with 93 wins thanks mostly to a +6 WAA pitching staff led by starters Cory Kluber (3.5 WAA) and Carlos Carrasco (1.7) and reliever Dan Otero (2 in 71 innings). The only stars in their +3 WAA lineup was DH Carlos Santana (2.9 WAA) and shortstop Francisco Lindor (2). Although third baseman Jose Ramirez cracked the superstar barrier with 4.3 WAA in 2017, while DH/first basemen Santana and Edwin Encarnacion combined for 4.2 and Lindor added 1.8, the injury-ridden lineup contributed just +2 WAA overall. But the 2017 pitching staff was, quite simply, the best in the history of baseball, earning an amazing +24 WAA. Corey Kluber, the best pitcher in the majors, led with 6.3, and starters Carlos Carrasco (3.9), Trevor Bower (2), and Mike Clevinger (2.3) were stars. Andrew Miller led the bullpen with 2.2 WAA in 63 innings, and astonishingly, not one of the 19 pitchers on the staff was worse than -0.1 WAA. With a run differential worth 108 wins, the Indians were unlucky to win only 102. Their starters, however, could not perform at their peak level in the playoffs and they lost to the Yankees in the first round. It will be very interesting to see if the Indians manage to sustain anywhere near that level of pitching performance in the years to come.

The strongest team in the AL West from 2005 through 2009 was the Los Angeles Angels of Anaheim, who made the playoffs in four years out of five with between 94 and 100 wins—all with not a single superstar season in the whole five-year period. Darin Erstad, the star of the team earlier in the decade, had slipped to average by 2005, and the only players in the lineup with significant value were Vladimir Guerrero (3.9 WAA) and Chone Figgins, who earned 2.4 playing nearly every position on the field. The line-up earned only +5 WAA, and the pitching staff added +6 with the help of star starters Bartolo Colon, John Lackey, and Jarrod Washburn. The team won 95 games and lost the ALCS to the hitless wonder White Sox. Both hitting and pitching fell off badly in 2006, but the team managed to return to the playoffs in 2007 with a +3 WAA lineup, a +6 WAA pitching staff, and four wins' worth of Pythagorean luck. This time Guerrero (3.3 WAA) accounted for the line-up's entire positive value, with 11 other offensive players within one run of average on either side of the ledger. John Lackey led the pitchers with a 3.8 WAA star season followed by Kelvim Escobar (2.8), both starters. They did not win a game against the Red Sox in the ALDS. The 2008 team was even weaker, with a +2 WAA line-up (Guerrero slumped to average) and +5 WAA pitching staff, but a remarkable 12 wins' worth of Pythagorean luck enabled them to win 100 games. Their new ace starters were Ervin Santana and Joe Saunders, with 4.5 WAA between them. In 2009, the line-up suddenly showed tremendous improvement, earning + 14 WAA. Figgins, now the third baseman, 35-year-old outfielder Bobby Abreu, veteran center fielder Torii Hunter and first baseman Kendrys Morales, all had star seasons, but the pitching staff fell below average. The team finally got revenge over the Red Sox in the ALDS, sweeping them after three consecutive defeats, but lost the ALCS to the Yankees.

The Angels fell into the neighborhood of .500 in 2010–2011, but since then, they have demonstrated an extraordinary combination of good fortune and ineptitude. After 40 games and 123 at-bats in 2011, when he turned 20, Mike Trout became their regular center fielder the next year. Trout so far has had one of the greatest careers in this history of baseball. Only Ted Williams has had six opening seasons better than his. Hitting between .287 and .326, with 27 to 41 home runs, and 67 to 110 walks in every season, Trout earned 7.5, 6.6, 6.5 and 6, 6.6, and 5 WAA (in just 114 games in 2017) in his first six years. That streak is very reminiscent of another right-handed-hitting outfielder, Henry Aaron, but Trout started his run a year earlier than Aaron and has a slightly higher average for his first four years. He was the genuine league MVP in 2012–2013 and the most valuable offensive player in 2015, winning the MVP Award only in 2014, when he ironically ranked just behind Jose Bautista of the Blue Jays in WAA. He is only an average center fielder, and the Angels might be well advised to move him to a corner position soon, but he is obviously on his way to Cooperstown and seems most likely, at this point, to emerge as the greatest player of the Millennial Generation. Yet amazingly, despite having one player who gets them at least halfway to the playoffs every year, the Angels have managed to get to post-season play with Trout in the line-up only once.

The 2012 Angels fielded the best lineup they had had in years, including not only Trout (7.5 WAA as a 20-year-old rookie), but also 3.9 WAA from first basemen Albert Pujols, an all-time great with 11 consecutive superstar seasons under his belt whom they had just signed from St. Louis at the age of 31, and a remarkable 3.1 WAA from 36-year-old outfielder Torii Hunter. But while the line-up earned +13 WAA (the most in many years), the pitching collapsed, with five starters averaging 30 years of age costing the team -6.1 WAA. The team won 89 games and missed the wild card by one game. In 2013, everything went wrong. Pujols missed much of the year with injury and earned less than 2 WAA. Meanwhile the Angels had signed a much more speculative free agent, 32-year-old Josh Hamilton, an outfielder who had had one superstar season in 2010 and a couple of star seasons with the Texas Rangers. Hamilton earned $15 million and 0.7 WAA for the Angels in 2013, and the team is still paying him more than $20 million annually even though he is now back with Texas and did not play in 2016. Shortstop Eric Aybar and outfielder J. B. Shuck were additional liabilities, and the whole line-up was -2 WAA despite Trout, while the pitching staff was average, leaving the team with 78 wins.

The team turned around impressively in 2014, when Trout's 6.1 WAA were complemented by Pujols (1.9), second baseman Howie Kendrick (2.5), outfielder Kole Calhoun (2.6), and shortstop Aybar, who improved all the way to 1.4 WAA. Hamilton also posted 1.7 WAA in 89 games, and although the pitching staff was slightly below average, the line-up's +16 WAA allowed the team to win a league-leading 98 games. Yet the Royals swept them in the ALDS, which remains, so far, Mike Trout's only appearance in post-season play. In 2015, Trout, Pujols and Calhoun combined for 9.9 WAA, but Aybar (-2.6 WAA) returned to form, and a disastrous bench pulled the whole line-up down to just +3 WAA. The pitching was worse, and only luck allowed the Angels to top .500 and win 85 games. Of the very few players who have had a remotely comparable impact at such an early age, Mike Trout has surely received the least media attention. Had the Angels managed to develop as many average young players as the Rays, he would already have appeared in post-season at least three times. Trout was the AL MVP again in 2016 with 6.7 WAA, his fifth consecutive superstar season at age 24, but Calhoun and Pujols (now a DH) slumped to average, first baseman C. J. Cron was the only other above-average player in the line-up, and second baseman Johnny Giavotella surrendered -29 runs in the field and cost the team -3.8 WAA. Trout kept his streak alive in 2017 with 5 WAA despite missing nearly a third of the season with a thumb injury, but that represented the entire positive value of the lineup, and the pitching staff cost them -5 WAA. Trout is now signed with the Angels through 2020, and it is to be hoped that they can find more worthy teammates for him.

The Texas Rangers, meanwhile, reached post-season play five times in seven years from 2010 through 2016 and played in two World Series, even though they topped off at 96 wins in 2011. Their always-uneven line-up also peaked in that year with +8 WAA. Their best player in these years was second baseman Ian Kinsler, who had superstar seasons of 4.3 WAA in 2011 and 4.3 in 2013, before he was most unwisely traded to Detroit for Prince Fielder. Josh Hamilton had a tremendous 6.3 WAA season in 2010 as well before falling to 2.1 WAA and 1.7 in the next two seasons. Nelson Cruz (4.4 WAA in 2010), Mike Napoli (4.5 WAA in 2011), and pitcher Matt Harrison (4.1 in 2012) also had superstar seasons, in these years. So did outfielder Shin-Soo Choo in 2014—a Korean who has had one of the best and unluckiest careers within the Millennial Generation. Although Choo consistently hit very well in the minors after the Seattle Mariners signed him at 18 in 2000, not until 2009, when he was 26, did he play a full major league season with the Cleveland Indians. He promptly earned 4.2 WAA, and he has turned in superstar seasons in four of the last six seasons for the Indians, the Cincinnati Reds, and the Rangers, peaking with Texas in 2015 at 5.3 WAA. Choo is one of seven offensive players from the Millennial generation who now has at least four superstar seasons. Third baseman Adrian Beltre, acquired as a free agent, remained a star in 2011–2013, but by 2014 his fielding was so bad that he had fallen to average. A well-balanced Rangers pitching staff contributed +8 WAA in 2010 and +11 WAA in 2011, but fell off thereafter.

Several of these Rangers teams presented interesting features. The 2011 team—the best one—should have been even better. Individually, its hitters generated enough walks and hits to have made the team +90 runs, or about ten wins, better than average, but in fact their runs scored totals beat the league average by only 54. The 2014 team finished well below .500 because of incredibly dreadful fielding, bad enough to cost the team a full -13 WAA. Chief among the culprits were 11 first basemen, led by Prince Fielder, who cost them a combined -71 runs. The 2015 team won a divisional championship with just 88 wins, including five wins' worth of Pythagorean luck.

Most extraordinary of all was the 2016 team. While the team's hitting was perfectly average, excellent fielding by 22-year-old Rougned Odor (+26 runs), rookie right fielder Nomar Mazara (+20), and first baseman Mitch Moreland (+29) allowed the line-up to post +6 WAA. Beltre was still a star with 2.3 WAA, but Odor led the team with 3.6. Choo was now down to average and Fielder surrendered -1.7 WAA as a DH. But the pitchers surrendered -5 WAA, and the team won an extraordinary 95 games thanks to 13 wins' worth of Pythagorean luck, *the highest figure in the history of baseball.* Their luck ran out in the division series, where they lost three games to Toronto. Like the Yankees in the early 2000s, the Rangers' record illustrates the perils of relying on aging players with one or two good seasons in their past.

In 2012, the Oakland A's started a new, three-year playoff run, winning 94 and 96 games in 2012–2013 and only 88 in 2014, when they had by far their best run differential, thanks to a dreadful -11 games' worth of Pythagorean luck. For the first time in many years, Billy Beane and the A's had come up with a genuine superstar, third baseman Josh Donaldson, whose career path had been most unfortunate. After attending Auburn University for three years, Donaldson was signed by the Chicago Cubs at 21 in 2007 and traded to the A's a year later. It took him until halfway through the 2012 season, when he was 26, to become a regular, and he became a superstar thanks to both hitting and fielding for the next four seasons. Other important assets were Cuban outfielder Yoenis Cespedes, signed in 2012 at the age of 26, and Josh Reddick, an outfielder whom Billy Beane had just plucked from the Red Sox for two very average young players. In 2012, Cespedes and Reddick earned 2.7 and 2.4 WAA, respectively, while Donaldson had a good half-season and 28-year-old shortstop Cliff Pennington, a homegrown product, had his second fantastic season in the field in three years, saving +32 runs and earning 1.7 WAA overall. The line-up earned +7 wins, and a well-balanced pitching staff added +4. Although Cespedes and Reddick both slipped to average in 2013, Donaldson earned 4 WAA in his first full season, and Beane replaced disastrous second baseman Jemile Weeks (-2 WAA in 2012) with Eric Sogard, who was nearly average. He was less lucky at shortstop, where Pennington had departed as a free agent and Jed Lowrie fielded so badly as to fall below average. Center fielder Coco Crisp also improved to 2.1 WAA, and the pitching staff earned +4 WAA again to complement the line-up's +10. The A's lost the ALDS to the Tigers in five games for the second consecutive year.

The 2014 team was most unlucky. Its run differential was good enough to win 99 games, but they in fact won just 88 and lost the wild card game to the much inferior Royals. Donaldson, hitting his peak at 28, earned 5.2 WAA, and Cespedes and Reddick earned 3.6 WAA between them. Although Crisp and DH Alberto Callaspo were significant liabilities, first baseman Brandon Moss had a great year in the field and earned 2.7 WAA, and the double-play combination was average. The pitching staff cost the team -1 WAA. Unfortunately, Donaldson was just one year away from free agency, and in November 2014 Beane traded him to the Toronto Blue Jays for four young players—none of whom so far has produced any significant results at the major league level. During 2015, he traded Cespedes to the Red Sox as well. The 2015 team fell to well below average, and Billy Beane is back to square one again. Even though Josh Donaldson was 29 when Beane traded him, he was, in this writer's opinion, simply too great a player to trade.

Donaldson's trade allowed the 2015 Toronto Blue Jays to field one of the best teams of the Xer-Millennial era. Although they won only 93 games, their adjusted run differential of +219 projected to make them a superior pennant winner with 103 wins. All the team's strength was in their line-up, which finished the season +24 WAA, while the pitching staff, despite the late-season acquisition of David Price, was -2 WAA. Donaldson led the team with 5.7 WAA, his third consecutive superstar season, but 32-year-old designated hitter Edwin Encarnacion was not far behind with 5. Encarnacion, who came up with Cincinnati in 2005 at the age of 22, had been an average hitter and a terrible third baseman with the Reds for about four seasons, but in 2012, a year after being traded to the Blue Jays, he became a star, splitting time between first base, the outfield, and DH. He remained one for three years before peaking in 2015 at the age of 32, when he also posted positive fielding numbers in limited duty at first base. Right fielder Jose Bautista, who had been the genuine AL MVP in 2014 with 6.4 WAA—0.2 more than Mike Trout—barely missed his fourth superstar season with 3.8 WAA. After bouncing from team to team, Bautista had reached the majors to stay with Pittsburgh in 2006, but was generally a below-average player through 2008. He suddenly became a superstar at age 29 in 2010, when he hit 54 home runs. Exactly how Encarnacion and Bautista became great at relatively advanced ages after reaching the Blue Jays is a mystery. Another major asset in 2015 was homegrown: center fielder Kevin Pillar, who saved +24 runs in the field in his first full season at age 26, and earned 2.9 WAA. Rookie second baseman Devon Travis earned 2 WAA in just 62 games, and the line-up did not include any below average players. Late-season acquisition David Price earned 1.4 WAA in just 74⅓ innings for the Blue Jays, finishing the year, which he had begun with Detroit, with 3.4. The pitching staff, however, still finished below average, and Price joined the Red Sox in the offseason.

The Blue Jays' adjusted run differential of +219 was the highest in the American League during this era, and their 103 projected wins edged out the projections for the 2007 and 2013 Red Sox (102 and 101) and the 2011 Yankees (102) as the best as well. Yet while those two Red Sox teams won the World Series, the Blue Jays barely made it through the ALDS and lost the league championship series to a Royals team whose run differential was 138 runs worse. The 2011 Yankees had also gone out in the first round. Sadly, in an era of three rounds of playoffs, putting together a truly superior team does not guarantee even reaching—much less winning—the World Series. Baseball's highest honor has become a lottery to which ten teams are admitted every year, often on the basis of very marginal superiority.

Josh Donaldson posted his fourth consecutive superstar season with 4 WAA in 2016, but Encarnacion slumped to 1.9 and Bautista to average. Troy Tulowitzki was also average in a full season, and the whole line-up earned just +2 WAA and the pitchers added +6, led by Aaron Sanchez (3 WAA) and J. A. Happ (2.7). The Jays easily survived the loss of David Price, who earned about 1 WAA for the Red Sox. The Blue Jays lost the ALCS to the Indians in three games.

After finishing over .500 twice and making the playoffs once in 2015–16, the Houston Astros blossomed in 2017, winning 101 games and the AL West with the help of a lineup worth +21 WAA. The lineup featured a remarkable six players with at least 2 WAA. Second baseman Jose Altuve, who hit brilliantly but had a poor year in the field, earned 4 WAA, and 22-year old shortstop Carlos Correa did the same in just 109 games, promising great things for the future. Then came center fielder George Springer (3.6) and third baseman Alex Bregman (3 WAA at just 22 years old.), outfielders Marwin Gonzales (2.9) and veteran Josh Reddick (2.6), and first baseman Yuli Gurriel (1.9.) Five of these players had been signed by the Astros. The pitching staff, on which no hurler threw more than 153 innings, added only +2 WAA, with starters Dallas Keuchel and Brad Peacock combining for 4.9. Houston made short work of the Red Sox in the division series and overcame a 3–2 deficit to beat the Yankees in the ALCS and move to the World Series. With its wealth of young talent, Houston seems poised to contend for some time.

The Books Are Nearly Closed on Generation X

In 2016, David Ortiz, 40 years old and in his last season, firmly established himself as an all-time great with his fifth superstar season, earning 4.2 WAA. No Gen Xer posted a superstar season during 2017, however, and the youngest members of that generation will turn 37 during 2018, suggesting that they have few, if any, additional superstar seasons to post. Only two Gen Xers who have already made the all-time list of players with at least four superstar seasons, Albert Pujols and CC Sabathia, are still active, and neither one of them has performed at that level for a number of years now. Nor do any members of this generation seem poised to enter that charmed circle, with the possible exception of Adam Wainwright, who needs only one more superstar season, but whose 2017 season does not promise future greatness. We may thus summarize, as we have for every other generation since the Lost, what their greatest players have accomplished.

The hitters of generation X repeatedly put up extraordinary numbers, turning 50 home runs into a figure that every major power hitter was likely to reach at least once. As it turns out, however, these stats reflected a general increase in offense throughout the major leagues, rather than the emergence of an unusual number a all-time greats. Thirteen offensive players from Generation X have five superstar seasons or more, compared to 15 GIs, 14 Silents, and 15 Boomers. The number of all-time greats has *not* expanded in proportion either to the total population of the U.S. and the Caribbean nations from which nearly every player comes, or in proportion to the size of the major leagues.

Barry Bonds, not surprisingly, leads the list of Generation X superstars with 17 seasons of 4 WAA or more—tied for all-time leader with Babe Ruth, who also had 17, and one ahead of Willie Mays and Henry Aaron, with 17 each. Bonds's career is unique, of course, because PEDs enabled him to post four seasons averaging 9 WAA at ages 36 through 39. This had a most unfortunate distorting effect on the record books, but it should be noted that Bonds had never fallen below the superstar level in his career up until that time, and it is entirely possible that he might have at least tied Mays and Aaron, albeit with less spectacular

WAA totals, had he not developed an entirely new physique in his late 30s. However the voters choose to assess his Hall of Fame candidacy, he is one of the greatest performers of all time. Albert Pujols, whom we have not yet discussed in detail, ranks second in their generation with 11 superstar seasons, and because of his defensive value, his greatest season, in 2009, was slightly superior to Bonds's, 10.3 to 10.1. Pujols is still contributing wins to the Los Angeles Angels of Anaheim but he has not approached the superstar level with them. Next come two first basemen, Jeff Bagwell with ten superstar seasons, and Frank Thomas with seven. There is no obvious reason why Thomas, but not Bagwell, should be in the Hall of Fame. Then comes Edgar Martinez, the greatest DH of all time, with seven superstar seasons, all between the ages of 29 and 38.

No other generation has produced two shortstops as dominant as Alex Rodriguez (seven superstar seasons overall, five of them at short), and Barry Larkin (six). The Gen X all-time great list does not include a single second baseman, and only one player, Jim Thome (five), who played third base for part of his career. Tied with Larkin are Ken Griffey, Jr. (six) and first baseman Todd Helton, who toiled in obscurity for the Colorado Rockies for 17 years, posting six superstar seasons and peaking at 8.6 WAA, trailing only Bonds and Pujols among hitters, in 2003. Then come Jim Thome, Sammy Sosa, Jim Edmonds, Vladimir Guerrero, and David Ortiz with five each. (Thome, Guerrero, Chipper Jones [3 superstar seasons] and reliever Trevor Hoffman [0] have just been elected to the Hall of Fame.)

Mike Piazza, as noted, has a strong claim as the second-greatest catcher in history, behind Johnny Bench, with two superstar seasons, four more over 3 WAA, and two more over 2 WAA. Behind him comes Ivan Rodriguez, who peaked at 3.2 WAA in 2004 and had six seasons over 2 WAA, and Jorge Posada, with one superstar season and three over 2 WAA.

Behind these players come 10 more hitters with four superstar seasons—compared to seven such players from the Boom Generation. These Xers include Don Mattingly, Mark McGwire, Rafael Palmeiro, Albert Belle, Jason Giambi, Gary Sheffield, Manny Ramirez, David Ortiz, Lance Berkman, and Larry Walker. Six of those 11 players have definitely been linked to PEDs. It is worth noting that of their counterparts among the Boomers—Jose Cruz, Bobby Grich, Buddy Bell, Dave Parker, Willie Wilson, Jesse Barfield, and Tony Gwynn— only Gwynn has ever even gotten serious consideration for the Hall of Fame. The only reason those players had less impressive traditional statistics was the era in which they played.

It was the pitchers of Generation X, not the hitters, who did truly extraordinary and unprecedented things. Eight different Gen X pitchers posted five or more superstar seasons, compared to four from the Lost Generation, two GI, two Silents and two Boomers. They were led by Roger Clemens, whose 12 superstar seasons beat out Walter Johnson and Lefty Grove (11) for the all-time record. He is followed by Randy Johnson (nine); Greg Maddux (eight), Pedro Martinez (six), and Roy Halladay, Curt Schilling, Tom Glavine, and Mike Mussina, with five each. Although most of these men pitched significantly fewer innings per season than their counterparts in earlier generations, they were so superior to average in their high-offense era that they earned as many extra wins for their teams anyway. As we have seen, they also sustained extraordinary performance at much greater ages than almost anyone from earlier generations. Generation X also includes pitchers Bret Saberhagen, Kevin Brown, and Johan Santana, who had four seasons of 4 WAA or more apiece. Jon Smoltz topped 4 WAA only once, with 5.5 in 1996, but he had four more seasons over 3 WAA and eight over 2, and has been elected to the Hall of Fame. We shall find that the Millennial Generation has not produced a comparable crop of outstanding pitchers.

We will never know who did and who did not use performance enhancing drugs in the years before testing, but some players have either confessed or have been clearly linked to such drugs by actual evidence, and some players' career pattern inevitably arouses suspicion because they were almost without precedent in earlier eras. In several cases, players fall into both categories; in others they do not. I am glad I do not have to try to decide who does and does not belong in the Hall of Fame.

Mediocrity has been even more pronounced in the National League than in the American during the Xer-Millennial era, and the winning percentages of playoff teams have been even lower—partly because of interleague play, in which the American League has consistently beaten the National, causing the total winning percentages of National League teams to fall below .500. During these 13 years, three clubs in particular have dominated postseason play: the Cardinals (eight appearances), the Dodgers (eight), and the Phillies (six). The Braves, Cubs, Reds, Pirates, and Giants have reached post-season play between three and five times each. No club has taken better advantage of the randomness of modern baseball than the Giants, who have not only reached the playoffs three times without ever winning more than 94 games, but also won the World Series three times.

We left the Cardinals in the last chapter after a poor season in 2003, when their line-up already included Albert Pujols, Jim Edmonds, and third baseman Scott Rolen. The National League in 2004 featured five offensive players with 6 WAA or more, including Bonds (9.6), Todd Helton of Colorado (8), and Adrian Beltre of Los Angeles (6.7), and the Cardinals had two, Pujols (second behind Bonds at 8.1) and Rolen (6.3). All three had outstanding years in the field, as did Edmonds, a third superstar with 5.6 WAA at age 34. Second baseman Tony Womack, outfielder Reggie Sanders, and late-season acquisition Larry Walker—who had had four superstar seasons with other clubs—were modest assets as well. The line-up posted +19 WAA despite a dismal season at bat and in the field from shortstop Edgar Renteria (-2 WAA), and the team won 105 games with the help of four wins' worth of Pythagorean luck. The pitching staff was average. Reaching the World Series, the Cardinals lost in four games to the Red Sox, whose Pythagorean percentage had been only slightly lower. The 2005 Cardinals duplicated the 2004 season almost exactly, with an average pitching staff, a line-up worth +18 WAA, and 100 wins. Once again Pujols (an outstanding first baseman) and Edmonds led the way with 7.5 and 4.4 WAA. A new double-play combination—30-year-old David Eckstein and 35-year-old Mark Grudzielanek—showed a vast improvement over Renteria and Womack, adding more than 3 WAA, and Abraham Nunez filled in capably for Rolen, who missed most of the year. Fielding earned fully half of the line-up's +18 WAA, suggesting once again that Tony LaRussa, now the Cardinals manager, understood its importance. This time, however, the Cardinals could not get past the pitching-rich Houston Astros in the NLDS.

As so often seems to happen in our current era, a much weaker Cardinals club won the World Series in 2006. Although Pujols had another fantastic season (7.6 WAA, +2 of them in the field) and Rolen added 4.1 more, age caught up to Edmonds and Eckstein, who were average, and catcher Yadier Molina, another superb fielder, had a dreadful year at the plate.

The line-up (+4 WAA) included no other significant assets, and the pitchers were a full -3 WAA. Winners of just 83 games, the Cardinals beat the Padres in the Division Series and barely got past the Mets, who had won 97 games, in the NLCS. They proceeded to beat the Tigers, winners of 95 games in the AL, in just five games. But the decline of the team was all too real, and although Pujols led the National League with 7.3 and 7.7 WAA in 2007–2008, the Cardinals won just 79 and 86 games, missing the playoffs both times.

A very different Cardinals team returned to post-season in 2009 with 91 wins. Few teams since the Giants of the early 1960s had combined such dramatic strengths and weaknesses. The 29-year-old Pujols had his best season yet, hitting .327 with 47 homers and 115 walks, saving an amazing 39 runs in the field, and topping the league yet again with 10.7 WAA.[45] Two starting pitchers, 34-year-old Chris Carpenter (17–4) and 27-year-old Adam Wainwright (19–8), earned 4.2 and 3.8 WAA. But the only other overall asset in the line-up was shortstop Brendan Ryan (2.3 WAA), and the line-up without Pujols and Ryan totaled -5 WAA. Pitchers not named Carpenter or Wainwright cost the Cardinals -3.2 WAA. A poor performance by Carpenter in Game 1 and a blown save in Game 2 by Ryan Franklin led to a sweep by the Dodgers in the NLDS. The same pattern continued in 2010, when Pujols (6.4 WAA, the best offensive player in the NL again), Wainwright (3.7) and outfielder Matt Holliday (5.1) posted superstar seasons worth 15 wins above .500, but the team won only 86 games (losing five wins to Pythagorean luck) and missed the playoffs.

The 2011 team was almost exactly as good, but its luck was better, and it won 90 games and the World Series. The line-up earned +12 WAA thanks to Pujols (5 WAA) and two older free agent signings, 35-year-old Lance Berkman (2.8) and Matt Holliday (2.6). Adam Wainwright missed the entire season with injury, and the pitching staff cost the team -5 WAA. The Cardinals were fortunate not to face the Phillies, one of the most extraordinary teams of the 21st century, whom we shall encounter in due course.

Albert Pujols's contract with the Cardinals, which he had signed after the 2004 season, ran out in 2011, and they did not re-sign him. At the age of 32, he signed a ten-year contract with the Los Angeles Angels of Anaheim that stands to pay him $30 million in 2021, when he will be 41 years old. The Cardinals' decision appears to have been a wise one since Pujols has suffered from injuries and has never reached the superstar level in the American League. Yet Pujols, with 11 consecutive superstar seasons, not only ranks behind Barry Bonds (17 superstar seasons) and Roger Clemens (12) as the third-greatest player of Generation X, but also ranks just behind Lou Gehrig (12 superstar seasons) as the greatest first baseman of all time. His best season in 2009 was better than Gehrig's (9 WAA in 1927). And from 2004 through 2009, he was one of the greatest fielding first basemen of all time, saving an average of 22 runs a season—enough to win his team two more games. If Pujols, now 37, could have one more superstar season, he would legitimately rank as the greatest first baseman of all time.

---

45. Michael Humphreys has told me privately that after incorporating new play-by-play data he is inclined to reduce Pujols' fielding runs saved somewhat, cutting his 2009 WAA to 9.7. The 10.7 figure is, however, consistent with the rest of the data in this book. It is also superior to any season of Barry Bonds's.

Despite Pujols' departure, the 2012 team was very similar in overall performance, with a +9 WAA line-up and a +3 WAA pitching staff. Remarkably, catcher Yadier Molina—until now a brilliant fielder but a very poor hitter—had a great year at the plate at age 29 and had a superstar season of 4.2 WAA—that is, a better season than either Yogi Berra or Roy Campanella ever had. New center fielder Jon Jay earned 3 WAA (mostly in the field), and third baseman David Freese, Holliday, and 35-year-old Carlos Beltran all contributed significantly. Wainwright, returning from Tommy John surgery, was only average on the mound. The team won only 88 games, five below its projection, and made the playoffs as a wild card, eventually losing the NLCS in seven games to the Giants. The 2013 team looked much stronger, and only four games' worth of bad Pythagorean luck prevented it from winning 101 games. This was, however, deceptive. Based on their walks, hits, and base running, the Cardinals projected to score 711 runs. They actually scored 783, good for about seven extra wins, indicating a phenomenal and most unusual ability to bunch hits and walks. Only five teams in the history of baseball have exceeded their projected runs scored by this much.[46] Second baseman Matt Carpenter just missed superstardom with 3.9 WAA, and Molina, who had another fine year at bat, added 2.4. Holliday and Allen Craig contributed 1.6 WAA each, but David Freese had a disastrous year in the field and cost the team -2.8 WAA. Wainwright returned to form with a 19–9 record in 241⅔ innings and 3.3 WAA, representing nearly the whole positive value of the pitching staff. The team, the strongest in the league thanks to their run luck, reached the World Series but lost to the Red Sox in six games.

Another form of luck carried the Cardinals to a division title in 2014. While their line-up fell from +16 WAA overall to -2, and Wainwright once again contributed the total positive value of the pitching staff with 4.9 WAA, the Cardinals managed to win 90 games with the help of seven wins' worth of Pythagorean luck. This time they lost the NLCS to the Giants. The 2015 team showed an extraordinary turnaround. Although Wainwright was injured and missed nearly the entire season, the pitching staff contributed an astonishing +16 WAA. That, along with four wins' worth of Pythagorean luck, allowed a perfectly average line-up to win 100 games and the division. Thirty-six-year-old John Lackey, signed from the American League, led the staff with 3.4 WAA, and Jamie Garcia (2.4), Carlos Martinez (2.2), Lance Lynn (1.6), and Michael Wacha (1.2) filled in a brilliant starting rotation. Relief aces Kevin Siegrist and Trevor Rosenthal combined for 2.6 WAA in 143⅓ innings. A weaker Mets team, however, eliminated them in the NLDS. In 2016, the pitchers suddenly regressed all the way to average, and the team won just 86 games and missed the playoffs. The Cardinals since 2009 are certainly one of the prototypes of a successful modern franchise. Helped enormously by one all-time great (Pujols) and an excellent pitcher (Wainwright), they have filled out most (but not all) of the team with average or slightly above-average players, generally earning over 90 wins and making the playoffs in almost every season. Luck has carried them into the playoffs on two occasions and has consistently determined their course through the post-season—as it has for every other team, as well.

The Cardinals also benefited from a highly balanced division in which every team made

---

46. This figure is based on the linear weights system developed by Pete Palmer, who kindly provided the data.

6. The Gen X and Millennial Era, 2005–2017   211

post-season play at least twice from 2004 through 2016. The Houston Astros managed to buy their way into postseason in 2004–2005 by signing 41-year-old Roger Clemens and 32-year-old Andy Pettitte from the Yankees. Although Pettitte missed most of 2004 with injury, Clemens posted a remarkable 4.5 WAA, Roy Oswalt and Brad Lidge added 3.2 and 2.8 WAA, and the pitching staff as a whole contributed +8 WAA. Outfielder Lance Berkman's 4.2 WAA exceeded the line-up's net contribution, as the team won 92 games. Clemens shattered all records for 42-year-old pitchers in 2005, finishing with a 1.87 ERA and 5.4 WAA, while Pettitte added 4.5 and Oswalt 3.6. Although the rest of the staff was weaker, the pitchers as a whole earned +8 WAA again, but won only 89 games thanks to a very mediocre line-up. Somehow beating the Braves and Cardinals, they were swept by an equally punchless White Sox club in the World Series. That was the end of their playoff run, one made possible by the performances of elderly, free agent pitchers.

The least successful team in the Central Division were the Milwaukee Brewers, who earned a wild card in 2008 with a projected 87 wins (90 in actual fact), thanks mostly to 3.3 WAA from pitcher CC Sabathia, and again in 2011, winning 96 games with the help of six wins' worth of Pythagorean luck and 6.9 WAA from outfielder Ryan Braun, who was later caught using PEDs. The Chicago Cubs won the Central Division in 2007 with just 85 wins (Arizona and Colorado tied for the league lead with 90, the lowest total in history), and again in 2008 with 97 wins. The 2007 team suffered from the same park illusions as so many Cubs teams of the past. Although six regulars in the line-up had averages over .280, the team's hitters were -5 WAA overall. The much stronger 2008 team relied even more heavily on its pitching, including superstar Ryan Dempster (4.7 WAA with a 17–6 record), Carlos Zambrano (2.5 WAA) and Ted Lilly (2.1). It was, however, eliminated by the Dodgers in the NLDS without winning a game.

Three years later, in late 2011, Theo Epstein, who had taken the Red Sox to the World Series twice, became the Cubs' general manager. The 2015 Cubs managed to win one of two wild card spots with 97 wins, but their prospects were not especially bright. Their line-up—weak in the field—cost the team -3 WAA, and they owed their record to +12 WAA from the pitching staff and seven wins' worth of Pythagorean luck. The star of the pitching staff was Jake Arrieta, who turned in a 22–6 record and an amazing 6.5 WAA. In an impressive turnaround, the 2016 lineup improved all the way from -4 WAA to +22, including +9 in the field, and the team projected to win 107 games actually won 103, a superior pennant winner. The Cubs featured the National League's true MVP, Kris Bryant, who fielded very well at third base and all over the outfield, hit 39 home runs, and earned 6.1 WAA. Second-year shortstop Addison Russell, just 22, and right fielder Jason Heyward saved +19 and +18 runs in the field and earned 1.4 and 0.6 WAA despite poor hitting, while second baseman Ben Zobrist, although well past his peak, earned 1. Center fielder Dexter Fowler and young utility infielder Javier Baez, another great fielder, both starred with 2 and 2.6 WAA. The pitching staff added +6 WAA thanks to three starters. Thirty-two-year-old Jon Lester had his best season in some time with 3.2 WAA, Kyle Hendrix added 3, and Jake Arrieta slipped to 1.4. The Cubs, the strongest team in the Xer-Millennial era to date, managed to pull out a close World Series against the much inferior Indians, winning their first title since 1908.

With their lineup falling from +22 WAA to +13 and their pitching staff from +6 to average, the Cubs in 2017 still managed to win their division again with just 92 wins. Bryant was a superstar again with 4.3 WAA, and first baseman Anthony Rizzo and catcher Wilson Contreras added 3.5 and 2.9. Pitchers Lester, Lackey and Arrieta all feel to average or below, but Kyle Hendricks (2 WAA) and Mike Montgomery (1.1) picked up some of the slack. The Cubs managed to advance to the NLDS, but lost to the Dodgers in just five games.

After a long drought, the Cincinnati Reds made the playoffs in 2010, 2012 and 2013 thanks mainly to the contributions of one of the great players of the Millennial Generation, first baseman Joey Votto. A Canadian, Votto was signed by the Reds in 2002 when he was still only 18, but inexplicably spent five and a half seasons in the minors. A strong hitter who has had three very fine fielding seasons at first base, Votto posted 2.7 WAA as a rookie in 2008, when he was 24, and followed that up with five consecutive superstar seasons, peaking in 2011 with 6.1 WAA. The rest of the Reds' line-up was very poor in 2008–2009, but in 2010 Votto was complemented by 23-year-old right fielder Jay Bruce, who posted 4.6 WAA thanks to saving 27 runs in the field, and 35-year-old Scott Rolen, who performed brilliantly once again at third base and added 3.3 WAA in 133 games. The pitching staff was average but the line-up earned +11 WAA, enough to win a weak division with 91 victories. The Phillies quickly eliminated them in the playoffs. The 2011 Reds won only 79 games despite Votto's best season, but the 2012 club returned to its 2010 level and added six wins' worth of Pythagorean luck, winning 97 games and their division. The lineup continued to decline, with Bruce earning 1.9 WAA, center fielder Franklin Stubbs (whom Bruce should surely have replaced by now) a disastrous -4.3 WAA, and shortstop Zack Cozart and utility man Wilson Valdez a total of -4.4 WAA. But the pitching staff earned +13 WAA, ten more than any other team in the league. Led by Johnny Cueto (19–9 with 3.9 WAA), five starters averaged over 200 innings apiece and totaled 8.3 WAA, and closer Arnoldis Chapman added 2.2 WAA in just 71⅔ innings. This time the Reds lost a five-game NLDS to the Giants. Four of the five starters were in their mid-20s, but the staff slumped back to average in 2013. This time, however, Votto's 5.6 WAA combined with 4 WAA from outfielder Shin-Soo Choo, acquired from the Indians in a clever three-way trade, and 3.5 WAA from Bruce. Despite some weak spots, the line-up earned +11 WAA and the team won 90 games, earning a wild card berth but losing to the Pirates. Votto missed most of 2014 and the line-up slumped, and in 2015 the Reds fielded one of the worst line-ups in recent memory. A long string of below-average players—including Bruce, who had a miserable year—more than outweighed Votto's superb 5.8 WAA, and the team's adjusted runs scored missed the league average by -149 runs. The pattern repeated itself in 2017 when Votto, now 33, had his greatest season, leading the NL with 7.1 WAA, but the team won just 70 games.

In 2013–2015 the Pittsburgh Pirates stepped into the role of the Tampa Bay Rays of the AL East a few years earlier, with center fielder Andrew McCutchen in the role of Evan Longoria. Although McCutchen already has three superstar seasons, his career may wind up looking more like that of Roy White than Roberto Clemente or Barry Bonds, to whom he was frequently compared. Signed at the age of 18 in 2005, he spent four seasons in the minors. He was average in his first two major league seasons and a star in 2011, when he was

24. Although graceful, he began as a poor fielder in center and has improved only to average. He became a superstar in 2012, hitting .327 with 5.1 WAA, but the Pirates won just 79 games because of terrible pitching. The 2013 line-up featured mediocre hitting, with McCutchen supplying the majority of its runs above average, but outstanding fielding by third baseman Pedro Alvarez (2.2 WAA), left fielder Starling Marte (2.2 WAA) and catcher Russell Martin (2.2 WAA) gave the line-up + 9 WAA overall with shortstop Clint Barmes the only serious weakness. Six wins' worth of Pythagorean luck made up for a -2 WAA pitching staff, and the team won a wild card berth, beat the Reds, and narrowly lost the NLDS to the Cardinals. Fielding was again a major strength in 2014, featuring great defensive performances from Martin (3.9 WAA in just 111 games), Alvarez (2.8 WAA in 122 games), and utility man Josh Harrison (3.6 WAA in 143 games). Although Marte's fielding fell off badly, his hitting improved and he added 1.8 WAA to McCutchen's 4.9. The line-up had no weaknesses and earned +13 WAA, but the pitching staff gave back -7 WAA, and the team won only 88 games thanks to bad Pythagorean luck. This time they lost the wild card playoff to the Giants, who managed to parlay *their* 88 wins into their third world championship in five years. The line-up fell off badly in 2015, as McCutcheon fell to 2.7 WAA and catcher Russell Martin left for Toronto. Pedro Alvarez moved to first base, where he was far less valuable (1.5 WAA), and Marte fell to 1 WAA. The whole line-up lost two-thirds of its positive value, falling to +4 WAA, but the pitching staff showed an amazing improvement to +7 WAA, led by 24-year-old Gerrit Cole, with 2.3 WAA. The team improved all the way to 98 victories with the help of six wins' worth of luck, but lost the wild card game. While the Pirates had done a good job of keeping below-average players out of their line-up, they had never become more than a moderately good team.

Although several of their hitters were never as good as their ballpark made them seem, the Philadelphia Phillies had the longest run at the top in the NL East, making the playoffs each year from 2007 through 2011. But only in 2011 did they win more than 97 games, and their line-up was never much more than mediocre.

The nucleus of the team included three infielders, first baseman Ryan Howard, second baseman Chase Utley, and shortstop Jimmy Rollins, all born in 1978–1979. Of the three, only Utley could by any stretch of the imagination be called a great player. He did not become a major league regular until 2005, when he was 26, and promptly became a star, with 2.5 and 2.2 WAA in the next two seasons, during which the Phillies finished second. But he barely missed four superstar seasons in a row from 2007 through 2010, with 4.6, 3.9, 5.2 and 4.1 WAA. Only in 2010 was he a significant asset in the field. Rollins, a year older, became a regular at 22 but was only an average player overall for the next six seasons (2001–2006), despite batting averages in the high .200s and 25 homers in 2006. In 2007, he hit .296 with 20 triples and 30 homers and was rewarded with the league MVP Award, even though he earned only 2.4 WAA, *the only time in his entire long career that he earned more than 2 WAA*. The league included 11 players with more than 4 WAA, led by Pujols, and including another Phillie (Utley) and another shortstop (Troy Tulowitzki of Denver.) In that same year of 2006, first baseman Ryan Howard spent his first full year as a regular at age 26 after six seasons in the minors, and managed to hit 58 home runs and drive in 149 runs while earning only 3.6 WAA, mainly because he gave up -13 runs in the field. During the next three years, Howard averaged 47 homers and 141 RBI while earning 1.7, 2.4, and 3.1 WAA. He declined to 1.1 WAA a year in the next two years. Outfielders Shane Victorino and Jayson Werth were also assets during these years, but never superstars.

Utley remained the only superstar in the Phillies' lineup during their run and will be a strong but not overwhelming candidate for the Hall of Fame. With Rollins and Howard as the other leading lights of the team, it is not surprising that the line-up earned +10 WAA in 2007, +2 WAA in 2008, +4 WAA in 2009, +8 WAA in 2010, and +2 in 2011. The real strength of these teams—initially concealed by the ball park—was on the mound. The 2008 team, which beat Tampa Bay in the World Series, featured 4 WAA from 24-year-old Cole Hamels, 2.6 WAA from 45-year-old Jamie Moyer, and 1.9 WAA from reliever Brad Lidge, and a total of +10 WAA from the staff. Hamels and Moyer slumped in 2009, when the team returned to the World Series but lost to the Yankees, but J. A. Happ earned 3.6 WAA and the staff earned +7 WAA. They added +6 in 2010, when the Phillies were eliminated in the NLCS, thanks to Roy Halladay, owner of three superstar seasons with the Toronto Blue Jays and improved to 5.2 WAA in his first year with the Phillies, who had traded for him, and Hamels, who added 3.1 WAA.

The 2011 Phillies were by far the best team of this run, winning 102 games thanks entirely to one of the greatest pitching staffs in the history of baseball. Halladay, in his second year with the Phillies, earned another 5. WAA with a 19–6 record. (He immediately fell to below average and retired after two more years.) Free agent Cliff Lee, 32 years old, who had had an extraordinarily erratic career with several teams, was right behind Halladay with a 17–8 record and 5.5 WAA. Hamels nearly gave the team three superstar starters with 3.9 WAA, and the last three starters—Vance Worley, Roy Oswalt, and Kyle Kendrick—had 3.3 WAA between them. All told, the Phillies' pitching staff—whose starters cost them more than $56 million that year—earned +19 WAA, about +5 more than the 1954 Indians. The team, to repeat, won 102 games with a generally mediocre line-up—but lost the Division Series, 3–2, to the St. Louis Cardinals, to become another victim of the playoff system. The Phillies played in a mediocre division and a mediocre league, and their five consecutive playoff appearances and two trips to the World Series gave several of their players an aura of stardom that they did not deserve. But the 2011 pitching staff remains one of the very greatest in the history of the game.

The New York Mets had preceded the Phillies at the top of the NL East with 97 wins in 2006, thanks to an interesting combination of homegrown players and high-priced free agents. Their best player by far was Carlos Beltran, a switch-hitting outfielder who had come to them after fine seasons with Kansas City and Houston, and who peaked in that year with 6.9 WAA, second only to Pujols in the National League. This was by far Beltran's greatest season and the third and last superstar season of his long career. In the infield, homegrown shortstop Jose Reyes earned 1.2 WAA (despite -10 runs in the field), and third baseman David Wright—also 23—earned 2.6, down from 5 WAA in 2005. Second baseman Jose Valentin, a free agent, had a fantastic year in the field and added 3.1 WAA, but Carlos Delgado, another high-priced free agent at first base, added only 1.3, and the bench was weak. Overall the line-up was +11 WAA and the pitching staff -1. Six wins' worth of Pythagorean luck got the Mets up to 97 wins, and nearly to the World Series, but they lost to the Cardinals in the last game of the NLCS with the tying and winning runs on base in the ninth inning. During the next two years, Wright earned 5.8 and 3.9 WAA, but the rest of the team slumped, failed to win 90 games overall, and twice missed wild card berths on the last day of the season. Wright, now in the decline phase of his career, still has just three superstar seasons. Although Reyes hit for a good average and stole a great many bases, he was never a good fielder and never close to a superstar.

After several more mediocre years, the Mets returned to the postseason in 2015 with 90 wins, a very poor lineup (-3 WAA) and a brilliant pitching staff (+12 WAA.) Their line-up was actually somewhat stronger than that by the end of the season and might have been average had Yoenis Cespedes, who earned 5 WAA in a season split between the two leagues, played more than 57 games with them. The stars of the pitching staff were starters Jacob deGrom and Matt Harvey, with 2.7 and 2.4 WAA. Forty-two-year-old Bartolo Colon, who tied for the team lead in wins, was a below-average hurler on the year. Injuries plagued the Mets in 2016 and their line-up slumped all the way to -6 WAA, but they managed to win a wild card berth with just 87 victories thanks to their +13 WAA pitching staff. Noah Syndergaard just missed superstar status with 3.9 WAA in 183⅔ innings, Jacob deGrom and 43-year-old Bartolo Colon added 2.7 and 2.1, Steve Matz had 1.8, and Jeurys Familia, Addison Reed, Seth Lugo and Robert Gsellman combined for 5.8 WAA in 264 innings. The Mets lost the wild card game.

The Atlanta Braves returned to postseason with 91 wins and a wild card berth in 2010, and did it again in 2012 with one of the most bizarre teams in history. Their pitching staff was essentially average, and of the +10 WAA earned by their line-up, +8 WAA came from their fielding. Michael Bourn in center and 22-year-old Jason Heyward in right saved a combined +46 runs (+28 by Heyward); second baseman Dan Uggla added +23; and a trio of shortstops saved +22 more. The team lost the single wild card game to the Cardinals, however, and in 2013 Bourn departed, Heyward missed one-third of the season, and the fielding reverted to average. A very balanced pitching staff earned +9 WAA, allowing them to win their division. This time they lost the NLDS.

The new kids on the playoff block were the Washington Nationals, who won the NL East in 2012 and 2014 with 98 and 96 wins, respectively, thanks in large part to the most promising young player in the National League, outfielder Bryce Harper. So far Harper's career bears a striking resemblance to that of 1950s bonus baby Al Kaline, who deservedly wound up in the Hall of Fame. Signed at age 17, Harper spent just one full season in the minors and earned 3.8 WAA as a 19-year-old rookie in 138 games in 2012. The Nationals' line-up earned +12 WAA—a full +7 WAA in the field—thanks to Harper (who had a great year in center field), first baseman Adam LaRoche (a superstar at 4.4 WAA), and third baseman Ryan Zimmerman (3.1 WAA.) The pitchers added +3 WAA. The line-up could not repeat its great performance in the field in 2013 and the team slipped nearly to .500. Harper missed a good deal of 2014 with injuries and performed at an average level, but the team finished with a league-leading 96 wins thanks to a great pitching staff, worth +13 WAA. Among the starters, Jordan Zimmermann earned 3.4 WAA, Tanner Roark had 3.5, Doug Fister had 3.2, and Stephen Strasburg, who had begun his career sensationally before undergoing Tommy John surgery, added 1.5 WAA, his usual level. Once again the Nationals were eliminated in the NLDS. 2015 was a strange year for the Nationals. Harper hit .330 with 42 homers and 124 walks and earned 7.9 WAA, the most by any hitter in either league since Pujols in 2009. Meanwhile, Max Scherzer, signed as a free agent from Detroit, added 5.3 WAA of his own, and the pitching staff finished with +12. Unfortunately, most of the line-up was mediocre, and outfielder Jayson Werth and infielder Anthony Rendon surrendered a combined -5.3 WAA between them in a little more than a full season's worth of play. Thanks to dreadful fielding, the lineup as a whole was -9 WAA despite Harper's 7.9. The other pitchers who had done so well in 2014 slumped to the neighborhood of average, and the team won just 83 games, due in part to -6 games of bad Pythagorean luck.

Although Harper fell all the way to average in 2016, the Nationals improved all the way to 95 wins and won their division. Scherzer just missed another superstar season with 3.7 WAA, but Tanner Roark and Steven Strasburg joined him with 3.2 and 1.9, and the staff earned +10 WAA. The line-up improved dramatically to +7 WAA thanks mainly to second baseman Daniel Murphy (3.3 WAA) and sensational rookie Trea Turner, who divided his time between center field, shortstop, and second base while earning a fantastic 2.9 WAA in just 73 games at age 23, a McCovey-like performance, and earning the status of a key player to watch in 2017. The Nationals lost the NLDS to the Dodgers. Their lineup improved to +8 WAA in 2017 while the pitching staff fell to +6, and the team won 97 games. Murphy, third baseman Rendon, and Harper (who missed about one third of the season) remained stars, with 3.4, 3.2 and 2.6 WAA, but Turner fell to average in just 98 games. Among the pitchers, Scherzer (4.4 WAA), Stephen Strasberg (3.9) and Gio Gonzales (3.9) accounted for 12.2 WAA among them, but the rest of the staff was about -6 WAA. But their pitchers performed relatively poorly in the NLDS, and they lost to the Cubs in five games.

The NL West has been the most mediocre division of the Xer-Millennial era, and the division as a whole has finished over .500 only four times in the last 13 years. Only two teams from this division ever won as many as 95 games during this period. All its teams have reached post-season at least twice, but we will confine our attention to teams that had sustained success or somehow found their way to the World Series.

The NL West teams reaching the postseason include the San Diego Padres in 2006 (with 88 wins), the Arizona Diamondbacks in 2007 (with 90 wins, but a negative overall run differential) and in 2011 (with a very fortunate 94 wins), and the Colorado Rockies, who went all the way to the World Series in 2007 after winning just 90 games. None of these teams had enough distinction or impact to warrant detailed analysis. Remarkably, the San Francisco Giants, who won three World Series in 2008, 2010, and 2012, were only marginally better. The 2008 team won 92 games thanks largely to its fielding, which earned the team +6 WAA. Its best players were two veterans in their early thirties, first baseman Aubrey Huff, who posted a remarkable 5.8 WAA, and outfielder Andre Torres, with 3.7. Buster Posey added 2.2 more behind the plate. They beat a mediocre Texas Rangers team in five games in the World Series. The team's fielding improved still more in 2011, earning +9 WAA, but its hitting collapsed completely and they finished last in the league in runs scored and missed the playoffs. The 2012 team featured a strong lineup, including superstars Posey (4.6 WAA, his only superstar season to date) and former Yankee outfielder Melky Cabrera, who earned

6. The Gen X and Millennial Era, 2005–2017   217

4 WAA in 113 games. The pitching staff was -3 WAA, but the team luckily managed 94 wins and swept the Tigers in the World Series. After winning only 76 games in 2013—due largely to poor fielding—they won 88 in 2014 with a +8 WAA lineup and an average pitching staff. Right fielder Hunter Pence, third baseman Pablo Sandoval, catcher Posey and outfielder Gregor Blanco combined for 9.1 WAA, and the lineup had no significant weak spots. On the mound, however, Madison Bumgarner, the hero of the World Series, was the only positive factor among the starting pitchers with 2.4 WAA, and the staff as a whole was average. The Giants beat the Royals in seven games in one of the weakest matchups in the history of the World Series. In 2016 they won a wild card berth again with just 87 victories. Their lineup earned +7 WAA thanks mainly to good fielding, led by first baseman Brandon Belt (2.1 WAA) and left fielder Angel Pagan (2.1), while Posey and Pence fell below 2. Johnny Cueto (3 WAA) and Madison Bumgarner (2.5) accounted for nearly double the +3 WAA earned by the pitching staff as a whole. This time their playoff luck ran out, and they lost to the Cubs in the division series. Before 1994, such a team would have been extraordinarily lucky ever to reach the postseason; now, in the era of two wild cards, the Giants had won three World Series in five years.

The Los Angeles Dodgers eked out division titles with 88 and 84 wins in 2006 and 2008, reaching the NLCS once, but put one of the strongest teams of the era in the field in 2009, good enough to win 99 games but held to 95 by bad luck. The line-up featured three star performances by center fielder Matt Kemp (3.5 WAA), third baseman Casey Blake (2.8) and second baseman Orlando Hudson (2.1), and positive contributions from virtually the entire rest of the line-up. On the mound, 24-year-old Clayton Kershaw earned 2.9 WAA in just 171 innings in the second full season of his career, and Randy Wolf (2 WAA) and a strong bullpen allowed the staff to add +6 WAA to the line-up's +12. They lost the NLCS to the Phillies. Kershaw is already an all-time great: he followed up the 2009 season with two more star seasons and five superstar seasons through 2017. Sadly for him, the rest of the team was not good enough to return to the playoffs until 2013, when the line-up earned just +4 WAA and the rest of the pitching staff was below average. Dodgers hurlers in 2014 were exactly average overall despite Kershaw's 5.6 WAA and Zach Greinke's 2.8. Luck helped them win their division in both seasons. They did it again in 2015 with a two-man team. The 31-year-old Greinke, who had begun his career at age 20 with Kansas City in 2004 and earned 6.3 WAA for the Royals five years later, eclipsed Kershaw with a fantastic season of 6.1 WAA and a record of 19–3. Between them, Kershaw and Greinke had 10.7 WAA, but the pitching staff as a whole had only +6. Their line-up was perfectly average, partly because of very poor run luck. It featured three stars—Adrian Gonzalez, Andre Ethier and Justin Turner—but also included 36-year-old Jimmy Rollins, who was bad enough (-3.9 WAA) to cancel out almost two of them. The Dodgers lost the NLDS to the Mets.

Zach Greinke signed with Arizona as a free agent for the 2016 season and promptly slumped almost all the way to average. Kershaw, although limited to 149 innings by injuries, pitched brilliantly and posted his fifth superstar season in six years with 4.2 WAA at age 28. He would clearly deserve to be elected to the Hall of Fame if his career tended tomorrow. This year, Dodgers pitchers earned +6 WAA while the line-up earned +5, and the team won a very weak division with 91 victories. Twenty-two-year-old rookie shortstop Corey Seager hit very well but earned only 2.2 WAA because of -11 runs in the field. Veterans Gonzalez and Utley were now average. The Dodgers lost the NLDS to the Cubs.

The 2017 Dodgers won a superior 104 games with a +6 WAA lineup and a very strong +13 pitching staff that tied their division rivals, the Arizona Diamondbacks, for the best in the league. Their lineup featured four stars: left fielder Chris Taylor (3.9 WAA), third baseman Justin Turner (3), 21-year old first baseman Cody Bellinger (2.4), and shortstop Seager (2), but they missed an average of 25 games a season and the Dodger bench was weak. Starters Kershaw (3.5 WAA), Alex Wood (2.4) and Rich Hill (1.6) and closer Kenley Jansen (2) led the pitchers.[47]

Although they lacked a single superstar, their seven stars suggest that they will be a strong team for years to come. The Dodgers swept their division rivals and wild card winners the Arizona Diamondbacks in the division series and defeated the defending World Series champion Cubs in the NLCS in five games. The 2017 World Series pitted them against the Houston Astros—the first time since 1970 that the fall classic involved two teams that had won more than 100 games. The series, featuring excellent starting pitching, great fielding, and a raft of home runs, lived up to its billing. The Astros defeated the Dodgers in seven games. How many more teams can reach the level of superior pennant winners, and how often the two best teams in baseball can meet in the World Series, remains to be seen.

The Millennial Generation: A Midterm Report

Twenty seventeen marked the 13th year that Millennials had posted at least one superstar season. The Boom Generation—which we shall use as a basis for comparison in place of Gen X so as to control for the PED factor—finished its 13th season at the top in 1979. At that time, the Boomers destined to become all-time greats had put up the following numbers of superstar seasons.

Reggie Jackson	8
Bobby Bonds	6
Rod Carew	5
Joe Morgan	5
Mike Schmidt	5
George Brett	3
Jim Rice	3
Bert Blyleven	4

Rickey Henderson, Wade Boggs, Eddie Murray, Paul Molitor, Tim Raines, Ryne Sandberg and Dave Stieb had not posted a single superstar season, and most of them had not yet played in the major leagues.

---

47. The 2017 Dodgers gave up a park-adjusted total of 611 runs, 139 fewer than the league average of 750. Apparently, however, they saved some of those 139 runs simply because they played a very high proportion of their games against low-scoring teams. This created an unusual discrepancy between their individual pitchers' totals of WAA and the team total amounting to about 3 games.

The tally for the Millennial Generation as 2017 drew to a close was as follows:

Miguel Cabrera	7
Joey Votto	7
Mike Trout	6
Paul Goldschmidt	5
Clayton Kershaw	5
Shin-Soo Choo	4
Josh Donaldson	4
Robinson Cano	4
Max Scherzer	4
Andrew McCutchen	3
David Wright	3

The top eight Boomers averaged 4.9 superstar seasons each after 1979; the top 11 Millennials averaged 4.7. The best Millennial pitchers are putting up superstar seasons at a faster rate than their Boomer counterparts, suggesting that seven innings every five days, instead of up to nine innings every four days, does allow a great pitcher to have a greater and longer impact upon his team's fortunes. Of the players on the list, Votto and Trout are already all-time greats. Kershaw and Scherzer may well have more great seasons in them. Clearly we must assume that there will be other Millennial all-timers who have not yet reached the majors. This new generation has already produced players comparable to the all-time greats from earlier generations, but it has produced fewer superstar seasons overall than any of them. We shall shortly examine the reasons why.

By the time this book appears, the 2018 season will be underway. Annual updates to the book will appear beginning in November 2018 at<http://baseballgreatness.com>, analyzing the year's successful teams and detailing new superstar performances. That site will also feature the tables of all-time hitters and pitchers from each generation, with suitable updates for Gen X, the Millennials, and the next generation that will reach the major leagues within ten years. The story will go on.

Epilogue
The Nature of Greatness

This book has explained how great players make great teams—a subject with implications for the writers and veterans who make new selections to the Hall of Fame. Election to Cooperstown always has and always will depend on many different aspects of a player's career, but the findings of this book, in my opinion, suggest that the voters might pay more attention to the number of dominant seasons candidates had. Not for nothing did Bill James pose the question, "If this guy were the best player on your team, would it be likely that you could win the pennant?" as one that should be asked about every Hall of Famer. And while there is no point in listing the Hall of Famers for whom the answer is generally "no," there is every reason to review those for whom the answer was "yes" for large portions of their career, but whom the voters, for whatever reason, have chosen to ignore.

We have defined an all-time great as a player with at least five seasons good enough to be the MVP on a pennant winner—which, empirically, means 4 WAA or more. Only 15–20 men from each generation, as we have seen, meet that standard. Yet a number of them have never been elected. Let us revisit some of these cases.

Wes Ferrell pitched in the big leagues from 1927 through 1941, mostly for the Indians (1927–1933) and the Red Sox (1934–1937. During the years in which he pitched at least 50 innings, his teams had an average winning percentage of .513, but he finished his career with a 193–128 record and a .601 winning percentage—a far better record relative to his team than many Hall of Famers. More importantly, among the GI Generation, he is the only pitcher other than Hal Newhouser to have as many as five seasons with 4 WAA or more. Any measurement of pitching skill that is independent of team performance and adjusts for the era the pitcher played in would confirm that he was one of the greatest pitchers of his generation. It is not his fault that such measurements had not been developed when he became eligible for the Hall, and he more than deserves election.

Insofar as a hitter can be compared to a pitcher, Charlie Keller's record is quite similar to that of Sandy Koufax—but in one respect it is slightly better. Koufax had four consecutive seasons of 4 WAA or more, but Keller had five, 1940–1943 and 1946 (missing 1944–1945 in military service). Although wartime conditions undoubtedly helped Keller achieve his best season in 1943 with 6.8 WAA, other seasons made clear that this was no fluke. His career was cut short by serious back problems after the war and his lifetime totals are not impressive—but the same is true of Koufax. In 1940–1946 he was about as valuable as Joe DiMaggio, and he deserves election.

Gil Hodges has been regarded as a sentimental favorite for the Hall of Fame because he played for the Boys of Summer and managed the Miracle Mets. DRA fielding statistics, however, have shown that he was a great first baseman, and the combination of his hitting and fielding made him the second-most valuable member of that team, behind Jackie Robinson but ahead of Duke Snider and Roy Campanella, who are in the Hall of Fame. Hodges definitely belongs as well.

Jim Wynn's life and career seem have to have been designed to obscure his greatness. He reached the majors in the midst of one of the worst eras for hitting in the history of the game and played most of his best years in the Houston Astrodome, the worst hitters' park in baseball. He also hit for a relatively low average but made up for it with walks. But he played center field well for most of his career, and he had superstar seasons in 1965, 1967–1970, 1972, and 1974, when he was the true MVP on an outstanding Los Angeles Dodgers team. Wynn is an exact contemporary of Dick Allen, who was nearly elected to the Hall by the Veterans Committee recently, but Allen had only six superstar seasons to Wynn's seven, and Wynn never caused any of the tremendous turmoil that Allen did. He is overqualified for Cooperstown and should be selected.

Luis Tiant finished his career with a won-lost record of 229–167, which is nearly identical to Catfish Hunter's and superior to Don Drysdale's. The Red Sox teams for which he pitched, it turns out, tended to be very weak in the field, making his contribution that much more significant. Like Sandy Koufax, Robin Roberts, Jim Bunning, and Juan Marichal, he had four seasons of 4 WAA or more. All of those pitchers are in the Hall of Fame; he is not. He should be.

Keith Hernandez possesses one of the oft-cited intangible qualifications for the Hall of Fame—having played on a world championship team from New York, the 1986 Mets. More importantly, he, like Jim Wynn, had seven seasons of 4 WAA or more, because he combined great hitting and great fielding. He was a key figure on the World Championship Cardinals as well. Yet he has not been selected.

Dave Stieb got no serious consideration from the BBWAA for the Hall and will always be a hard sell for the Veterans Committee. For reasons that are certainly not clear from his record, he never managed to win 20 games in a season and finished his career with a record of 176–137. Yet Stieb had six seasons of 4 WAA or more—including an adjusted figure for strike-shortened 1981—a figure that was exceeded only by Bob Gibson *among all pitchers from the GI, Silent and Boom generations*. He was clearly a very dominant pitcher but of all these candidates he remains the least likely to succeed.

Eligible players from Generation X, of course, include some of the most distinguished records in baseball, including Barry Bonds, who ties Babe Ruth with 17 superstar seasons for the all-time lead, and Roger Clemens, who leads all pitchers in history with 12. These and many other candidates and future candidates are shadowed by the issue of steroids. I have done what I could to shed light on this question in the text of the book, and I do not envy the task of the writers and veterans who will have to pass on these candidates.

In general, the BBWAA and the Veterans Committee would in my opinion do well to pay more attention to players' greatest seasons and the number of times that they have exceeded 4 WAA, and less to their lifetime totals of hits and home runs. We have just lived through a very high-offense era, the treatment of injuries has improved, the schedule is longer, and it has been much easier to reach milestones like 500 home runs and 3,000 hits. Such totals in the Boomer-Xer era simply did not represent the same level of dominance as they did in earlier eras. Willie Mays hit 660 home runs and Alex Rodriguez hit 696, but Mays had 16 superstar seasons and Rodriguez had seven.

Professional baseball took its present shape in 1901 in the midst of an age of greatness. Humankind was making extraordinary progress in every walk of life in 1901, transforming the economies of the north Atlantic world, creating a vast new system of higher education, inventing new media of communication, developing modern democracy, and pushing back artistic frontiers. It was also an era of fierce competition, not least on the international stage, where great-power imperialism helped unleash the first of two world wars in 1914. Because of the statistics that had already been part of professional baseball for a couple of decades, the sport provided a riveting arena in which men could demonstrate their greatness. Christy Mathewson, Honus Wagner, Ty Cobb, Tris Speaker, Walter Johnson, Babe Ruth, and many more deservedly became national heroes. As we have seen, they demonstrated extraordinary skill in an endeavor to which thousands of young men were devoting their lives. They rightly captured the imagination of their countrymen, and of much of Latin America and Japan as well. The annual drama of major league baseball required sustained effort in which eight teams in each league tried to prevail over a 154-game season. Because of the high degree of randomness within any individual game, players, teams, and fans had to contend with triumph and disaster on a daily basis. Not for nothing did many serious fans learn the lists of pennant and World Series winners by heart.

In response to a growing and spreading population, change came to baseball in 1961–1962, and more drastically in 1969, when the leagues expanded for the second time and split themselves into two divisions. Major league franchises no longer had to work quite so hard and assemble quite so many fine players to reach post-season play and the ultimate reward that it offered. The pace of these changes has accelerated rapidly in the last 25 years, leaving us with 30 teams, one-third of whom reach post-season play every year, each needing a great deal of good fortune to survive three or even four rounds of playoffs and win the World Championship. Within that group of playoff teams, the distribution of World Series winners is almost random, only occasionally reflecting their actual strength. Let us hope that the 2016 and 2017 World Series are soon followed by others in which victory goes to a deserving team.

The current governing structure of Major League Baseball—entirely dominated by the interests of the 30 owners—has militated against greatness. The addition of more and more post-season teams has been designed to keep the largest number of teams in contention for as long as possible, in order to boost interest and attendance. Surprisingly enough, this has not been successful. Major league attendance averaged 2.5 million per team in 1993, the last year in which only four teams made the post-season, but just 2.4 million in 2015, when ten of them did. The introduction of three rounds of playoffs and two wild cards, however, has clearly reduced the incentive to develop and maintain a superior pennant winner that could consistently win at least 103 games a year. While there is, obviously, a significant advantage to winning a division rather than reaching post-season as one of two wild card teams, since a division winner does not have to risk its chances for further progress on a single game, it is clear that winning 103 games instead of 93 does not significantly increase a team's chances of winning the World Series. And it has been a very long time since any team sustained that level of performance for a period of years. The luxury tax on high payrolls, which discourages the richest clubs from spending whatever they could to assemble the best possible teams, and the changes in contract rules that have allowed small market teams to hold on to superstars in their prime, have also worked to prevent the concentration of talent and the development of great teams.

And the expansion of post-season play has had another most unfortunate effect. Before 1969, the World Series was without question the biggest sporting event of the year and the focus of the nation's attention. Now, the seemingly endless round of post-season games running late into the night—far more than any fan could watch—has diluted interest, just as it has become impossible to build a dynasty and capture the imagination of the American people over a period of years. The NFL in general and the Super Bowl in particular eclipsed baseball in the nation's imagination long ago. The nation's attitude towards the game's history is also much affected. Until 1995, I and thousands of other fans would have had no trouble remembering every World Series or playoff team since 1901. Now to recall who has been in the playoffs every year since 1995 would be quite an extraordinary feat of memory. While fans a half-century ago experienced the extraordinary catharsis of season-long pennant races—the greatest of which I had the great privilege of chronicling for the ages many years ago[48]—we live today in an age of instant gratification, symbolized by highlight shows and the growing popularity of daily fantasy sports. They give consumers a different experience and teach different lessons about life. In my opinion those lessons are not, in the long run, more useful.

The proliferation of teams and the expansion of playoffs has also reduced the visibility of great individual players. Mike Trout, as we have seen, has begun his career with six seasons comparable to those of Ty Cobb, Ted Williams, Willie Mays or Henry Aaron, and superior to Mickey Mantle. Yet even though he plays in one of the nation's largest media markets, he does not remotely enjoy the national stature that those men did. But this leads us to the other source of mediocrity which this book has uncovered: the shortage of high-level talent. Among the Millennial Generation, Trout and Miguel Cabrera, Joey Votto and Robinson Cano, and Clayton Kershaw and Max Scherzer all have an excellent chance of posting lifetime records that are indeed the equal of any of the greats of the past. The combination of talent and dedication that produces extraordinary greatness still exists—but there are suddenly far fewer examples of it, relative to the size of major league baseball. As we have seen, from 1901 through 2004, the number of superstar seasons per team per year was remarkably consistent from era to era, holding steady in the 0.72 range—nearly three superstar seasons for every four teams. But after 2016, in which the AL had only eight superstars and the NL four, the average for 2005–2016 was down to 0.54 per team per year—just a little more than

---

48. David Kaiser, *Epic Season: The 1948 American League Pennant Race* (Amherst: University of Massachusetts Press, 1998).

one for every two teams. This is also a major cause of the general mediocrity that has overtaken the standings of major league baseball. Why has it happened?

The reason, I believe, is quite simple. Unlike the NFL and the NBA, which draw upon huge networks of high school and college programs, baseball no longer has a nationwide structure that allows a great mass of young players to develop their skills at an early age. And Major League Baseball, for reasons of its own, is doing very little about this.

Eighty years ago, when the place of baseball and organized baseball in American life had reached its peak, the path to the majors was open to every young American regardless of his economic status—with the exception, of course, of the 10 percent of young Americans who were barred by segregation. High school kids played on American Legion teams, rural kids played on town teams, urban youth played on factory teams. From there, if they could impress a scout at a tryout, they could enter the huge minor league structure, which would winnow out the few among them good enough to reach the majors and the even smaller number who could become great. Today nothing comparable exists. An excellent recent newspaper article on the development of young American players states the problem very clearly and supplies some key data. While baseball, like football and basketball today, was formerly a route out of poverty, that is no longer the case for those born in the U.S. "Without the finances to train and participate in showcases," individual instruction and travel baseball, writes a man in a position to know, "the low income player has no avenue to the Major League, College, Travel, or High School teams." *Only overseas*, mainly in the Dominican Republic, have the major league clubs established academies which offer poor youth a chance. That is why the Dominican Republic, with a population of 10.5 million people—3 percent of the population of the United States—supplies about 11 percent of the players on major league rosters. Even more astonishing, largely because of the academies in the Dominican Republic and Venezuela maintained by MLB clubs, 42 percent of the players in the minor leagues are Hispanic.[49] To a significant extent, the production of major league baseball players, like the production of clothing and electronics and the recruitment of customer service personnel, has been outsourced outside the United States, to areas where young, ambitious, and poor youth will work for less. But because the baseball-mad regions of the rest of the world remain quite small, this new talent base has not been large enough to sustain the necessary number of great players. Baseball will never regain the place it occupied among American sports before 1950, but MLB could do more do develop U.S. talent. Some of the $100 million contracts spent on free agent pitchers would be much better spent, for all concerned, on programs that would give young Americans a chance.

Let us return to our main theme. Greatness in any human activity—scientific, artistic, intellectual or athletic—is extraordinarily rare. The beauty of baseball, a highly complex and demanding sport to which hundreds of thousands of young men have given large parts of their lives, is that the statistical tools we have developed over the decades allow us to measure greatness so precisely. About 19,000 men have played major league baseball since

---

49. Tim Goodrum, "The Disappearance of African-Americans in Major League Baseball, *Fayette News*, October 6, 2016, http://fayette-news.com/the-disappearance-of-african-americans-in-major-league-baseball/. The 42 percent figure includes Hispanics of U.S. origin.

1901. Of them, 97—one-half of 1 percent—have had at least five superstar seasons. Unlike so many of the men and women whose extraordinary ability and dedication makes them outliers in their fields, the great baseball players have statistical proof of their stature, and have generally, although not always, received appropriate rewards. Our age is even more unfriendly to greatness in other realms of endeavor than in sports. In the arts, in intellectual pursuits, in journalism, and most certainly in politics, it would be very difficult to argue that we enjoy as much great talent as we have in certain periods in the past. And in many other fields, uniquely talented individuals often find themselves pushed to the sidelines and resented, rather than celebrated, for their talents. Baseball is not enjoying its greatest era, but it remains an endless source of fascination and inspiration, both for the challenge of measuring its intricate mix of skills, and the examples of extraordinary achievement that it continues to provide.

Appendix

For those particularly interested in how statistical sausages are made, this appendix will discuss some of the more difficult issues that arose in putting this book together.

WAA Computations for Short Seasons

In an ideal world, all seasons of 4 WAA or more would be created equal; in reality this is not quite true. For the period 1901–1903 the two leagues played fewer than 140 games a season, adopting 154 only in 1904. In 1917–1918, war and its aftermath cut the schedules to about 124 and 138 games, respectively. In 1972, the first serious work stoppage in the era of the Players' Association cut the schedules to about 155 games instead of 162. Most seriously of all, lengthy strikes in 1981 and 1994 cut those seasons to about 109 games in 1981 and 112 games in 1994, and the shortened 1995 season included about 144 games for each team.

At first glance, it might seem reasonable to project the total WAA players earned during these short seasons out to a full 154 or 162 games, but a close look at the data immediately makes clear that that would lead to severe distortions of performance. The shorter the sample of games that will make up a season, the more extreme deviations from average will be. Every fan has learned that it is very unlikely that the league-leading figures for home runs, batting average and ERA halfway through the season will almost never be doubled when the season comes to an end. Thus, in 1917, when about ⅕ of the season was not played, Ty Cobb and Pete Alexander earned 6–7 WAA as it was, and it is very unlikely that even they would have sustained that pace through another 30 games or so. A careful check of the performances of all-time greats in 1917 revealed, surprisingly, that no one was actually deprived of a superstar season by missing those games—they were all either over 4 WAA already, or too far away from it to reach it. Thus I made no adjustment for 1917–1918. I also saw no reason to adjust for 1972, since that season was essentially identical in length to the 154-game seasons that players had played for decades.

1981, 1994 and 1995 presented the biggest problems. Simply projecting 110 games or so out to 162 would have created a most unusual and obviously unrealistic number of superstar performances. It was clearly very unlikely that some of the players who would have exceeded 4 WAA by that method would in fact have sustained their level of performance over 162 games—since they had never done so in the past. And that became my rule of thumb for 1981, 1994, and 1995. If a projected season was both comfortably in excess of 4

WAA, and in line with the player's normal statistics in surrounding years, it was counted as a superstar season. If it would have been his only such season, it was not. In all three cases, if the player had already earned more than 4 WAA in the short season, I left the figure as it was.

The Computation of Pitcher WAA

The accurate calculation of pitcher WAA was the most difficult problem involved in this book and went through several iterations. While this discussion will be too technical for many readers, I want to make clear how it was done.

My initial decision on calculating numbers of runs saved by a team's pitchers grew naturally out of my reliance on Michael Humphreys's DRA calculations of fielding performance. If a team's fielders, according to his methods, had saved 50 runs, and if the team overall had given up 100 runs less than the league average (both figures having been park-adjusted), I concluded that the team's pitchers had saved 50 runs. This is not a perfect calculation, in part because it takes no account of defensive run luck. Humphrey's calculations of the number of runs fielders saved is based on the number of hits they prevented. He used Pete Palmer's linear weights to convert hits to runs. This is a very accurate method, but it assumes a random distribution of hits within games. Depending on exactly *when* fielders saved those runs—for instance, whether a great catch took place with outs and the bases empty (probably saving no runs), or two outs and the bases full (saving three runs), the calculation that turned Willie Mays's extra outs into runs might over- or underestimate how many runs he actually saved. That in turn would affect the accuracy of my overall calculation of how many runs had been saved by the team's pitchers. Since, however, there is no database that gives the amount of defensive run luck for each team in every season, I could not build it into my calculations.[50]

My next step was to reconcile my overall calculation of runs saved by a teams' pitchers with the calculations of runs saved by individual pitchers in baseball-reference.com. Baseball-reference.com calculates the runs above or below average for every pitcher for every season using its own formula. That formula begins with the runs (not earned runs) that the pitcher actually allowed, and comparing it to an estimate of what an average pitcher, pitching against the same teams in the same ball parks and with the same defense behind him, would have allowed. The question I faced was whether the sum of the runs saved/runs allowed for the pitchers on a particular team would add up pretty closely to the figure I had independently arrived at for pitchers' runs saved for that team. Sometimes it did; other times, there was a significant discrepancy.

The biggest reason for the discrepancy was that while baseball-reference.com takes account of the team's fielding, it uses different methods to compute fielding performance. In many cases those methods reached very different results for fielding performance than DRA. I was convinced that DRA was much more accurate than the Total Zone method that

---

50. Michael Humphreys is at work on such a database, but it will be very hard, even if his work is completed, to apportion run luck between pitching and fielding.

baseball-reference uses for most of the history of baseball and confident that it was not significantly less accurate than the Baseball Info Solutions Defensive Runs saved that it uses for more recent seasons. Thus, I changed the baseball-reference figures for pitchers' runs saved to reflect the difference between DRA results for a team's defense and the results it was using. In other words, if baseball-reference rated a defense to have saved 50 runs while DRA showed that defense to be perfectly average, I assumed that the team's pitchers, as a group, had saved 50 runs more than the baseball-reference estimate. I then parceled out those 50 runs among the team's individual pitchers, based upon their percentage of the team's total innings pitched.

It then developed, however, that the difference in fielding statistics did not in some cases account for all the difference between baseball-reference's estimates of a pitching staff's contribution and mine. In some cases, a substantial difference of several dozen runs remained. Sometimes that delta produced very extreme results for individual pitchers. There were several possible reasons for this, including the possible influence of run luck. I decided to solve the remaining problem by cutting the remaining delta in half. That method is not perfect, but it produced a very reasonable and relatively consistent set of results across the decades. Because of that last adjustment, the results for WAA for individual pitchers for certain teams, when added up, might differ by 1–2 WAA from my estimate of the pitching staff as a whole. I did not want to penalize any pitchers for imperfections in my method, however, and these were, in my opinion, the most accurate results I could come up with.

Bibliography

Online Resources

Baseball-Reference.com
Seamheads.com

Books and Articles

Durocher, Leo, with Ed Linn. *Nice Guys Finish Last*. New York: Simon & Schuster, 1975.
Tim Goodrum. "The Disappearance of African-Americans in Major League Baseball." *Fayette (GA) Daily News*. Accessed October 6, 2016. http://fayette-news.com/the-disappearance-of-african-americans-in-major-league-baseball/.
Humphreys, Michael. *Wizardry: Baseball's All-Time Greatest Fielders Revealed*. New York: Oxford University Press, 2011.
James, Bill. *The Bill James Baseball Abstract 1984*. New York: Ballantine, 1984.
_____. *The Bill James Guide to Baseball Managers from 1870 to Today*. New York: Scribner, 1997.
_____. *The Politics of Glory: How Baseball's Hall of Fame Really Works*. New York: Macmillan, 1994.
Kaiser, David. *Epic Season: The 1948 American League Pennant Race*. Amherst: University of Massachusetts Press, 1998.
_____. *No End Save Victory: How FDR Led the Nation into War*. New York: Basic Books, 2014.
Lamb, William F. *Black Sox in the Courtroom: The Grand Jury, Criminal Trial and Civil Litigation*. Jefferson, NC: McFarland, 2013.

Index

Aaron, Henry 4, 13, 52, 72, 96, 102, 106, 114, 121, 131, 144, 152, 164, 202, 206
Aase, Don 125
Abreu, Bobby 194–95, 202
Acker, Tom 95
Adair, Jerry 114
Adams, Babe 14
Adams, Franklin P. 24
Adcock, Joe 97
Agee, Tommie 132
Alderson, Sandy 186
Alexander, Doyle 124, 147
Alexander, Grover Cleveland 12, 35, 37, 39, 60
Alexander, Pete 55, 160
Alfonzo, Edgardo 169
Allen, Bernie 113
Allen, Dick (Richie) 60, 106, 108, 134, 139–41, 172, 221
Allen, Johnny 49
Allison, Bob 113–14
Alomar, Roberto 153, 174
Alomar, Sandy 174
Alou, Felipe 100–103
Alou, Jesus 105
Alou, Moises 167–68, 171
Altuve, Jose 206
Alvarez, Pedro 213
American League, leading teams, analysis: (1901–25) 27–38; (1926–39) 43–54; (1940–42) 55–59; (1946–56) 72–85; (1957–66) 108, 111–15; (1967–83) 116–30; (1984–93) 146–54; (1994–2004) 173–86; (2005–2017) 190–206
Ames, Red 27
Anderson, Greg 164
Anderson, Larry 165
Andujar, Joaquin 155
Antonelli, Johnny 94

Aparicio, Luis 29, 104, 111, 114, 118, 139, 146
Appling, Luke 75, 80, 110, 146
Armas, Tony 130, 148
Armbrister, Ed 134
Arnovich, Morrie 65
Arrieta 212; Jake, 211
Arroyo, Luis 112
Ashburn, Richie 13, 70–71, 91–92, 112, 139
Autry, Gene 128
Avery, Steve 160
Avila, Bobby 81, 97
Aybar, Eric 202–3

Backman, Wally 156
Baerga, Carlos 173–74
Baez, Javier 211
Bagby, Jim 16, 34
Bagwell, Jeff 14, 150, 165–66, 196, 207
Bailey, Ed 94–95, 102
Baker, Dusty 138
Baker, Frank "Home Run" 30–31, 49, 55
Bamberger, George 130
Bancroft, Dave 39, 41, 182
Bando, Sal 122, 129
Banks, Ernie 100, 102, 112, 133
Bannister, Alan 128
Barber, Red 66
Barfield, Jesse 147–48, 172, 207
Barnes, Clint 213
Barrett, Marty 148
Barrios, Francisco 128
Barrow, Ed 35, 43, 51, 65
Barry, Jack 30–31
Bartell, Dick 64
Battey, Earl 111, 113
Bauer, Hank 76, 78, 83, 118
Bautista, Jose 202, 205

Bay, Jason 191
Beane, Billy 1, 184, 197, 204–5
Bearden, Gene 76
Beaumont, Ginger 26
Beazley, Johnny 67
Beckett, Josh 191–92
Belanger, Mark 20, 119
Bell, Buddy 172, 207
Bell, David 176
Bell, Derek 167, 169
Bell, George 147–48
Bell, Gus 94, 172
Bell, Jay 168
Bell, Les 60, 94–95
Belle, Albert 173–74, 207
Bellhorn, Mark 184
Belliard, Rafael 160
Bellinger, Cody 218
Belt, Brandon 217
Beltran, Carlos 195, 214
Beltre, Adrian 191, 203, 208
Bench, Johnny 16, 46, 133–34, 136, 143, 156, 169, 172, 207
Bender, Chief 31
Benintendi, Andrew 193
Benitez, Armando 169
Benton, Larry 62
Bergman, Dave 146
Bergman, Lance 207
Berkman, Lance 209, 211
Berra, Yogi 46–47, 53, 77–78, 82–85, 108, 110, 124, 210
Berryhill, Damon 160
Betts, Mookie 193
Bickford, Vern 87
Biggio, Craig 166–67, 173
Billingham, Jack 134
Bishop, Max 48
Black, Joe 90
Blades, Roy 60
Blair, Paul 13, 20, 116, 118–19, 189
Blake, Casey 217

Blanco, Gregor 217
Blasingame, Don 99
Blass, Steve 136
Blefary, Curt 118
Blue, Vida 121, 129
Blyleven, Bert 13, 133, 137, 146, 148, 172, 218
Boddicker, Mike 130
Boesch, Brennan 200
Bogaerts, Xander 193
Boggs, Wade 13, 148–49, 171–72, 178–79, 192, 218
Boley, Joe 47
Bolin, Bob 105
Bonds, Barry 1, 4, 9, 14, 17, 95, 150, 158, 164, 168, 196, 206, 209, 212, 221
Bonds, Bobby 106, 124, 170–72, 218
Bonham, Tiny 58
Bonilla, Bobby 159, 162, 167, 170
Boom Generation 13, 118, 171–73
Boone, Bob 150
Boone, Bret 16, 177
Borders, Pat 174
Boswell, Dave 121
Bottomley, Jim 60–61
Boudreau, Lou 2, 57, 67–69, 74–75, 79, 110, 146
Bourn, Michael 215
Bouton, Jim 113
Bowa, Larry 141
Bower, Trevor 201
Boyer, Clete 111, 113
Boyer, Ken 71, 88, 96, 100, 114, 139–40, 172
Bradley, Jackie 193
Branca, Ralph 86, 90
Brandt, Jackie 100, 114
Braun, Ryan 211
Brazle, Al 87
Breadon, Sam 60
Bream, Sid 159
Brecheen, Harry 86–87
Bregman, Alex 206
Bresnahan, Roger 26
Brett, George 46, 127, 150, 218
Bridges, Tommy 51, 56
Brinkman, Eddie 124
Brock, Lou 131
Broglio, Ernie 104
Brookens, Tom 146
Brosius, Scott 179
Brown, Kevin 167, 207
Brown, Mordecai "Three Finger" 25, 27

Brown, Ollie 105
Bruce, Jay 212
Bruton, Billy 96–97
Bryant, Kris 211–12
Buchholz, Clay 192
Bucker, Bill 148
Buckner, Bill 138
Buehrle, Mark 199
Buford, Don 20, 119
Buhl, Bob 98, 107
Buhner, Jay 175
Bumgarner, Madison 217
Bunning, Jim 91, 106–7, 112, 126, 221
Burdette, Lew 98
Burgess, Smokey 95
Burkett, Jesse 23
Burkett, John 162
Burks, Ellis 148, 165
Burleson, Rick 125–26
Burnett, A.J. 194
Burns, George 40
Bush, Bullet Joe 31
Bush, Joe 31, 36
Butler, Brett 157
Byrne, Tommy 76–77, 85

Cabrera, Melky 194–95, 216
Cabrera, Miguel 6, 12, 14, 199, 219, 223
Cadore, Leon 40
Cain, Lorenzo 200
Cairo, Miguel 184
Calhoun, Kole 203
Callaspo, Alberto 204
Callison, Johnny 106, 111, 140
Cameron, Mike 16, 176–77
Camilli, Dolph 66–67
Campanella, Roy 46–47, 72, 84–85, 88–89, 110, 136, 210, 221
Campaneris, Bert 122
Campbell, Bill 125
Candelaria, John 137
Candiotti, Tom 140
Cano, Robinson 174, 193, 195, 219, 223
Canseco, Jose 151
Carbo, Bernie 125, 134
Cardenas, Leo 120
Carew, Rod 13, 120, 128–29, 146, 154, 172, 176, 218
Carey, Max 59
Carlton, Steve 137–38, 141–44, 149, 173
Carpenter, Chris 209
Carpenter, Max 210
Carrasco, Carlos 201

Carter, Gary 143, 156, 172
Carter, Joe 153
Casey, Hugh 66–67
Cash, Norm 111–12, 117, 166
Catchers, value of 46–47
Cavarretta, Phil 69
Cedeno, Cesar 134, 137
Cedeno, Roger 169
Cepeda, Orlando 16, 100, 105, 115, 130, 135
Cespedes, Yoenis 204, 215
Cey, Ron 138
Chance, Dean 131
Chance, Frank 24–25
Chandler, Spud 72
Chapman, Arnoldis 212
Chapman, Ben 48, 51
Chapman, Ray 16, 34
Chapman, Sam 58
Chavez, Eric 185, 195
Chesbro, Jack 26
Chiozza, Lou 64
Choo, Shin-Soo 203, 212, 219
Cicotte, Eddie 34
Cirillo, Jeff 177
Clark, Jack 155
Clark, Tony 184
Clark, Will 164, 170
Clarke, Fred 26
Clayton, Royce 164
Clemens, Roger 4, 14, 37, 149, 163, 180, 194, 207, 209, 211, 221
Clemente, Roberto 13, 17, 25, 99, 102, 106, 131, 136, 139, 152, 176, 212
Cleveland, Reggie 125
Clevinger, Mike 201
Clift, Harland 110
Cobb, Ty 4, 12, 28, 32, 36, 39, 54, 81, 104, 116, 142, 151, 189, 222–23
Cochrane, Mickey 46, 51, 85, 110
Cohen, Andy 62
Colavito, Rocky 112
Cole, Gerrit 213
Cole, Leonard "King" 25
Coleman, Vince 155
Collins, Eddie 12, 28, 30–31, 33, 35, 39, 42, 49, 54, 57, 78
Collins, Joe 78, 83
Collins, Pat 44
Collins, Rip 35, 63
Colon, Bartolo 174, 201, 215
Colt, Houston 101
Combs, Earle 16, 37, 43–45, 48–51, 153

Index

Concepcion, Dave 134–36
Cone, David 157, 178–79, 207
Conigliaro, Tony 117
Conley, Gene 98
Conte, Victor 164–65
Contreras, Jose 199
Contreras, Wilson 212
Coombs, Jack 12, 31
Cooper, Cecil 125, 129
Cooper, Mort 67
Cora, Joey 175–76
Cordero, Will 174
Correa, Carlos 206
Cotts, Neil 199
Coveleski, Stan 16, 34–35, 38, 55
Covington, Wes 97
Cowens, Al 127
Cox, Billy 88, 90
Cozart, Zack 212
Craft, Harry 65
Cramer, Doc 57
Cramer, Richard 77, 141
Crandall, Del 97
Crandall, Doc 27
Cravath, Gavvy 39
Crawford, Carl 192, 197
Crawford, Sam 29
Crawford, Willie 138
Crisp, Coco 190–91, 204
Critz, Hughie 62
Cron, C.J. 203
Crone, Ray 98
Cronin, Joe 43, 50, 57, 70, 110, 146
Crosetti, Frankie 51, 57
Crowder, General 56
Cruz, Jose 172, 207
Cruz, Nelson 203
Cuellar, Mike 119
Cueto, Johnny 212, 217
Curtis, Chad 179
Cuyler, Kiki 55

Daal, Omar 168
Dahlen, Bill 26
Dahlgren, Babe 53, 56, 58
Dailey, Bill 113
Dalton, Harry 118
Damon, Johnny 183, 185, 190, 194, 197
Dark, Alvin 93
Darling, Ron 157
Davenport, Jim 102, 105
Davis, Chili 153
Davis, Curt 65–67
Davis, Kiddo 62
Davis, Russ 176

Davis, Tommy 102, 104
Davis, Wade 200
Davis, Willie 103–5
Dawson, Andre 143
Dean, Dizzy 63, 65, 67, 109
DeCinces, Doug 129, 150
deGrom, Jacob 215
DeJesus, Ivan 154
Delgado, Carlos 214
Demaree, Al 27
Dempster, Ryan 211
Denny, John 143
Derringer, Paul 61
Devine, Joe 51
Devlin, Art 26
Dickey, Bill 45–47, 51–52, 85, 110
Dickson, Murray 87
DiMaggio, Dom 57–58, 73–74, 79–80
DiMaggio, Joe 2, 5, 13, 16, 35, 46, 52–53, 55, 57–58, 67–68, 72–74, 76–78, 86, 106, 109
Ditmar, Art 111
Dobson, Pat 117, 119
Doby, Larry 75, 78, 81
Doerr, Bobby 57, 68, 73, 75, 79–80, 97, 110
Donald, Atley 58
Donaldson, Josh 4, 204–5, 219
Donlin, Mike 26–27
Donovan, Wild Bill 29
Douthit, Taylor 60–61
Downing, Brian 129
Doyle, Denny 126
Drew, J.D. 162
Drew, Stephen 192
Dropo, Walt 80
Drysdale, Don 90, 99, 103, 105, 126, 140, 221
Dugan, Joe 36–37, 44
Duncan, Mariano 178
Duren, Ryne 108
Durocher, Leo 44, 63, 66, 92, 132
Dye, Jermaine 186
Dykes, Jimmy 48–49
Dykstra, Lenny 156

Earnshaw, George 48
Easter, Luke 81, 195
Eastwick, Rawley 136
Eckersley, Dennis 125, 148, 153–54
Eckstein, David 208
Edmonds, Jim 170, 207–8

Edwards, Johnny 99
Elliott, Bob 87
Ellis, Doc 124
Ellsbury, Jacoby 191, 195
Elster, Kevin 157
Encarnacion, Edwin 201, 205
Ennis, Del 13–14, 70, 72, 88, 92, 189
Epstein, Mike 122
Epstein, Theo 183, 192, 211
Erikson, Scott 153
Ermer, Cal 120
Erskine, Carl 90
Erstad, Darin 186, 201
Escobar, Kelvim 202
Essick, Bill 51
Ethier, Andre 217
Evans, Darrell 147
Evans, Dwight 124, 126, 148
Evans, Joe 34
Everett, Carl 167
Evers, Johnny 24–25

Faber, Red 34
Face, Elroy 99
Fain, Ferris 78, 84
Fairly, Ron 105
Falkenberg, Cy 16, 28
Familia, Jeurys 215
Farrell, Turk 101
Fassero, Jeff 171
Feller, Bob 2, 13, 27, 45, 56–58, 67, 72–74, 76, 82, 85–86, 95, 103, 109–10, 140, 168
Ferguson, Joe 138
Fernandez, Alex 167
Fernandez, Sid 147, 157
Fernandez, Tony 148, 174
Ferrell, Wes 54, 56, 70, 73, 83, 85, 109, 126, 140, 147, 220
Fielder, Cecil 178
Fielder, Prince 200, 203–4
Figgins, Chone 201–2
Figueroa, Ed 124
Fingers, Rollie 122, 129, 181
Finley, Charlie 31, 121–22, 129
Finley, Steve 168
Fisk, Carlton 46, 124, 126, 172
Fister, Doug 215
Flanagan, Mike 126
Fletcher, Art 39–41, 55, 64
Flick, Elmer 28
Flood, Curt 104, 130
Foli, Tim 129
Ford, Whitey 71, 77, 79, 83–84, 108, 112–14, 122, 126, 140

Foster, George 135
Foster, Rube 32
Foulke, Keith 184
Fournier, Jack 41, 55
Fowler, Dexter 211
Fox, Nellie 83, 111, 139
Fox, Pete 59
Foxx, Jimmy 43, 45–49, 51, 57–59, 70, 109, 175
Franco, John 169
Franco, Julio 174
Francona, Terry 192
Franklin, Ryan 209
Frazee, Harry 35
Freehan, Bill 117
Freeman, Hershel 95
Freese, David 210
Freese, Gene 111
French, Larry 67
Frey, Lonnie 64
Friend, Bob 99
Frisch, Frankie 9, 38, 41, 55, 59–61, 63
Fryman, Travis 174
Fuentes, Tito 105
Fuld, Sam 197
Furcal, Rafael 162
Furillo, Carl 86, 88–89, 193

Gabrielson, Len 105
Galan, Augie 64, 69
Galarraga, Andres 161–62
Gant, Ron 160
Gantner, Jim 129
Garcia, Damaso 147
Garcia, Freddy 177, 199
Garcia, Jamie 210
Garcia, Mike 82
Garciaparra, Nomar 182–83
Gardner, Brett 195–96
Gardner, Larry 31, 34
Garland, Jon 199
Garr, Ralph 128
Garrett, Wayne 132
Garver, Ned 13, 70
Garvey, Steve 138
Gehrig, Lou 13–14, 16, 35, 37, 43–45, 48–53, 58, 60, 68, 70, 96, 109, 130, 142, 209
Gehringer, Charlie 43, 50, 75, 88, 97, 176
Generation X 13–4, 135, 206–8
Gentile, Jim 112
Gentry, Gary 132
Gerardi, Joe 179
Gerber, Wally 36
Geronimo, Cesar 134–35
GI Generation 13, 43, 109–10

Giambi, Jason 180–81, 184–85, 193–94, 207
Giavotella, Johnny 203
Gibson, Bob 13, 102, 131, 140, 146, 149, 172, 221
Gibson, Kirk 146, 157
Gilbert, Billy 26
Giles, Brian 174
Giles, Marcus 162
Gilliam, Jim 90, 104–5, 138
Girardi, Joe 178, 194
Gladwell, Malcolm 2
Glavine, Tom 160, 207
Godden, Dwight 178
Goldschmidt, Paul 219
Gomez, Lefty 49, 53, 84, 109, 122, 138; Ruben, 94
Gonzales, Gio 216
Gonzales, Marwin 206
Gonzalez, Adrian 192, 217
Gonzalez, Alex 190–91
Gonzalez, Juan 174
Gonzalez, Luis 168
Gonzalez, Tony 106–7
Gooden, Dwight 157
Goodman, Billy 79–80
Goodman, Ival 65
Gordon, Alex 200
Gordon, Joe 16, 53, 58, 67, 69, 74–75, 88, 97, 109
Gordon, Sid 92
Goslin, Goose 37, 50–51, 54
Gossage, Rich 125, 181
Gowdy, Hank 41
Graffanino, Tony 161
Granderson, Curtis 195, 199
Green, Chad 196
Green, Dick 122
Green, Nick 191
Greenberg, Hank 13, 50, 52, 58, 67, 72
Greenwell, Mike 148
Gregg, Vean 16
Gregorius, Didi 196
Greinke, Zack 217
Grich, Bobby 119, 127–28, 146, 150, 172, 207
Griffey, Ken 135, 175, 207
Griffin, Doug 125
Griffith, Calvin 120–21
Griffith, Clark 50, 57
Griffith, Tommy 41
Grim, Bob 83
Grimes, Burleigh 40, 61
Grissom, Marquis 171, 174
Grissom, Marv 94
Groat, Dick 99, 104, 107
Groh, Heinie 40–41

Gross, Don 95
Grove, Lefty 45–49, 55, 57, 61, 175
Grubb, Johnny 146
Gsellman, Robert 215
Guerrero, Pedro 157
Guerrero, Vladimir 157, 201–2, 207
Guidry, Ron 125–26
Guillen, Carlos 177
Gullett, Don 136
Gura, Larry 128
Gurriel, Yuli 206
Guzman, Juan 154
Gwynn, Tony 154, 171–72, 207

Haak, Howie 158
Haas, Mule 48–49
Hack, Stan 64, 69
Hafey, Chick 61
Haines, Jesse 61
Hale, Sammy 47
Hall, Jimmie 113–14
Halladay, Roy 150, 207, 214
Hallahan, Wild Bill 61
Haller, Tom 102, 105
Hamels, Cole 214
Hamilton, Josh 202–3
Hampton, Mike 167, 169
Haney, Frank 97
Haney, Fred 97–98
Hanigan, Ryan 193
Hansen, Ron 114
Harper, Bryce 215
Harper, George 61
Harrelson, Bud 132
Harris, Bucky 38
Harrison, Josh 213
Harrison, Matt 203
Hart, Jim Ray 103, 105
Hartnett, Gabby 64, 110
Harvey, Matt 215
Hatteberg, Scott 185
Hayes, Charlie 179
Hazle, Bob 97
Hearn, Jim 87
Heath, Jeff 87
Hegan, Jim 46
Heilmann, Harry 30, 54, 175
Helms, Tommy 134
Helton, Todd 164, 207–8
Henderson, Dave 148, 151–52
Henderson, Rickey 9, 13, 17, 130, 147, 151–52, 158, 169, 171, 218
Hendricks, Kyle 211, 212
Henrich, Tommy 76
Henry, Butch 171

Henry, John 1, 183
Hentgen, Pat 154
Herman, Billy 64, 66
Hernandez, Keith 155–56, 171, 221
Hernandez, Orlando 179–80
Hernandez, Roberto 199
Hernandez, Willie 146
Herr, Tommy 155
Herrera, Kelvin 200
Hershiser, Orel 157, 173
Herzog, Whitey 156
Heyward, Jason 211, 215
Higbe, Kirby 66
Hill, Ken 171
Hill, Rich 218
Hiller, Chuck 102
Hiller, John 117
Hinske, Eric 197
Hoak, Don 99
Hobson, Butch 126, 148
Hodges, Gil 88–89, 109, 136, 172, 221
Hoffmann, Glenn 148
Holland, Greg 200
Holliday, Matt 209
Holmes, Tommy 69
Holt, Brock 193
Holtzman, Ken 122, 124–25, 129, 133
Hooper, Harry 32–33
Hooton, Burt 138
Hopp, Johnny 67
Horlen, Joel 114
Hornsby, Rogers 12, 28, 39–40, 54, 60
Horton, Willie 117
Houk, Ralph 84, 112
Houtteman, Art 82
Howard, Elston 108, 112
Howard, Frank 104
Howard, Ryan 213
Howe, Neil 12
Howsam, Bob 134
Hubbard, Glenn 152
Hubbell, Carl 62, 67, 109, 140
Hudson, Orlando 217
Huff, Aubrey 216
Huggins, Miller 1, 48, 56
Hughson, Tex 59, 73
Huizenga, Wayne 168
Humphreys, Michael 2, 20, 24, 40, 73, 136, 155, 161, 172, 209
Hunter, Brian 176
Hunter, Catfish 122, 124–25, 129, 173, 221
Hunter, Torii 202

Ibanez, Raul 195
Iglesias, Jose 192
Infante, Omar 200
Inge, Brandon 199–200
Irvin, Monte 72, 92–93, 110

Jablonski, Ray 95
Jackson, Austin 200
Jackson, Joe 12, 16, 35, 39, 54–55, 134
Jackson, Larry 107
Jackson, Michael 174
Jackson, Reggie 13, 46, 121, 123–24, 127–30, 148, 150, 171–72, 218
Jackson, Shoeless Joe 28, 31, 33, 122
Jackson, Travis 29, 40, 61–62, 64, 110, 182
Jansen, Kenley 218
Jansen, Larry 93
Javier, Julian 131
Javier, Stan 152
Jay, Joey 98–99
Jay, Jon 210
Jeffcoat, Hal 95
Jenkins, Ferguson 107, 125, 133
Jeter, Derek 29–30, 40, 146, 162, 178, 181, 183, 196, 200
Johnson, Alex 107
Johnson, Ban 23, 31
Johnson, Byron Bancroft 27
Johnson, Davey 20, 119
Johnson, Deron 107
Johnson, Lou 105
Johnson, Randy 14, 37, 149, 160, 163, 167–68, 175–76, 193–94, 207
Johnson, Syl 61
Johnson, Walter 4, 12, 35, 37, 42, 45, 55, 60, 140, 157, 160, 207, 222
Johnstone, Jay 141
Jones, Chipper 160–62
Jones, Cleon 132
Jones, Nippy 87
Jones, Ruppert 146
Joost, Eddie 78
Jordan, Brian 162
Joss, Addie 28
Joyce, Matthew 197
Judge, Aaron 4–6, 196
Jurges, Billy 64
Justice, David 160, 180, 185

Kaat, Jim 141
Kaline, Al 71, 84, 108, 112, 117, 139, 215

Kasko, Eddie 88, 99
Katt, Ray 94, 100
Keller, Charlie 16, 53, 67, 72, 86, 109, 176, 220
Kelly, George "High Pockets" 41, 62
Keltner, Ken 2, 75, 81, 110
Kemp, Matt 217
Kendrick, Howie 203
Kendrick, Kyle 214
Kennedy, Adam 186
Kennedy, John 13
Kent, Jeff 165
Kerr, Dickie 34
Kershaw, Clayton 11, 14, 217, 219, 223
Keuchel, Dallas 206
Key, Jimmy 147–48, 207
Killebrew, Harmon 71, 112–13
Killian, Ed 29
Kimbrel, Craig 193
Kinder, Ellis 80
Kiner, Ralph 81, 86, 93, 110
Kinsler, Ian 203
Kirkland, Willie 100
Kling, Johnny 25
Klippstein, Johnny 95
Kluber, Corey 7, 10, 201
Kluszewski, Ted 94–95
Knight, Ray 156
Knoblauch, Chuck 153, 179
Koenig, Mark 44
Konstanty, Jim 92
Koosman, Jerry 14, 132
Koufax, Sandy 4, 8, 27, 71, 73, 85, 90–91, 102–3, 106, 137, 182, 187, 220–21
Kremer, Ray 60
Kubek, Tony 108, 111
Kubiak, Ted 122
Kucks, Johnny 85
Kuenn, Harvey 102
Kuhn, Bowie 31, 129
Kurowski, Whitey 86

Labine, Clem 90
Lackey, John 201, 210
Lajoie, Nap 12, 16, 28–29
Landis, Jim 111
Langston, Mark 171
Lanier, Hal 105
Lanier, Max 67
Lannin, Joseph J. 33
Lansford, Carney 148
Larkin, Barry 158, 182, 196, 207
LaRoche, Adam 215
Larsen, Don 85

LaRussa, Tony 151, 208
Lary, Lyn 49
Lavagetto, Cookie 67, 86
Lawrence, Brooks 95
Lazzeri, Tony 16, 44, 70, 75, 110, 153
Leach, Tommy 26
Leaver, Sam 26
Lee, Bill 64, 125
Lee, Cliff 214
Lefebvre, Jim 105
Leibrandt, Charlie 150, 160
Leiter, Al 169
Lemke, Mark 160–61
Lemon, Bob 76, 82, 109, 140
Lemon, Chet 128, 146
Leon, Sandy 193
Leonard, Dutch 30, 32, 128
Lester, Jon 191, 211–12
Lewis, Darren 164, 183
Lewis, Duffy 32
Lidge, Brad 211, 214
Lima, Jose 167
Lind, Jose 159
Lindell, Johnny 74
Lindor, Francisco 201
Lindstrom, Freddie 62, 70
Linz, Phil 114
Linzy, Frank 105
Lockhart, Keith 162
Lockman, Whitey 93–94, 100
Loes, Billy 90
Lofton, Kenny 161, 174
Logan, Johnny 96
Lolich, Mickey 117
Lombardi, Ernie 110
Lonborg, Jim 117, 141
Loney, James 197
Long, Terrence 185
Longoria, Evan 197, 212
Lopat, Ed 76–78
Lopes, Davey 138
Lopez, Hector 111
Lopez, Javier 47, 160–61
Loretta, Mark 190
Lost Generation 12, 54–5
Lowe, Derek 183
Lowell, Mike 190
Lowrie, Jed 191–92, 204
Luderus, Fred 39
Lugo, Julio 191
Lugo, Seth 215
Lumpe, Jerry 108
Lupien, Tony 59
Luzinski, Greg 141
Lyle, Sparky 125
Lynn, Fred 124, 129
Lynn, Lance 210

Mack, Connie 21, 31, 45, 48–49, 56–57
Mack, Shane 153
Macon, Max 67
MacPhail, Larry 65–66, 69, 72
Maddux, Gary 141
Maddux, Greg 14, 149, 160, 207
Madson, Ryan 200–201
Magee, Sherry 12, 14, 54, 189
Maglie, Sal 90, 93
Malone, Pat 52
Maloney, Jim 107, 187
Manley, Effa 92
Mantilla, Felix 97
Mantle, Mickey 1, 13, 35, 71–72, 78, 81, 83, 96, 108, 113, 117, 139, 223
Manush, Heinie 50, 70
Mapes, Cliff 76
Maranville, Rabbit 39
Marichal, Juan 16, 62, 91, 100, 103–6, 126, 172, 187, 221
Marion, Marty 87
Maris, Roger 9, 101, 112
Marquard, Rube 27
Marshall, Mike 138
Marshall, Willard 92
Marte, Starling 213
Martin, Billy 1, 78, 108, 120, 123–25, 129, 151
Martin, Pepper 61, 63
Martin, Russell 213
Martinez, Carlos 210
Martinez, Dennis 173
Martinez, Edgar 16, 150, 175–77, 207
Martinez, Pedro 150, 163, 171, 182–83, 207
Martinez, Tino 170, 175, 178–79, 193
Martinez, Victor 192
Marty, Joe 67
Matheny, Mike 170
Mathews, Eddie 30, 71, 88, 95, 110, 112, 114, 117, 139
Mathewson, Christy 12, 26, 222
Matsui, Hideki 181
Matsuzaka, Daisuke 191
Mattingly, Don 13–14, 145, 147, 189, 207
Matz, Steve 215
Mauch, Gene 129
Mauer, Joe 46, 198–99
May, Lee 134
May, Rudy 127
Mayberry, John 127

Mays, Carl 35, 106
Mays, Willie 13, 16–17, 29–30, 71–72, 93–94, 99–100, 102–6, 108–9, 114, 117–18, 121, 139, 172, 175–77, 222–23
Mazara, Nomar 204
Mazeroski, Bill 99, 139, 155
McBride, Bake 142
McCarthy, Joe 1, 48–49, 51–52, 56, 72
McCarver, Tim 130
McCormick, Mike 65
McCosky, Barney 56, 74
McCovey, Willie 16, 62, 100, 132, 139, 172
McCoy, Benny 58
McCracken, Voros 21
McCutchen, Andrew 212–13, 219
McDougald, Gil 78, 84, 108
McEnaney, Will 136
McGann, Dan 26
McGee, Willie 155
McGinnity, Joe "Iron Man" 26, 168–69
McGraw, John 26, 38, 41
McGraw, Tug 142
McGregor, Scott 130
McGriff, Fred 160–61
McGwire, Mark 9, 151–52, 164, 167, 170, 175–76, 207
McInnis, Stuffy 30–31
McLain, Denny 117, 124, 131
McMillan, Roy 95
McNally, Dave 118–19
McQuinn, George 74
McRae, Hal 127, 150
McReynolds, Kevin 157
Medich, Doc 124
Medwick, Joe 63, 65
Menke, Denis 134
Merkle, Fred 24
Merritt, Jim 13, 116, 120, 189
Mertes, Sam 26
Mesa, Jose 173–74
Messersmith, Andy 138
Meusel, Bob 35–36, 44
Meusel, Irish 41
Millar, Kevin 183
Millennial Generation 14, 199, 218–19
Miller, Andrew 201
Miller, Bing 47–48
Millwood, Kevin 160, 162
Mincher, Don 111
Minoso, Minnie 81, 83, 111, 115, 140
Missionary Generation 12

Index

Mitchell, Clarence 61
Mitchell, Dale 75
Mitchell, Kevin 156–57
Mitchell, Willie 28
Mize, Johnny 62, 67, 86, 92, 109
Molina, Bengie 186
Molina, Jose 197
Molina, Yadier 208, 210
Molitor, Paul 129, 153, 171–72, 218
Monday, Rick 138
Montgomery, Jordan 196
Montgomery, Mike 212
Moon, Wally 88, 99
Moore, Jo-Jo 64
Moore, Terry 65, 86
Moore, Wilcy 44
Morales, Kendrys 200, 202
Moreland, Mitch 204
Moret, Roger 125
Morgan, Joe 13, 16, 129, 134–36, 143, 146, 154, 172, 176, 218
Morris, Jack 147, 153
Moseby, Lloyd 148
Moss, Brandon 204
Mossi, Don 82
Moustakas, Mike 200
Moyer, Jamie 177–78, 214
Mueller, Bill 183
Mueller, Don 93–94, 100, 183, 190
Munger, Red 87
Munson, Thurman 46, 124, 172
Murphy, Daniel 216
Murphy, Duane 130
Murphy, Johnny 52
Murray, Eddie 126, 130, 148, 171, 173–74, 218
Musial, Stan 13, 17, 50, 52, 55, 65, 67–69, 71, 86–88, 93
Mussina, Mike 180, 194, 207
Myer, Buddy 50
Myers, Billy 65
Myers, Randy 157

Nagy, Charles 174
Napoli, Mike 192, 203
Narleski, Ray 82
Neagle, Denny 161
National League, leading teams analysis: (1901–13) 24–27; (1914–24) 38–42; (1925–42) 59–66; (1946–66) 85–108; (1967–78) 130–38; (1976–83) 139–44; (1984–2004) 154–71; (2005–17) 208–18
Neal, Charlie 99
Nettles, Graig 123, 172
Newcombe, Don 88, 90, 153
Newhouser, Hal 68–69, 82, 109, 140, 220
Newsom, Bobo 56, 74
Niekro, Phil 139–40, 146, 172
Nixon, Otis 160
Nixon, Trot 183
Nolan, Gary 13–14, 116, 136, 189
Noren, Irv 78, 82–84
Norris, Mike 130
North, Billy 122
Northrup, Jim 117
Nunez, Abraham 208
Nuxhall, Joe 95

O'Dell, Billy 102
Odom, Blue Moon 122
O'Farrell, Bob 60
Offerman, Jose 183
Ogea, Chad 173
Oglivie, Ben 129
Ojeda, Bob 157
Okajima, Hideki 191
Olerud, John 153, 169, 177
Oliva, Tony 113–15, 121
Oliver, Al 46
O'Neill, Paul 178–79
O'Neill, Steve 34
Ordonez, Maglio 200
Ordonez, Rey 169, 173
Orosco, Jesse 157
Orta, Jorge 128
Ortiz, David 193
Osteen, Claude 105
Oswalt, Roy 207, 211, 214
Otero, Dan 201
Otis, Amos 127
O'Toole, Jim 99, 107
Ott, Mel 13, 43, 62, 69–70, 109
Overall, Orvie 25
Owen, Mickey 66
Oyler, Ray 117

Pafko, Andy 90
Pagan, Angel 217
Pagan, Jose 102
Page, Joe 74, 77
Paige, Satchel 76
Palmeiro, Rafael 207
Palmer, Jim 20, 118–20, 137, 173
Palmer, Pete 4, 19, 21, 77, 210

Papelbon, Jonathan 190, 201
Pappas, Milt 118
Parker, Dave 137, 172, 207
Parker, Wes 105
Parnell, Mel 80
Parrish, Lance 146
Pascual, Camilo 111, 113
Patek, Freddie 127
Peach, Georgia 30
Peacock, Brad 206
Pearson, Monte 52
Peckinpaugh, Roger 35, 37
Pedroia, Dustin 191, 193
Pena, Carlos 197
Pena, Tony 155, 174
Pence, Hunter 217
Pendleton, Terry 155, 160–61
Pennington, Cliff 204
Pennock, Herb 36, 45, 55
Pepitone, Joe 113
Peralta, Johnny 200
Perez, Tony 16, 108, 115, 133–36, 143
performance enhancing drugs (PEDs) and steroids 14, 16, 145–46, 151, 164, 165, 168, 176, 181, 185–86, 188–89, 196, 206–8, 211
Perranoski, Ron 105
Perry, Gaylord 103, 105, 126, 140, 172
Perry, Jim 120
Pesky, John 58, 74, 80
Pesky, Johnny 58, 73, 79, 110
Peterson, Cap 105
Petrocelli, Rico 125
Pettis, Gary 150
Pettitte, Andy 178, 194, 211
Pfeffer, Jeff 39
Pfister, Jack 25
Phillips, Adolfo 107
Phillips, Tony 152, 171
Piazza, Mike 46, 169, 207
Pierce, Billy 83–84, 102, 140, 147
Pillar, Kevin 205
Piniella, Lou 125
Pinson, Vada 99, 107
Pipgras, George 48
Pizarro, Juan 98
Plank, Eddie 28, 31
Plunk, Eric 173–74
Plunk, Erik 173–74
Podres, Johnny 90, 103
Polanco, Placido 170
Politte, Cliff 199
Pollet, Howie 86
Polonia, Luis 152

Index

Pomeranz, Drew 193
Porcello, Rick 193
Posada, Jorge 179, 181, 207
Posey, Buster 46, 216–17
Post, Wally 94–95
Powell, Boog 20, 114, 118
Price, David 193, 197, 205
Puckett, Kirby 153
Pujols, Albert 6, 12, 14, 17, 150, 164, 166, 170, 196, 202–3, 206–10, 213–14, 216
Pythagorean formula 3–4
Pythagorean luck 19
Pytlak, Frankie 58

Raburn, Ryan 200
Raines, Tim 172, 178, 218
Ramirez, Hanley 193
Ramirez, Josh 201
Ramirez, Manny 173, 183, 207
Randolph, Willie 123, 127, 147
Raschi, Vic 76–78
Ravine, Chavez 103
Reddick, Josh 206
Reed, Addison 215
Reed, Rick 169
Reed, Ron 141
Reese, Andy 61
Reese, Pee Wee 40, 66, 77, 86, 90, 93, 110, 136, 155, 182
Regan, Phil 105
Reiser, Pete 67
Remy, Jerry 126
Rendon, Anthony 216
Renteria, Edgar 167, 170, 190, 208
Rettenmund, Merv 119
Reulbach, Edward "Big Ed" 25
Reuther, Dutch 40
Reyes, Jose 214
Reynolds, Allie 69, 74, 76–78
Reynolds, Shane 167
Rhodes, Arthur 177
Rhodes, Dusty 100
Rice, Jim 37–38, 46, 124, 126, 148, 172, 218
Rice, Sam 37
Richardson, Bobby 108, 111–12
Rickey, Branch 60–61, 65–67, 69, 86–88, 92
Rigney, Bill 121
Rijo, Jose 152, 158, 207
Ring, Johnny 40
Ripken, Cal 30, 50, 130, 142, 146–47, 155, 158, 172
Rivers, Mickey 123
Rizzo, Anthony 212

Rizzuto, Phil 2, 16, 29, 40, 58, 76–77, 79, 93, 110, 155, 182
Roark, Tanner 215–16
Roberts, Brian 195
Roberts, Robin 91, 106, 126, 221
Robertson, Bob 136
Robertson, Dave 195
Robinson, Brooks 20, 114, 118–19, 126, 172
Robinson, Frank 94–95, 99
Robinson, Jackie 13, 46, 72, 75, 87–88, 109, 136, 221
Rodney, Fernando 197
Rodriguez, Alex 158, 175–77, 182, 184, 193–96, 207, 222
Rodriguez, Eduardo 193
Rodriguez, Ivan 199, 207
Rodriquez, Aurelio 124
Roe, Preacher 69, 88, 90
Roebuck, Ed 90
Roenicke, Gary 126
Rogell, Billy 51
Rogers, Steve 143
Rojas, Cookie 107
Rolen, Scott 170, 208, 212
Rolfe, Red 51–52, 56
Rollins, Jimmy 213, 217
Rollins, Rich 120
Romano, John 111
Roosevelt, Franklin 13
Rose, Pete 30, 107, 134–35, 140, 142, 152, 166
Roseboro, John 104–5
Rosen, Al 81, 83, 110
Rosenthal, Trevor 210
Roush, Edd 40, 61
Rowe, Schoolboy 51, 56
Rowell, Bama 67
Rucker, Nap 55
Rudi, Joe 122, 129
Rudolph, Dick 39
Ruffing, Red 48–49, 53, 109, 122, 138
run luck 19–20
Rusch, Glendon 169
Russell, Addison 211
Russell, Bill 138
Russell, Reb 34
Ruth, Babe 1, 4, 12, 17, 32, 35–36, 39, 54, 139, 206, 221–22
Ryan, Brendan 209
Ryan, Nolan 132, 137, 173

Sabathia, CC 194–96, 199, 206, 208, 211
Saberhagen, Bret 150, 183, 207
Sadecki, Ray 105

Sain, Johnny 87
Sale, Chris 7, 193
Sallee, Slim 40
Sanchez, Aaron 205
Sanchez, Anibal 200
Sanchez, Gary 196
Sandberg, Ryne 147, 154, 172, 218
Sanders, Reggie 208
Sanderson, Scott 154
Sandoval, Pablo 217
Sanguillen, Manny 136
Santana, Carlos 201
Santana, Ervin 202
Santana, Johan 198, 207
Santana, Rafael 157
Santiago, Ramon 200
Santo, Ron 133, 139
Sarni, Bill 100
Saunders, Joe 202
Schang, Wally 31
Scherzer, Max 7, 199, 216, 219, 223
Schilling, Curt 168, 184, 207
Schmidt, Jason 165
Schmidt, Mike 4, 13, 141, 148, 152, 171–72, 218
Schoendienst, Red 86, 97
Schofield, Dick 105, 150
Schulte, Frank 24–25
Schulte, Fred 50
Score, Herb 84
Scott, Everett 35–36
Scott, George 117, 119, 126
Scott, Jim 34
Scott, Mike 157
Seager, Corey 217–18
Seaver, Tom 132–33, 138, 143, 173
Segui, David 176
Selkirk, George 51–53
Selma, Dick 133
Seminick, Andy 92
Severino, Luis 196
Shannon, Mike 131
Shantz, Bobby 78, 108
Shaw, Bob 103, 105, 111
Shawkey, Bob 31, 35, 48
Shea, Frank 74, 76
Sheckard, Jimmy 24–25
Sheffield, Gary 162, 167, 184, 207
Sherdel, Bill 61
Shields, James 197
Shocker, Urban 36, 44
Shore, Ernie 32
Short, Chris 106
Shuck, J.B. 202

Index

Shuey, Paul 174
Siebern, Norm 108
Siegrist, Kevin 210
Sierra, Ruben 177–78, 184
Sievers, Roy 111
Silent Generation 13, 70–1, 139–41
Simmons, Al 43, 45, 49, 54
Simmons, Curt 104
Simmons, Ted 46
Singleton, Chris 186
Singleton, Ken 126
Sisler, George 36, 39
Sizemore, Ted 141
Skowron, Bill 83
Slagle, Jimmy 24–25
Slaughter, Enos 65, 67, 86–87
Smith, Al 82
Smith, Elmer 34
Smith, Lonnie 155
Smith, Ozzie 146, 155
Smith, Reggie 138
Smith, Sherry 40
Smoltz, John 160
Snider, Duke 46, 88–89, 91, 140, 221
Snyder, Frank 41
Sogard, Eric 204
Sojo, Luis 175, 176, 179
Soriano, Alfonso 180
Sosa, Sammy 207
Southworth, Billy 60
Spahn, Warren 28, 85, 87, 89, 95, 97, 109, 140, 173
Speaker, Tris 12, 16–17, 28, 30, 32–35, 39, 54, 161, 222
Spencer, Daryl 100
Springer, George 206
Stafford, Bill 112
Stange, Lee 113, 117
Stanky, Eddie 86, 93
Stanley, Bob 125
Stanton, Mike 180
Stargell, Willie 136
Staub, Rusty 134–35
Steinfeldt, Harry 24–25
Stengel, Casey 1, 41, 51, 76, 82, 118, 121
Stephens, Gene 114
Stephens, Junior 2
Stephens, Vern 79–80, 110
Stephenson, Riggs 63
steroids *see* performance enhancing drugs
Stewart, Dave 152
Stewart, Jimmy 134
Stieb, Dave 146–47, 172–73, 218, 221

Stirnweiss, Snuffy 69, 72, 76
Stock, Milt 41
Stoneham, Horace 62
Stottlemyre, Mel 114
Strasburg, Stephen 215, 216
Strauss, William 12
Strawberry, Darryl 156, 178–79
Strunk, Amos 31
Stubbs, Franklin 212
Sturdivant, Tom 85, 108
Sturm, Johnny 58
Sutcliffe, Rick 154
Sutter, Bruce 181
Sutton, Don 105, 138, 173
Suzuki, Ichiro 16, 36, 177, 195
Swisher, Nick 194
Syndergaard, Noah 215

Tabor, Jim 59
Tanner, Chuck 140
Tapani, Kevin 153
Tartabull, Jose 117
Taylor, Chris 218
Taylor, Jack 61
Taylor, Tony 106
Teixeira, Mark 194–95
Tejada, Miguel 185–86
Temple, Johnny 95
Tenace, Gene 122
Terry, Bill 54, 61–62, 175
Terry, Ralph 113
Tesreau, Jeff 27
Teufel, Tim 156–57
Thevenow, Tommy 60
Thomas, Frank 150, 196, 207
Thome, Jim 173, 207
Thompson, Hank 92–94, 99
Thompson, Robby 164
Thomson, Bobby 92–93
Thorn, John 21
Thrift, Syd 158
Tiant, Luis 91, 106, 125–26, 221
Tinker, Joe 24–25, 41
Tinsley, Lee 182
Tolan, Bobby 134–35, 141
Toney, Fred 40
Torre, Frank 97
Torre, Joe 1, 46, 194
Torrez, Mike 125
Tovar, Cesar 120
Tracewski, Dick 117
Trammell, Alan 146, 155, 172, 182
Travis, Devon 205
Traynor, Pie 59
Tresh, Tom 113
Trillo, Manny 142

Trout, Dizzy 73
Trout, Mike 11, 14, 73, 154, 193, 202–3, 205, 219, 223
Trout, Steve 154
Tudor, John 155
Tulowitzki, Troy 205, 213
Turley, Bob 108, 111
Turner, Justin 217–18
Turner, Terry 28
Turner, Trea 216
Tyler, Lefty 40

Uggla, Dan 215
Uhlaender, Ted 120
Upton, B.J. 197
Uribe, Jose 157
Utley, Chase 174, 213

Valdez, Wilson 212
Valentin, John 182–83
Valentin, Jose 214
Valentine, Ellis 143
Vance, Dazzy 41, 55, 168
Van Slyke, Andy 95, 155, 158–59
Varitek, Jason 183
Vaughan, Arky 67, 75, 80, 110, 146
Vaughn, Hippo 40, 55
Vaughn, Mo 182
Vazquez, Javier 195, 207
Veeck, Bill 73, 75, 83, 111, 128
Ventura, Robin 169, 180
Verlander, Justin 199
Versalles, Zoilo 114
Victorino, Shane 192, 214
Vina, Fernando 170–71
Viola, Frank 150
Virdon, Bill 99
Vitt, Oscar 57
Vizcaino, Jose 174
Vizquel, Omar 173
Voiselle, Bill 87
Votto, Joey 4–6, 10, 14, 203, 212, 219, 223

Wacha, Michael 210
Waddell, Rube 12, 27, 73
Wagner, Billy 167
Wagner, Honus 12, 25, 158, 196, 222
Wagner, Leon 100
Wainwright, Adam 162, 206, 208–9
Wakefield, Tim 140, 182–83, 190
Walberg, Rube 48
Walker, Dixie 66, 86, 89

Index

Walker, Larry 171, 207–8
Walker, Todd 183–84
Walsh, Ed 160
Walters, Bucky 65
Waner, Lloyd 59–60, 70
Waner, Paul 59, 70, 109, 189
Wang, Chien-Ming 194
Ward, Aaron 35–36
Ward, Duane 154
Ward, Pete 114
Washburn, Jarrod 201
Watkins, George 61
Weaver, Buck 34
Weaver, Earl 118, 130
Weeks, Jemile 204
Weis, Al 132
Weiss, Walt 152
Welch, Bob 138, 153
Wells, David 179–80
Wells, Vernon 195
Wendell, Turk 169
Werber, Billy 65
Wert, Don 117
Werth, Jayson 214, 216
Wertz, Vic 82
Westrum, Wes 93–94, 100
Wheat, Zack 39, 41
Whitaker, Lou 146
White, Bill 100, 104, 107
White, Devon 167
White, Frank 127, 150
White, Roy 46, 123, 212
Whiten, Mark 179
Wilhelm, Hoyt 14, 94, 109, 111, 140
Willey, Carlton 98
Williams, Bernie 178, 180–81, 193
Williams, Billy 133, 139, 176
Williams, Davey 94, 100
Williams, Dick 122
Williams, Ken 36
Williams, Matt 164, 168, 174
Williams, Ted 2, 4–5, 8–9, 50, 52, 57, 65, 67, 74, 77–80, 82, 84, 87, 106, 108
Willis, Dontrelle 14, 189
Wills, Maury 104–5, 130, 138, 152
Wilson, Dan 176
Wilson, Earl 117
Wilson, Enrique 184
Wilson, Hack 63
Wilson, Mookie 156
Wilson, Willie 127, 150, 161, 172, 207
Wiltse, Hooks 27
Wine, Bobby 107
Winfield, Dave 153
wins above average (WAA) 4–11, 227–29
Witt, Mike 150
Witt, Whitey 37
Wolf, Randy 217
Womack, Tony 193, 208
Wood, Alex 218
Wood, Smokey Joe 32, 140, 218
Wood, Wilbur 140
Woodling, Gene 76, 78
Woodward, Woody 134
Worley, Vance 214
Wright, David 189, 214, 219
Wright, Jim 125
Wright, Steven 193
Wyatt, Whitlow 66
Wynn, Early 82–84, 109, 111, 138, 140, 152, 173
Wynn, Jim 108, 115, 134, 136, 138–39, 221

Yastrzemski, Carl 8–9, 13, 17, 96, 108, 116–17, 125–26, 139
Yawkey, Tom 45, 49
Yaz see Yastrzemski, Carl
Yeager, Steve 138
York, Rudy 56, 73
Youkilis, Kevin 183, 190
Young, Chris 193
Young, Cy 12, 23
Youngs, Ross 41
Yount, Robin 129, 146

Zachry, Pat 136
Zambrano, Carlos 211
Zeile, Todd 169
Zimmer, Don 125
Zimmerman, Heinie 40
Zimmerman, Jerry 99
Zimmerman, Ryan 215
Zimmermann, Jordan 215
Zisk, Richie 128
Zito, Barry 185
Zobrist, Ben 197, 211

www.ingramcontent.com/pod-product-compliance
Lightning Source LLC
Chambersburg PA
CBHW060259240426
43661CB00060B/2837